P. Kropotkin

Memoirs of a Revolutionist

BY

PETER KROPOTKIN

With a New Introduction and Notes by
NICOLAS WALTER

DOVER PUBLICATIONS, INC.
MINEOLA, NEW YORK

Bibliographical Note

This Dover edition, first published in 1971 and republished in 2010, is an unabridged and unaltered republication of the work first published in 1899 by Houghton, Mifflin & Company, Boston and New York. A new Introduction and Notes (pp. 503–540), written by Nicolas Walter, have been added to the present edition.

International Standard Book Number
ISBN-13: 978-0-486-47316-1
ISBN-10: 0-486-47316-3

Manufactured in the United States by Courier Corporation
47316301
www.doverpublications.com

INTRODUCTION
TO THE DOVER EDITION

PETER KROPOTKIN was the best known of all the Russian revolutionary exiles before 1917, and *Memoirs of a Revolutionist* is the best known of all his books. One can certainly appreciate it without knowing anything about him, and in a way it needs no introduction. But he was not a simple man, and it is not a simple book; moreover, the story it tells comes to an end long before he wrote it, and he lived long after he had written it. So one can certainly appreciate it more if one knows something about his life—especially his later life—and about the problems the book raises.

The first problem is that the title is misleading;* Kropotkin was an active revolutionist for a relatively short time. He was born in 1842, a member of the Russian aristocracy, and brought up to carry on its tradition, which he did for a third of his life. Like many of his contemporaries, he had doubts about the Tsarist regime from an early age, but it was not until 1867 that he broke with it decisively by leaving the army, and it was not until 1872 that he opposed it positively by entering the Chaikovski Circle.† This process of growth and change is described in great detail in the first half of the *Memoirs*, but it is necessary to emphasize that Kropotkin's revolutionary activity began only when he was almost thirty years old.

---

* It is perhaps significant that Kropotkin himself would have preferred the more neutral title *Around One's Life* (which was in fact used for the French edition); but he was overruled by his editors.

† In this Introduction and the new Notes section, a more modern (and less Gallicized) transliteration is used for Russian names; thus, the "Tchaykóvsky" of the text is here "Chaikovski," "Joukóvsky" has become "Zhukovski," and so on.

From 1872 to 1886 Kropotkin led the life of a typical nineteenth-century revolutionary agitator. He visited Western Europe to learn about the socialist movement, returned to Russia and joined the populist movement, was arrested and imprisoned without trial, escaped and fled from Russia, took refuge in Western Europe and joined the anarchist movement, was expelled from Switzerland and moved to France, was arrested and imprisoned after a fake trial, was amnestied and took refuge in England. This period of intense agitation is described in great detail in the second half of the *Memoirs*, but again it is necessary to emphasize that Kropotkin's revolutionary activity lasted for only fourteen years (of which he spent five in prison).

From 1886 to 1917 Kropotkin lived in England, and it was during this period that he wrote the *Memoirs*. In 1897 he visited North America for the first time, to attend the meeting of the British Association for the Advancement of Science in Toronto, and he took the opportunity to travel across Canada and also to give lectures in several places in the United States. In New York he met Walter Hines Page, editor of the *Atlantic Monthly*, who commissioned a series of autobiographical articles from him. These appeared from September, 1898, to September, 1899, with the title "The Autobiography of a Revolutionist"; a longer version was published in book form in England and the United States in 1899, with the title *Memoirs of a Revolutionist*. The introduction was by Georg Brandes (1842–1927), the Danish critic, who met Kropotkin in London in 1895, and with whom he corresponded from 1896 to 1919; Kropotkin asked him to write the introduction in 1899.

The *Memoirs* is perhaps the best thing Kropotkin wrote,*

* The style is distinctly better than that of his other writings in English, presumably because it was revised by Richard Heath (1831–1912), a friend of his who was a Christian Socialist writer.

and it gives an unforgettable picture of Russia in the middle of the nineteenth century, of the populist movement there in the 1870's, and of the anarchist movement in Western Europe in the 1870's and 1880's. But this is where we come to the second problem raised by the book: the twelve years between coming to England and writing the *Memoirs*, far from being described in the same kind of rich detail as the previous forty, are dismissed in a dozen pages at the end. Moreover, Kropotkin lived for another twenty-two years after writing the book and, though he suffered increasingly severe attacks of bronchial illness every year, he remained active to the end.

The result is that the *Memoirs* says a great deal about the first half of Kropotkin's life, but virtually nothing about the second half. It is a great pity that he cut the book short at the end, and that he did not bring it up to date before his death. Unfortunately no really satisfactory biography of him has appeared, and the best study so far— *The Anarchist Prince* by George Woodcock and Ivan Avakumović—is twenty years old and has long been out of print. It is therefore worth giving a brief account of Kropotkin's life between 1886 and 1921, so that readers will know about some of the things which are not in the *Memoirs*, before dealing with the problems raised by some of the things which are in the book.

By 1886 Kropotkin was the most famous anarchist in the world. He maintained his revolutionary opinions, but he was never again directly involved in revolutionary activity. He arrived in England at a time when the socialist movement was flourishing, and for a few years he took an important part in it. He immediately helped to found the Freedom Press, which has been the main vehicle of anarchist propaganda in Britain ever since. Though he was identified

with the anarchist section of the socialist movement, he
was not confined to it. He addressed left-wing audiences
of all kinds all over the country, and frequently attended
meetings to commemorate such events as the Paris Commune
or the Chicago Martyrs or to welcome some distinguished
foreign visitor to London. He took a minor part in such
episodes as the Bloody Sunday riot in 1887 and the Great
Dock Strike in 1889. He was on good terms with several
political groups on the left, and was friendly with such
leaders as William Morris and H. M. Hyndman, Keir
Hardie and Bernard Shaw. But his main influence was for
anarchism, and the rise of the anarchist movement in
Britain during the late 1880's owed much to his presence.

Within the anarchist movement his main influence was
for intelligence and against extremism. Indeed Kropotkin
himself became more and more intellectual and less and
less militant. After 1890 he still wrote the occasional
article for *Freedom* and went to the occasional meeting,
but he took little part in political activity—except in
special circumstances, as when he spoke at the meeting
to protest against the exclusion of the anarchists from the
London Congress of the Second International in 1896, or
when he intervened with a Liberal cabinet minister (who
had once been a socialist leader) to prevent the deportation
of the Italian anarchist Malatesta in 1912 (previously he
intervened with the police to secure the release of another
foreign revolutionary—none other than the Bolshevik
leader, Lenin!).*

Kropotkin was more closely involved in the French
movement, though he was unable to visit France for eighteen years. He wrote far more for the French than for the

* This is the story told by Horace Brust in the first volume of his
"memoirs of a political police officer," *I Guarded Kings* (London,
1935), but his general standard of accuracy is so low that it must be
treated with caution.

British anarchist press, and most of his political articles, pamphlets and books were first published in France and only later translated into English (as well as many other languages). In 1892 he was named in a secret police report in Paris as one of the leading members of a group believed to be running the international anarchist movement from London; though the details were nonsense, the story gives a fair indication of his importance. In 1896 the French authorities refused to allow him into the country to give some lectures, and he was not let in until 1905.

In England Kropotkin gave a very different impression. So far as is known, there was never any question of deporting him; the only brush he had with the authorities was for keeping a dog without the necessary license! He lived a life of almost bourgeois respectability with his wife and daughter—and sometimes a single servant—in a series of small suburban houses (near London in Harrow, Acton, Bromley and Highgate, and then in Brighton Kemp Town). Unlike many other Russian exiles, he made no attempt to recover the substantial property he had left behind, and he worked hard earning his own living by writing scientific articles for newspapers, magazines and reference books.

Kropotkin was not merely a journalist. Though he did no more original scientific work after leaving Russia, he enjoyed a reputation as a scientist in his own right for what he had achieved in the past. His theories about the orography, glaciation and desiccation of Asia, which had appeared in Russia during the 1870's, were published in England thirty years later, and they are still recognized as valuable contributions to physical geography. But he was active in many other fields, and he was always particularly interested in the application of the findings of natural science to the improvement of human society. Thus in *Fields, Factories and Workshops* (1899) he suggested that advanced agricultural techniques could be used to rationalize and humanize the economies of industrial countries; in *Mutual Aid* (1902) he suggested that the principle of cooperation, which was at least as important as that of competition in biological evolution, could be used to assist the social evolution of mankind; and in *Modern Science and Anarchism* (1901) he suggested that the movement of both natural and social science was in the direction of the anarchist ideal.

Two of Kropotkin's later writings are important enough to mention separately. His single major venture into the field of history—*The Great French Revolution* (1909)—was one of the earliest attempts to describe the French Revolution from the point of view of the common people and also to make proper use of the material on the popular movements of the 1790's. His work on ethics, which extended over many years and took up most of his attention towards the end of his life, was never completed and was published in a fragmentary form the year after his death.

In continental Europe Kropotkin was thought of as an anarchist who happened to be a scientist; in the Anglo-Saxon world he was thought of more as a scientist who happened to be an anarchist. As a prominent intellectual—and as a Russian prince—he was widely respected in Britain and North America, sometimes to an embarrassing extent. In 1894 the British *Contemporary Review* published an account of him called "Our Most Distinguished Refugee," and this kind of treatment—however much he discouraged it—was bound to have an effect. His political opinions were accepted as a romantic eccentricity, and it was difficult for him to make people take them seriously. On the other hand his fame did make the idea of anarchism more acceptable for many who would otherwise have rejected it without question, and he managed to exert a strong personal influence even in apparently unfavorable circumstances.

When my grandfather met him in 1902, it was at the home of Sir Hugh Low, a former colonial administrator—and yet he succeeded in converting my grandfather to anarchism!

There are many anecdotes of Kropotkin's obstinacy in maintaining his convictions. He refused to rise for the toast to the King's health at a banquet given for him by the Royal Geographical Society; he refused to accept the Fellowship of the Society because it was under royal patronage; he refused to consider the suggestion that he might become professor of geography at Cambridge (England) in case his freedom of speech and action might be limited; he refused to make any kind of deal with the Russian or French governments when they tried to open negotiations with him; and he consistently refused to give interviews to the press.

Nevertheless, though he would not compromise with authority, Kropotkin did modify his opinions—especially about war. Internationalism and antimilitarism have always been fundamental principles of the anarchist movement. He was himself very much a cosmopolitan; he lived in several countries, he spoke many languages and read even more, and he had friends and correspondents all over the world. He never showed a trace of racial feeling—his wife, incidentally, was Jewish. He wrote an eloquent attack on war which was included in his first anarchist book and reprinted as a pamphlet, and another which was included in his last anarchist book and also reprinted as a pamphlet. But in the 1890's he began to write in terms suggesting that the Hohenzollern regime and the Marxist Social Democrats in Germany were both expressions of a national character, and showing prejudice against Germany and in favor of England (the country which had given him refuge and allowed him freedom) and France (the country of the Revolution and the Commune).

This tendency became stronger in 1905, when the revolution in Russia made Kropotkin include it among the countries which should be defended. In private he went so far in his abandonment of anarchist tradition as to support the idea of a war by the Entente against Germany and the extension of conscription to prepare for it. So when the war which he had long expected finally came in 1914, it was not really surprising that Kropotkin—like many other left-wing leaders—gave immediate and unqualified support to the Allies. This won him the approval of liberals and patriots, but it cut him off from the movement he had been associated with for forty years. He made virtually no headway among anarchists in the West, and the most crushing rebuke came in an article by his old friend Malatesta in his old paper *Freedom* (November, 1914). The only place where he had much influence was Russia, and here it is necessary to go back and trace his relationship with his native land during his long exile.

When Kropotkin left Russia in 1876 he intended to return as soon as possible, but it soon became clear that he would never be able to cross the frontier without immediate arrest and eventual death in prison or Siberia. At the same time the Russian revolutionary movement grew away from the anarchist ideas which had previously influenced it; the preoccupation with constitutional government as an end and with assassination as a means repelled Kropotkin, and he ceased to have direct links with the movement soon after the death of the Tsar in 1881.

But most of Kropotkin's friends were Russian revolutionary exiles like himself, and he was always interested in what was happening in Russia—especially when anarchism revived. From 1892, groups of Russian exiles began to send anarchist propaganda from Western Europe into Russia, and they naturally made contact with Kropotkin and gave prominence to his writings. The most influential of these was his book, *The Conquest of Bread*, which was translated in 1902 with the title *Khleb i Volya* (Bread and Liberty); in 1903 a group with that name was formed in Switzerland which began a paper, also called *Khleb i Volya*, and produced another series of publications, again headed by Kropotkin's writings.

Anarchism became more widespread in Russia than ever before, and many anarchists were active in the 1905 Revolution. By then they were roughly divided into two sections—those who favored extreme methods such as robbery and assassination, and those who favored the traditional methods of propaganda and agitation; the latter acknowledged the leadership of Kropotkin, and he played a significant part in conferences of Russian anarchists in London and Paris between 1904 and 1906. Most of the exiles returned to Russia during the revolution, and *Khleb i Volya* ceased publication. Kropotkin hoped to follow them, and made preparations for the journey (including visits to a shooting-gallery to practice his marksmanship—at the age of sixty-three!). But while the situation was uncertain he ran a new paper called *Listki "Khleb i Volya"* (Leaves from *Khleb i Volya*), and when the reaction came in 1907 the anarchist movement was suppressed; he had to abandon hope of returning yet, though he contributed to Russian anarchist papers right up to the First World War.

Kropotkin's renewed involvement in Russian affairs was not derived only from his anarchism. An instance of his wider interests came when he suggested after his visit to North America in 1897 that the Dukhobors who had left Russia and were living unhappily in Cyprus might settle more happily in Canada—and, partly through his efforts, they did. Another prominent Russian intellectual who

championed their cause was Tolstoy, and at about the same
time Kropotkin began a correspondence with him (through
Tolstoy's disciple Chertkov) which lasted for several years.
Kropotkin was of course passionately fond of Russian
literature, and when he made a second visit to North America, in 1901, it was to give a series of lectures on this
subject at the Lowell Institute in Boston; these were the
basis of his book, *Ideals and Realities in Russian Literature*,
which was published in London and New York in 1905.
(He was never able to visit the United States again, because
of the change in the immigration laws following the assassination of President McKinley by the anarchist Czolgosz in
1901.)

A more important factor was that most of Kropotkin's
Russian friends were not anarchists at all, but moderate
socialists, and especially populists of the kind he had worked
with in the 1870's. Stepniak, who had once gone to the Balkans to join the Slav rising against the Turks and had gone
back to Russia to assassinate a police chief, and who was for
a time an anarchist, became so moderate that he joined the
Independent Labour Party (the precursor of the British
Labour Party) when it was formed in 1893. Nikolai Chaikovski, who had once led the remarkable group which Kropotkin
belonged to, and who was also for a time an anarchist,
became a right-wing populist leader in Russia, and after the
1917 Revolution he became the head of a short-lived anti-
Bolshevik government at Archangel. At the end of the
1890's, the bulk of the populists formed the Social Revolutionary Party, and many of Kropotkin's old colleagues
in the Chaikovski Circle became prominent members of it.
When the first Russian translation of his *Memoirs* was
published in London in 1902, it was mainly Social Revolutionaries who circulated it inside Russia. When the
Social Revolutionary journalist Burtsev accused the Social

Revolutionary leader Azev of being a police spy, in 1908, Kropotkin presided at the court of honor in Paris which found the accusation proved. His personal links with the party were strengthened in 1910, when his daughter married a young Social Revolutionary called Boris Lebedev.

Twenty years after leaving Russia, Kropotkin came to enjoy the status of a veteran among the revolutionary exiles, and, though his anarchist opinions were well known, he was able to represent the movement as a whole. In Britain he acted as its unofficial spokesman, writing on its behalf to the liberal press on many occasions. During the reaction after the 1905 Revolution, he was involved in the work of the Parliamentary Russian Committee, a pressure group uniting Russian exiles and British radicals, and he wrote a booklet for it called *The Terror in Russia* (1909).

Again, though Kropotkin never abandoned his anarchist identity, he did shift his position. By 1905 he expected a Russian revolution to go only as far as the French Revolution of 1789—that is, to replace Tsarism by a parliamentary republic rather than a socialist regime—and when the First World War began he went even further to the right than the Social Revolutionaries by establishing relations with the "Cadets" (the liberal Constitutional Democrats) and writing in favor of the war in their paper, *Russkiye Vedomosti* (Russian Gazette). His support of the war and his new political associations gave ammunition to left-wing opponents of the war who also opposed anarchism, and his example was used—above all by the Bolsheviks—to discredit the whole anarchist movement. But even in Russia his influence was limited, and he lost touch with those revolutionary groups which stuck to their principles.

When the 1917 Revolution began, Kropotkin returned to Russia after more than forty years in exile. He made contact

not with the anarchists or the Social Revolutionaries, but
with such figures as Lvov, the liberal who was the first
prime minister of the Provisional Government, and Kerensky, the moderate socialist who succeeded him. Kerensky
indeed offered him a place in the cabinet and, though
Kropotkin was still enough of an anarchist to refuse, the
offer was a fair indication of his position. When he spoke at
the all-party State Conference in Moscow in August, 1917,
his intervention was a call for the declaration of a republic
and a renewal of the offensive against Germany. His
comment on the Bolshevik seizure of power in November,
1917—"This buries the revolution"—was perhaps prompted
more by their opposition to the war than by their tendency
towards dictatorship, though it turned out to be prophetic.

The fall of the Provisional Government in 1917 and the
end of the war in 1918 released Kropotkin from his awkward
situation, and his open disapproval of the communist regime
brought him back to the anarchists. He resumed contact
with the leaders of the Russian movement, as well as many
foreign visitors. He also met Lenin, in 1919, and did what he
could—which was not much—to prevent some of the early
excesses of the new regime. In his last political writings—
the *Letter to the Workers of the West* and *What Is To Be
Done?*, both written in 1920—he made two apparently
contradictory but actually complementary points: that
the communists were destroying the revolution, and that
foreign intervention in Russia should stop. In his early
life he had swung from the moderate to the extreme left—
from the liberalism of the Russian Enlightenment in the
1860's (the *prosvetitelstvo*) through the socialism of the
Russian populist movement in the early 1870's (the *narod-
nichestvo*) to the anarchism of the West European labor
movement in the late 1870's; in his later life he had gradually swung back to a moderate position; but now at the end

of his life he returned to the unequivocal anarchism he had maintained at the peak of his career, insisting that the people themselves should take control of their own fate.

Kropotkin died on February 8, 1921, in the town of Dmitrov near Moscow. The government offered a state funeral, but his family refused, and in the event his funeral in Moscow was the last great anarchist demonstration in Russia. Later in the same year the anarchist movement there was suppressed once and for all. The editions of Kropotkin's political writings, which had begun to appear in 1918, came to an end. The house he was born in was made the Kropotkin Museum and kept his memory alive for a time, but it was closed soon after his wife's death in 1938. He was not forgotten: his name was given not only to the lane where he was born, but also to another street in Moscow, as well as a small square and a Metro station; a large town in Caucasia and a small one in Siberia are called Kropotkin; and the Siberian mountain range he was the first to cross in 1866 is also named after him. His grave may be seen today in the Novodevichi Monastery. He is still generally respected in the land of his birth, even if he is little read there.

Returning to the *Memoirs of a Revolutionist*, the first task is to clear up the bibliographical problems. When it was commissioned in 1897, Kropotkin had already begun to write it, in Russian; but he wrote the full text for publication in English, and did not have time to complete a Russian version—so that the Russian editions of 1902, 1906 and so on were in fact translations from his English. However, he rewrote several passages and also wrote new ones at various times, again in Russian, and some of these were included in the Russian editions of 1925 and 1929. By the end of his life he had written almost the whole text in

Russian, and his manuscript was used for the Russian edition of 1933; the most recent Russian edition, of 1966, reproduces this text (with a few omissions). Some of the additional material appeared in English for the first time in the abridged edition published by Doubleday in 1962 (and reprinted by Peter Smith in 1967). The present edition is an unabridged reprint of the first American edition, which was published by Houghton Mifflin in November, 1899 (it was slightly shorter than the first British edition, which was published by Smith Elder in London at the same time, and also varied in several unimportant details). None of the additional material has been included, but it has of course been taken into account in this introduction and in the notes to the text, which appear on pages 503–540.

Most of the book is so clear that it needs no comment, apart from the explanation of references to particular people and events in the notes. But it is worth discussing a few general problems. One small point is that Kropotkin tended to be inaccurate about minor details. This was natural enough, since he was writing in haste a long time afterwards. Some of his errors have been corrected in the notes, but no doubt others could be detected by more thorough research. Another small point is that Kropotkin was extremely reticent about his personal life. So far as sex is concerned, for example, he was a typical nineteenth-century puritan, and he raised the subject only to criticize other people's misconduct; his own relations with women were not mentioned at all, and even his wife was mentioned only in passing. In other areas the pattern was similar. He described his interest in the arts, but not his own enthusiastic if amateurish piano playing and landscape painting. We learn that he liked tea, but little more about his tastes; drinking and gambling, those favorite occupations of the Russian leisured classes, seem to have passed him by. He described ideas and characters, but not faces or voices.

Thus there is no point looking for intimate revelations in this book; Kropotkin's memoirs were essentially political. Here we come to the larger problem that he was rather evasive about some aspects of the two political episodes he was involved in before he settled in England—the Russian populist movement from 1872 to 1874, and the West European anarchist movement from 1876 to 1882. Again, this was natural enough, since he did not wish to injure old comrades by exposing their former activities too frankly, but he also tended to idealize the past and to play down his own particular role. To set the record completely straight would require a long historical analysis with frequent reference to other sources, which would be quite out of place here; but it is necessary to indicate where Kropotkin's testimony should be treated with caution.

In the Chaikovski Circle, according to Kropotkin, there was not even temporary friction. But according to other members there was in fact considerable friction, and it was moreover frequently centered on Kropotkin himself. There was disagreement about allowing a prince into the group at all, and later he was found to be rigid in his views and dogmatic in his exposition of them. Kropotkin himself, in one of his additions to the *Memoirs*, made more of the differences between the moderates, who were in the majority, and the extremists, of which he was a leading spokesman; he recalled "strong arguments" about the program he drew up for the group in 1873, and his criticism of those members who objected to his revolutionary proposals was resented. Kropotkin's part in the Chaikovski Circle was altogether more turbulent than one might guess from his *Memoirs*.

In the anarchist movement, Kropotkin again blurred the

disagreements among the various factions. There was a deep division within the Jura Federation between old members who followed Bakunin and were collectivists chiefly interested in the labor movement, and newcomers— including Kropotkin himself—who tacitly rejected many of Bakunin's ideas and were communists interested in a wider struggle altogether. The Jura Federation was won over to anarchist-communism in 1880, and the withdrawal of Guillaume, Schwitzguébel and Spichiger was due not only to the difficulties described by Kropotkin but also to political and personal differences. Again, Kropotkin's part in the anarchist movement was altogether more controversial than one might guess from his *Memoirs*.

Another thing Kropotkin does not mention is that, though he was later a strong opponent of secrecy and terrorism, he was during the 1870's a leading conspirator and advocate of propaganda by deed. In 1877 he attended the last meeting of the International Social Democratic Alliance, which Bakunin had secretly formed in 1868 to infiltrate the First International, and at the London Congress in 1881 he spoke privately in favor of having secret alongside open organizations. Also in 1877 he helped to write an article calling for propaganda by deed, and in 1880 he published an article calling for action not only "by speech, by writing" and so on, but also "by dagger, gun and dynamite."* It is important to realize that Kropotkin was a much more aggressive character than one might guess from his *Memoirs* or from his later reputation.

And yet, though he played down what he had done, Kropotkin did not deny his past. Even when he had become acceptable enough for his memoirs to be printed in a re-

* This article, "Action," was written by Carlo Cafiero, not Kropotkin; but it was published in *Le Révolté* (the paper Kropotkin had founded in 1879) on December 25, 1880, when he was still the main editor.

spectable American magazine and then by respectable American and British publishers, he still proclaimed his revolutionary position right to the end of his book— and indeed to the end of his life. In his later years he came to occupy a position similar to those of Voltaire and Tolstoy before him and of Pasternak and Bertrand Russell after him —a subversive intellectual who was too obstinate to tame and too famous to silence, and who was important no longer so much for what he actually said or did as for what he stood for. At times, indeed, Kropotkin seems too good to be true, and today he can certainly be seen to have been overoptimistic about the future. A Kropotkin in Russia today would rebel against an even crueler regime; he would be arrested after a few days, not after several years; he would be treated far worse in prison, and he would find it far harder to escape; if he did manage to do so, he would not be able to travel freely across the world; if he went to Britain, he would be an undesirable alien rather than an honored guest; if he went to the United States he would not be let in at all; if he wrote what he believed, he would have difficulty in getting it published. Half a century after his death, this makes his example all the more admirable. We need more Kropotkins, and a good beginning is to read his magnificent account of his own life.

NICOLAS WALTER

November, 1969
LONDON, ENGLAND.

NOTE

THIS book probably would not have been written for some time to come, but for the kind invitation and most friendly encouragement of the editor and the publishers of "The Atlantic Monthly" to write it for serial publication in their magazine. I feel it a most pleasant duty to express here my very best thanks for the hospitality that was offered to me, and for the friendly pressure that was exercised to induce me to undertake this work. It was published in "The Atlantic Monthly" (September, 1898, to September, 1899), under the title, "The Autobiography of a Revolutionist." Preparing it now for publication in book form, I have added considerably to the original text in the parts dealing with my youth and my stay in Siberia, and especially in the Sixth Part, in which I have told the story of my life in Western Europe.

P. KROPÓTKIN.

BROMLEY, KENT, October, 1899.

CONTENTS

NOTE ON THE PORTRAITS

The frontispiece portrait of P. Kropótkin is from a photograph (about 1886) by Nadar, Paris. The one facing page 210 shows him at the age of twenty-two, and is from a photograph by Bergamasco, St. Petersburg. That of his mother, Ekaterína Nikoláevna Kropótkin (facing page 12), is from a painting.

INTRODUCTION
TO THE FIRST EDITION

THE autobiographies we owe to great minds have generally been of one of the three following types: "So far I went astray; thus I found the true path" (St. Augustine); or, "So bad was I, but who dare consider himself better?" (Rousseau); or, "This is the way a genius has slowly been evolved from within and by favorable surroundings" (Goethe). In all these forms of self-representation the author is mainly occupied with himself.

In the nineteenth century the autobiographies of men of mark are very often shaped on these lines: "So talented and attractive was I; such appreciation and admiration I won!" (Johanne Louise Heiberg, "A Life lived over in Recollection"). Or, "So talented was I and so worthy of being loved, but yet so unappreciated; and these were the hard struggles I went through before I won the crown of fame" (Hans Christian Andersen, "The Story of my Life"). In these two classes of life-records, the author is occupied only with what his fellow men have thought of him and said about him.

The author of the autobiography before us is not intent upon his own capabilities, and consequently describes no struggle to gain recognition. Still less does he care for the opinions of his fellow men about himself; what others have thought of him he mentions only once, with a single word.

There is in this work no gazing upon one's image. The author is not one of those who willingly speak of themselves; he does so reluctantly and with a certain shyness. There is here no confession that reveals the inner self, no

sentimentality, and no cynicism. The author speaks neither
of his sins nor of his virtues; he enters into no vulgar
intimacy with his reader. He does not say when he fell
in love, and so little touches upon his relations with the
other sex that he even does not mention his marriage; we
learn only incidentally that he is married at all. That he
is a father, and a very loving one, he finds time to mention
but once in his rapid review of the last sixteen years of
his life.

He is more anxious to give the psychology of his contemporaries than of himself. One finds in his book the
psychology of official Russia and of the masses underneath, of Russia struggling forward and of Russia stagnant.
And he strives to give the history of his contemporaries
rather than his own history. The record of his life contains, consequently, the history of Russia during his lifetime, as well as the history of the labor movement in
Europe during the last half-century. When he plunges
into his own inner world, we see the outer world reflected
in it.

There is, nevertheless, in this book, analogous with
Goethe's aim in "Dichtung und Wahrheit," a representation of how a remarkable mind has been shaped; and, in
analogy with the "Confessions" of St. Augustine, we have
the story of an inner crisis which corresponds with what in
olden times was called "conversion." In fact, this inner
crisis is the turning-point and the core of the book.

There are at this moment only two great Russians who
think for the Russian people, and whose thoughts belong
to mankind, — Leo Tolstóy and Peter Kropótkin. Tolstóy
has often told us, in poetical shape, parts of his life.
Kropótkin gives us here for the first time, without any
poetical recasting, a rapid survey of his whole career.

However radically different these two men are, there is
one parallel which can be drawn between their lives and

their views of life. Tolstóy is an artist, Kropótkin is a
man of science; but neither, at a certain period of his life,
could find peace in continuing the work to which he had
brought great inborn capacities. Religious considerations
brought Tolstóy, social considerations brought Kropótkin,
to abandon the paths they had first taken. Both are filled
with love for mankind; and they are at one in the severe
condemnation of the indifference, the thoughtlessness, the
crudeness, and brutality of the upper classes, as well as in
the attraction they both feel for the life of the downtrodden and ill-used man of the people. Both see more
cowardice than stupidity in the world. Both are idealists,
and both have the reformer's temperament. Both are peace-
loving natures, and Kropótkin is the more peaceful of the
two, — although Tolstóy always preaches peace and condemns those who take right into their own hands and
resort to force, while Kropótkin justifies their action and
was on friendly terms with the terrorists. The point
upon which they differ most is their attitude toward the
intelligent educated man and toward science, which in his
religious passion Tolstóy disdains and disparages, while
Kropótkin holds both in high esteem, although at the same
time he condemns men of science for forgetting the people
and the misery of the people.

Many a man and many a woman has accomplished a
great life-work without having led a great life. Many
people are interesting, although their lives may have been
quite insignificant and commonplace. Kropótkin's life is
both great and interesting.

One will find in this volume a combination of all the
elements out of which an intensely eventful life is composed : idyl and tragedy, drama and romance. The childhood
in Moscow and in the country, the portraits of his mother,
sisters, and teachers, or of the old and trusty servants, and
the many pictures of patriarchal life are done in such a

masterly way that every heart will be touched by them.
The landscapes, the story of the unusually intense love
between the two brothers, — all this is pure idyl. Side
by side with these things there is, unhappily, plenty of
sorrow and suffering : the harshness in family life, the
cruel treatment of the serfs, and the narrow-mindedness and
heartlessness which are the ruling stars of men's destinies.

There is variety and there are dramatic catastrophes; life
at court and life in prison; life in the highest Russian
society, with emperors and grand dukes, and life in poverty,
with the working proletariat, in London and in Switzerland. There are changes of costume as in a drama, the
chief actor having to appear during the day in fine dress in
the Winter Palace, and in the evening in peasant's clothes
in the suburbs, as a preacher of revolution. And there is,
too, the sensational element that belongs to the novel.
Although nobody could be simpler in tone and style than
Kropótkin, nevertheless parts of his tale, from the very
nature of the events he has to tell, are more intensely exciting than any part of those novels which aim only at
being sensational. One reads with breathless interest of
the preparations for the escape from the hospital of the
fortress of St. Peter and St. Paul, and the bold execution
of the plan.

Few men have moved, as Kropótkin did, in all classes of
society; few know all these classes as he does. What a
picture ! — Kropótkin, as a little boy with curled hair, in
a fancy dress costume, standing by the Emperor Nicholas,
or running after the Emperor Alexander as his page, with
the idea of protecting him. And then that other picture :
Kropótkin in a terrible prison, sending away the Grand
Duke Nicholas, or listening to the growing insanity of a
peasant who is confined in a cell under his very feet.

He has lived the life of the aristocrat and of the worker;
he has been page de chambre of the Emperor and an impecu-

nious writer; he has lived the life of the student, the officer, the man of science, the explorer of unknown lands, the administrator, and the hunted revolutionist.   In exile he has had at times to live upon tea and bread as a Russian peasant, and he has been exposed to espionage and murder plots like a Russian emperor.

Few men have had an equally wide field of experience. Just as Kropótkin is able, as a geologist, to survey prehistoric evolution for hundreds of thousands of years past, so too he has assimilated the whole historical evolution of his own times.   To the literary and scientific education which is won in the study and in the university (such as the knowledge of languages, belles-lettres, philosophy, and higher mathematics), he added at an early stage of his life that education which is gained in the workshop and the laboratory, as also in the open field, — the study of natural science, military science, fortification, machines, and factories.   His intellectual equipment is universal.

How this active mind must have suffered when he was reduced to the inactivity of prison life!   What a test of endurance, and what an exercise in stoicism!   Kropótkin says somewhere that a morally developed personality must be at the foundation of every organization.   That applies to him.   Life has made of him one of the corner-stones for the building of the future.

The crisis in Kropótkin's life has two turning-points which must be mentioned.

He approaches his thirtieth year, the decisive year in a man's life.   With heart and soul he is a man of science ; he has made a valuable scientific discovery.   He has found out that the maps of Northern Asia are incorrect; not only that the old conceptions of the geography of Asia are wrong, but that the theories of Humboldt are also in conflict with the facts.   For more than two years he has plunged into laborious research.   Then, all of a sudden, he sees on a certain day flash upon him the true relations of the facts; he understands that the main lines of structure in Asia are not from north to south or from west to east, but from the southwest to the northeast. He submits his discovery to test, he applies it to numerous separated facts, and it stands the test. Now he knows the joys of scientific revelation in the highest and purest form; he feels how elevating is their action on the mind.

Then comes the crisis. Sorrow follows, because these joys are the lot of so few. He asks himself whether he has the right to enjoy them alone. He feels that there is a higher duty, — to do his part in bringing to the mass of the people the knowledge already gained rather than to work at making new discoveries.

For my part I do not think that he was right. With such conceptions Pasteur would not have been the benefactor of mankind that he has been. After all, everything, in the last resort, is to the benefit of the mass of the people. I think that one does the utmost for the well-being of all when one achieves the most intense production that one can. But this fundamental notion is characteristic of Kropótkin; it gives his essence.

And this tendency of his mind carries him further. In Finland, where he has gone to make a new scientific discovery, as he comes to the idea — which was heresy then — that in prehistoric times all Northern Europe was buried under ice, he is so much impressed with compassion for the poor, the suffering, who often know hunger in their struggle for bread, that he considers it his highest, absolute duty to become a teacher and a helper of the great working and destitute masses. Soon after that a new world opens before him, — the life of the working classes, — and he *learns* from those whom he intends to *teach*.

Five or six years later the crisis appears in its second phase. It happens in Switzerland. Already during his

first stay in that country Kropótkin had abandoned the
group of state socialists, from fear of an economic despotism, from hatred of centralization, from love for the freedom of the individual and the community. However, it is
only after his long imprisonment in Russia, during his second stay among the intelligent workers of western Switzerland, that the conception, which has floated before his eyes,
of a new structure of society more distinctly dawns upon
him as a society of federated associations, coöperating in
about the same way as railway companies, or the postal
departments of separate countries, coöperate now. He
knows that he cannot dictate to the future the lines which
it will have to follow; he is convinced that all must grow
out of the constructive activity of the masses, but for illustration's sake he compares the coming structure with the
guilds and the mutual relations which existed in mediæval
times, and were worked out from below. He does not
believe at all in the distinction between leaders and led;
but I must confess that I am old-fashioned enough to feel
pleased when Kropótkin, by a slight inconsistency, says
once in praise of a friend that he was "a born leader."

The author describes himself as a revolutionist, and he
is surely quite right in so doing. But seldom have there
been revolutionists as humane and as mild as he is. One
feels astounded when in one passage — where he speaks of
the possibility of an armed conflict with the Swiss police —
a fighting instinct appears in his character, as it exists in
the characters of all of us. He cannot say precisely whether
he and his friends felt a relief at being spared a fight, or a
regret that the fight did not take place. This expression
of feeling stands alone. He has never been an avenger, but
always a martyr.

He does not impose sacrifices upon others : he makes
them himself. All his life he has done it, but in such a
way that the sacrifice seems to have cost him nothing, so

little does he make of it.   And with all his energy he is so little vindictive that of a disgusting prison doctor he only remarks: "The less said of him the better."

He is a revolutionist without emphasis, and without emblem.   He laughs at the oaths and ceremonies with which conspirators bind themselves in dramas and operas.   This man is simplicity personified.   In character he stands comparison with any of the fighters for freedom of any country.   None have been more disinterested than he, none have loved mankind more than he does.

But he would not permit me to say in the beginning of his book all the good that I think of him, and should I say it my words would outrun the limits of a reasonable Introduction.

GEORG BRANDES.

MEMOIRS OF A REVOLUTIONIST

PART FIRST

CHILDHOOD

I

Moscow is a city of slow historical growth, and down to the present time its different parts have wonderfully well retained the features which have been stamped upon them in the slow course of history. The Trans-Moskva River district, with its broad, sleepy streets and its monotonous gray-painted, low-roofed houses, of which the entrance-gates remain securely bolted day and night, has always been the secluded abode of the merchant class, and the stronghold of the outwardly austere, formalistic, and despotic Nonconformists of the "Old Faith." The citadel, or Kreml, is still the stronghold of church and state; and the immense space in front of it, covered with thousands of shops and warehouses, has been for centuries a crowded beehive of commerce, and still remains the heart of a great internal trade which spreads over the whole surface of the vast empire. The Tverskáya and the Smiths' Bridge have been for hundreds of years the chief centres for the fashionable shops; while the artisans' quarters, the Pluschíkha and the Dorogomílovka, retain the very same features which characterized their uproarious populations in the times of the Moscow Tsars. Each quarter is a little world in itself; each has its own physiognomy, and lives its own separate

life.   Even the railways — when they made an irruption
into the old capital — grouped apart in special centres on
the outskirts of the old town their stores and machine-
works, their heavily loaded carts and engines.

However, of all parts of Moscow, none, perhaps, is more
typical than that labyrinth of clean, quiet, winding streets
and lanes which lies at the back of the Kreml, between
two great radial streets, the Arbát and the Prechístenka,
and is still called the Old Equerries' Quarter, — the
Stáraya Konyúshennaya.

Some fifty years ago, there lived in this quarter, and
slowly died out, the old Moscow nobility, whose names
were so frequently mentioned in the pages of Russian
history before the times of Peter I., but who subsequently
disappeared to make room for the newcomers, "the men
of all ranks," called into service by the founder of the
Russian state.   Feeling themselves supplanted at the St.
Petersburg court, these nobles of the old stock retired
either to the Old Equerries' Quarter in Moscow, or to their
picturesque estates in the country round about the capital,
and they looked with a sort of contempt and secret jealousy
upon the motley crowd of families which came "from no
one knew where" to take possession of the highest functions of the government, in the new capital on the banks
of the Nevá.

In their younger days, most of them had tried their fortunes in the service of the state, chiefly in the army; but
for one reason or another they had soon abandoned it,
without having risen to high rank.   The more successful
ones obtained some quiet, almost honorary position in their
mother city, — my father was one of these, — while most
of the others simply retired from active service.   But
wheresoever they might have been shifted, in the course of
their careers, over the wide surface of Russia, they always
somehow managed to spend their old age in a house of

their own in the Old Equerries' Quarter, under the shadow of the church where they had been baptized, and where the last prayers had been pronounced at the burial of their parents.

New branches budded from the old stocks. Some of them achieved more or less distinction in different parts of Russia; some owned more luxurious houses in the new style in other quarters of Moscow or at St. Petersburg; but the branch which continued to reside in the Old Equerries' Quarter, somewhere near to the green, the yellow, the pink, or the brown church which was endeared through family associations, was considered as the true representative of the family, irrespective of the position it occupied in the family tree. Its old-fashioned head was treated with great respect, not devoid, I must say, of a slight tinge of irony, even by those younger representatives of the same stock who had left their mother city for a more brilliant career in the St. Petersburg Guard or in the court circles. He personified for them the antiquity of the family and its traditions.

In these quiet streets, far away from the noise and bustle of the commercial Moscow, all the houses had much the same appearance. They were mostly built of wood, with bright green sheet-iron roofs, the exteriors stuccoed and decorated with columns and porticoes; all were painted in gay colors. Nearly every house had but one story, with seven or nine big, gay-looking windows facing the street. A second story was admitted only in the back part of the house, which looked upon a spacious yard, surrounded by numbers of small buildings, used as kitchens, stables, cellars, coach-houses, and as dwellings for the retainers and servants. A wide gate opened upon this yard, and a brass plate on it usually bore the inscription, " House of So and So, Lieutenant or Colonel, and Commander," — very seldom " Major-General " or any similarly elevated civil rank.

But if a more luxurious house, embellished by a gilded iron railing and an iron gate, stood in one of those streets, the brass plate on the gate was sure to bear the name of "Commerce Counsel" or "Honorable Citizen" So and So. These were the intruders, those who came unasked to settle in this quarter, and were therefore ignored by their neighbors.

No shops were allowed in these select streets, except that in some small wooden house, belonging to the parish church, a tiny grocer's or greengrocer's shop might have been found ; but then, the policeman's lodge stood on the opposite corner, and in the daytime the policeman himself, armed with a halberd, would appear at the door to salute with his inoffensive weapon the officers passing by, and would retire inside when dusk came, to employ himself either as a cobbler, or in the manufacture of some special snuff patronized by the elder male servants of the neighborhood.

Life went on quietly and peacefully — at least for the outsider — in this Moscow Faubourg Saint-Germain. In the morning nobody was seen in the streets. About midday the children made their appearance under the guidance of French tutors and German nurses who took them out for a walk on the snow-covered boulevards. Later on in the day the ladies might be seen in their two-horse sledges, with a valet standing behind on a small plank fastened at the end of the runners, or ensconced in an old-fashioned carriage, immense and high, suspended on big curved springs and dragged by four horses, with a postilion in front and two valets standing behind. In the evening most of the houses were brightly illuminated, and, the blinds not being drawn down, the passers-by could admire the card-players or the waltzers in the saloons. "Opinions" were not in vogue in those days, and we were yet far from the years when in each one of these houses a struggle began between "fathers and sons," — a struggle that usually ended either in a family tragedy or in a nocturnal visit of the state police. Fifty years ago nothing of the sort was thought of; all was quiet and smooth, — at least on the surface.

In this old Equerries' Quarter I was born in 1842, and here I passed the first fifteen years of my life. Even after our father had sold the house in which our mother died, and bought another, and when again he had sold that house, and we spent several winters in hired houses, until he had found a third one to his taste, within a stone's-throw of the church where he had been baptized, we still remained in the Old Equerries' Quarter, leaving it only during the summer to go to our country-seat.

II

A high, spacious bedroom, the corner room of our house, with a white bed upon which our mother is lying, our baby chairs and tables standing close by, and the neatly served tables covered with sweets and jellies in pretty glass jars, — a room into which we children are ushered at a strange hour, — this is the first half-distinct reminiscence of my life.

Our mother was dying of consumption; she was only thirty-five years old. Before parting with us forever, she had wished to have us by her side, to caress us, to feel happy for a moment in our joys, and she had arranged this little treat by the side of her bed, which she could leave no more. I remember her pale thin face, her large, dark brown eyes. She looked at us with love, and invited us to eat, to climb upon her bed; then all of a sudden she burst into tears and began to cough, and we were told to go.

Some time after, we children — that is, my brother Alexander and myself — were removed from the big house to a small side house in the court-yard. The April sun filled the little rooms with its rays, but our German nurse, Madame Búrman, and Uliána our Russian nurse, told us to go to bed. Their faces wet with tears, they were sewing for us black shirts fringed with broad white tassels. We could not sleep: the unknown frightened us, and we listened to their subdued talk. They said something about our mother which we could not understand. We jumped out of our beds, asking, " Where is mamma ? Where is mamma ? "

Both of them burst into sobs, and began to pat our

curly heads, calling us " poor orphans," until Uliána could hold out no longer, and said, "Your mother is gone there, — to the sky, to the angels."

" How to the sky ? Why ? " our infantile imagination in vain demanded.

This was in April, 1846. I was only three and a half years old, and my brother Sásha not yet five. Where our elder brother and sister, Nicholas and Hélène, had gone I do not know : perhaps they were already at school. Nicholas was twelve years old, Hélène was eleven ; they kept together, and we knew them but little. So' we remained, Alexander and I, in this little house, in the hands of Madame Búrman and Uliána. The good old German lady, homeless and absolutely alone in the wide world, took toward us the place of our mother. She brought us up as well as she could, buying us from time to time some simple toys, and over-feeding us with ginger cakes when ever another old German, who used to sell such cakes, — probably as homeless and solitary as herself, — paid an occasional visit to our house. We seldom saw our father, and the next two years passed without leaving any impression on my memory.

III

Our father was very proud of the origin of his family, and would point with solemnity to a piece of parchment which hung on a wall of his study. It was decorated with our arms, — the arms of the principality of Smolénsk covered with the ermine mantle and the crown of the Monomáchs, — and there was written on it, and certified by the Heraldry Department, that our family originated with a grandson of Rostisláv Mstislávich the Bold (a name familiar in Russian history as that of a Grand Prince of Kíeff), and that our ancestors had been Grand Princes of Smolénsk.

"It cost me three hundred rubles to obtain that parchment," our father used to say. Like most people of his generation, he was not much versed in Russian history, and valued the parchment more for its cost than for its historical associations.

As a matter of fact, our family is of very ancient origin indeed ; but, like most descendants of Rurik who may be regarded as representative of the feudal period of Russian history, it was driven into the background when that period ended, and the Románoffs, enthroned at Moscow, began the work of consolidating the Russian state. In recent times, none of the Kropótkins seem to have had any special liking for state functions. Our great-grandfather and grandfather both retired from the military service when quite young men, and hastened to return to their family estates. It must also be said that of these estates the main one, Urúsovo, situated in the government of Ryazán, on a high hill at the border of fertile prairies, might tempt any one by the beauty of its shadowy forests, its winding rivers, and its endless meadows. Our grandfather was only a lieutenant when he left the service, and retired to Urúsovo, devoting himself to his estate, and to the purchase of other estates in the neighboring provinces.

Probably our generation would have done the same; but our grandfather married a Princess Gagárin, who belonged to a quite different family. Her brother was well known as a passionate lover of the stage. He kept a private theatre of his own, and went so far in his passion as to marry, to the scandal of all his relations, a serf, — the genial actress Semyónova, who was one of the creators of dramatic art in Russia, and undoubtedly one of its most sympathetic figures. To the horror of "all Moscow," she continued to appear on the stage.

I do not know if our grandmother had the same artistic and literary tastes as her brother, — I remember her when she was already paralyzed and could speak only in whispers; but it is certain that in the next generation a leaning toward literature became a characteristic of our family. One of the sons of the Princess Gagárin was a minor Russian poet, and issued a book of poems, — a fact which my father was ashamed of and always avoided mentioning; and in our own generation several of our cousins, as well as my brother and myself, have contributed more or less to the literature of our period.

Our father was a typical officer of the time of Nicholas I. Not that he was imbued with a warlike spirit or much in love with camp life; I doubt whether he spent a single night of his life at a bivouac fire, or took part in one battle. But under Nicholas I. that was of quite secondary importance. The true military man of those times was the officer who was enamored of the military uniform, and utterly despised all other sorts of attire; whose soldiers were trained to perform almost superhuman tricks with their legs and rifles (to break the wood of the rifle into pieces while "presenting arms" was one of those famous tricks); and who could show on parade a row of soldiers as perfectly aligned and as motionless as a row of toy-soldiers. "Very good," the Grand Duke Mikhael said once of a regiment, after having kept it for one hour presenting arms, — "only, *they breathe!*" To respond to the then current conception of a military man was certainly our father's ideal.

True, he took part in the Turkish campaign of 1828; but he managed to remain all the time on the staff of the chief commander; and if we children, taking advantage of a moment when he was in a particularly good temper, asked him to tell us something about the war, he had nothing to tell but of a fierce attack of hundreds of Turkish dogs which one night assailed him and his faithful servant, Frol, as they were riding with dispatches through an abandoned Turkish village. They had to use swords to extricate themselves from the hungry beasts. Bands of Turks would assuredly have better satisfied our imagination, but we accepted the dogs as a substitute. When, however, pressed by our questions, our father told us how he had won the cross of Saint Anne "for gallantry," and the golden sword which he wore, I must confess we felt really disappointed. His story was decidedly too prosaic. The officers of the general staff were lodged in a Turkish village, when it took fire. In a moment the houses were enveloped in flames, and in one of them a child had been left behind. Its mother uttered despairing cries. Thereupon, Frol, who always accompanied his master, rushed into the flames and saved the child. The chief commander, who saw the act, at once gave father the cross for gallantry.

"But, father," we exclaimed, "it was Frol who saved the child!"

"What of that?" replied he, in the most naïve way. "Was he not my man? It is all the same."

He also took some part in the campaign of 1831, during the Polish Revolution, and in Warsaw he made the acquaintance of, and fell in love with, the youngest daughter of the commander of an army corps, General Sulíma. The marriage was celebrated with great pomp, in the Lazienki palace; the lieutenant-governor, Count Paskiéwich, acting as nuptial godfather on the bridegroom's side. "But your mother," our father used to add, "brought me no fortune whatever."

This was true. Her father, Nikolái Semyónovich Sulíma, was not versed in the art of making a career or a fortune. He must have had in him too much of the blood of those Cossacks of the Dnyéper, who knew how to fight the well-equipped, warlike Poles or armies of the Turks, three times more than themselves, but knew not how to avoid the snares of the Moscow diplomacy, and, after having fought against the Poles in the terrible insurrection of 1648, which was the beginning of the end for the Polish republic, lost all their liberties in falling under the dominion of the Russian Tsars. One Sulíma was captured by the Poles and tortured to death at Warsaw, but the other "colonels" of the same stock only fought the more fiercely on that account, and Poland lost Little Russia. As to our grandfather, during Napoleon I.'s invasion he had cut his way, at the head of his regiment of cuirassiers, into a French infantry square bristling with bayonets, and, after having been left for dead on the battlefield, had recovered with a deep cut in his head; but he could not become a valet to the favorite of Alexander I., the omnipotent Arakchéeff, and was consequently sent into a sort of honorary exile, first as a governor-general of West Siberia, and later of East Siberia. In those times such a position was considered more lucrative than a gold mine, but our grandfather returned from Siberia as poor as he went, and left only modest fortunes to his three sons and three daughters. When I went to Siberia, in 1862, I often heard his name mentioned with respect. He was driven to despair by the wholesale stealing which went on in those provinces, and which he had no means to repress.

Our mother was undoubtedly a remarkable woman for the times she lived in. Many years after her death, I discovered, in a corner of a store-room of our country-house, a mass of papers covered with her firm but pretty handwriting: diaries in which she wrote with delight of the scenery of Germany, and spoke of her sorrows and her thirst for happiness; books which she had filled with Russian verses, prohibited by censorship, — among them the beautiful historical ballads of Ryléeff, the poet, whom Nicholas I. hanged in 1826; other books containing music, French dramas, verses of Lamartine, and Byron's poems that she had copied; and a great number of water-color paintings.

Tall, slim, adorned with a mass of dark chestnut hair, with dark brown eyes and a tiny mouth, she looks quite life-like in a portrait in oils that was painted *con amore* by a good artist. Always lively and often careless, she was fond of dancing, and the peasant women in our village would tell us how she would admire from a balcony their ring-dances, — slow and full of grace, — and how finally she would herself join in them. She had the nature of an artist. It was at a ball that she caught the cold that produced the inflammation of the lungs which brought her to the grave.

All who knew her loved her. The servants worshiped her memory. It was in her name that Madame Búrman took care of us, and in her name the Russian nurse bestowed upon us her love. While combing our hair, or signing us with the cross in our beds, Uliána would often say, "And your mamma must now look upon you from the skies, and shed tears on seeing you, poor orphans." Our whole childhood is irradiated by her memory. How often, in some

Ekaterina Nikoláevna Kropótkin
Mother of P. Kropótkin

dark passage, the hand of a servant would touch Alexander
or me with a caress; or a peasant woman, on meeting us in
the fields, would ask, "Will you be as good as your mother
was? She took compassion on us. You will, surely."
"Us" meant, of course, the serfs. I do not know what
would have become of us if we had not found in our house,
among the serf servants, that atmosphere of love which
children must have around them. We were her children,
we bore likeness to her, and they lavished their care upon
us, sometimes in a touching form, as will be seen later on.

Men passionately desire to live after death, but they often
pass away without noticing the fact that the memory of a
really good person always lives. It is impressed upon the
next generation, and is transmitted again to the children.
Is not that an immortality worth striving for?

IV

Two years after the death of our mother our father married again. He had already cast his eyes upon a nice-looking young person, who belonged to a wealthy family, when the fates decided another way. One morning, while he was still in his dressing-gown, the servants rushed madly into his room, announcing the arrival of General Timoféeff, the commander of the sixth army corps, to which our father belonged. This favorite of Nicholas I. was a terrible man. He would order a soldier to be flogged almost to death for a mistake made during a parade, or he would degrade an officer and send him as a private to Siberia because he had met him in the street with the hooks of his high, stiff collar unfastened. With Nicholas General Timoféeff's word was all-powerful.

The general, who had never before been in our house, came to propose to our father to marry his wife's niece, Mademoiselle Elisabeth Karandinó, one of several daughters of an admiral of the Black Sea fleet, — a young lady with a classical Greek profile, said to have been very beautiful. Father accepted, and his second wedding, like the first, was solemnized with great pomp.

"You young people understand nothing of this kind of thing," he said in conclusion, after having told me the story more than once, with a very fine humor which I will not attempt to reproduce. "But do you know what it meant at that time, — the commander of an army corps? Above all, that one-eyed devil, as we used to call him, coming himself to propose? Of course she had no dowry; only a big trunk filled with their ladies' finery, and that Martha, her one serf, dark as a gypsy, sitting upon it."

I have no recollection whatever of this event. I only remember a big drawing-room in a richly furnished house, and in that room a young lady, attractive, but with a rather too sharp southern look, gamboling with us, and saying, " You see what a jolly mamma you will have ; " to which Sásha and I, sulkily looking at her, replied, " Our mamma has flown away to the sky." We regarded so much liveliness with suspicion.

Winter came, and a new life began for us. Our house was sold, and another was bought and furnished completely anew. All that could convey a reminiscence of our mother disappeared, — her portraits, her paintings, her embroideries. In vain Madame Búrman implored to be retained in our house, and promised to devote herself to the baby our stepmother was expecting as to her own child : she was sent away. "Nothing of the Sulímas in my house," she was told. All connection with our uncles and aunts and our grandmother was broken. Uliána was married to Frol, who became a major-domo, while she was made housekeeper ; and for our education a richly paid French tutor, M. Poulain, and a miserably paid Russian student, N. P. Smirnóff, were engaged.

Many of the sons of the Moscow nobles were educated at that time by Frenchmen, who represented the débris of Napoleon's Grande Armée. M. Poulain was one of them. He had just finished the education of the youngest son of the novelist Zagóskin, and his pupil, Serge, enjoyed in the Old Equerries' Quarter the reputation of being so well brought up that our father did not hesitate to engage M. Poulain for the considerable sum of six hundred rubles a year.

M. Poulain brought with him his setter, Trésor, his coffee-pot Napoléon, and his French textbooks, and he began to rule over us and the serf Matvéi who was attached to our service.

His plan of education was very simple. After having woke us up he attended to his coffee, which he used to take in his room. While we were preparing the morning lessons he made his toilet with minute care : he shampooed his gray hair so as to conceal his growing baldness, put on his tail-coat, sprinkled and washed himself with eau-de-cologne, and then escorted us downstairs to say good-morning to our parents. We used to find our father and stepmother at breakfast, and on approaching them we recited in the most official way, "Bonjour, mon cher papa," and "Bonjour, ma chère maman," and kissed their hands. M. Poulain made a very complicated and elegant obeisance in pronouncing the words, "Bonjour, monsieur le prince," and "Bonjour, madame la princesse," after which the procession immediately withdrew and retired upstairs. This ceremony was repeated every morning.

Then our work began. M. Poulain changed his tail-coat for a dressing-gown, covered his head with a leather cap, and dropping into an easy-chair said, "Recite the lesson."

We recited it "by heart," from one mark which was made in the book with the nail to the next mark. M. Poulain had brought with him the grammar of Noël and Chapsal, memorable to more than one generation of Russian boys and girls; a book of French dialogues; a history of the world, in one volume; and a universal geography, also in one volume. We had to commit to memory the grammar, the dialogues, the history, and the geography.

The grammar, with its well-known sentences, "What is grammar?" "The art of speaking and writing correctly," went all right. But the history book, unfortunately, had a preface, which contained an enumeration of all the advantages which can be derived from a knowledge of history. Things went on smoothly enough with the first sentences. We recited : "The prince finds in it magnanimous exam-

ples for governing his subjects; the military commander
learns from it the noble art of warfare." But the moment
we came to law all went wrong. "The jurisconsult meets
in it" — but what the learned lawyer meets in history we
never came to know. That terrible word "jurisconsult"
spoiled all the game. As soon as we reached it we stopped.

"On your knees, *gros pouff!*" exclaimed Poulain.
(That was for me.) "On your knees, *grand dada!*"
(That was for my brother.) And there we knelt, shedding tears and vainly endeavoring to learn all about the
jurisconsult.

It cost us many pains, that preface! We were already
learning all about the Romans, and used to put our sticks
in Uliána's scales when she was weighing rice, "just like
Brennus;" we jumped from our table and other precipices
for the salvation of our country, in imitation of Curtius;
but M. Poulain would still from time to time return to the
preface, and again put us on our knees for that very same
jurisconsult. Was it strange that later on both my brother
and I should entertain an undisguised contempt for jurisprudence?

I do not know what would have happened with geography if Monsieur Poulain's book had had a preface. But
happily the first twenty pages of the book had been torn
away (Serge Zagóskin, I suppose, rendered us that notable
service), and so our lessons commenced with the twenty-
first page, which began, " of the rivers which water France."

It must be confessed that things did not always end with
kneeling. There was in the class-room a birch rod, and
Poulain resorted to it when there was no hope of progress
with the preface or with some dialogue on virtue and propriety; but one day sister Hélène, who by this time had
left the Catherine Institut des Demoiselles, and now occupied a room underneath ours, hearing our cries, rushed,
all in tears, into our father's study, and bitterly reproached

him with having handed us over to our stepmother, who had abandoned us to "a retired French drummer." "Of course," she cried, "there is no one to take their part, but I cannot see my brothers being treated in this way by a drummer!"

Taken thus unprepared, our father could not make a stand. He began to scold Hélène, but ended by approving her devotion to her brothers. Thereafter the birch rod was reserved for teaching the rules of propriety to the setter, Trésor.

No sooner had M. Poulain discharged himself of his heavy educational duties than he became quite another man, — a lively comrade instead of a gruesome teacher. After lunch he took us out for a walk, and there was no end to his tales: we chattered like birds. Though we never went with him beyond the first pages of syntax, we soon learned, nevertheless, "to speak correctly;" we used to *think* in French; and when he had dictated to us half through a book of mythology, correcting our faults by the book, without ever trying to explain to us why a word must be written in a particular way, we had learned "to write correctly."

After dinner we had our lesson with the Russian teacher, a student of the faculty of law in the Moscow University. He taught us all "Russian" subjects, — grammar, arithmetic, history, and so on. But in those years serious teaching had not yet begun. In the meantime he dictated to us every day a page of history, and in that practical way we quickly learned to write Russian quite correctly.

Our best time was on Sundays, when all the family, with the exception of us children, went to dine with Madame la Générale Timoféeff. It would also happen occasionally that both M. Poulain and N. P. Smirnóff would be allowed to leave the house, and when this occurred we were placed under the care of Uliána. After a hurriedly eaten dinner we hastened to the great hall, to which the younger housemaids soon repaired. All sorts of games were started, — blind man, vulture and chickens, and so on; and then, all of a sudden, Tíkhon, the Jack-of-all-trades, would appear with a violin. Dancing began; not that measured and tiresome dancing, under the direction of a French dancing-master "on india-rubber legs," which made part of our education, but free dancing which was not a lesson, and in which a score of couples turned round any way; and this was only preparatory to the still more animated and rather wild Cossack dance. Tíkhon would then hand the violin to one of the older men, and would begin to perform with his legs such wonderful feats that the doors leading to the hall would soon be filled by the cooks and even the coachmen, who came to see the dance so dear to the Russian heart.

About nine o'clock the big carriage was sent to fetch the family home. Tíkhon, brush in hand, crawled on the floor, to make it shine with its virgin glance, and perfect order was restored in the house. And if, next morning, we two had been submitted to the most severe cross-examination, not a word would have been dropped concerning the previous evening's amusements. We never would have betrayed any one of the servants, nor would they have betrayed us. One Sunday, my brother and I, playing alone in the wide hall, ran against a bracket which supported a costly lamp. The lamp was broken to pieces. Immediately a council was held by the servants. No one scolded us; but it was decided that early next morning Tíkhon should at his risk and peril slip out of the house, and run to the Smiths' Bridge in order to buy another lamp of the same pattern. It cost fifteen rubles, — an enormous sum for the servants; but it was bought, and we never heard a word of reproach about it.

When I think of it now, and all these scenes come back

to my memory, I remember that we never heard coarse language in any of the games, nor saw in the dances anything like the kind of dancing which children are now taken to admire in the theatres. In the servants' house, among themselves, they assuredly used coarse expressions; but we were children, — *her* children, — and that protected us from anything of the sort.

In those days children were not bewildered by a profusion of toys, as they are now. We had almost none, and were thus compelled to rely upon our own inventiveness. Besides, we both had early acquired a taste for the theatre. The inferior carnival theatres, with the thieving and fighting shows, produced no lasting impression upon us: we ourselves played enough at robbers and soldiers. But the great star of the ballet, Fanny Elssler, came to Moscow, and we saw her. When father took a box in the theatre, he always secured one of the best, and paid for it well; but then he insisted that all the members of the family should enjoy it to its full value. Small though I was at that time, Fanny Elssler left upon me the impression of a being so full of grace, so light, and so artistic in all her movements that ever since I have been unable to feel the slightest interest in a dance which belongs more to the domain of gymnastics than to the domain of art.

Of course, the ballet that we saw — Gitana, the Spanish Gypsy — had to be repeated at home; its substance, not the dances. We had a ready-made stage, as the doorway which led from our bedroom into the class-room had a curtain instead of a door. A few chairs put in a half-circle in front of the curtain, with an easy-chair for M. Poulain, became the hall and the imperial lodge, and an audience could easily be mustered with the Russian teacher, Uliána, and a couple of maids from the servants' rooms.

Two scenes of the ballet had to be represented by some

means or other : the one where the little Gitana is brought
by the gypsies into their camp in a wheelbarrow, and that
in which Gitana makes her first appearance on the stage,
descending from a hill and crossing a bridge over a brook
which reflects her image. The audience burst into frantic
applause at this point, and the cheers were evidently called
forth — so we thought, at least — by the reflection in the
brook.

We found our Gitana in one of the youngest girls in the
maid-servants' room. Her rather shabby blue cotton dress
was no obstacle to personifying Fanny Elssler. An over-
turned chair, pushed along by its legs, head downwards,
was an acceptable substitute for the wheelbarrow. But the
brook ! Two chairs and the long ironing-board of Andréi,
the tailor, made the bridge, and a piece of blue cotton
made the brook. The image in the brook, however, would
not appear full size, do what we might with M. Poulain's
little shaving-glass. After many unsuccessful endeavors we
had to give it up, but we bribed Uliána to behave as if she
saw the image, and to applaud loudly at this passage, so
that finally we began to believe that perhaps something of
it could be seen.

Racine's " Phèdre," or at least the last act of it, also
went off nicely ; that is, Sásha recited the melodious verses
beautifully, —

"A peine nous sortions des portes de Trézène;"

and I sat absolutely motionless and unconcerned during the
whole length of the tragic monologue intended to apprise
me of the death of my son, down to the place where, according to the book, I had to exclaim, " O, dieux ! "

But whatsoever we might impersonate, all our performances invariably ended with hell. All candles save one
were put out, and this one was placed behind a transparent
paper to imitate flames, while my brother and I, concealed

from view, howled in the most appalling way as the condemned. Uliána, who did not like to have any allusion
to the Evil One made at bedtime, looked horrified; but I
ask myself now whether this extremely concrete representation of hell, with a candle and a sheet of paper, did not
contribute to free us both at an early age from the fear of
eternal fire. Our conception of it was too realistic to resist
skepticism.

I must have been very much of a child when I saw the
great Moscow actors: Schépkin, Sadóvskiy, and Shúmski,
in Gogol's "Revisór" and another comedy; still, I remember not only the salient scenes of the two plays, but even
the forms and expressions of these great actors of the
realistic school which is now so admirably represented by
Duse. I remembered them so well that when I saw the
same plays given at St. Petersburg, by actors belonging to
the French declamatory school, I found no pleasure in
their acting, always comparing them with Schépkin and
Sadóvskiy, by whom my taste in dramatic art was settled.

This makes me think that parents who wish to develop
artistic taste in their children ought to take them occasionally to really well-acted, good plays, instead of feeding
them on a profusion of so-called "children's pantomimes."

V

WHEN I was in my eighth year, the next step in my career was taken, in a quite unforeseen way. I do not know exactly on what occasion it happened, but probably it was on the twenty-fifth anniversary of Nicholas I.'s accession, when great festivities were arranged for at Moscow. The imperial family were coming to the old capital, and the Moscow nobility intended to celebrate this event by a fancy-dress ball, in which children were to play an important part. It was agreed that the whole motley crowd of nationalities of which the population of the Russian Empire is composed should be represented at this ball to greet the monarch. Great preparations went on in our house, as well as in all the houses of our neighborhood. Some sort of remarkable Russian costume was made for our stepmother. Our father, being a military man, had to appear, of course, in his uniform ; but those of our relatives who were not in the military service were as busy with their Russian, Greek, Caucasian, and Mongolian costumes as the ladies themselves. When the Moscow nobility gives a ball to the imperial family, it must be something extraordinary. As for my brother Alexander and myself, we were considered too young to take part in so important a ceremonial.

And yet, after all, I did take part in it. Our mother was an intimate friend of Madame Nazímoff, the wife of the general who was governor of Wilno when the emancipation of the serfs began to be spoken of. Madame Nazímoff, who was a very beautiful woman, was expected to be present at the ball with her child, about ten years old, and to wear some wonderfully beautiful costume of a Persian princess, in harmony with which the costume of a young Persian prince, exceedingly rich, with a belt covered with jewels, was made ready for her son.   But the boy fell ill just before the ball, and Madame Nazímoff thought that one of the children of her best friend would be the best substitute for her own child.   Alexander and I were taken to her house to try on the costume.   It proved to be too short for Alexander, who was much taller than I, but it fitted me exactly, and therefore it was decided that I should impersonate the Persian prince.

The immense hall of the house of the Moscow nobility was crowded with guests.   Each of the children received a standard bearing at its top the arms of one of the sixty provinces of the Russian Empire.   I had an eagle floating over a blue sea, which represented, as I learned later on, the arms of the government of Astrakhan, on the Caspian Sea. We were then ranged at the back of the great hall, and slowly marched in two rows toward the raised platform upon which the Emperor and his family stood.   As we reached it we marched right and left, and thus stood aligned in one row before the platform.   At a given signal all standards were lowered before the Emperor.   The apotheosis of autocracy was made most impressive : Nicholas was enchanted.   All provinces of the empire worshiped the supreme ruler.   Then we children slowly retired to the rear of the hall.

But here some confusion occurred.   Chamberlains in their gold-embroidered uniforms were running about, and I was taken out of the ranks; my uncle, Prince Gagárin, dressed as a Tungus (I was dizzy with admiration of his fine leather coat, his bow, and his quiver full of arrows), lifted me up in his arms, and planted me on the imperial platform.

Whether it was because I was the tiniest in the row of

boys, or that my round face, framed in curls, looked funny under the high Astrakhan fur bonnet I wore, I know not, but Nicholas wanted to have me on the platform; and there I stood amidst generals and ladies looking down upon me with curiosity. I was told later on that Nicholas I., who was always fond of barrack jokes, took me by the arm, and, leading me to Marie Alexándrovna (the wife of the heir to the throne), who was then expecting her third child, said in his military way, " That is the sort of boy you must bring me," — a joke which made her blush deeply. I well remember, at any rate, Nicholas asking me whether I would have sweets; but I replied that I should like to have some of those tiny biscuits which were served with tea (we were never over-fed at home), and he called a waiter and emptied a full tray into my tall bonnet. "I will take them to Sásha," I said to him.

However, the soldier-like brother of Nicholas, Mikhael, who had the reputation of being a wit, managed to make me cry. "When you are a good boy," he said, "they treat you so," and he passed his big hand over my face downwards; "but when you are naughty, they treat you so," and he passed the hand upwards, rubbing my nose, which already had a marked tendency toward growing in that direction. Tears, which I vainly tried to stop, came into my eyes. The ladies at once took my part, and the good-hearted Marie Alexándrovna took me under her protection. She set me by her side, in a high velvet chair with a gilded back, and our people told me afterward that I very soon put my head in her lap and went to sleep. She did not leave her chair during the whole time the ball was going on.

I remember also that, as we were waiting in the entrance-hall for our carriage, our relatives petted and kissed me, saying, "Pétya, you have been made a page;" but I answered, "I am not a page. I will go home," and was very anxious about my bonnet which contained the pretty little biscuits that I was taking home for Sásha.

I do not know whether Sásha got many of those biscuits, but I recollect what a hug he gave me when he was told about my anxiety concerning the bonnet.

To be inscribed as a candidate for the corps of pages was then a great favor, which Nicholas seldom bestowed on the Moscow nobility. My father was delighted, and already dreamed of a brilliant court career for his son. My step-mother, every time she told the story, never failed to add, "It is all because I gave him my blessing before he went to the ball."

Madame Nazímoff was delighted, too, and insisted upon having her portrait painted in the costume in which she looked so beautiful, with me standing at her side.

My brother Alexander's fate, also, was decided next year. The jubilee of the Izmáylovsk regiment, to which my father had belonged in his youth, was celebrated about this time at St. Petersburg. One night, while all the household was plunged in deep sleep, a three-horse carriage, ringing with the bells attached to the harnesses, stopped at our gate. A man jumped out of it, loudly shouting, "Open! An ordinance from his Majesty the Emperor."

One can easily imagine the terror which this nocturnal visit spread in our house. My father, trembling, went down to his study. "Court-martial, degradation as a soldier," were words which rang then in the ears of every military man; it was a terrible epoch. But Nicholas simply wanted to have the names of the sons of all the officers who had once belonged to the regiment, in order to send the boys to military schools, if that had not yet been done. A special messenger had been dispatched for that purpose from St. Petersburg to Moscow, and was now calling day and night at the houses of the ex-Izmáylovsk officers.

With a shaking hand my father wrote that his eldest son, Nicholas, was already in the first corps of cadets at Moscow;

that his youngest son, Peter, was a candidate for the corps of pages; and that there remained only his second son, Alexander, who had not yet entered the military career. A few weeks later came a paper informing father of the "monarch's favor." Alexander was ordered to enter a corps of cadets in Orel, a small provincial town. It cost my father a deal of trouble and a large sum of money to get Alexander sent to a corps of cadets at Moscow. This new "favor" was obtained only in consideration of the fact that our elder brother was in that corps.

And thus, owing to the will of Nicholas I., we had both to receive a military education, though, before we were many years older, we simply hated the military career for its absurdity. But Nicholas was watchful that none of the sons cf the nobility should embrace any other profession than the military one, unless they were of infirm health; and so we had all three to be officers, to the great satisfaction of my father.

VI

WEALTH was measured in those times by the number of "souls" that a landed proprietor owned. So many "souls" meant so many male serfs: women did not count. My father, who owned nearly twelve hundred souls, in three different provinces, and who had, in addition to his peasants' holdings, large tracts of land which were cultivated by these peasants, was accounted a rich man. He lived up to his reputation, which meant that his house was open to any number of visitors, and that he kept a very large household.

We were a family of eight, occasionally of ten or twelve; but fifty servants at Moscow, and half as many more in the country, were considered not one too many. Four coachmen to attend a dozen horses, three cooks for the masters and two more for the servants, a dozen men to wait upon us at dinner-time (one man, plate in hand, standing behind each person seated at the table), and girls innumerable in the maid-servants' room, — how could any one do with less than this?

Besides, the ambition of every landed proprietor was that everything required for his household should be made at home, by his own men.

"How nicely your piano is always tuned! I suppose Herr Schimmel must be your tuner?" perhaps a visitor would remark.

To be able to answer, "I have my own piano-tuner," was in those times the correct thing.

"What beautiful pastry!" the guests would exclaim, when a work of art, composed of ices and pastry, appeared toward the end of the dinner. "Confess, prince, that it comes from Tremblé" (the fashionable pastry-cook).

"It is made by my own confectioner, a pupil of Tremblé, whom I have allowed to show what he can do," was a reply which elicited general admiration.

To have embroideries, harnesses, furniture, — in fact, everything, — made by one's own men was the ideal of the rich and respected landed proprietor. As soon as the children of the servants attained the age of ten, they were sent as apprentices to the fashionable shops, where they were obliged to spend five or seven years chiefly in sweeping, in receiving an incredible number of thrashings, and in running about town on errands of all sorts. I must own that few of them became masters of their respective arts. The tailors and the shoemakers were found only skillful enough to make clothes or shoes for the servants, and when a really good pastry was required for a dinner-party it was ordered at Tremblé's, while our own confectioner was beating the drum in the band.

That band was another of my father's ambitions, and almost every one of his male servants, in addition to other accomplishments, was a bass-viol or a clarinet in the band. Makár, the piano-tuner, alias under-butler, was also a flutist; Andréi, the tailor, played the French horn; the confectioner was first put to beat the drum, but he misused his instrument to such a deafening degree that a tremendous trumpet was bought for him, in the hope that his lungs would not have the power to make the same noise as his hands; when, however, this last hope had to be abandoned, he was sent to be a soldier. As to "spotted Tíkhon," in addition to his numerous functions in the household as lamp-cleaner, floor-polisher, and footman, he rendered himself useful in the band, — to-day as a trombone, to-morrow as a bassoon, and occasionally as second violin.

The two first violins were the only exceptions to the rule : they were "violins," and nothing else. My father had bought them, with their large families, for a handsome

sum of money, from his sisters (he never bought serfs from
nor sold them to strangers). In the evenings when he was
not at his club, or when there was a dinner or an evening
party at our house, the band of twelve to fifteen musicians
was summoned. They played very nicely, and were in
great demand for dancing-parties in the neighborhood; still
more when we were in the country. This was, of course, a
constant source of gratification to my father, whose permission had to be asked to get the assistance of his band.

Nothing, indeed, gave him more pleasure than to be
asked for help, either in the way mentioned or in any
other : for instance, to obtain free education for a boy, or to
save somebody from a punishment inflicted upon him by a
law court. Although he was liable to fall into fits of rage,
he was undoubtedly possessed of a natural instinct toward
leniency, and when his patronage was requested he would
write scores of letters in all possible directions, to all
sorts of persons of high standing, in favor of his protégé.
At such times, his mail, which was always heavy, would be
swollen by half a dozen special letters, written in a most original, semi-official, and semi-humorous style; each of them
sealed, of course, with his arms, in a big square envelope,
which rattled like a baby-rattle on account of the quantity
of sand it contained, — the use of blotting-paper being then
unknown. The more difficult the case, the more energy he
would display, until he secured the favor he asked for his
protégé, whom in many cases he never saw.

My father liked to have plenty of guests in his house.
Our dinner-hour was four, and at seven the family gathered
round the *samovar* (tea-urn) for tea. Every one belonging
to our circle could drop in at that hour, and from the time
my sister Hélène was again with us there was no lack of
visitors, old and young, who took advantage of the privilege. When the windows facing the street showed bright
light inside, that was enough to let people know that the
family was at home and friends would be welcome.

Nearly every night we had visitors. The green tables were opened in the hall for the card-players, while the ladies and the young people stayed in the reception-room or around Hélène's piano. When the ladies had gone, card-playing continued sometimes till the small hours of the morning, and considerable sums of money changed hands among the players. Father invariably lost. But the real danger for him was not at home: it was at the English Club, where the stakes were much higher than in private houses, and especially when he was induced to join a party of "very respectable" gentlemen, in one of the "most respectable" houses of the Old Equerries' Quarter, where gambling went on all night. On an occasion of this kind his losses were sure to be heavy.

Dancing-parties were not infrequent, to say nothing of a couple of obligatory balls every winter. Father's way, in such cases, was to have everything done in a good style, whatever the expense. But at the same time such niggardliness was practiced in our house in daily life that if I were to recount it, I should be accused of exaggeration. It is said of a family of pretenders to the throne of France, renowned for their truly regal hunting-parties, that in their every-day life even the tallow candles are minutely counted. The same sort of miserly economy ruled in our house with regard to everything; so much so that when we, the children of the house, grew up, we detested all saving and counting. However, in the Old Equerries' Quarter such a mode of life only raised my father in public esteem. "The old prince," it was said, "seems to be sharp over money at home; but he knows how a nobleman ought to live."

In our quiet and clean lanes that was the kind of life which was most in respect. One of our neighbors, General D——, kept his house up in very grand style; and yet the most comical scenes took place every morning between

him and his cook. Breakfast over, the old general, smoking his pipe, would himself order the dinner.

" Well, my boy," he would say to the cook, who appeared
in snow-white attire, " to-day we shall not be many; only
a couple of guests. You will make us a soup, you know,
with some spring delicacies, — green peas, French beans,
and so on. You have not given us any as yet, and madam,
you know, likes a good French spring soup."

" Yes, sir."

" Then, anything you like as an entrée."

" Yes, sir."

" Of course, asparagus is not yet in season, but I saw
yesterday such nice bundles of it in the shops."

" Yes, sir; eight shillings the bundle."

" Quite right!   Then, we are sick of your roasted
chickens and turkeys; you ought to get something for a
change."

" Some venison, sir ? "

" Yes, yes ; anything for a change.'

And when the six courses of the dinner had been decided
on, the old general would ask, " Now, how much shall I
give you for to-day's expenses?   Six shillings will do, I
suppose ? "

" One pound, sir."

" What nonsense, my boy!   Here are six shillings; I
assure you that 's quite enough."

" Eight shillings for asparagus, five for the vegetables."

" Now, look here, my dear boy, be reasonable. I 'll go
as high as seven-and-six, and you must be economical."

And the bargaining would go on thus for half an hour,
until the two would agree upon fourteen shillings and sixpence, with the understanding that the morrow's dinner
should not cost more than three shillings. Whereupon the
general, quite happy at having made such a good bargain,
would take his sledge, make a round of the fashionable

shops, and return quite radiant, bringing for his wife a bottle of exquisite perfume, for which he had paid a fancy price in a French shop, and announcing to his only daughter that a new velvet mantle — "something very simple" and very costly — would be sent for her to try on that afternoon.

All our relatives, who were numerous on my father's side, lived exactly in the same way; and if a new spirit occasionally made its appearance, it usually took the form of some religious passion. Thus, a Prince Gagárin joined the Jesuit order, again to the scandal of "all Moscow;" another young prince entered a monastery, while several older ladies became fanatic devotees.

There was a single exception. One of our nearest relatives, Prince — let me call him Mírski, had spent his youth at St. Petersburg as an officer of the guard. He took no interest in keeping his own tailors and cabinet-makers, for his house was furnished in a grand modern style, and his wearing apparel was all made in the best St. Petersburg shops. Gambling was not his propensity, — he played cards only when in company with ladies; but his weak point was his dinner-table, upon which he spent incredible sums of money.

Lent and Easter were his chief epochs of extravagance. When the Great Lent came, and it would not have been proper to eat meat, cream, or butter, he seized the opportunity to invent all sorts of delicacies in the way of fish. The best shops of the two capitals were ransacked for that purpose; special emissaries were dispatched from his estate to the mouth of the Vólga, to bring back on post-horses (there was no railway at that time) a sturgeon of great size or some extraordinarily cured fish. And when Easter came, there was no end to his inventions.

Easter, in Russia, is the most venerated and also the gayest of the yearly festivals. It is the festival of spring.

The immense heaps of snow which have been lying during the winter along the streets rapidly thaw, and roaring streams run down the streets; not like a thief who creeps in by insensible degrees, but frankly and openly spring comes, — every day bringing with it a change in the state of the snow and the progress of the buds on the trees; the night frosts only keep the thaw within reasonable bounds.   The last week of the Great Lent, Passion Week, was kept in Moscow, in my childhood, with extreme solemnity; it was a time of general mourning, and crowds of people went to the churches to listen to the impressive reading of those passages of the Gospels which relate the sufferings of the Christ.   Not only were meat, eggs, and butter not eaten, but even fish was refused; some of the most rigorous taking no food at all on Good Friday.   The more striking was the contrast when Easter came.

On Saturday every one attended the night service, which began in a mournful way.   Then, suddenly, at midnight, the resurrection news was announced.   All the churches were at once illuminated, and gay peals of bells resounded from hundreds of bell-towers.   General rejoicing began. All the people kissed one another thrice on the cheeks, repeating the resurrection words, and the churches, now flooded with light, shone with the gay toilettes of the ladies. The poorest woman had a new dress; if she had only one new dress a year, she would get it for that night.

At the same time, Easter was, and is still, the signal for a real debauch in eating.   Special Easter cream cheeses (*páskha*) and Easter bread (*koolích*) are prepared; and every one, no matter how poor he or she may be, must have be it only a small paskha and a small koolich, with at least one egg painted red, to be consecrated in the church, and to be used afterward to break the Lent.   With most old Russians, eating began at night, after a short Easter mass, immediately after the consecrated food had been brought

from church ; but in the houses of the nobility the ceremony
was postponed till Sunday morning, when a table was covered with all sorts of viands, cheeses and pastry, and all the
servants came to exchange with their masters three kisses
and a red-painted egg. Throughout Easter week a table
spread with Easter food stood in the great hall, and every
visitor was invited to partake.

On this occasion Prince Mírski surpassed himself.
Whether he was at St. Petersburg or at Moscow, messengers
brought to his house, from his estate, a specially prepared
cream cheese for the paskha, and his cook managed to make
out of it a piece of artistic confectionery. Other messengers were dispatched to the province of Nóvgorod to get a
bear's ham, which was cured for the prince's Easter table.
And while the princess, with her two daughters, visited the
most austere monasteries, in which the night service would
last three or four hours in succession, and spent all Passion
Week in the most mournful condition of mind, eating only
a piece of dry bread between the visits she paid to Russian,
Roman, and Protestant preachers, her husband made every
morning the tour of the well-known Milútin shops at St.
Petersburg, where all possible delicacies are brought from
the ends of the earth. There he used to select the most
extravagant dainties for his Easter table. Hundreds of
visitors came to his house, and were asked " just to taste "
this or that extraordinary thing.

The end of it was that the prince managed literally to eat
up a considerable fortune. His richly furnished house and
beautiful estate were sold, and when he and his wife were
old they had nothing left, not even a home, and were compelled to live with their children.

No wonder that when the emancipation of the serfs came,
nearly all these families of the Old Equerries' Quarter were
ruined. But I must not anticipate events.

VII

To maintain such numbers of servants as were kept in our house would have been simply ruinous, if all provisions had to be bought at Moscow; but in those times of serfdom things were managed very simply. When winter came, father sat at his table and wrote the following : —

"To the manager of my estate, Nikólskoye, situated in the government of Kalúga, district of Meschóvsk, on the river Siréna, from the Prince Alexéi Petróvich Kropótkin, Colonel and Commander of various orders.

"On receipt of this, and as soon as winter communication is established, thou art ordered to send to my house, situated in the city of Moscow, twenty-five peasant-sledges, drawn by two horses each, one horse from each house, and one sledge and one man from each second house, and to load them with [so many] quarters of oats, [so many] of wheat, and [so many] of rye, as also with all the poultry and geese and ducks, well frozen, which have to be killed this winter, well packed and accompanied by a complete list, under the supervision of a well-chosen man;" and so it went on for a couple of pages, till the next full stop was reached. After this there followed an enumeration of the penalties which would be inflicted in case the provisions should not reach the house situated in such a street, number so and so, in due time and in good condition.

Some time before Christmas the twenty-five peasant-sledges really entered our gates, and covered the surface of the wide yard.

"Frol!" shouted my father, as soon as the report of this great event reached him. "Kiryúshka! Yegórka!

Where are they? Everything will be stolen! Frol, go and receive the oats! Uliána, go and receive the poultry! Kiryúshka, call the princess!"

All the household was in commotion, the servants running wildly in every direction, from the hall to the yard, and from the yard to the hall, but chiefly to the maid-servants' room, to communicate there the Nikólskoye news: "Pásha is going to marry after Christmas. Aunt Anna has surrendered her soul to God," and so on. Letters had also come from the country, and very soon one of the maids would steal upstairs into my room.

"Are you alone? The teacher is not in?"

"No, he is at the university."

"Well, then, be kind and read me this letter from mother."

And I would read to her the naïve letter, which always began with the words, "Father and mother send you their blessings for ages not to be broken." After this came the news: "Aunt Eupraxie lies ill, all her bones aching; and your cousin is not yet married, but hopes to be after Easter; and Aunt Stepanída's cow died on All Saints' day." Following the news came the greetings, two pages of them: "Brother Paul sends you his greetings, and the sisters Mary and Dária send their greetings, and then Uncle Dmítri sends his many greetings," and so on. However, notwithstanding the monotony of the enumeration, each name awakened some remarks: "Then she is still alive, poor soul, if she sends her greetings; it is nine years since she has lain motionless." Or, "Oh, he has not forgotten me; he must be back, then, for Christmas; such a nice boy. You will write me a letter, won't you? and I must not forget him then." I promised, of course, and when the time came I wrote a letter in exactly the same style.

When the sledges had been unloaded, the hall filled with peasants. They had put on their best coats over their

sheepskins, and waited until father should call them into
his room to have a talk about the snow and the prospects
of the next crops.   They hardly dared to walk in their
heavy boots on the polished floor.   A few ventured to sit
down on the edge of an oak bench; they emphatically
refused to make use of chairs.   So they waited for hours,
looking with alarm upon every one who entered father's
room or issued from it.

Some time later on, usually next morning, one of the
servants would run slyly upstairs to the class-room.

" Are you alone ? "

" Yes."

" Then go quickly to the hall.   The peasants want to
see you; something from your nurse."

When I went down to the hall, one of the peasants
would give me a little bundle containing perhaps a few
rye cakes, half a dozen hard-boiled eggs, and some apples,
tied in a motley colored cotton kerchief.   " Take that: it
is your nurse, Vasilísa, who sends it to you.   Look if the
apples are not frozen.   I hope not : I kept them all the
journey on my breast.   Such a fearful frost we had."   And
the broad, bearded face, covered with frost-bites, would smile
radiantly, showing two rows of beautiful white teeth from
beneath quite a forest of hair.

" And this is for your brother, from his nurse Anna,"
another peasant would say, handing me a similar bundle.
" ' Poor boy,' she says, ' he can never have enough at
school.' "

Blushing and not knowing what to say, I would mur-
mur at last, " Tell Vasilísa that I kiss her, and Anna too,
for my brother."   At which all faces would become still
more radiant.

" Yes, I will, to be sure."

Then Kiríla, who kept watch at father's door, would
whisper suddenly, " Run quickly upstairs; your father may

come out in a moment.   Don't forget the kerchief; they
want to take it back."

As I carefully folded the worn kerchief, I most passionately desired to send Vasilísa something.   But I had
nothing to send, not even a toy, and we never had pocket-
money.

Our best time, of course, was in the country.   As soon
as Easter and Whitsuntide had passed, all our thoughts
were directed toward Nikólskoye.   However, time went
on, — the lilacs must be past blooming at Nikólskoye, —
and father had still thousands of affairs to keep him in
town.   At last, five or six peasant-carts entered our yard:
they came to take all sorts of things which had to be sent
to the country-house.   The great old coach and the other
coaches in which we were going to make the journey were
taken out and inspected once more.   The boxes began to
be packed.   Our lessons made slow progress; at every moment we interrupted our teachers, asking whether this or
that book should be taken with us, and long before all
others we began packing our books, our slates, and the toys
that we ourselves had made.

Everything was ready: the peasant-carts stood heavily
loaded with furniture for the country-house, boxes containing the kitchen utensils, and almost countless empty glass
jars which were to be brought back in the autumn filled
with all kinds of preserves.   The peasants waited every
morning for hours in the hall; but the order for leaving
did not come.   Father continued to write all the morning in
his room, and disappeared at night.   Finally, our stepmother
interfered, her maid having ventured to report that the peasants were very anxious to return, as haymaking was near.

Next afternoon, Frol, the major-domo, and Mikhael
Aléeff, the first violin, were called into father's room.
A sack containing the "food money" — that is, a few cop-

pers a day — for each of the forty or fifty souls who were
to accompany the household to Nikólskoye, was handed to
Frol, with a list.   All were enumerated in that list : the
band in full; then the cooks and the under-cooks, the laun-
dresses, the under-laundress who was blessed with a family
of six mites, " Polka Squinting," " Domna the Big One,"
" Domna the Small One," and the rest of them.

The first violin received an " order of march."   I knew
it well, because father, seeing that he never would be
ready, had called me to copy it into the book in which he
used to copy all " outgoing papers : " —

" To my house servant, Mikhael Aléeff, from Prince
Alexéi Petróvich Kropótkin, Colonel and Commander.

" Thou art ordered, on May 29th, at six A. M., to march
out with my loads, from the city of Moscow, for my
estate, situated in the government of Kalúga, district of
Meschóvsk, on the river Siréna, representing a distance of
one hundred and sixty miles from this house ; to look after
the good conduct of the men entrusted to thee, and if any
one of them proves to be guilty of misconduct or of drunk-
enness or of insubordination, to bring the said man before
the commander of the garrison detachment of the separate
corps of the interior garrisons, with the inclosed circular
letter, and to ask that he may be punished by flogging
[the first violin knew who was meant], as an example to
the others.

" Thou art ordered, moreover, to look especially after
the integrity of the goods entrusted to thy care, and to
march according to the following order : First day, stop at
village So and So, to feed the horses ; second day, spend
the night at the town of Podólsk ; " and so on for all the
seven or eight days that the journey would last.

Next day, at ten instead of at six, — punctuality is not
a Russian virtue ("Thank God, we are not Germans," true
Russians used to say), — the carts left the house.   The

servants had to make the journey on foot; only the children were accommodated with a seat in a bath-tub or basket, on the top of a loaded cart, and some of the women might find an occasional resting-place on the rim of a cart. The others had to walk all the hundred and sixty miles. As long as they were marching through Moscow, discipline was maintained : it was peremptorily forbidden to wear top-boots, or to pass a belt over the coat. But when they were on the road, and we overtook them a couple of days later, and especially when it was known that father would stay a few days longer at Moscow, the men and the women — dressed in all sorts of impossible coats, belted with cotton handkerchiefs, burned by the sun or dripping under the rain, and helping themselves along with sticks cut in the woods — certainly looked more like a wandering band of gypsies than the household of a wealthy landowner. Similar peregrinations were made by every household in those times, and when we saw a file of servants marching along one of our streets, we at once knew that the Apúkhtins or the Pryánishnikoffs were migrating.

The carts were gone, yet the family did not move. All of us were sick of waiting; but father still continued to write interminable orders to the managers of his estates, and I copied them diligently into the big " outgoing book." At last the order to start was given. We were called downstairs. My father read aloud the order of march, addressed to "the Princess Kropótkin, wife of Prince Alexéi Petróvich Kropótkin, Colonel and Commander," in which the halting-places during the five days' journey were duly enumerated. True, the order was written for May 30, and the departure was fixed for nine A. M.,though May was gone, and the departure took place in the afternoon: this upset all calculations. But, as is usual in military marching-orders, this circumstance had been foreseen, and was provided for in the following paragraph : —

"If, however, contrary to expectation, the departure of your highness does not take place at the said day and hour, you are requested to act according to the best of your understanding, in order to bring the said journey to its best issue."

Then, all present, the family and the servants, sat down for a moment, signed themselves with the cross, and bade my father good-by. "I entreat you, Alexis, don't go to the club," our stepmother whispered to him. The great coach, drawn by four horses, with a postilion, stood at the door, with its little folding ladder to facilitate climbing in; the other coaches also were there. Our seats were enumerated in the marching-orders, but our stepmother had to exercise "the best of her understanding" even at that early stage of the proceedings, and we started to the great satisfaction of all.

The journey was an inexhaustible source of enjoyment for us children. The stages were short, and we stopped twice a day to feed the horses. As the ladies screamed at the slightest declivity of the road, it was found more convenient to alight each time the road went up or down hill, which it did continually, and we took advantage of this to have a peep into the woods by the roadside, or a run along some crystal brook. The beautifully kept highroad from Moscow to Warsaw, which we followed for some distance, was covered, moreover, with a variety of interesting objects: files of loaded carts, groups of pilgrims, and all sorts of people. Twice a day we stopped in big, animated villages, and after a good deal of bargaining about the prices to be charged for hay and oats, as well as for the samovárs, we dismounted at the gates of an inn. Cook Andréi bought a chicken and made the soup, while we ran in the meantime to the next wood, or examined the yard of the great inn.

At Máloyaroslávetz, where a battle was fought in 1812, when the Russian army vainly attempted to stop Napoleon

in his retreat from Moscow, we usually spent the night.
M. Poulain, who had been wounded in the Spanish campaign, knew, or pretended to know, everything about the
battle at Máloyaroslávetz. He took us to the battlefield,
and explained how the Russians tried to check Napoleon's
advance, and how the Grande Armée crushed them and
made its way through the Russian lines. He explained
it as well as if he himself had taken part in the battle.
Here the Cossacks attempted *un mouvement tournant,* but
Davoust, or some other marshal, routed them and pursued
them just beyond these hills on the right. There the left
wing of Napoleon crushed the Russian infantry, and here
Napoleon himself, at the head of the Old Guard, charged
Kutúzoff's centre, and covered himself and his Guard with
undying glory.

We once took the old Kalúga route, and stopped at Tarú-
tino; but here Poulain was much less eloquent. For it
was at this place that Napoleon, who intended to retreat by
a southern route, was compelled, after a bloody battle, to
abandon that plan, and was forced to follow the Smolénsk
route, which his army had laid waste during its march on
Moscow. But still — so it appeared in Poulain's narrative
— Napoleon was deceived by his marshals; otherwise he
would have marched straight upon Kíeff and Odéssa, and
his eagles would have floated over the Black Sea.

Beyond Kalúga we had to cross for a stretch of five
miles a beautiful pine forest, which remains connected in
my memory with some of the happiest reminiscences of my
childhood. The sand in that forest was as deep as in an
African desert, and we went all the way on foot, while the
horses, stopping every moment, slowly dragged the carriages
in the sand. When I was in my teens, it was my delight
to leave the family behind, and to walk the whole distance
by myself. Immense red pines, centuries old, rose on every
side, and not a sound reached the ear except the voices

of the lofty trees. In a small ravine a fresh crystal spring
murmured, and a passer-by had left in it, for the use of
those who should come after him, a small funnel-shaped
ladle, made of birch bark, with a split stick for a handle.
Noiselessly a squirrel ran up a tree, and the underwood
was as full of mysteries as were the trees. In that forest
my first love of nature and my first dim perception of its
incessant life were born.

Beyond the forest, and past the ferry which took us over
the Ugrá, we left the highroad and entered narrow country
lanes, where green ears of rye bent toward the coach, and
the horses managed to bite mouthfuls of grass on either
side of the way, as they ran, closely pressed to one another
in the narrow, trenchlike road. At last we caught sight of
the willows which marked the approach to our village, and
all of a sudden we saw the elegant pale yellow bell tower
of the Nikólskoye church.

For the quiet life of the landlords of those times Nikólskoye was admirably suited. There was nothing in it of
the luxury which is seen in richer estates; but an artistic
hand was visible in the planning of the buildings and gardens, and in the general arrangement of things. Besides
the main house, which father had recently built, there were,
round a spacious and well-kept yard, several smaller houses,
which, while they gave a greater degree of independence
to their inhabitants, did not destroy the close intercourse
of the family life. An immense "upper garden" was
devoted to fruit trees, and through it the church was
reached; the southern slope of the land, which led to the
river, was entirely given up to a pleasure garden, where
flower-beds were intermingled with alleys of lime-trees,
lilacs, and acacias. From the balcony of the main house
there was a beautiful view of the river, with the ruins of
an old earthen fortress where the Russians offered a stub-

born resistance during the Mongol invasion, and further on
a great area of yellow grain-fields bordered on the horizon
by woods.

In the early years of my childhood we occupied with
M. Poulain one of the separate houses entirely by ourselves;
and after his method of education was softened by the
intervention of our sister Hélène, we were on the best possible terms with him. Father was invariably absent from
home in the summer, which he spent in military inspec-
tions, and our stepmother did not pay much attention to
us, especially after her own child, Pauline, was born. We
were thus always with M. Poulain, who thoroughly enjoyed
the stay in the country, and let us enjoy it. The woods;
the walks along the river; the climbing over the hills to
the old fortress, which Poulain made alive for us as he
told how it was defended by the Russians, and how it was
captured by the Tartars; the little adventures, in one of
which Poulain became our hero by saving Alexander from
drowning; an occasional encounter with wolves, — there
was no end of new and delightful impressions.

Large parties were organized, also, in which all the
family took part, sometimes picking mushrooms in the
woods, and afterward having tea in the midst of the forest,
where a man a hundred years old lived alone with his little
grandson, taking care of bees. At other times we went to
one of father's villages where a big pond had been dug, in
which golden carp were caught by the thousand, — part of
them being taken for the landlord and the remainder being
distributed among all the peasants. My former nurse lived
in that village. Her family was one of the poorest; besides
her husband, she had only a small boy to help her, and
a girl, my foster-sister, who became later on a preacher
and a " virgin " in the Nonconformist sect to which they
belonged. There was no bound to her joy when I came
to see her. Cream, eggs, apples, and honey were all that

she could offer; but the way in which she offered them, in
bright wooden plates, after having covered the table with
a fine snow-white linen tablecloth of her own make (with
the Russian Nonconformists absolute cleanliness is a matter
of religion), and the fond words with which she addressed
me, treating me as her own son, left the warmest feelings
in my heart.   I must say the same of the nurses of my
elder brothers, Nicholas and Alexander, who belonged to
prominent families of two other Nonconformist sects in
Nikólskoye.   Few know what treasuries of goodness can be
found in the hearts of Russian peasants, even after centuries of the most cruel oppression, which might well have
embittered them.

On stormy days M. Poulain had an abundance of tales to
tell us, especially about the campaign in Spain.   Over and
over again we induced him to tell us how he was wounded
in a battle, and every time he came to the point when he
felt warm blood streaming into his boot, we jumped to kiss
him and gave him all sorts of pet names.

Everything seemed to prepare us for the military career:
the predilection of our father (the only toys that I remember his having bought for us were a rifle and a real sentry-
box); the war tales of M. Poulain; nay, even the library
which we had at our disposal.   This library, which had
once belonged to General Repnínsky, our mother's grandfather, a learned military man of the eighteenth century,
consisted exclusively of books on military warfare, adorned
with rich plates and beautifully bound in leather.   It was
our chief recreation, on wet days, to look over the plates
of these books, representing the weapons of warfare since
the times of the Hebrews, and giving plans of all the battles that had been fought since Alexander of Macedonia.
These heavy books also offered excellent material for building out of them strong fortresses which would stand for
some time the blows of a battering-ram, and the projectiles

of an Archimedean catapult (which, however, persisted in sending stones into the windows, and was soon prohibited). Yet neither Alexander nor I became a military man. The literature of the sixties wiped out the teachings of our childhood.

M. Poulain's opinions about revolutions were those of the Orleanist "Illustration Française," of which he received back numbers, and of which we knew all the woodcuts. For a long time I could not imagine a revolution otherwise than in the shape of Death riding on a horse, the red flag in one hand and a scythe in the other, mowing down men right and left. So it was pictured in the "Illustration." But I now think that M. Poulain's dislike was limited to the uprising of 1848, for one of his tales about the Revolution of 1789 deeply impressed my mind.

The title of prince was used in our house with and without occasion. M. Poulain must have been shocked by it, for he began once to tell us what he knew of the great Revolution. I cannot now recall what he said, but one thing I remember, namely, that Count Mirabeau and other nobles one day renounced their titles, and that Count Mirabeau, to show his contempt for aristocratic pretensions, opened a shop decorated with a signboard which bore the inscription, "Mirabeau, tailor." (I tell the story as I had it from M. Poulain.) For a long time after that I worried myself thinking what trade I should take up so as to write, "Kropótkin, such and such a handicraft man." Later on, my Russian teacher, Nikolái Pávlovich Smirnóff, and the general republican tone of Russian literature influenced me in the same way; and when I began to write novels — that is, in my twelfth year — I adopted the signature P. Kropótkin, which I never have departed from, notwithstanding the remonstrances of my chiefs when I was in the military service.

VIII

In the autumn of 1852 my brother Alexander was sent to the corps of cadets, and from that time we saw each other only during the holidays and occasionally on Sundays. The corps of cadets was five miles from our house, and although we had a dozen horses, it always happened that when the time came to send a sledge to the corps there was no horse free for that purpose. My eldest brother, Nicholas, came home very seldom. The relative freedom which Alexander found at school, and especially the influence of two of his teachers in literature, developed his intellect rapidly, and later on I shall have ample occasion to speak of the beneficial influence that he exercised upon my own development. It is a great privilege to have had a loving, intelligent elder brother.

In the meantime I remained at home. I had to wait till my turn to enter the corps of pages should come, and that did not happen until I was nearly fifteen years of age. M. Poulain was dismissed, and a German tutor was engaged instead. He was one of those idealistic men who are not uncommon among Germans, but I remember him chiefly on account of the enthusiastic way in which he used to recite Schiller's poetry, accompanying it by a most naïve kind of acting that delighted me. He stayed with us only one winter.

The next winter I was sent to attend the classes at a Moscow gymnasium ; and finally I remained with our Russian teacher, Smirnóff. We soon became friends, especially after my father took both of us for a journey to his Ryazán estate. During this journey we indulged in all sorts of fun,

and we used to invent humorous stories in connection with
the men and the things that we saw; while the impression produced upon me by the hilly tracts we crossed added
some new and fine touches to my growing love of nature.
Under the impulse given me by Smirnóff, my literary tastes
also began to grow, and during the years from 1854 to
1857 I had full opportunity to develop them. My teacher,
who had by this time finished his studies at the university,
obtained a small clerkship in a law court, and spent his
mornings there. I was thus left to myself till dinner-time,
and after having prepared my lessons and taken a walk, I
had plenty of time to read, and especially to write. In the
autumn, when my teacher returned to his office at Moscow,
while we remained in the country, I was left again to myself,
and though in continual intercourse with the family, and
spending a good deal of time in playing with my little sister
Pauline, I could in fact dispose of my time as I liked for
reading and writing.

Serfdom was then in the last years of its existence. It
is recent history, — it seems to be only of yesterday; and
yet, even in Russia, few realize what serfdom was in reality.
There is a dim conception that the conditions which it
created were very bad; but those conditions, as they affected
human beings bodily and mentally, are not generally understood. It is amazing, indeed, to see how quickly an institution and its social consequences are forgotten when the
institution has ceased to exist, and with what rapidity men
and things change. I will try to recall the conditions of
serfdom by telling, not what I heard, but what I saw.

Uliána, the housekeeper, stands in the passage leading
to father's room, and crosses herself; she dares neither to
advance nor to retreat. At last, after having recited a
prayer, she enters the room, and reports, in a hardly audible
voice, that the store of tea is nearly at an end, that there

are only twenty pounds of sugar left, and that the other provisions will soon be exhausted.

"Thieves, robbers!" shouts my father. "And you, you are in league with them!" His voice thunders throughout the house. Our stepmother leaves Uliána to face the storm. But father cries, "Frol, call the princess! Where is she?" And when she enters, he receives her with the same reproaches.

"You also are in league with this progeny of Ham; you are standing up for them;" and so on, for half an hour or more.

Then he commences to verify the accounts. At the same time, he thinks about the hay. Frol is sent to weigh what is left of that, and our stepmother is sent to be present during the weighing, while father calculates how much of it ought to be in the barn. A considerable quantity of hay appears to be missing, and Uliána cannot account for several pounds of such and such provisions. Father's voice becomes more and more menacing; Uliána is trembling; but it is the coachman who now enters the room, and is stormed at by his master. Father springs at him, strikes him, but he keeps repeating, "Your highness must have made a mistake."

Father repeats his calculations, and this time it appears that there is more hay in the barn than there ought to be. The shouting continues; he now reproaches the coachman with not having given the horses their daily rations in full; but the coachman calls on all the saints to witness that he gave the animals their due, and Frol invokes the Virgin to confirm the coachman's appeal.

But father will not be appeased. He calls in Makár, the piano-tuner and sub-butler, and reminds him of all his recent sins. He was drunk last week, and must have been drunk yesterday, for he broke half a dozen plates. In fact, the breaking of these plates was the real cause of all the disturbance: our stepmother had reported the fact to father in the morning, and that was why Uliána was received with more scolding than was usually the case, why the verification of the hay was undertaken, and why father now continues to shout that "this progeny of Ham" deserve all the punishments on earth.

Of a sudden there is a lull in the storm. My father takes his seat at the table and writes a note. "Take Makár with this note to the police station, and let a hundred lashes with the birch rod be given to him."

Terror and absolute muteness reign in the house.

The clock strikes four, and we all go down to dinner; but no one has any appetite, and the soup remains in the plates untouched. We are ten at table, and behind each of us a violinist or a trombone-player stands, with a clean plate in his left hand; but Makár is not among them.

"Where is Makár?" our stepmother asks. "Call him in."

Makár does not appear, and the order is repeated. He enters at last, pale, with a distorted face, ashamed, his eyes cast down. Father looks into his plate, while our stepmother, seeing that no one has touched the soup, tries to encourage us.

"Don't you find, children," she says, "that the soup is delicious?"

Tears suffocate me, and immediately after dinner is over I run out, catch Makár in a dark passage, and try to kiss his hand; but he tears it away, and says, either as a reproach or as a question, "Let me alone; you, too, when you are grown up, will you not be just the same?"

"No, no, never!"

Yet father was not among the worst of landowners. On the contrary, the servants and the peasants considered him one of the best. What we saw in our house was going on everywhere, often in much more cruel forms. The flogging of the serfs was a regular part of the duties of the police and of the fire brigade.

A landowner once made the remark to another, "Why is it that the number of souls on your estate increases so slowly? You probably do not look after their marriages."

A few days later the general returned to his estate. He had a list of all the inhabitants of his village brought him, and picked out from it the names of the boys who had attained the age of eighteen, and the girls just past sixteen, — these are the legal ages for marriage in Russia. Then he wrote, "John to marry Anna, Paul to marry Paráshka," and so on with five couples. "The five weddings," he added, "must take place in ten days, the next Sunday but one."

A general cry of despair rose from the village. Women, young and old, wept in every house. Anna had hoped to marry Gregory; Paul's parents had already had a talk with the Fedótoffs about their girl, who would soon be of age. Moreover, it was the season for ploughing, not for weddings; and what wedding can be prepared in ten days? Dozens of peasants came to see the landowner; peasant women stood in groups at the back entrance of the estate, with pieces of fine linen for the landowner's spouse, to secure her intervention. All in vain. The master had said that the weddings should take place at such a date, and so it must be.

At the appointed time, the nuptial processions, in this case more like burial processions, went to the church. The women cried with loud voices, as they are wont to cry during burials. One of the house valets was sent to the church, to report to the master as soon as the wedding ceremonies were over; but soon he came running back, cap in hand, pale and distressed.

"Paráshka," he said, "makes a stand; she refuses to be married to Paul. Father" (that is, the priest) "asked her, 'Do you agree?' but she replied in a loud voice, 'No, I don't.'"

The landowner grew furious. "Go and tell that long-maned drunkard" (meaning the priest; the Russian clergy wear their hair long) "that if Paráshka is not married at once, I will report him as a drunkard to the archbishop. How dares he, clerical dirt, disobey me? Tell him he shall be sent to rot in a monastery, and I shall exile Paráshka's family to the steppes."

The valet transmitted the message. Paráshka's relatives and the priest surrounded the girl; her mother, weeping, fell on her knees before her, entreating her not to ruin the whole family. The girl continued to say "I won't," but in a weaker and weaker voice, then in a whisper, until at last she stood silent. The nuptial crown was put on her head; she made no resistance, and the valet ran full speed to the mansion to announce, "They are married."

Half an hour later, the small bells of the nuptial processions resounded at the gate of the mansion. The five couples alighted from the cars, crossed the yard, and entered the hall. The landlord received them, offering them glasses of wine, while the parents, standing behind the crying daughters, ordered them to bow to the earth before their lord.

Marriages by order were so common that amongst our servants, each time a young couple foresaw that they might be ordered to marry, although they had no mutual inclination for each other, they took the precaution of standing together as godfather and godmother at the christening of a child in one of the peasant families. This rendered marriage impossible, according to Russian Church law. The stratagem was usually successful, but once it ended in a tragedy. Andréi, the tailor, fell in love with a girl belonging to one of our neighbors. He hoped that my father would permit him to go free, as a tailor, in exchange for a certain yearly payment, and that by working hard at his trade he could manage to lay aside some money and to buy freedom for the girl. Otherwise, in marrying one of my father's serfs she would have become the serf of her hus-

band's master.   However, as Andréi and one of the maids
of our household foresaw that they might be ordered to
marry, they agreed to unite as god-parents in the christening
of a child.   What they had feared happened : one day they
were called to the master, and the dreaded order was given.

"We are always obedient to your will," they replied,
"but a few weeks ago we acted as godfather and godmother
at a christening."   Andréi also explained his wishes and
intentions.   The result was that he was sent to the recruiting board to become a soldier.

Under Nicholas I. there was no obligatory military service for all, such as now exists.   Nobles and merchants
were exempt, and when a new levy of recruits was ordered,
the landowners had to supply a certain number of men from
their serfs.   As a rule, the peasants, within their village
communities, kept a roll amongst themselves ; but the house
servants were entirely at the mercy of their lord, and if he
was dissatisfied with one of them, he sent him to the recruiting board and took a recruit acquittance, which had a considerable money value, as it could be sold to any one whose
turn it was to become a soldier.

Military service in those times was terrible.   A man was
required to serve twenty-five years under the colors, and
the life of a soldier was hard in the extreme.   To become
a soldier meant to be torn away forever from one's native
village and surroundings, and to be at the mercy of officers
like Timoféeff, whom I have already mentioned.   Blows
from the officers, flogging with birch rods and with sticks,
for the slightest fault, were normal affairs.   The cruelty
that was displayed surpasses all imagination.   Even in the
corps of cadets, where only noblemen's sons were educated,
a thousand blows with birch rods were sometimes administered, in the presence of all the corps, for a cigarette, — the
doctor standing by the tortured boy, and ordering the punishment to end only when he ascertained that the pulse was

about to stop beating. The bleeding victim was carried away unconscious to the hospital. The commander of the military schools, the Grand Duke Mikhael, would quickly have removed the director of a corps who had not had one or two such cases every year. "No discipline," he would have said.

With common soldiers it was far worse. When one of them appeared before a court-martial, the sentence was that a thousand men should be placed in two ranks facing each other, every soldier armed with a stick of the thickness of the little finger (these sticks were known under their German name of *Spitzruthen*), and that the condemned man should be dragged three, four, five, and seven times between these two rows, each soldier administering a blow. Sergeants followed to see that full force was used. After one or two thousand blows had been given, the victim, spitting blood, was taken to the hospital and attended to, in order that the punishment might be finished as soon as he had more or less recovered from the effects of the first part of it. If he died under the torture, the execution of the sentence was completed upon the corpse. Nicholas I. and his brother Mikhael were pitiless; no remittance of the punishment was ever possible. "I will send you through the ranks; you shall be skinned under the sticks," were threats which made part of the current language.

A gloomy terror used to spread through our house when it became known that one of the servants was to be sent to the recruiting board. The man was chained and placed under guard in the office, to prevent suicide. A peasant-cart was brought to the office door, and the doomed man was taken out between two watchmen. All the servants surrounded him. He made a deep bow, asking every one to pardon him his willing or unwilling offenses. If his father and mother lived in our village, they came to see him off. He bowed to the ground before them, and his mother and his other female relatives began loudly to sing out their lamentations, — a sort of half-song and half-recitative : " To whom do you abandon us ? Who will take care of you in the strange lands ? Who will protect you from cruel men ? " — exactly in the same way in which they sang their lamentations at a burial, and with the same words.

Thus Andréi had now to face for twenty-five years the terrible fate of a soldier : all his schemes of happiness had come to a violent end.

The fate of one of the maids, Pauline, or Pólya, as she used to be called, was even more tragical. She had been apprenticed to make fine embroidery, and was an artist at the work. At Nikólskoye her embroidery frame stood in sister Hélène's room, and she often took part in the conversations that went on between our sister and a sister of our stepmother who stayed with Hélène. Altogether, by her behavior and talk Pólya was more like an educated young person than a housemaid.

A misfortune befell her : she realized that she would soon be a mother. She told all to our stepmother, who burst into reproaches : " I will not have that creature in my house any longer ! I will not permit such a shame in my house ! oh, the shameless creature ! " and so on. The tears of Hélène made no difference. Pólya had her hair cut short, and was exiled to the dairy ; but as she was just embroidering an extraordinary skirt, she had to finish it at the dairy, in a dirty cottage, at a microscopical window. She finished it, and made many more fine embroideries, all in the hope of obtaining her pardon. But pardon did not come.

The father of her child, a servant of one of our neighbors, implored permission to marry her ; but as he had no money to offer, his request was refused. Pólya's " too gentlewoman-like manners " were taken as an offense, and a

•most bitter fate was kept in reserve for her. There was in our household a man employed as a postilion, on account of his small size; he went under the name of "bandy-legged Fílka." In his boyhood a horse had kicked him terribly, and he did not grow. His legs were crooked, his feet were turned inward, his nose was broken and turned to one side, his jaw was deformed. To this monster it was decided to marry Pólya, — and she was married by force. The couple were sent to become peasants at my father's estate in Ryazán.

Human feelings were not recognized, not even suspected, in serfs, and when Turguéneff published his little story "Mumú," and Grigoróvich began to issue his thrilling novels, in which he made his readers weep over the misfortunes of the serfs, it was to a great number of persons a startling revelation. "They love just as we do; is it possible?" exclaimed the sentimental ladies who could not read a French novel without shedding tears over the troubles of the noble heroes and heroines.

The education which the owners occasionally gave to some of their serfs was only another source of misfortune for the latter. My father once picked out in a peasant house a clever boy, and sent him to be educated as a doctor's assistant. The boy was diligent, and after a few years' apprenticeship made a decided success. When he returned home, my father bought all that was required for a well-equipped dispensary, which was arranged very nicely in one of the side houses of Nikólskoye. In summer time, Sásha the Doctor — that was the familiar name under which this young man went in the household — was busy gathering and preparing all sorts of medical herbs, and in a short time he became most popular in the region round Nikólskoye. The sick people among the peasants came from the neighboring villages, and my father was proud of the success of his dispensary. But this condition of things did not last. One winter, my father came to Nikól-skoye, stayed there for a few days, and left. That night Sásha the Doctor shot himself, — by accident, it was reported; but there was a love-story at the bottom of it. He was in love with a girl whom he could not marry, as she belonged to another landowner.

The case of another young man, Gherásim Kruglóff, whom my father educated at the Moscow Agricultural Institute, was almost equally sad. He passed his examinations most brilliantly, getting a gold medal, and the director of the Institute made all possible endeavors to induce my father to give him freedom and to let him go to the university, — serfs not being allowed to enter there. " He is sure to become a remarkable man," the director said, " perhaps one of the glories of Russia, and it will be an honor for you to have recognized his capacities and to have given such a man to Russian science."

" I need him for my own estate," my father replied to the many applications made on the young man's behalf. In reality, with the primitive methods of agriculture which were then in use, and from which my father would never have departed, Gherásim Kruglóff was absolutely useless. He made a survey of the estate, but when that was done he was ordered to sit in the servants' room and to stand with a plate at dinner-time. Of course Gherásim resented it very much; his dreams carried him to the university, to scientific work. His looks betrayed his discontent, and our stepmother seemed to find an especial pleasure in offending him at every opportunity. One day in the autumn, a rush of wind having opened the entrance gate, she called out to him, " Garáska, go and shut the gate."

That was the last drop. He answered, " You have a porter for that," and went his way.

My stepmother ran into father's room, crying, "Your servants insult me in your house!"

Immediately Gherásim was put under arrest and chained, to be sent away as a soldier. The parting of his old father and mother with him was one of the most heart-rending scenes I ever saw.

This time, however, fate took its revenge. Nicholas I. died, and military service became more tolerable. Gherásim's great ability was soon remarked, and in a few years he was one of the chief clerks, and the real working force in one of the departments of the ministry of war. Meanwhile, my father, who was absolutely honest, and, at a time when almost every one was receiving bribes and making fortunes, had never let himself be bribed, departed once from the strict rules of the service, in order to oblige the commander of the corps to which he belonged, and consented to allow an irregularity of some kind. It nearly cost him his promotion to the rank of general; the only object of his thirty-five years' service in the army seemed on the point of being lost. My stepmother went to St. Petersburg to remove the difficulty, and one day, after many applications, she was told that the only way to obtain what she wanted was to address herself to a particular clerk in a certain department of the ministry. Although he was a mere clerk, he was the real head of his superiors, and could do everything. This man's name was — Gherásim Ivánovich Kruglóff!

"Imagine, our Garáska!" she said to me afterward. "I always knew that he had great capacity. I went to see him, and spoke to him about this affair, and he said, 'I have nothing against the old prince, and I will do all I can for him.'"

Gherásim kept his word: he made a favorable report, and my father got his promotion. At last he could put on the long-coveted red trousers and the red-lined overcoat, and could wear the plumage on his helmet.

These were things which I myself saw in my childhood. If, however, I were to relate what I heard of in those years, it would be a much more gruesome narrative : stories of men and women torn from their families and their villages, and sold, or lost in gambling, or exchanged for a couple of hunting dogs, and then transported to some remote part of Russia for the sake of creating a new estate ; of children taken from their parents and sold to cruel or dissolute masters ; of flogging " in the stables," which occurred every day with unheard-of cruelty ; of a girl who found her only salvation in drowning herself ; of an old man who had grown gray-haired in his master's service, and at last hanged himself under his master's window ; and of revolts of serfs, which were suppressed by Nicholas I.'s generals by flogging to death each tenth or fifth man taken out of the ranks, and by laying waste the village, whose inhabitants, after a military execution, went begging for bread in the neighboring provinces.   As to the poverty which I saw during our journeys in certain villages, especially in those which belonged to the imperial family, no words would be adequate to describe the misery to readers who have not seen it.

To become free was the constant dream of the serfs, — a dream not easily realized, for a heavy sum of money was required to induce a landowner to part with a serf.

"Do you know," my father said to me, once, " that your mother appeared to me after her death ?   You young people do not believe in these things, but it was so.   I sat one night very late in this chair, at my writing-table, and slumbered, when I saw her enter from behind, all in white, quite pale, and with her eyes gleaming.   When she was dying she begged me to promise that I would give liberty to her maid, Másha, and I did promise ; but then, what with one thing and another, nearly a whole year passed without my having fulfilled my intention. Then she appeared, and said to me in a low voice, 'Alexis, you promised me to give liberty to Másha; have you forgotten it?' I was quite terrified; I jumped out of my chair, but she had vanished. I called the servants, but no one had seen anything. Next morning I went to her grave and had a litany sung, and immediately gave liberty to Másha."

When my father died, Másha came to his burial, and I spoke to her. She was married, and quite happy in her family life. My brother Alexander, in his jocose way, told her what my father had said, and we asked her what she knew of it.

"These things," she replied, "happened a long time ago, so I may tell you the truth. I saw that your father had quite forgotten his promise, so I dressed up in white and spoke like your mother. I recalled the promise he had made to her, — you won't bear a grudge against me, will you?"

"Of course not!"

Ten or twelve years after the scenes described in the early part of this chapter, I sat one night in my father's room, and we talked of things past. Serfdom had been abolished, and my father complained of the new conditions, though not very severely; he had accepted them without much grumbling.

"You must agree, father," I said, "that you often punished your servants cruelly, and even without reason."

"With the people," he replied, "it was impossible to do otherwise;" and, leaning back in his easy-chair, he remained plunged in thought. "But what I did was nothing worth speaking of," he said, after a long pause. "Take that same Sábleff: he looks so soft, and talks in such a thin voice; but he was really terrible with his serfs. How many

times they plotted to kill him! I, at least, never took
advantage of my maids, whereas that old devil T—— went
on in such a way that the peasant women were going to
inflict a terrible punishment upon him. . . . Good-by,
bonne nuit!"

IX

I WELL remember the Crimean war. At Moscow it affected people but little. Of course, in every house lint and bandages for the wounded were made at evening parties: not much of it, however, reached the Russian armies, immense quantities being stolen and sold to the armies of the enemy. My sister Hélène and other young ladies sang patriotic songs, but the general tone of life in society was hardly influenced by the great struggle that was going on. In the country, on the contrary, the war caused terrible gloominess. The levies of recruits followed one another rapidly, and we continually heard the peasant women singing their funereal songs. The Russian people look upon war as a calamity which is being sent upon them by Providence, and they accepted this war with a solemnity that contrasted strangely with the levity I saw elsewhere under similar circumstances. Young though I was, I realized that feeling of solemn resignation which pervaded our villages.

My brother Nicholas was smitten like many others by the war fever, and before he had ended his course at the corps he joined the army in the Caucasus. I never saw him again.

In the autumn of 1854 our family was increased by the arrival of two sisters of our stepmother. They had had their own house and some vineyards at Sebastopol, but now they were homeless, and came to stay with us. When the allies landed in the Crimea, the inhabitants of Sebastopol were told that they need not be afraid, and had only to stay where they were; but after the defeat at the Alma, they were ordered to leave with all haste, as the city would be invested within a few days.   There were few conveyances, and there was no way of moving along the roads in face of the troops which were marching southward.   To hire a cart was almost impossible, and the ladies, having abandoned all they had on the road, had a very hard time of it before they reached Moscow.

I soon made friends with the younger of the two sisters, a lady of about thirty, who used to smoke one cigarette after another, and to tell me of all the horrors of their journey.   She spoke with tears in her eyes of the beautiful battle-ships which had to be sunk at the entrance of the harbor of Sebastopol, and she could not understand how the Russians would be able to defend Sebastopol from the land; there was no wall even worth speaking of.

I was in my thirteenth year when Nicholas I. died.   It was late in the afternoon, the 18th of February (2d of March), that the policemen distributed in all the houses of Moscow a bulletin announcing the illness of the Tsar, and inviting the inhabitants to pray in the churches for his recovery.   At that time he was already dead, and the authorities knew it, as there was telegraphic communication between Moscow and St. Petersburg; but not a word having been previously uttered about his illness, they thought that the people must be gradually prepared for the announcement of his death.   We all went to church and prayed most piously.

Next day, Saturday, the same thing was done, and even on Sunday morning bulletins about the Tsar's health were distributed.   The news of the death of Nicholas reached us only about midday, through some servants who had been to the market.   A real terror reigned in our house and in the houses of our relatives, as the information spread.   It was said that the people in the market behaved in a strange way, showing no regret, but indulging in dangerous talk.   Full-grown people spoke in whispers, and our stepmother kept repeating, "Don't talk before the men;" while the servants whispered among themselves, probably about the coming "freedom." The nobles expected at every moment a revolt of the serfs, — a new uprising of Pugachóff.

At St. Petersburg, in the meantime, men of the educated classes, as they communicated to one another the news, embraced in the streets. Every one felt that the end of the war and the end of the terrible conditions which prevailed under the "iron despot" were near at hand. Poisoning was talked about, the more so as the Tsar's body decomposed very rapidly, but the true reason only gradually leaked out: a too strong dose of an invigorating medicine that Nicholas had taken.

In the country, during the summer of 1855, the heroic struggle which was going on in Sebastopol for every yard of ground and every bit of its dismantled bastions was followed with a solemn interest. A messenger was sent regularly twice a week from our house to the district town to get the papers; and on his return, even before he had dismounted, the papers were taken from his hands and opened. Hélène or I read them aloud to the family, and the news was at once transmitted to the servants' room, and thence to the kitchen, the office, the priest's house, and the houses of the peasants. The reports which came of the last days of Sebastopol, of the awful bombardment, and finally of the evacuation of the town by our troops were received with tears. In every country-house round about, the loss of Sebastopol was mourned over with as much grief as the loss of a near relative would have been, although every one understood that now the terrible war would soon come to an end.

X

It was in August, 1857, when I was nearly fifteen, that my turn came to enter the corps of pages, and I was taken to St. Petersburg. When I left home I was still a child; but human character is usually settled in a definite way at an earlier age than is generally supposed, and it is evident to me that under my childish appearance I was then very much what I was to be later on. My tastes, my inclinations, were already determined.

The first impulse to my intellectual development was given, as I have said, by my Russian teacher. It is an excellent habit in Russian families — a habit now, unhappily, on the decline — to have in the house a student who aids the boys and the girls with their lessons, even when they are at a gymnasium. For a better assimilation of what they learn at school, and for a widening of their conceptions about what they learn, his aid is invaluable. Moreover, he introduces an intellectual element into the family, and becomes an elder brother to the young people, — often something better than an elder brother, because the student has a certain responsibility for the progress of his pupils; and as the methods of teaching change rapidly, from one generation to another, he can assist his pupils much better than the best educated parents could.

Nikolái Pávlovich Smirnóff had literary tastes. At that time, under the wild censorship of Nicholas I., many quite inoffensive works by our best writers could not be published; others were so mutilated as to deprive some passages in them of any meaning. In the genial comedy by Griboyédoff, "Misfortune from Intelligence," which ranks with the best comedies of Molière, Colonel Skalozúb had to be named " Mr. Skalozúb," to the detriment of the sense and even of the verses ; for the representation of a colonel in a comical light would have been considered an insult to the army. Of so innocent a book as Gógol's "Dead Souls" the second part was not allowed to appear, nor the first part to be reprinted, although it had long been out of print. Numerous verses of Púshkin, Lérmontoff, A. K. Tolstói, Ryléeff, and other poets were not permitted to see the light; to say nothing of such verses as had any political meaning or contained a criticism of the prevailing conditions. All these circulated in manuscript, and Smirnóff used to copy whole books of Gógol and Púshkin for himself and his friends, a task in which I occasionally helped him. As a true child of Moscow he was also imbued with the deepest veneration for those of our writers who lived in Moscow, — some of them in the Old Equerries' Quarter. He pointed out to me with respect the house of the Countess Saliàs (Eugénie Tour), who was our near neighbor, while the house of the noted exile Alexander Hérzen always was associated with a certain mysterious feeling of respect and awe. The house where Gógol lived was for us an object of deep respect, and though I was not nine when he died (in 1851), and had read none of his works, I remember well the sadness his death produced at Moscow. Turguéneff well expressed that feeling in a note, for which Nicholas I. ordered him to be put under arrest and sent into exile to his estate.

Púshkin's great poem, "Evghéniy Onyéghin," made but little impression upon me, and I still admire the marvelous simplicity and beauty of his style in that poem more than its contents. But Gógol's works, which I read when I was eleven or twelve, had a powerful effect on my mind, and my first literary essays were in imitation of his humorous manner. An historical novel by Zagóskin, "Yuriy Milosláv-

skiy," about the times of the great uprising of 1612, Púsh
kin's "The Captain's Daughter," dealing with the Pugachóff uprising, and Dumas's "Queen Marguerite" awakened
in me a lasting interest in history. As to other French
novels, I have only begun to read them since Daudet and
Zola came to the front. Nekrásoff's poetry was my favorite
from early years; I knew many of his verses by heart.

Nikolái Pávlovich early began to make me write, and with
his aid I wrote a long "History of a Sixpence," for which
we invented all sorts of characters, into whose possession
the sixpence fell. My brother Alexander had at that time
a much more poetical turn of mind. He wrote most romantic stories, and began early to make verses, which he did
with wonderful facility and in a most musical and easy
style. If his mind had not subsequently been taken up by
natural history and philosophical studies, he undoubtedly
would have become a poet of mark. In those years his
favorite resort for finding poetical inspiration was the gently
slooping roof underneath our window. This aroused in me
a constant desire to tease him. "There is the poet sitting under the chimney-pot, trying to write his verses," I
used to say; and the teasing ended in a fierce scrimmage,
which brought our sister Hélène to a state of despair. But
Alexander was so devoid of revengefulness that peace
was soon concluded, and we loved each other immensely.
Among boys, scrimmage and love seem to go hand in hand.

I had even then taken to journalism. In my twelfth
year I began to edit a daily journal. Paper was not to be
had at will in our house, and my journal was in 32° only.
As the Crimean war had not yet broken out, and the only
newspaper which my father used to receive was the Gazette
of the Moscow police, I had not a great choice of models.
As a result my own Gazette consisted merely of short paragraphs announcing the news of the day: as, " Went out to
the woods. N. P. Smirnóff shot two thrushes," and so on.

This soon ceased to satisfy me, and in 1855 I started a monthly review, which contained Alexander's verses, my novelettes, and some sort of "varieties." The material existence of this review was fully guaranteed, for it had plenty of subscribers; that is, the editor himself and Smirnóff, who regularly paid his subscription, of so many sheets of paper, even after he had left our house. In return, I accurately wrote out for my faithful subscriber a second copy.

When Smirnóff left us, and a student of medicine, N. M. Pávloff, took his place, the latter helped me in my editorial duties. He obtained for the review a poem by one of his friends, and — still more important — the introductory lecture on physical geography by one of the Moscow professors. Of course this had not been printed before : a reproduction would never have found its way into the review.

Alexander, I need not say, took a lively interest in the paper, and its renown soon reached the corps of cadets. Some young writers on the way to fame undertook the publication of a rival. The matter was serious : in poems and novels we could hold our own ; but they had a " critic," and a " critic " who writes, in connection with the characters of some new novel, all sorts of things about the conditions of life, and touches upon a thousand questions which could not be touched upon anywhere else, makes the soul of a Russian review. They had a critic, and we had none ! He wrote an article for the first number, and his article was shown to my brother. It was rather pretentious and weak. Alexander at once wrote an anti-criticism, ridiculing and demolishing the critic in a violent manner. There was great consternation in the rival camp when they learned that this anti-criticism would appear in our next issue ; they gave up publishing their paper, their best writers joined our staff, and we triumphantly announced the future " exclusive collaboration " of so many distinguished writers.

In August, 1857, the review had to be suspended, after nearly two years' existence. New surroundings and a quite new life were before me. I went away from home with regret, the more so because the whole distance between Moscow and St. Petersburg would be between me and Alexander, and I already considered it a misfortune that I had to enter a military school.

PART SECOND

THE CORPS OF PAGES

I

THE long-cherished ambition of my father was thus real‑ized. There was a vacancy in the corps of pages which I could fill before I had got beyond the age to which admis‑sion was limited, and I was taken to St. Petersburg and entered the school. Only a hundred and fifty boys — mostly children of the nobility belonging to the court — received education in this privileged corps, which combined the character of a military school endowed with special rights and of a court institution attached to the imperial house‑hold. After a stay of four or five years in the corps of pages, those who had passed the final examinations were received as officers in any regiment of the guard or of the army they chose, irrespective of the number of vacancies in that regiment; and each year the first sixteen pupils of the highest form were nominated *pages de chambre ;* that is, they were personally attached to the several members of the imperial family, — the emperor, the empress, the grand duchesses, and the grand dukes. That was considered, of course, a great honor; and, moreover, the young men upon whom this honor was bestowed became known at the court, and had afterward every chance of being nominated aides‑de‑camp of the emperor or of one of the grand dukes, and consequently had every facility for making a brilliant career in the service of the state. Fathers and mothers of families connected with the court took due care, therefore, that their boys should not miss entering the corps of pages, even though entrance had to be secured at the expense of other candidates who never saw a vacancy opening for them. Now that I was in the select corps my father could give free play to his ambitious dreams.

The corps was divided into five forms, of which the highest was the first, and the lowest the fifth, and the intention was that I should enter the fourth form. However, as it appeared at the examinations that I was not sufficiently familiar with decimal fractions, and as the fourth form contained that year over forty pupils, while only twenty had been mustered for the fifth form, I was enrolled in the latter.

I felt extremely vexed at this decision. It was with reluctance that I entered a military school, and now I should have to stay in it five years instead of four. What should I do in the fifth form, when I knew already all that would be taught in it ? With tears in my eyes I spoke of it to the inspector (the head of the educational department), but he answered me with a joke. " You know," he remarked, "what Cæsar said, — better to be the first in a village than the second in Rome." To which I warmly replied that I should prefer to be the very last, if only I could leave the military school as soon as possible. " Perhaps, after some time, you will like the school," he remarked, and from that day he became friendly to me.

To the teacher of arithmetic, who also tried to console me, I gave my word of honor that I would never cast a glance into his textbook ; "and nevertheless you will have to give me the highest marks." I kept my word ; but thinking now of this scene, I fancy that the pupil was not of a very docile disposition.

And yet, as I look back upon that remote past, I cannot but feel grateful for having been put in the lower form. Having only to repeat during the first year what I already knew, I got into the habit of learning my lessons by merely listening to what the teachers said in the class-room; and, the lessons over, I had plenty of time to read and to write to my heart's content. I never prepared for the examinations, and used to spend the time which was allowed for that in reading aloud, to a few friends, dramas of Shakespeare or of Ostróvsky. When I reached the higher "special" forms, I was also better prepared to master the variety of subjects we had to study. Besides, I spent more than half of the first winter in the hospital. Like all children who are not born at St. Petersburg, I had to pay a heavy tribute to "the capital on the swamps of Finland," in the shape of several attacks of local cholera, and finally one of typhoid fever.

When I entered the corps of pages, its inner life was undergoing a profound change. All Russia awakened at that time from the heavy slumber and the terrible nightmare of Nicholas I.'s reign. Our school also felt the effects of that revival. I do not know, in fact, what would have become of me, had I entered the corps of pages one or two years sooner. Either my will would have been totally broken, or I should have been excluded from the school with no one knows what consequences. Happily, the transition period was already in full sway in the year 1857.

The director of the corps was an excellent old man, General Zheltúkhin. But he was the nominal head only. The real master of the school was "the Colonel," — Colonel Girardot, a Frenchman in the Russian service. People said he was a Jesuit, and so he was, I believe. His ways, at any rate, were thoroughly imbued with the teachings of Loyola, and his educational methods were those of the French Jesuit colleges.

Imagine a short, extremely thin man, with dark, piercing, and furtive eyes, wearing short clipped mustaches, which gave him the expression of a cat; very quiet and firm; not remarkably intelligent, but exceedingly cunning; a despot at the bottom of his heart, who was capable of hating — intensely hating — the boy who would not fall under his fascination, and of expressing that hatred, not by silly persecutions, but unceasingly, by his general behavior, — by an occasionally dropped word, a gesture, a smile, an interjection. His walk was more like gliding along, and the exploring glances he used to cast round without turning his head completed the illusion. A stamp of cold dryness was impressed on his lips, even when he tried to look well disposed, and that expression became still more harsh when his mouth was contorted by a smile of discontent or of contempt. With all this there was nothing of a commander in him; you would rather think, at first sight, of a benevolent father who talks to his children as if they were full-grown people. And yet, you soon felt that every one and everything had to bend before his will. Woe to the boy who would not feel happy or unhappy according to the degree of good disposition shown toward him by the Colonel.

The words "the Colonel" were continually on all lips. Other officers went by their nicknames, but no one dared to give a nickname to Girardot. A sort of mystery hung about him, as if he were omniscient and everywhere present. True, he spent all the day and part of the night in the school. Even when we were in the classes he prowled about, visiting our drawers, which he opened with his own keys. As to the night, he gave a good portion of it to the task of inscribing in small books, — of which he had quite a library, — in separate columns, by special signs and in inks of different colors, all the faults and virtues of each boy.

Play, jokes, and conversation stopped when we saw him slowly moving along through our spacious rooms, hand in hand with one of his favorites, balancing his body forward and backward; smiling at one boy, keenly looking into the eyes of another, casting an indifferent glance upon a third, and giving a slight contortion to his lip as he passed a fourth : and from these looks every one knew that he liked the first boy, that to the second he was indifferent, that he intentionally did not notice the third, and that he disliked the fourth. This dislike was enough to terrify most of his victims, — the more so as no reason could be given for it. Impressionable boys had been brought to despair by that mute, unceasingly displayed aversion and those suspicious looks; in others the result had been a total annihilation of will, as one of the Tolstois — Theodor, also a pupil of Girardot — has shown in an autobiographic novel, "The Diseases of the Will."

The inner life of the corps was miserable under the rule of the Colonel. In all boarding-schools the newly entered boys are subjected to petty persecutions. The "greenhorns" are put in this way to a test. What are they worth? Are they not going to turn "sneaks"? And then the "old hands" like to show to newcomers the superiority of an established brotherhood. So it is in all schools and in prisons. But under Girardot's rule these persecutions took on a harsher aspect, and they came, not from the comrades of the same form, but from the first form, — the pages de chambre, who were non-commissoned officers, and whom Girardot had placed in a quite exceptional, superior position. His system was to give them carte blanche; to pretend that he did not know even the horrors they were enacting; and to maintain through them a severe discipline. To answer a blow received from a page de chambre would have meant, in the times of Nicholas I., to be sent to a battalion of soldiers' sons, if the fact became public; and to revolt in any way against the mere caprice of a page de chambre meant that the twenty youths of the first form, armed with their heavy oak rulers, would assemble in a room, and, with Girardot's tacit approval, administer a severe beating to the boy who had shown such a spirit of insubordination.

Accordingly, the first form did what they liked; and not further back than the preceding winter one of their favorite games had been to assemble the "greenhorns" at night in a room, in their night-shirts, and to make them run round, like horses in a circus, while the pages de chambre, armed with thick india-rubber whips, standing some in the centre and the others on the outside, pitilessly whipped the boys. As a rule the "circus" ended in an Oriental fashion, in an abominable way. The moral conceptions which prevailed at that time, and the foul talk which went on in the school concerning what occurred at night after circus, were such that the least said about them the better.

The Colonel knew all this. He had a perfectly organized system of espionage, and nothing escaped his knowledge. But so long as he was not known to know it, all was right. To shut his eyes to what was done by the first form was the foundation of his system of maintaining discipline.

However, a new spirit was awakened in the school, and only a few months before I entered it a revolution had taken place. That year the third form was different from what it had hitherto been. It contained a number of young men who really studied and read a good deal; some of them became, later, men of mark. My first acquaintance with one of them — let me call him von Schauff — was when he was reading Kant's "Critique of Pure Reason." Besides, they had amongst them some of the strongest youths of the school. The tallest member of the corps was in that form, as also a very strong young man, Kóshtoff, a great friend of von Schauff. The third form did not bear the yoke of the pages de chambre with the same docility as their predecessors; they were disgusted with what was going on; and in consequence of an incident, which I prefer not to describe, a fight took place between the third and the first form, with the result that the pages de chambre got a very severe thrashing from their subordinates. Girardot hushed up the affair, but the authority of the first form was broken down. The india-rubber whips remained, but were never again brought into use. The circuses and the like became things of the past.

That much was won; but the lowest form, the fifth, composed almost entirely of very young boys who had just entered the school, had still to obey the petty caprices of the pages de chambre. We had a beautiful garden, filled with old trees, but the boys of the fifth form could enjoy it little: they were forced to run a roundabout, while the pages de chambre sat in it and chattered, or to send back the balls when these gentlemen played ninepins. A couple of days after I had entered the school, seeing how things stood in the garden, I did not go there, but remained upstairs. I was reading, when a page de chambre, with carroty hair and a face covered with freckles, came upon me, and ordered me to go at once to the garden to run the roundabout.

"I shan't; don't you see I am reading?" was my reply.

Anger disfigured his never too pleasant face. He was ready to jump upon me. I took the defensive. He tried to give me blows on the face with his cap. I fenced as best I could. Then he flung his cap on the floor.

"Pick it up."

"Pick it up yourself."

Such an act of disobedience was unheard of in the school. Why he did not beat me unmercifully on the spot I do not know. He was much older and stronger than I was.

Next day and the following days I received similar

commands, but obstinately remained upstairs. Then began
the most exasperating petty persecutions at every step,
— enough to drive a boy to desperation. Happily, I was
always of a jovial disposition, and answered them with
jokes, or took little heed of them.

Moreover, it all soon came to an end. The weather
turned rainy, and we spent most of our time indoors. In
the garden the first form smoked freely enough, but when
we were indoors the smoking club was "the tower." It
was kept beautifully clean, and a fire was always burning
there. The pages de chambre severely punished any of
the other boys whom they caught smoking, but they
themselves sat continually at the fireside chattering and
enjoying cigarettes. Their favorite smoking time was after
ten o'clock at night, when all were supposed to have gone
to bed; they kept up their club till half past eleven, and,
to protect themselves from an unexpected interruption by
Girardot, they ordered us to be on the watch. The small
boys of the fifth form were taken out of their beds in
turn, two at a time, and they had to loiter about the
staircase till half past eleven, to give notice of the approach
of the Colonel.

We decided to put an end to these night watches. Long
were the discussions, and the higher forms were consulted
as to what was to be done. At last the decision came:
"Refuse, all of you, to keep the watch; and when they
begin to beat you, which they are sure to do, go, as many
of you as can, in a block, and call in Girardot. He knows
it all, but then he will be bound to stop it." The question
whether that would not be "reporting" was settled in the
negative by experts in matters of honor: the pages de
chambre did not behave toward the others like comrades.

The turn to watch fell that night to a Shahovskóy, an old
hand, and to Selánoff, a newcomer, an extremely timid boy,
who even spoke in a girlish voice. Shahovskóy was called

upon first, but refused to go, and was left alone.   Then two pages de chambre went to the timid Selánoff, who was in bed; as he refused to obey, they began to flog him brutally with heavy leather braces.   Shahovskóy woke up several comrades who were near at hand, and they all ran to find Girardot.

I was also in bed when the two came upon me, ordering me to take the watch.   I refused.   Thereupon, seizing two pairs of braces, — we always used to put our clothes in perfect order on a bench by the bedside, braces uppermost, and the necktie across them, — they began to flog me.   Sitting up in bed, I fenced with my hands, and had already received several heavy blows, when a command resounded, — " The first form to the Colonel ! "   The fierce fighters became tame at once, and hurriedly put my things in order.

" Don't say a word," they whispered.

" The necktie across, in good order," I said to them, while my shoulders and arms burned from the blows.

What Girardot's talk with the first form was we did not know; but next day, as we stood in the ranks before marching downstairs to the dining-room, he addressed us in a minor key, saying how sad it was that pages de chambre should have fallen upon a boy who was right in his refusal.   And upon whom ?   A newcomer, and so timid a boy as Selánoff was.   The whole school was disgusted at this Jesuitic speech.

No need to say that that was the end of the watch-keeping, and that it gave a final blow to the worrying of the newcomers : it has never been renewed.

It surely was also a blow to Girardot's authority, and he resented it very much.   He regarded our form, and me especially, with great dislike (the roundabout affair had been reported to him), and he manifested it at every opportunity.

During the first winter, I was a frequent inmate of the hospital.   After suffering from typhoid fever, during which the director and the doctor bestowed on me a really parental care, I had very bad and persistently recurring gastric attacks.   Girardot, as he made his daily rounds of the hospital, seeing me so often there, began to say to me every morning, half jokingly, in French, "Here is a young man who is as healthy as the New Bridge, and loiters in the hospital."   Once or twice I replied jestingly, but at last, seeing malice in this constant repetition, I lost patience and grew very angry.

"How dare you say that?" I exclaimed.   "I shall ask the doctor to forbid your entering this room," and so on.

Girardot recoiled two steps; his dark eyes glittered, his thin lip became still thinner.   At last he said, "I have offended you, have I?   Well, we have in the hall two artillery guns: shall we have a duel?"

"I don't make jokes, and I tell you that I shall bear no more of your insinuations," I continued.

He did not repeat his joke, but regarded me with even more dislike than before.

Every one spoke of Girardot's dislike for me; but I paid no attention to it, and probably increased it by my indifference.   For full eighteen months he refused to give me the epaulets, which were usually given to newly entered boys after one or two months' stay at the school, when they had learned some of the rudiments of military drill; but I felt quite happy without that military decoration.   At last, an officer — the best teacher of drill in the school, a man simply enamored of drill — volunteered to teach me; and when he saw me performing all the tricks to his entire satisfaction, he undertook to introduce me to Girardot.   The Colonel refused again, twice in succession, so that the officer took it as a personal offense; and when the director of the corps once asked him why I had no epaulets yet, he bluntly answered, "The boy is all right; it is the Colonel who does not want him;" whereupon, probably after a remark of the director, Girardot himself asked to examine me again, and gave me the epaulets that very day.

But the Colonel's influence was rapidly vanishing. The whole character of the school was changing. For twenty years Girardot had realized his ideal, which was to have the boys nicely combed, curled, and girlish looking, and to send to the court pages as refined as courtiers of Louis XIV. Whether they learned or not, he cared little; his favorites were those whose clothes-baskets were best filled with all sorts of nail-brushes and scent bottles, whose "private" uniform (which could be put on when we went home on Sundays) was of the best make, and who knew how to make the most elegant *salut oblique*. Formerly, when Girardot had held rehearsals of court ceremonies, wrapping up a page in a striped red cotton cover taken from one of our beds, in order that he might represent the Empress at a *baisemain*, the boys almost religiously approached the imaginary Empress, seriously performed the ceremony of kissing the hand, and retired with a most elegant oblique bow; but now, though they were very elegant at court, they would perform at the rehearsals such bearlike bows that all roared with laughter, while Girardot was simply raging. Formerly, the younger boys who had been taken to a court levee, and had been curled for that purpose, used to keep their curls as long as they would last; now, on returning from the palace, they hurried to put their heads under the cold-water tap, to get rid of the curls. An effeminate appearance was laughed at. To be sent to a levee, to stand there as a decoration, was now considered a drudgery rather than a favor. And when the small boys who were occasionally taken to the palace to play with the little grand dukes remarked that one of the latter used, in some game, to make a hard whip out of his handkerchief, and use it freely, one of our boys did the same, and so whipped the grand duke that he cried. Girardot was terrified, while the old Sebastopol admiral who was tutor of the grand duke only praised our boy.

A new spirit, studious and serious, developed in the corps, as in all other schools. In former years, the pages, being sure that in one way or another they would get the necessary marks for being promoted officers of the guard, spent the first years in the school hardly learning at all, and only began to study more or less in the last two forms; now the lower forms learned very well. The moral tone also became quite different from what it was a few years before. Oriental amusements were looked upon with disgust, and an attempt or two to revert to old manners resulted in scandals which reached the St. Petersburg drawing-rooms. Girardot was dismissed. He was only allowed to retain his bachelor apartment in the building of the corps, and we often saw him afterward, wrapped in his long military cloak, pacing along, plunged in reflections, — sad, I suppose, because he could not but condemn the new spirit which rapidly developed in the corps of pages.

II

ALL over Russia people were talking of education. As soon as peace had been concluded at Paris, and the severity of censorship had been slightly relaxed, educational matters began to be eagerly discussed. The ignorance of the masses of the people, the obstacles that had hitherto been put in the way of those who wanted to learn, the absence of schools in the country, the obsolete methods of teaching, and the remedies for these evils became favorite themes of discussion in educated circles, in the press, and even in the drawing-rooms of the aristocracy. The first high schools for girls had been opened in 1857, on an excellent plan and with a splendid teaching staff. As by magic a number of men and women came to the front, who have not only devoted their lives to education, but have proved to be remarkable practical pedagogists : their writings would occupy a place of honor in every civilized literature, if they were known abroad.

The corps of pages also felt the effect of that revival. Apart from a few exceptions, the general tendency of the three younger forms was to study. The head of the educational department, the inspector, Winkler, who was a well-educated colonel of artillery, a good mathematician, and a man of progressive opinions, hit upon an excellent plan for stimulating that spirit. Instead of the indifferent teachers who formerly used to teach in the lower forms, he endeavored to secure the best ones. In his opinion, no professor was too good to teach the very beginnings of a subject to the youngest boys. Thus, to teach the elements of algebra in the fourth form he invited a first-rate mathematician and

a born teacher, Captain Sukhónin, and the form took at
once to mathematics. By the way, it so happened that this
captain was a tutor of the heir of the throne (Nikolái Alexándrovich, who died at the age of twenty-two), and the heir
apparent was brought once a week to the corps of pages to
be present at the algebra lessons of Captain Sukhónin.
Empress Marie Alexándrovna, who was an educated woman,
thought that perhaps the contact with studious boys would
stimulate her son to learning. He sat amongst us, and had
to answer questions like all the others. But he managed
mostly, while the teacher spoke, to make drawings very
nicely, or to whisper all sorts of droll things to his neighbors. He was good-natured and very gentle in his behavior,
but superficial in learning, and still more so in his affections.

For the fifth form the inspector secured two remarkable
men. He entered our class-room one day, quite radiant,
and told us that we should have a rare chance. Professor
Klasóvsky, a great classical scholar and expert in Russian
literature, had consented to teach us Russian grammar, and
would take us through all the five forms in succession,
shifting with us every year to the next form. Another
university professor, Herr Becker, librarian of the imperial
(national) library, would do the same in German. Professor
Klasóvsky, he added, was in weak health that winter, but
the inspector was sure that we would be very quiet in his
class. The chance of having such a teacher was too good
to be lost.

He had thought aright. We became very proud of
having university professors for teachers, and although
there came voices from the Kamchátka (in Russia, the back
benches of each class bear the name of that remote and
uncivilized peninsula) to the effect that "the sausage-
maker" — that is, the German — must be kept by all means
in obedience, public opinion in our form was decidedly in
favor of the professors.

"The sausage-maker" won our respect at once. A tall man, with an immense forehead and very kind, intelligent eyes, not devoid of a touch of humor, came into our class, and told us in quite good Russian that he intended to divide our form into three sections. The first section would be composed of Germans, who already knew the language, and from whom he would require more serious work; to the second section he would teach grammar, and later on German literature, in accordance with the established programmes; and the third section, he concluded with a charming smile, would be the Kamchátka. "From you," he said, "I shall only require that at each lesson you copy four lines which I will choose for you from a book. The four lines copied, you can do what you like; only do not hinder the rest. And I promise you that in five years you will learn something of German and German literature. Now, who joins the Germans? You, Stackelberg? You, Lamsdorf? Perhaps some one of the Russians? And who joins the Kamchátka?" Five or six boys, who knew not a word of German, took residence in the peninsula. They most conscientiously copied their four lines, — a dozen or a score of lines in the higher forms, — and Becker chose the lines so well, and bestowed so much attention upon the boys, that by the end of the five years they really knew something of the language and its literature.

I joined the Germans. My brother Alexander insisted so much in his letters upon my acquiring German, which possesses so rich a literature and into which every book of value is translated, that I set myself assiduously to learn it. I translated and studied most thoroughly one page of a rather difficult poetical description of a thunderstorm; I learned by heart, as the professor had advised me, the conjugations, the adverbs, and the prepositions, and began to read. A splendid method it is for learning languages. Becker advised me, moreover, to subscribe to a cheap illus-

trated weekly, and its illustrations and short stories were a
continual inducement to read a few lines or a column. I
soon mastered the language.

Toward the end of the winter I asked Herr Becker to
lend me a copy of Goethe's " Faust." I had read it in a
Russian translation; I had also read Turguéneff's beautiful
novel, " Faust; " and I now longed to read the great work
in the original. " You will understand nothing in it; it is
too philosophical," Becker said, with his gentle smile; but
he brought me, nevertheless, a little square book, with the
pages yellowed by age, containing the immortal drama. He
little knew the unfathomable joy that that small square
book gave me. I drank in the sense and the music of
every line of it, beginning with the very first verses of the
ideally beautiful dedication, and soon knew full pages by
heart. Faust's monologue in the forest, and especially the
lines in which he speaks of his understanding of nature, —

> " Thou
> Not only cold, amazed acquaintance yield'st,
> But grantest that in her profoundest breast
> I gaze, as in the bosom of a friend," —

simply put me in ecstasy, and till now it has retained its
power over me. Every verse gradually became a dear
friend. And then, is there a higher æsthetic delight than
to read poetry in a language which one does not yet quite
thoroughly understand? The whole is veiled with a sort
of slight haze, which admirably suits poetry. Words, the
trivial meanings of which, when one knows the language
colloquially, sometimes interfere with the poetical image
they are intended to convey, retain but their subtle,
elevated sense; while the music of the poetry is only the
more strongly impressed upon the ear.

Professor Klasóvsky's first lesson was a revelation to us.
He was a small man, about fifty years of age, very rapid in

his movements, with bright, intelligent eyes and a slightly sarcastic expression, and the high forehead of a poet. When he came in for his first lesson, he said in a low voice that, suffering from a protracted illness, he could not speak loud enough, and asked us, therefore, to sit closer to him. He placed his chair near the first row of tables, and we clustered round him like a swarm of bees.

He was to teach us Russian grammar; but, instead of the dull grammar lesson, we heard something quite different from what we expected. It was grammar; but here came in a comparison of an old Russian folk-lore expression with a line from Homer or from the Sanskrit Mahabharata, the beauty of which was rendered in Russian words; there, a verse from Schiller was introduced, and was followed by a sarcastic remark about some modern society prejudice; then solid grammar again, and then some wide poetical or philosophical generalization.

Of course, there was much in it that we did not understand, or of which we missed the deeper sense. But do not the bewitching powers of all studies lie in that they continually open up to us new, unsuspected horizons, not yet understood, which entice us to proceed further and further in the penetration of what appears at first sight only in vague outline? Some with their hands placed on one another's shoulders, some leaning across the tables of the first row, others standing close behind Klasóvsky, our eyes glittering, we all hung on his lips. As toward the end of the hour, his voice fell, the more breathlessly we listened. The inspector opened the door of the class-room, to see how we behaved with our new teacher; but on seeing that motionless swarm he retired on tiptoe. Even Daúroff, a restless spirit, stared at Klasóvsky as if to say, "That is the sort of man you are?" Even von Kleinau, a hopelessly obtuse Circassian with a German name, sat motionless. In most of the others something good and elevated

simmered at the bottom of their hearts, as if a vision of an
unsuspected world was opening before them. Upon me
Klasóvsky had an immense influence, which only grew
with years. Winkler's prophecy, that, after all, I might
like the school, was fulfilled.

In Western Europe, and probably in America, this type
of teacher seems not to be generally known, but in Russia there is not a man or woman of mark, in literature
or in political life, who does not owe the first impulse
toward a higher development to his or her teacher of literature. Every school in the world ought to have such a
teacher. Each teacher in a school has his own subject,
and there is no link between the different subjects. Only
the teacher of literature, guided by the general outlines of
the programme, but left free to treat it as he likes, can
bind together the separate historical and humanitarian
sciences, unify them by a broad philosophical and humane
conception, and awaken higher ideas and inspirations in the
brains and hearts of the young people. In Russia, that
necessary task falls quite naturally upon the teacher of
Russian literature. As he speaks of the development of
the language, of the contents of the early epic poetry,
of popular songs and music, and, later on, of modern fiction,
of the scientific, political, and philosophical literature of
his own country, and the divers æsthetical, political, and
philosophical currents it has reflected, he is bound to introduce that generalized conception of the development of
human mind which lies beyond the scope of each of the
subjects that are taught separately.

The same thing ought to be done for the natural sciences
as well. It is not enough to teach physics and chemistry,
astronomy and meteorology, zoölogy and botany. The
philosophy of all the natural sciences — a general view of
nature as a whole, something on the lines of the first
volume of Humboldt's "Cosmos"— must be conveyed to

the pupils and the students, whatsoever may be the extension given to the study of the natural sciences in the school. The philosophy and the poetry of nature, the methods of all the exact sciences, and an inspired conception of the life of nature must make part of education. Perhaps the teacher of geography might provisionally assume this function; but then we should require quite a different set of teachers of this subject, and a different set of professors of geography in the universities would be needed. What is now taught under this name is anything you like, but it is not geography.

Another teacher conquered our rather uproarious form in a quite different manner. It was the teacher of writing, the last one of the teaching staff. If the "heathen" — that is, the German and the French teachers — were regarded with little respect, the teacher of writing, Ebert, who was a German Jew, was a real martyr. To be insolent with him was a sort of *chic* amongst the pages. His poverty alone must have been the reason why he kept to his lesson in our corps. The old hands, who had stayed for two or three years in the fifth form without moving higher up, treated him very badly; but by some means or other he had made an agreement with them: "One frolic during each lesson, but no more," — an agreement which, I am afraid, was not always honestly kept on our side.

One day, one of the residents of the remote peninsula soaked the blackboard sponge with ink and chalk and flung it at the caligraphy martyr. "Get it, Ebert!" he shouted, with a stupid smile. The sponge touched Ebert's shoulder, the grimy ink spirted into his face and down on to his white shirt.

We were sure that this time Ebert would leave the room and report the fact to the inspector. But he only exclaimed, as he took out his cotton handkerchief and

wiped his face, "Gentlemen, one frolic, — no more to-
day!" "The shirt is spoiled," he added, in a subdued
voice, and continued to correct some one's book.

We looked stupefied and ashamed. Why, instead of
reporting, he had thought at once of the agreement! The
feeling of the class turned in his favor. "What you have
done is stupid," we reproached our comrade. "He is
a poor man, and you have spoiled his shirt! Shame!"
somebody cried.

The culprit went at once to make excuses. "One must
learn, learn, sir," was all that Ebert said in reply, with
sadness in his voice.

All became silent after that, and at the next lesson, as
if we had settled it beforehand, most of us wrote in our
best possible handwriting, and took our books to Ebert,
asking him to correct them. He was radiant; he felt
happy that day.

This fact deeply impressed me, and was never wiped out
from my memory. To this day I feel grateful to that
remarkable man for his lesson.

With our teacher of drawing, who was named Ganz, we
never arrived at living on good terms. He continually reported those who played in his class. This, in our opinion, he had no right to do, because he was only a teacher
of drawing, but especially because he was not an honest
man. In the class he paid little attention to most of us,
and spent his time in improving the drawings of those who
took private lessons from him, or paid him in order to show
at the examinations a good drawing and to get a good mark
for it. Against those comrades who did so we had no
grudge. On the contrary, we thought it quite right that
those who had no capacity for mathematics or no memory
for geography, and had but poor marks in these subjects,
should improve their total of marks by ordering from a

draughtsman a drawing or a topographical map for which they would get "a full twelve." Only for the first two pupils of the form it would not have been fair to resort to such means, while the remainder could do it with untroubled consciences. But the teacher had no business to make drawings to order; and if he chose to act in this way, he ought to bear with resignation the noise and the tricks of his pupils. Instead of this, no lesson passed without his lodging complaints, and each time he grew more arrogant.

As soon as we were moved to the fourth form, and felt ourselves naturalized citizens of the corps, we decided to tighten the bridle upon him. "It is your own fault," our elder comrades told us, "that he takes such airs with you; *we* used to keep him in obedience." So we decided to bring him into subjection.

One day, two excellent comrades of our form approached Ganz with cigarettes in their mouths, and asked him to oblige them with a light. Of course, that was only meant for a joke, — no one ever thought of smoking in the classrooms, — and, according to our rules of propriety, Ganz had merely to send the two boys away; but he inscribed them in the journal, and they were severely punished. That was the last drop. We decided to give him a " benefit night." That meant that one day all the form, provided with rulers borrowed from the upper forms, would start an outrageous noise by striking the rulers against the tables, and send the teacher out of the class. However, the plot offered many difficulties. We had in our form a lot of "goody" boys who would promise to join in the demonstration, but at the last moment would grow nervous and draw back, and then the teacher would name the others. In such enterprises unanimity is the first requisite, because the punishment, whatsoever it may be, is always lighter when it falls on the whole class instead of on a few.

The difficulties were overcome with a truly Machiavel‧ lian craft. At a given signal all were to turn their backs to Ganz, and then, with the rulers laid in readiness on the desks of the next row, they would produce the required noise. In this way the goody boys would not feel terrified at Ganz's staring at them. But the signal? Whistling, as in robbers' tales, shouting, or even sneezing would not do: Ganz would be capable of naming any one of us as having whistled or sneezed. The signal must be a silent one. One of us, who drew nicely, would take his drawing to show it to Ganz, and the moment he returned and took his seat, — that was to be the time!

All went on admirably. Nesádoff took up his drawing, and Ganz corrected it in a few minutes, which seemed to us an eternity. He returned at last to his seat; he stopped for a moment, looking at us; he sat down. . . . All the form turned suddenly on their seats, and the rulers rattled merrily within the desks, while some of us shouted amidst the noise, "Ganz out! Down with him!" The noise was deafening; all the forms knew that Ganz had got his benefit night. He stood there, murmuring something, and finally went out. An officer ran in, — the noise continued; then the sub-inspector dashed in, and after him the inspector. The noise stopped at once. Scolding began.

"The elder under arrest at once!" the inspector commanded; and I, who was the first in the form, and consequently the elder, was marched to the black cell. That spared me seeing what followed. The director came; Ganz was asked to name the ringleaders, but he could name nobody. "They all turned their backs to me, and began the noise," was his reply. Thereupon the form was taken downstairs, and although flogging had been completely abandoned in our school, this time the two who had been reported because they asked for a light were flogged with the birch rod, under the pretext that the benefit night was a revenge for their punishment.

I learned this ten days later, when I was allowed to return to the class. My name, which had been inscribed on the red board in the class, was wiped off. To this I was indifferent; but I must confess that the ten days in the cell, without books, seemed to me rather long, so that I composed (in horrible verses) a poem, in which the deeds of the fourth form were duly glorified.

Of course, our form became now the heroes of the school. For a month or so we had to tell and retell all about the affair to the other forms, and received congratulations for having managed it with such unanimity that nobody was caught separately. And then came the Sundays — all the Sundays down to Christmas — that the form had to remain at the school, not being allowed to go home. Being all kept together, we managed to make those Sundays very gay. The mammas of the goody boys brought them heaps of sweets; those who had some money spent it in buying mountains of pastry, — substantial before dinner, and sweet after it; while in the evenings the friends from the other forms smuggled in quantities of fruit for the brave fourth form.

Ganz gave up inscribing any one; but drawing was totally lost for us. No one wanted to learn drawing from that mercenary man.

III

My brother Alexander was at that time at Moscow, in a corps of cadets, and we maintained a lively correspondence. As long as I stayed at home this was impossible, because our father considered it his prerogative to read all letters addressed to our house, and he would soon have put an end to any but a commonplace correspondence. Now we were free to discuss in our letters whatever we liked. The only difficulty was to get money for stamps; but we soon learned to write in such fine characters that we could convey an incredible amount of matter in each letter. Alexander, whose handwriting was beautiful, contrived to get four printed pages on one single page of note-paper, and his microscopic lines were as legible as the best small type print. It is a pity that these letters, which he kept as precious relics, have disappeared. The state police, during one of their raids, robbed him even of these treasures.

Our first letters were mostly about the little details of my new surroundings, but our correspondence soon took a more serious character. My brother could not write about trifles. Even in society he became animated only when some serious discussion was engaged in, and he complained of feeling "a dull pain in the brain"—a physical pain, as he used to say—when he was with people who cared only for small talk. He was very much in advance of me in his intellectual development, and he urged me forward, raising new scientific and philosophical questions one after another, and advising me what to read or to study. What a happiness it was for me to have such a brother!—a brother who, moreover, loved me passionately. To him I owe the best part of my development.

Sometimes he would advise me to read poetry, and would send me in his letters quantities of verses and whole poems, which he wrote from memory.   " Read poetry," he wrote : " poetry makes men better."   How often, in my after life, I realized the truth of this remark of his !   Read poetry : it makes men better.   He himself was a poet, and had a wonderful facility for writing most musical verses ; indeed, I think it a great pity that he abandoned poetry.   But the reaction against art, which arose among the Russian youth in the early sixties, and which Turguéneff has depicted in Bazráoff ("Fathers and Sons"), induced him to look upon his verses with contempt, and to plunge headlong into the natural sciences.   I must say, however, that my favorite poet was none of those whom his poetical gift, his musical ear, and his philosophical turn of mind made him like best. His favorite Russian poet was Venevítinoff, while mine was Nekrásoff, whose verses were very often unmusical, but appealed most to my heart by their sympathy for " the downtrodden and ill-treated."

" One must have a set purpose in his life," he wrote me once.   " Without an aim, without a purpose, life is not life."   And he advised me to get a purpose in my life worth living for.   I was too young then to find one ; but something undetermined, vague, " good " altogether, already rose under that appeal, even though I could not say what that " good " would be.

Our father gave us very little spending money, and I never had any to buy a single book; but if Alexander got a few rubles from some aunt, he never spent a penny of it for pleasure, but bought a book and sent it to me.   He objected, though, to indiscriminate reading.   " One must have some question," he wrote, " addressed to the book one is going to read."   However, I did not then appreciate this remark, and cannot think now without amazement of the number of books, often of a quite special character, which I read in all branches, but particularly in the domain of history. I did not waste my time upon French novels, since Alexander, years before, had characterized them in one blunt sentence: " They are stupid and full of bad language."

The great questions concerning the conception we should form of the universe — our *Weltanschauung*, as the Germans say — were, of course, the dominant subjects in our correspondence. In our childhood we had never been religious. We were taken to church; but in a Russian church, in a small parish or in a village, the solemn attitude of the people is far more impressive than the mass itself. Of all that I ever had heard in church only two things had impressed me: the twelve passages from the Gospels, relative to the sufferings of the Christ, which are read in Russia at the night service on the eve of Good Friday, and the short prayer condemning the spirit of domination, which is recited during the Great Lent, and is really beautiful by reason of its simple, unpretentious words and feeling. Púshkin has rendered it into Russian verse.

Later on, at St. Petersburg, I went several times to a Roman Catholic church, but the theatrical character of the service and the absence of real feeling in it shocked me, the more so when I saw there with what simple faith some retired Polish soldier or a peasant woman would pray in a remote corner. I also went to a Protestant church; but coming out of it I caught myself murmuring Goethe's words: —

> "But you will never link hearts together
> Unless the linking springs from your own heart."

Alexander, in the meantime, had embraced with his usual passion the Lutheran faith. He had read Michelet's book on Servetus, and had worked out for himself a religion on the lines of that great fighter. He studied with enthusiasm the Augsburg declaration, which he copied out and sent me, and our letters now became full of discussions about grace, and of texts from the apostles Paul and James. I followed my brother, but theological discussions did not deeply interest me. Since I had recovered from the typhoid fever I had taken to quite different reading.

Our sister Hélène, who was now married, was at St. Petersburg, and every Saturday night I went to visit her. Her husband had a good library, in which the French philosophers of the last century and the modern French historians were well represented, and I plunged into them. Such books were prohibited in Russia, and evidently could not be taken to school; so I spent most of the night, every Saturday, in reading the works of the encyclopædists, the philosophical dictionary of Voltaire, the writings of the Stoics, especially Marcus Aurelius, and so on. The infinite immensity of the universe, the greatness of nature, its poetry, its ever throbbing life, impressed me more and more; and that never ceasing life and its harmonies gave me the ecstasy of admiration which the young soul thirsts for, while my favorite poets supplied me with an expression in words of that awakening love of mankind and faith in its progress which make the best part of youth and impress man for a life.

Alexander, by this time, had gradually come to a Kantian agnosticism, and the "relativity of perceptions," "perceptions in time and space, and time only," and so on, filled pages and pages in our letters, the writing of which became more and more microscopical as the subjects under discussion grew in importance. But neither then nor later on, when we used to spend hours and hours in discussing Kant's philosophy, could my brother convert me to become a disciple of the Königsberg philosopher.

Natural sciences — that is, mathematics, physics, and astronomy — were my chief studies. In the year 1858, before Darwin had brought out his immortal work, a professor of zoölogy at the Moscow University, Roulier, published three lectures on transformism, and my brother took up at once his ideas concerning the variability of species. He was not satisfied, however, with approximate proofs only, and began to study a number of special books on heredity and the like; communicating to me in his letters the main facts, as well as his ideas and his doubts. The appearance of "The Origin of Species" did not settle his doubts on several special points, but only raised new questions and gave him the impulse for further studies. We afterward discussed — and that discussion lasted for many years — various questions relative to the origin of variations, their chances of being transmitted and being accentuated; in short, those questions which have been raised quite lately in the Weismann-Spencer controversy, in Galton's researches, and in the works of the modern Neo-Lamarckians. Owing to his philosophical and critical mind, Alexander had noticed at once the fundamental importance of these questions for the theory of variability of species, even though they were so often overlooked then by many naturalists.

I must also mention a temporary excursion into the domain of political economy. In the years 1858 and 1859 every one in Russia talked of political economy; lectures on free trade and protective duties attracted crowds of people, and my brother, who was not yet absorbed by the variability of species, took a lively though temporary interest in economical matters, sending me for reading the "Political Economy" of Jean Baptiste Say. I read a few chapters only: tariffs and banking operations did not interest me in the least; but Alexander took up these matters so passionately that he even wrote letters to our stepmother, trying to interest her in the intricacies of the customs duties. Later on, in Siberia, as we were re-reading some of the letters of that period, we laughed like children when we fell upon one of his epistles in which he complained of our stepmother's incapacity to be moved even by such burning questions, and raged against a greengrocer whom he had caught in the street, and who, "would you believe it," he wrote with signs of exclamation, "although he was a trades-man, affected a pig-headed indifference to tariff questions!"

Every summer about one half of the pages were taken to a camp at Peterhof. The lower forms, however, were dispensed from joining the camp, and I spent the first two summers at Nikólskoye. To leave the school, to take the train to Moscow, and there to meet Alexander was such a happy prospect that I used to count the days that had to pass till that glorious one should arrive. But on one occasion a great disappointment awaited me at Moscow. Alexander had not passed his examinations, and was left for another year in the same form. He was, in fact, too young to enter the special classes; but our father was very angry with him, nevertheless, and would not permit us to see each other. I felt very sad. We were not children any more, and had so much to say to each other. I tried to obtain permission to go to our aunt Sulíma, at whose house I might meet Alexander, but it was absolutely refused. After our father remarried we were never allowed to see our mother's relations.

That spring our Moscow house was full of guests. Every night the reception-rooms were flooded with lights, the band played, the confectioner was busy making ices and pastry, and card-playing went on in the great hall till a late hour. I strolled aimlessly about in the brilliantly illuminated rooms, and felt unhappy.

One night, after ten, a servant beckoned me, telling me to come out to the entrance hall. I went. "Come to the coachmen's house," the old major-domo Frol whispered to me. "Alexander Alexéievich is here."

I dashed across the yard, up the flight of steps leading to

the coachmen's house, and into a wide, half-dark room, where, at the immense dining-table of the servants, I saw Alexander.

"Sásha, dear, how did you come?" and in a moment we rushed into each other's arms, hugging each other and unable to speak from emotion.

"Hush, hush! they may overhear you," said the servants' cook, Praskóvia, wiping away her tears with her apron. "Poor orphans! If your mother were only alive" —

Old Frol stood, his head deeply bent, his eyes also twinkling.

"Look here, Pétya, not a word to any one; to no one," he said, while Praskóvia placed on the table an earthenware jar full of porridge for Alexander.

He, glowing with health, in his cadet uniform, already had begun to talk about all sorts of matters, while he rapidly emptied the porridge pot. I could hardly make him tell me how he came there at such a late hour. We lived then near the Smolénsky boulevard, within a stone's throw of the house where our mother died, and the corps of cadets was at the opposite outskirts of Moscow, full five miles away.

He had made a doll out of bedclothes, and had put it in his bed, under the blankets; then he went to the tower, descended from a window, came out unnoticed, and walked the whole distance.

"Were you not afraid at night, in the deserted fields round your corps?" I asked.

"What had I to fear? Only lots of dogs were upon me; I had teased them myself. To-morrow I shall take my sword with me."

The coachmen and other servants came in and out; they sighed as they looked at us, and took seats at a distance, along the walls, exchanging words in a subdued tone, so as not to disturb us; while we two, in each other's arms, sat there till midnight, talking about nebulæ and Laplace's hypothesis, the structure of matter, the struggles of the papacy under Boniface VIII. with the imperial power, and so on.

From time to time one of the servants would hurriedly run in, saying, "Pétinka, go and show thyself in the hall; they are moving about and may ask for thee."

I implored Sásha not to come next night; but he came, nevertheless, — not without having had a scrimmage with the dogs, against whom he had taken his sword. I responded with feverish haste, when, earlier than the day before, I was called once more to the coachmen's house. Alexander had made part of the journey in a cab. The previous night, one of the servants had brought him what he had got from the card-players and asked him to take it. He took some small coin to hire a cab, and so he came earlier than on his first visit.

He intended to come next night, too, but for some reason it would have been dangerous for the servants, and we decided to part till the autumn. A short "official" note made me understand next day that his nocturnal escapades had passed unnoticed. How terrible would have been the punishment, if they had been discovered! It is awful to think of it: flogging before the corps till he was carried away unconscious on a sheet, and then degradation to a soldiers' sons' battalion, — anything was possible, in those times.

What our servants would have suffered for hiding us, if information of the affair had reached our father's ears, would have been equally terrible; but they knew how to keep secrets, and not to betray one another. They all knew of the visits of Alexander, but none of them whispered a word to any one of the family. They and I were the only ones in the house who ever knew anything about it.

IV

THAT same year I made my start as an investigator of popular life. This work brought me one step nearer to our peasants, making me see them under a new light; later, it also helped me a great deal in Siberia.

Every year, in July, on the day of "The Holy Virgin of Kazan," which was the fête of our church, a pretty large fair was held in Nikólskoye. Tradesmen came from all the neighboring towns, and many thousands of peasants flocked from thirty miles round to our village, which for a couple of days had a most animated aspect. A remarkable description of the village fairs of South Russia had been published that year by the Slavophile Aksákoff, and my brother, who was then at the height of his politico-economical enthusiasm, advised me to make a statistical description of our fair, and to determine the returns of goods brought in and sold. I followed his advice, and to my great amazement I really succeeded: my estimate of returns, so far as I can judge now, was not more unreliable than many similar estimates in books of statistics.

Our fair lasted only a little more than twenty-four hours. On the eve of the fête the great open space given to the fair was full of life and animation. Long rows of stalls, to be used for the sale of cottons, ribbons, and all sorts of peasant women's attire, were hurriedly built. The restaurant, a substantial stone building, was furnished with tables, chairs, and benches, and its floor was strewn over with bright yellow sand. Three wine shops were erected, and freshly cut brooms, planted on high poles, rose high in the air, to attract the peasants from a distance. Rows and rows of smaller stalls, for the sale of crockery, boots, stoneware, gingerbread, and all sorts of small things, rose as if by a magic wand, while in a special corner of the fair ground holes were dug to receive immense cauldrons, in which bushels of millet and sarrazin and whole sheep were boiled, for supplying the thousands of visitors with hot *schi* and *kásha* (soup and porridge). In the afternoon, the four roads leading to the fair were blocked by hundreds of peasant carts, and heaps of pottery, casks filled with tar, corn, and cattle were exhibited along the roadsides.

The night service on the eve of the fête was performed in our church with great solemnity. Half a dozen priests and deacons, from the neighboring villages, took part in it, and their chanters, reinforced by young tradespeople, sang in the choirs such ritornellos as could usually be heard only at the bishop's in Kalúga. The church was crowded; all prayed fervently. The tradespeople vied with one another in the number and sizes of the wax candles which they lighted before the ikons, as offerings to the local saints for the success of their trade, and the crowd being so great as not to allow the last comers to reach the altar, candles of all sizes — thick and thin, white and yellow, according to the offerer's wealth — were handed from the back of the church through the crowd, with whispers: "To the Holy Virgin of Kazan, our Protector;" "To Nicholas the Favorite;" "To Frol and Laur" (the horse saints, — that was from those who had horses to sell); or simply to "The Saints," without further specification.

Immediately after the night service was over, the "forefair" began, and I had now to plunge headlong into my work of asking hundreds of people what was the value of the goods they had brought in. To my great astonishment I got on admirably. Of course, I was myself asked questions: "Why do you do this?" "Is it not for the old prince, who intends increasing the market dues?" But the assurance that the "old prince" knew and would know nothing of it (he would have thought it a disgraceful occupation) settled all doubts at once. I soon caught the proper way of asking questions, and after I had taken half a dozen cups of tea, in the restaurant, with some tradespeople (oh, horror, if my father had learned that!), all went on very well. Vasíly Ivánoff, the elder of Nikólskoye, a beautiful young peasant, with a fine intelligent face and a silky fair beard, took an interest in my work. "Well, if thou wantest it for thy learning, get at it; thou wilt tell us later on what thou hast found out," was his conclusion, and he told some of the people that it was "all right."

In short, the imports were determined very nicely. But next day the sales offered certain difficulties, chiefly with the drygoods merchants, who did not themselves yet know how much they had sold. On the day of the fête the young peasant women simply stormed the shops; each of them, having sold some linen of her own make, was now buying some cotton print and a bright kerchief for herself, a colored handkerchief for her husband, perhaps some lace, a ribbon or two, and a number of small gifts for grandmother, grandfather, and the children who had remained at home. As to the peasants who sold crockery, or ginger cakes, or cattle, or hemp, they at once determined their sales, especially the old women. "Good sale, grandmother?" I would ask. "No need to complain, my son. Why should I anger God! Nearly all is sold." And out of their small items tens of thousands of rubles grew in my notebook. One point only remained unsettled. A wide space was given up to many hundreds of peasant women who stood in the burning sun, each with her piece of hand-woven linen, sometimes exquisitely fine, which she had brought for sale. Scores of buyers, with gypsy faces and shark-like looks, moved about in the crowd, buying. Only rough estimates of these sales could be made.

I made no reflections at that time about this new experience of mine; I was simply happy to see that it was not a failure. But the serious good sense and sound judgment of the Russian peasants which I witnessed during this couple of days left upon me a lasting impression. Later, when we were spreading socialist doctrines amongst the peasants, I could not but wonder why some of my friends, who had received a seemingly far more democratic education than myself, did not know how to talk to the peasants or to the factory workers from the country. They tried to imitate the "peasants' talk" by introducing a profusion of so-called "popular phrases," but they only rendered themselves the more incomprehensible.

Nothing of the sort is needed, either in talking to peasants or in writing for them. The Great Russian peasant perfectly well understands the educated man's talk, provided it is not stuffed with words taken from foreign languages. What the peasant does not understand is abstract notions when they are not illustrated by concrete examples. But my experience is that when you speak to the Russian peasant plainly, and start from concrete facts, — and the same is true with regard to village folk of all nationalities, — there is no generalization from the whole world of science, social or natural, which cannot be conveyed to a man of average intelligence, if you yourself understand it concretely. The chief difference between the educated and the uneducated man is, I should say, that the latter is not able to follow a chain of conclusions. He grasps the first of them, and may be the second, but he gets tired at the third, if he does not see what you are driving at. But how often do we meet the same difficulty in educated people.

One more impression I gathered from that work of my boyhood, an impression which I did not formulate till afterward, and which will probably astonish many a reader. It is the spirit of equality which is highly developed in the

Russian peasant, and in fact in the rural population everywhere. The Russian peasant is capable of much servile
obedience to the landlord and the police officer ; he will
bend before their will in a servile manner ; but he does not
consider them superior men, and if the next moment that
same landlord or officer talks to the same peasant about
hay or ducks, the latter will reply to him as an equal to
an equal. I never saw in a Russian peasant that servility,
grown to be a second nature, with which a small functionary talks to one of high rank, or a valet to his master.
The peasant too easily submits to force, but he does not
worship it.

I returned that summer from Nikólskoye to Moscow in a
new fashion. There being then no railway between Kalúga
and Moscow, there was a man, Buck by name, who kept
some sort of carriages running between the two towns. Our
people never thought of traveling in these carriages : they
had their own horses and conveyances ; but when my father,
in order to save my stepmother a double journey, proposed
to me, half in joke, that I should travel alone in that way,
I accepted his offer with delight.

A tradesman's wife, old and very stout, and myself on
the back seats, and a tradesman or artisan on the front seat,
were the only occupants of the carriage. I found the
journey very pleasant, — first of all because I was traveling
by myself (I was not yet sixteen), and next because the
old lady, who had brought with her for a three days'
journey a colossal hamper full of provisions, treated me to
all sorts of home-made delicacies. The surroundings during
that journey were delightful. One evening especially is
still vivid in my memory. We came to one of the great
villages and stopped at an inn. The old lady ordered a
samovar for herself, while I went out into the street,
walking about anywhere. A small " white inn," at which

only food is served, but no drinks, attracted my attention, and I went in. Numbers of peasants sat round the small tables, which were covered with white napkins, and enjoyed their tea. I followed their example.

Everything there was new to me. It was a village of "Crown peasants," that is, peasants who had not been serfs, and enjoyed a relative well-being, probably owing to the weaving of linen, which they carried on as a home industry. Slow, serious conversations, with occasional laughter, were going on at the tables, and after the usual introductory questions, I soon found myself engaged in a conversation with a dozen peasants about the crops in our neighborhood, and answering all sorts of inquiries. They wanted to know all about St. Petersburg, and especially about the rumors concerning the coming abolition of serfdom. A feeling of simplicity and of natural relations of equality, as well as of hearty goodwill, which I always felt afterwards when among peasants or in their houses, pervaded me at that inn. Nothing extraordinary happened that night, so that I even ask myself whether the incident is worth mentioning at all; and yet, that warm dark night in the village, that small inn, that talk with the peasants, and the keen interest they took in hundreds of things lying far beyond their habitual surroundings, have made a poor "white inn" more attractive to me ever since than the best restaurant in the world.

V

Stormy times came now in the life of our corps. When
Girardot was dismissed, his place was taken by one of our
officers, Captain B——. He was rather good-natured than
otherwise, but he had got it into his head that he was not
treated by us with due reverence corresponding to the high
position which he now occupied, and he tried to enforce
upon us more respect and awe towards himself. He began
by quarreling over all sorts of petty things with the upper
form, and — what was still worse in our opinion — he attempted to destroy our "liberties," the origin of which was
lost in "the darkness of time," and which, insignificant in
themselves, were perhaps on that very account only the
dearer to us.

The result of it was that for several days the school was
in an open revolt, which ended in wholesale punishment,
and in the exclusion from the corps of two of our favorite
pages de chambre.

Then the same captain began to intrude into the class-
rooms, where we used to spend one hour in the morning in
preparing our lessons, before the classes began. We were
considered to be there under our teaching staff, and were
happy to have nothing to do with our military officers. We
resented that intrusion very much, and one day I loudly expressed our discontent by telling the captain that this was
the place of the inspector of the classes, not his. I spent
weeks under arrest for that frankness, and perhaps would
have been excluded from the school, had it not been that
the inspector of the classes, his aid, and even our old
director judged that, after all, I had only expressed aloud
what they all used to say to themselves.

No sooner were these troubles over, than the death of the Dowager-Empress, the widow of Nicholas I., brought a new interruption in our work.

The burial of crowned heads is always so arranged as to produce a deep impression on the crowds. The body of the Empress was brought from Tsárkoye Seló, where she died, to St. Petersburg, and here, followed by the imperial family, all the high dignitaries of the state, and scores of thousands of functionaries and corporations, and preceded by hundreds of clergy and choirs, it was taken from the railway station, through the main thoroughfares, to the fortress, where it had to lie in state for several weeks. A hundred thousand men of the guard were placed along the streets, and thousands of people, dressed in the most gorgeous uniforms, preceded, accompanied, and followed the hearse in a solemn procession. Litanies were sung at every important crossing of the streets, and here the ringing of the bells on the church towers, the voices of the vast choirs, and the sounds of the military bands united in the most impressive way, so as to make people believe that the immense crowds really mourned the loss of the Empress.

As long as the body lay in state in the cathedral of the fortress, the pages, among others, had to keep watch round it, night and day. Three pages de chambre and three maids of honor always stood close by the coffin, which was placed on a high pedestal, while some twenty pages were stationed on the platform, upon which litanies were sung twice every day, in the presence of the Emperor and all his family. Consequently, every week nearly one half of the corps was taken in turns to the fortress, to lodge there. We were relieved every two hours, and in the daytime our service was not difficult; but when we had to rise in the night, to dress in our court uniforms, and then to walk through the dark and gloomy inner courts of the fortress to the cathedral, to the sound of the gloomy chime of the fortress bells, a cold shiver seized me at the thought of the prisoners who were immured somewhere in this Russian Bastille. "Who knows," thought I, "whether in my turn I shall not also have to join them some day."

The burial did not pass without an accident, which might have had serious consequences. An immense canopy had been erected under the dome of the cathedral, over the coffin. A huge gilded crown rose above it, and from this crown an immense purple mantle, lined with ermine, hung towards the four thick pilasters which support the dome of the cathedral. It was impressive, but we boys soon made out that the crown was of gilded cardboard and wood, the mantle of velvet only in its lower part, while higher up it was red cotton, and that the ermine lining was simply cotton flannelette or swansdown, to which tails of black squirrels had been sewn; the escutcheons, which represented the arms of Russia, veiled with black crêpe, were simple cardboard. But the crowds, which were allowed at certain hours of the night to pass by the coffin, and to kiss in a hurry the gold brocade which covered it, surely had no time to closely examine the flannelette ermine or the cardboard escutcheons, and the desired theatrical effect was obtained even by such cheap means.

When a litany is sung in Russia, all people present hold lighted wax candles, which have to be put out after certain prayers have been read. The imperial family also held such candles, and one day, the young son of the Grand Duke Constantine, seeing that the others put out their wax candles by turning them upside down, did the same. The black gauze which hung behind him from an escutcheon took fire, and in a second the escutcheon and the cotton stuff were ablaze. An immense tongue of fire ran up the heavy folds of the supposed ermine mantle.

The service was stopped. All looks were directed with

terror upon the tongue of fire, which went higher and higher toward the cardboard crown and the woodwork that supported the whole structure. Bits of burning stuff began to fall, threatening to set fire to the black gauze veils of the ladies present.

Alexander II. lost his presence of mind for a couple of seconds only, but he recovered immediately, and said in a composed voice: "The coffin must be taken !" The pages de chambre at once covered it with the thick gold brocade, and we all advanced to lift it; but in the meantime the big tongue of flame had broken into a number of smaller ones, which now slowly devoured only the fluffy outside of the cotton stuff and, meeting more and more dust and soot in the upper parts of the structure, gradually died out in its folds.

I cannot say what I looked at most : the creeping fire or the stately slender figures of the three ladies who stood by the coffin, the long trains of their black dresses spreading over the steps which led to the upper platform, and their black lace veils hanging down their shoulders. None of them had made the slightest movement : they stood like three beautiful carved images. Only in the dark eyes of one of them, Mademoiselle Gamaléya, tears glittered like pearls. She was a daughter of South Russia, and was the only really handsome lady amongst the maids of honor at the court.

At the corps everything was upside down. The classes were interrupted ; those of us who returned from the fortress were lodged in temporary quarters, and, having nothing to do, spent the whole day in all sorts of frolics. In one of them we managed to open a cupboard which stood in the room, and contained a splendid collection of models of all kinds of animals, for the teaching of natural history. That was its official purpose, but it was never even so much as shown to us, and now that we got hold of it we utilized it in our own way. With a human skull, which was in the collection, we made a ghostly figure wherewith to frighten other comrades and the officers at night.   As to the animals, we placed them in the most ludicrous positions and groups: monkeys were seen riding on lions, sheep were playing with leopards, the giraffe danced with the elephant, and so on. The worst was that a few days later one of the Prussian princes, who had come to assist at the burial ceremony (it was the one, I think, who became later on the Emperor Frederic), visited our school, and was shown all that concerned our education.   Our director did not fail to boast of the excellent educational appliances which we had, and brought his guest to that unfortunate cupboard.   When the German prince caught a glimpse of our zoölogical classification, he drew a long face and quickly turned away.   The director looked horrified; he had lost the power of speech, and only pointed repeatedly with his hand at some sea stars, which were placed in glass boxes on the walls beside the cupboard.   The suite of the prince tried to look as if they had noticed nothing, and only threw rapid glances at the cause of so much disturbance, while we wicked boys made all sorts of faces in order not to burst with laughter.

THE school years of a Russian youth are so different from the corresponding period in west European schools, that I must dwell further on my school life. Russian boys, as a rule, while they are yet at a lyceum or in a military school, take an interest in a wide circle of social, political, and philosophical matters. It is true that the corps of pages was, of all schools, the least congenial place for such a development; but in those years of general revival, broader ideas penetrated even there, and carried some of us away, without, however, preventing us from taking a very lively part in "benefit nights" and all sorts of frolics.

While I was in the fourth form I became interested in history, and with the aid of notes made during the lessons, and helping myself with reading, I wrote quite a course of early mediaeval history for my own use. Next year, the struggle between Pope Boniface VIII. and the imperial power attracted my special attention, and now it became my ambition to be admitted to the Imperial Library as a reader, to study that great struggle. That was contrary to the rules of the library, pupils of secondary schools not being admitted; our good Herr Becker, however, smoothed the way out of the difficulty, and I was allowed at last to enter the sanctuary, and to take a seat at one of the readers' small tables, on one of the red velvet sofas which then formed a part of the furniture of the reading-room.

From various textbooks and some books from our own library, I soon got to the sources. Knowing no Latin, I discovered, nevertheless, a rich supply of original sources in Old Teutonic and Old French, and found an immense æsthetic enjoyment in the quaint structure and expressiveness of the Old French in the chronicles. Quite a new structure of society and quite a world of complicated relations opened before me; and from that time I learned to value far more highly the original sources of history than the works of modernized generalizations in which the prejudices of modern politics, or even mere current formulæ, are often substituted for the real life of the period. Nothing gives more impetus to one's intellectual development than some sort of independent research, and these studies of mine afterwards helped me very much.

Unhappily I had to abandon them when we reached the second form (the last but one). The pages had to study during the last two years nearly all that was taught in other military schools in three special forms, and we had a vast amount of work to do for the school. Natural sciences, mathematics, and military sciences necessarily relegated history to the background.

In the second form we began seriously to study physics. We had an excellent teacher, a very intelligent man with a sarcastic turn of mind, who hated learning from memory, and managed to make us *think*, instead of merely learning facts. He was a good mathematician, and taught us physics on a mathematical basis, admirably explaining at the same time the leading ideas of physical research and physical apparatus. Some of his questions were so original and his explanations so good that they engraved themselves forever in my memory.

Our textbook of physics was not bad (most textbooks for the military schools had been written by the best men at the time), but it was rather old, and our teacher, who followed his own system in teaching, began to prepare a short summary of his lessons, — a sort of *aide-mémoire*. However, after a few weeks it so happened that the task of writing this summary fell upon me, and our teacher, acting as a true pedagogist, trusted it entirely to me, only reading the proofs. When we came to the chapters on heat, electricity, and magnetism, they had to be written entirely anew, with more developments, and this I did, thus preparing a nearly complete textbook of physics, which was printed for the use of the school.

In the second form we also began to study chemistry, and in this, too, we had a first-rate teacher, — a passionate lover of the subject, who had himself made valuable original researches. The years 1859–61 were years of a universal revival of taste for the exact sciences. Grove, Clausius, Joule, and Séguin showed that heat and all physical forces are but divers modes of motion ; Helmholtz began about that time his epoch-making researches in sound ; Tyndall, in his popular lectures, made one touch, so to say, the very atoms and molecules. Gerhardt and Avogadro introduced the theory of substitutions, and Mendeléeff, Lothar Meyer, and Newlands discovered the periodical law of elements ; Darwin, with his " Origin of Species," revolutionized all biological sciences ; while Karl Vogt and Moleschott, following Claude Bernard, laid the foundations of true psychology in physiology. It was a time of scientific revival, and the current which carried minds toward natural science was irresistible. Numbers of excellent books were published at that time in Russian translations, and I soon understood that whatever one's subsequent studies might be, a thorough knowledge of the natural sciences and familiarity with their methods must lie at the foundation. Five or six of us joined together to get some sort of laboratory for ourselves. With the elementary apparatus recommended for beginners in Stöckhardt's excellent textbook, we started our laboratory in a small bedroom of two of our comrades, the brothers Zasetsky. Their father, an old admiral in retirement, was delighted to see his sons engaged in so useful a pursuit, and did not object to our coming together on Sundays and during the holidays in that room, by the side of his own study.   With Stöckhardt's book as a guide, we systematically made all experiments. I must say that once we nearly set the house on fire, and that more than once we poisoned all the rooms with chlorine and similar stuffs.   But the old admiral, when we related the adventure at dinner time, took it very nicely, and told us how he and his comrades also nearly set a house on fire in the far less useful pursuit of punch making; while the mother only said, amidst her paroxysms of coughing: "Of course, if it *is* necessary for your learning to handle such nasty smelling things, then there's nothing to be done!"

After dinner she usually took her seat at the piano, and till late at night we would go on singing duets, trios, and choruses from the operas. Or we would take the score of some Italian or Russian opera and go through it from the beginning to the end, — the mother and her daughter acting as the prima donnas, while we managed more or less successfully to maintain all the other parts. Chemistry and music thus went hand in hand.

Higher mathematics also absorbed a great deal of my time. Several of us had already decided that we should not enter a regiment of the Guard, where all our time would be given to military drill and parades, and we intended to enter, after promotion, one of the military academies, — artillery or engineering. In order to do so we had to prepare in higher geometry, differential calculus, and the beginnings of integral calculus, and we took private lessons for that purpose. At the same time, elementary astronomy being taught to us under the name of mathematical geography, I plunged into astronomical reading, especially during the last year of my stay at school. The never-ceasing life of the universe, which I conceived as *life* and evolution, became for me an inexhaustible source of higher poetical thought, and gradually the sense of Man's oneness with Nature, both animate and inanimate — the Poetry of Nature — became the philosophy of my life.

If the teaching in our school had been limited to the subjects I have mentioned, our time would have been pretty well occupied. But we also had to study in the domain of humanitarian science, history, law, — that is, the main outlines of the Russian code, — and political economy in its essential leading principles, including a course of comparative statistics; and we had to master formidable courses of military science, — tactics, military history (the campaigns of 1812 and 1815 in all their details), artillery and field fortification. Looking back now upon this education, I think that apart from the subjects relating to military warfare, for which more detailed studies in the exact sciences might have been advantageously substituted, the variety of subjects which we were taught was not beyond the capacity of the average youth. Owing to a pretty good knowledge of elementary mathematics and physics, which we gained in the lower forms, most of us managed to do all the work. Some studies were neglected by the majority of us, especially law, as also modern history, for which we had unfortunately an old wreck of a master, who was kept at his post only in order to give him his full old-age pension. Moreover, some latitude was given us in the choice of the subjects we liked best, and while we underwent severe examinations in these chosen subjects, we were treated rather leniently in the remainder. But the chief cause of the relative success which was obtained in the school was that the teaching was rendered as concrete as possible. As soon as we had learned elementary geometry on paper, we relearned it in the field, with poles and the surveyor's chain, and

next with the astrolabe, the compass, and the surveyor's
table. After such a concrete training, elementary astronomy
offered no difficulties, while the surveys themselves were
an endless source of enjoyment.

The same system of concrete teaching was applied to
fortification. In the winter we solved such problems as,
for instance, the following: Having a thousand men and
a fortnight at your disposal, build the strongest fortification
you can build, to protect that bridge for a retreating army;
and we hotly discussed our schemes with the teacher when
he criticised them. In the summer we applied our knowledge in the field. To these practical exercises I attribute
the ease with which most of us mastered such a variety
of scientific subjects at the age of seventeen or eighteen.

With all that, we had plenty of time for amusement and
all sorts of frolics. Our best time was when the examinations were over, and we had three or four weeks quite
free before going to camp, or when we returned from camp,
and had another three weeks free before the beginning of
lessons. The few of us who remained then in the school
were allowed, during the vacations, to go out just as we
liked, always finding bed and food at the school. I worked
in the library, or visited the picture galleries of the Her-
mitage, studying one by one all the best pictures of each
school separately; or I went to the different Crown manufactories of playing-cards, cottons, iron, china, and glass
which are open to the public. Sometimes we went out
rowing on the Nevá, spending the whole night on the
river; sometimes in the Gulf of Finland with fishermen, —
a melancholy northern night, during which the morning
dawn meets the afterglow of the setting sun, and a book
can be read in the open air at midnight. For all this we
found plenty of time.

After my visits to the manufactories I took a liking to

strong and perfect machinery. Seeing how a gigantic paw, coming out of a shanty, grasps a log floating in the Nevá, pulls it inside, and puts it under the saws, which cut it into boards ; or how a huge red-hot iron bar is transformed into a rail after it has passed between two cylinders, I understood the poetry of machinery. In our present factories, machinery work is killing for the worker, because he becomes a lifelong servant to a given machine, and never is anything else. But this is a matter of bad organization, and has nothing to do with the machine itself. Overwork and lifelong monotony are equally bad whether the work is done with the hand, with plain tools, or with a machine. But apart from these, I fully understand the pleasure that man can derive from a consciousness of the might of his machine, the intelligent character of its work, the gracefulness of its movements, and the correctness of what it is doing; and I think that William Morris's hatred of machines only proved that the conception of the machine's power and gracefulness was missing in his great poetical genius.

Music also played a very great part in my development. From it I borrowed even greater joy and enthusiasm than from poetry. The Russian opera hardly existed in those times; but the Italian opera, which had a number of first-rate stars in it, was the most popular institution at St. Petersburg. When the prima donna Bosio fell ill, thousands of people, chiefly of the youth, stood till late at night at the door of her hotel to get news of her. She was not beautiful, but seemed so much so when she sang that young men madly in love with her could be counted by the hundred; and when she died, she had a burial such as no one had ever had at St. Petersburg before. All St. Petersburg was then divided into two camps: the admirers of the Italian opera, and those of the French stage, which even then was showing in germ the putrid Offenbachian current that a few years later infected all Europe. Our form was also divided, half and half, between these two camps, and I belonged to the former. We were not permitted to go to the pit or to the balcony, while all the boxes in the Italian opera were always taken months in advance, by subscription, and even transmitted in certain families as an hereditary possession. But we gained admission, on Saturday nights, to the passages in the uppermost gallery, and had to stand there in a Turkish bath atmosphere, while to conceal our showy uniforms we used to wear our black overcoats, lined with wadding and with a fur collar, tightly buttoned in spite of the heat. It is a wonder that none of us got pneumonia in this way, especially as we came out overheated with the ovations which we used to make to our favorite singers, and stood afterwards at the stage door to catch one more glimpse of our favorites, and to cheer them. The Italian opera, in those years, was in some strange way intimately connected with the radical movement, and the revolutionary recitatives in " Wilhelm Tell " and " The Puritans " were always met with stormy applause and vociferations which went straight to the heart of Alexander II.; while in the sixth-story galleries, and in the smoking-room of the opera, and at the stage door the best part of the St. Petersburg youth came together in a common idealist worship of a noble art. All this may seem childish; but many higher ideas and pure inspirations were kindled in us by this worship of our favorite artists.

VII

EVERY summer we went out camping at Peterhof, with
the other military schools of the St. Petersburg district.
On the whole, our life there was very pleasant, and certainly it was excellent for our health : we slept in spacious
tents, bathed in the sea, and spent a great deal of time
during the six weeks in open-air exercise.

In military schools the main purpose of camp life was
evidently military drill, which we all disliked very much,
but the dullness of which was occasionally relieved by making us take part in manœuvres. One night, as we were
going to bed, Alexander II. aroused the whole camp by
having the alert sounded. In a few minutes all the camp
was alive, — several thousand boys gathering round their
colors, and the guns of the artillery school booming in the
stillness of the night. All military Peterhof came gallop-
ing to the camp, but owing to some misunderstanding the
Emperor remained on foot. Orderlies hurried in all directions to get a horse for him, but there was none, and not
being a good rider, he would not ride any horse but one
of his own. He was very angry, and freely gave vent to
his anger. " Imbecile (durák), have I only one horse ? "
I heard him shout to an orderly who reported that his
horse was in another camp.

With the coming darkness, the booming of the guns, and
the rattling of the cavalry, we boys grew very much excited, and when Alexander ordered a charge, our column
charged straight upon him. Tightly packed in the ranks,
with lowered bayonets, we must have had a menacing aspect ; and I saw the Emperor, who was still on foot, clearing

the way for the column in three formidable jumps.   I
understood then the meaning of a column which marches
in serried ranks under the excitement of the music and the
march itself.   There stood before us the Emperor, our commander, whom we all venerated; but I felt that in this
moving mass not one page or cadet would have moved an
inch aside or stopped to make room for him.   We were
the marching column, he was but an obstacle, and the
column would have marched over him.   "Why should he
be in our way?" the pages said afterward.   Boys, rifle in
hand, are even more terrible in such cases than old soldiers.

Next year, when we took part in the great manœuvres
of the St. Petersburg garrison, I saw some of the sidelights
of warfare.   For two days in succession we did nothing
but march up and down in a space of about twenty miles,
without having the slightest idea of what was going on
round us, or for what purpose we were marched.   Cannon
boomed now in our neighborhood and now far away; sharp
musketry fire was heard somewhere in the hills and the
woods; orderlies galloped up and down, bringing an order
to advance and next an order to retreat; and we marched,
marched, and marched, seeing no sense in all these movements and counter movements.   Masses of cavalry had
passed along the same road, making it a deep bed of
movable sand, and we had to advance and retreat several
times over the same ground, till at last our column broke all
discipline and became an incoherent mass of pilgrims rather
than a military unit.   The color guard alone remained in
the road; the remainder slowly paced along the sides of the
road in the wood.   The orders and the supplications of the
officers were of no avail.

Suddenly a shout came from behind: "The Emperor is
coming!   The Emperor!"   The officers ran about, begging
us to form ranks: nobody listened to them.

The Emperor came, and ordered a retreat once more.

"About!" the word of command rang out. "The Emperor is behind us; please turn round," the officers whispered; but the battalion took hardly any notice of the command, and none whatever of the presence of the Emperor. Happily, Alexander II. was no fanatic of militarism, and after having said a few words to cheer us, with a promise of rest, he galloped off.

I understood then how much depends in warfare upon the state of mind of the troops, and how little can be done by mere discipline when more than an average effort is required from the soldiers. What can discipline do when tired troops have to make a supreme effort to reach the field of battle at a given hour! It is absolutely powerless; only enthusiasm and confidence can at such moments induce the soldiers to do "the impossible," and it is the impossible that continually must be accomplished to secure success. How often I recalled to memory that object lesson later on, in Siberia, when we also had to do "the impossible" during our scientific expeditions!

Comparatively little of our time, however, during our stay in the camp was given to military drill and manœuvres. A good deal of it was employed in practical work in surveying and fortification. After a few preliminary exercises we were given a reflecting compass and told, "Go and make a plan of, say, this lake, or those roads, or that park, measuring the angles with the compass and the distances by pacing." Early in the morning, after a hurriedly swallowed breakfast, a boy would fill his capacious military pockets with slices of rye bread, and would go out for four or five hours in the parks, miles away, mapping with his compass and paces the beautiful shady roads, the rivulets, and the lakes. His work was afterward compared with accurate maps, and prizes in optical and drawing instruments, at the boy's choice, were awarded. For me, these surveys were a deep source of enjoyment. The independent work, the isolation under the centuries-old trees, the life of the forest which I could enjoy undisturbed, while there was at the same time the interest in the work, — all these left deep traces on my mind; and when I became an explorer of Siberia, and several of my comrades became explorers of central Asia, these surveys were found to have been an excellent preparation.

Finally, in the last form, parties of four boys were taken every second day to some villages at a considerable distance from the camp, and there they had to make a detailed survey of several square miles, with the aid of the surveyor's table and a telescopic ruler. Officers of the general staff came from time to time to verify their work and to advise them. This life amid the peasants in the villages had the best effect upon the intellectual and moral development of the boys.

At the same time there were exercises in the construction of natural size cross-sections of fortifications. We were taken out by an officer into the open field, and there we had to make the profile of a bastion, or of a complicated bridge head, nailing battens and poles together in exactly the same way as railway engineers do in tracing a railway. When it came to embrasures and barbettes, we had to calculate a great deal in order to obtain the inclinations of the different planes, and after that geometry ceased to be difficult to understand.

We delighted in such work, and once, in town, finding in our garden a heap of clay and gravel, we began to build a real fortification on a reduced scale, with well calculated straight and oblique embrasures and barbettes. All was done very neatly, and our ambition now was to obtain some planks for making the platforms for the guns, and to place upon them the model guns which we had in our class-rooms. But, alas! our trousers wore an alarming aspect.

"What are you doing there?" our captain exclaimed. "Look at yourselves! You look like navvies" (that was exactly what we were proud of). "What if the grand duke comes and finds you in such a state!"

"We will show him our fortification and ask him to get us tools and boards for the platforms."

All protests were vain. A dozen workmen were sent next day to cart away our beautiful structure as if it were a mere heap of mud!

I mention this to show how children and youths long for the application of what they learn at school in the abstract, and how stupid are the educators who are unable to see what a powerful aid they could find in this direction for helping their pupils to grasp the real sense of the things they learn. In our school, all was directed towards training us for warfare; we should have worked with the same enthusiasm, however, at laying out a railway, at building a log house, or at cultivating a garden or a field. But all this longing of children and youths for *real* work is wasted simply because our idea of the school is still the mediæval scholasticism, the mediæval monastery!

VIII

THE years 1857–61 were years of rich growth in the intellectual forces of Russia. All that had been whispered for the last decade, in the secrecy of friendly meetings, by the generation represented in Russian literature by Turguéneff, Tolstóy, Hérzen, Bakúnin, Ogaryóff, Kavélin, Dostoévsky, Grigoróvich, Ostróvsky, and Nekrásoff, began now to leak out in the press. Censorship was still very rigorous; but what could not be said openly in political articles was smuggled in under the form of novels, humorous sketches, or veiled comments on west European events, and every one read between the lines and understood.

Having no acquaintances at St. Petersburg apart from the school and a narrow circle of relatives, I stood outside the radical movement of those years, — miles, in fact, away from it. And yet, this was, perhaps, the main feature of the movement, — that it had the power to penetrate into so "well meaning" a school as our corps was, and to find an echo in such a circle as that of my Moscow relatives.

I used at that time to spend my Sundays and holidays at the house of my aunt, mentioned in a previous chapter under the name of Princess Mírski. Prince Mírski thought only of extraordinary lunches and dinners, while his wife and their young daughter led a very gay life. My cousin was a beautiful girl of nineteen, of a most amiable disposition, and nearly all her male cousins were madly in love with her. She, in turn, fell in love with one of them, and wanted to marry him. But to marry a cousin is considered a great sin by the Russian Church, and the old princess tried in vain to obtain a special permission from

the high ecclesiastical dignitaries. Now she brought her
daughter to St. Petersburg, hoping that she might choose
among her many admirers a more suitable husband than her
own cousin. It was labor lost, I must add; but their fashionable apartment was full of brilliant young men from the
Guards and from the diplomatic service.

Such a house would be the last to be thought of in connection with revolutionary ideas; and yet it was in that
house that I made my first acquaintance with the revolutionary literature of the times. The great refugee, Hérzen, had
just begun to issue at London his review, "The Polar Star,"
which made a commotion in Russia, even in the palace
circles, and was widely circulated secretly at St. Petersburg.
My cousin got it in some way, and we used to read it
together. Her heart revolted against the obstacles which
were put in the way of her happiness, and her mind was
the more open to the powerful criticisms which the great
writer launched against the Russian autocracy and all the
rotten system of misgovernment. With a feeling near to
worship I used to look on the medallion which was printed
on the paper cover of "The Polar Star," and which represented the noble heads of the five "Decembrists" whom
Nicholas I. had hanged after the rebellion of December 14,
1825, — Bestúzheff, Kahóvskiy, Péstel, Ryléeff, and Mu-
raviów-Apóstol.

The beauty of the style of Hérzen, — of whom Turguéneff has truly said that he wrote in tears and blood, and
that no other Russian had ever so written, — the breadth of
his ideas, and his deep love of Russia took possession of
me, and I used to read and re-read those pages, even more
full of heart than of brain.

In 1859, or early in 1860, I began to edit my first revolutionary paper. At that age, what could I be but a constitutionalist? — and my paper advocated the necessity
of a constitution for Russia. I wrote about the foolish

expenses of the court, the sums of money which were spent at Nice to keep quite a squadron of the navy in attendance on the Dowager-Empress, who died in 1860 ; I mentioned the misdeeds of the functionaries which I continually heard spoken of, and I urged the necessity of constitutional rule. I wrote three copies of my paper, and slipped them into the desks of three comrades of the higher forms, who, I thought, might be interested in public affairs. I asked my readers to put their remarks behind the Scotch clock in our library.

With a throbbing heart, I went next day to see if there was something for me behind the clock. Two notes were there, indeed. Two comrades wrote that they fully sympathized with my paper, and only advised me not to risk too much. I wrote my second number, still more vigorously insisting upon the necessity of uniting all forces in the name of liberty. But this time there was no reply behind the clock. Instead the two comrades came to me.

" We are sure," they said, " that it is you who edit the paper, and we want to talk about it. We are quite agreed with you, and we are here to say, ' Let us be friends.' Your paper has done its work, — it has brought us together ; but there is no need to continue it. In all the school there are only two more who would take any interest in such matters, while if it becomes known that there is a paper of this kind, the consequences will be terrible for all of us. Let us constitute a circle and talk about everything ; perhaps we shall put something into the heads of a few others."

This was so sensible that I could only agree, and we sealed our union by a hearty shaking of hands. From that time we three became firm friends, and used to read a great deal together and discuss all sorts of things.

The abolition of serfdom was the question which then engrossed the attention of all thinking men.

The revolution of 1848 had had its distant echo in the hearts of the Russian peasant folk, and from the year 1850 the insurrections of revolted serfs began to take serious proportions. When the Crimean war broke out, and militia was levied all over Russia, these revolts spread with a violence never before heard of. Several serf-owners were killed by their serfs, and the peasant uprisings became so serious that whole regiments, with artillery, were sent to quell them, whereas in former times small detachments of soldiers would have been sufficient to terrorize the peasants into obedience.

These outbreaks on the one side, and the profound aversion to serfdom which had grown up in the generation which came to the front with the advent of Alexander II. to the throne, rendered the emancipation of the peasants more and more imperative. The Emperor, himself averse to serfdom, and supported, or rather influenced, in his own family by his wife, his brother Constantine, and the Grand Duchess Hélène Pávlovna, took the first steps in that direction. His intention was that the initiative of the reform should come from the nobility, the serf-owners themselves. But in no province of Russia could the nobility be induced to send a petition to the Tsar to that effect. In March, 1856, he himself addressed the Moscow nobility on the necessity of such a step; but a stubborn silence was all their reply to his speech, so that Alexander II., growing quite angry, concluded with those memorable words of Hérzen : "It is better, gentlemen, that it should come from above than to wait till it comes from beneath." Even these words had no effect, and it was to the provinces of Old Poland, — Gródno, Wílno, and Kóvno, — where Napoleon I. had abolished serfdom (on paper) in 1812, that recourse was had. The governor-general of those provinces, Nazímoff, managed to obtain the desired address from the Polish nobility. In November, 1857, the famous "rescript" to the governor-

general of the Lithuanian provinces, announcing the intention of the Emperor to abolish serfdom, was launched, and
we read, with tears in our eyes, the beautiful article of
Hérzen, "Thou hast conquered, Galilean," in which the
refugees at London declared that they would no more look
upon Alexander II. as an enemy, but would support him in
the great work of emancipation.

The attitude of the peasants was very remarkable. No
sooner had the news spread that the liberation long sighed
for was coming than the insurrections nearly stopped. The
peasants waited now, and during a journey which Alexander
made in Middle Russia they flocked around him as he
passed, beseeching him to grant them liberty, — a petition,
however, which Alexander received with great repugnance.
It is most remarkable — so strong is the force of tradition
— that the rumor went among the peasants that it was
Napoleon III. who had required of the Tsar, in the treaty
of peace, that the peasants should be freed. I frequently
heard this rumor; and on the very eve of the emancipation they seemed to doubt that it would be done without
pressure from abroad. "Nothing will be done unless Gari-
baldi comes," was the reply which a peasant made at St.
Petersburg to a comrade of mine who talked to him about
"freedom coming."

But after these moments of general rejoicing years of incertitude and disquiet followed. Specially appointed committees in the provinces and at St. Petersburg discussed
the proposed liberation of the serfs, but the intentions of
Alexander II. seemed unsettled. A check was continually
put upon the press, in order to prevent it from discussing
details. Sinister rumors circulated at St. Petersburg and
reached our corps.

There was no lack of young men amongst the nobility
who earnestly worked for a frank abolition of the old servitude; but the serfdom party drew closer and closer round

the Emperor, and got power over his mind. They whis
pered into his ears that the day serfdom was abolished the
peasants would begin to kill the landlords wholesale, and
Russia would witness a new Pugachóff uprising, far more
terrible than that of 1773. Alexander, who was a man of
weak character, only too readily lent his ear to such predic-
tions. But the huge machine for working out the emancipation law had been set to work. The committees had
their sittings; scores of schemes of emancipation, addressed
to the Emperor, circulated in manuscript or were printed at
London. Hérzen, seconded by Turguéneff, who kept him
well informed about all that was going on in government
circles, discussed in his "Bell" and his "Polar Star" the
details of the various schemes, and Chernyshévsky in the
"Contemporary" (*Sovreménnik*). The Slavophiles, especially Aksákoff and Bélyáeff, had taken advantage of the
first moments of relative freedom allowed the press to give
the matter a wide publicity in Russia, and to discuss the
features of the emancipation with a thorough understanding
of its technical aspects. All intellectual St. Petersburg
was with Hérzen, and particularly with Chernyshévsky, and
I remember how the officers of the Horse Guards, whom I
saw on Sundays, after the church parade, at the home of
my cousin (Dmítri Nikoláevich Kropótkin, who was aide-
de-camp of that regiment and aide-de-camp of the Emperor),
used to side with Chernyshévsky, the leader of the advanced
party in the emancipation struggle. The whole disposition
of St. Petersburg, in the drawing-rooms and in the street
was such that it was impossible to go back. The liberation
of the serfs had to be accomplished; and another important point was won, — the liberated serfs would receive,
besides their homesteads, the land that they had hitherto
cultivated for themselves.

However, the party of the old nobility were not discouraged. They centred their efforts on obtaining a postpone-

ment of the reform, on reducing the size of the allotments, and on imposing upon the emancipated serfs so high a redemption tax for the land that it would render their economical freedom illusory; and in this they fully succeeded. Alexander II. dismissed the real soul of the whole business, Nicholas Milútin (brother of the minister of war), saying to him, "I am so sorry to part with you, but I must: the nobility describe you as one of the Reds." The first committees, which had worked out the scheme of emancipation, were dismissed, too, and new committees revised the whole work in the interest of the serf-owners; the press was muzzled once more.

Things assumed a very gloomy aspect. The question whether the liberation would take place at all was now asked. I feverishly followed the struggle, and every Sunday, when my comrades returned from their homes, I asked them what their parents said. By the end of 1860 the news became worse and worse. "The Valúeff party has got the upper hand." "They intend to revise the whole work." "The relatives of the Princess X. [a friend of the Tsar] work hard upon him." "The liberation will be postponed: they fear a revolution."

In January, 1861, slightly better rumors began to circulate, and it was generally hoped that something would be heard of the emancipation on the day of the Emperor's accession to the throne, the 19th of February.

The 19th came, but it brought nothing with it. I was on that day at the palace. There was no grand levee, only a small one; and pages of the second form were sent to such levees in order to get accustomed to the palace ways. It was my turn that day; and as I was seeing off one of the grand duchesses who came to the palace to assist at the mass, her husband did not appear, and I went to fetch him. He was called out of the Emperor's study, and I told him, in a half jocose way, of the perplexity of his wife, without having the slightest suspicion of the important matters that may have been talked of in the study at that time. Apart from a few of the initiated, no one in the palace suspected that the manifesto had been signed on the 19th of February, and was kept back for a fortnight only because the next Sunday, the 26th, was the beginning of the carnival week, and it was feared that, owing to the drinking which goes on in the villages during the carnival, peasant insurrections might break out. Even the carnival fair, which used to be held at St. Petersburg on the square near the winter palace, was removed that year to another square, from fear of a popular insurrection in the capital. Most terrible instructions had been issued to the army as to the ways of repressing peasant uprisings.

A fortnight later, on the last Sunday of the carnival (March 5, or rather March 17, New Style), I was at the corps, having to take part in the military parade at the riding-school. I was still in bed, when my soldier servant, Ivánoff, dashed in with the tea tray, exclaiming, "Prince, freedom! The manifesto is posted on the Gostínoi Dvor" (the shops opposite the corps).

"Did you see it yourself?"

"Yes. People stand round; one reads, the others listen. It *is* freedom!"

In a couple of minutes I was dressed, and out. A comrade was coming in.

"Kropótkin, freedom!" he shouted. "Here is the manifesto. My uncle learned last night that it would be read at the early mass at the Isaac Cathedral; so we went. There were not many people there; peasants only. The manifesto was read and distributed after the mass. They well understood what it meant. When I came out of the church, two peasants, who stood in the gateway, said to me in such a droll way, 'Well, sir? now — all gone?'"

And he mimicked how they had shown him the way out. Years of expectation were in that gesture of sending away the master.

I read and re-read the manifesto. It was written in an elevated style by the old Metropolitan of Moscow, Philarète, but with a useless mixture of Russian and Old Slavonian which obscured the sense. It was liberty; but it was not liberty yet, the peasants having to remain serfs for two years more, till the 19th of February, 1863. Notwithstanding all this, one thing was evident : serfdom was abolished, and the liberated serfs would get the land and their homesteads. They would have to pay for it, but the old stain of slavery was removed. They would be slaves no more; the reaction had *not* got the upper hand.

We went to the parade ; and when all the military performances were over, Alexander II., remaining on horseback, loudly called out, "The officers to me!" They gathered round him, and he began, in a loud voice, a speech about the great event of the day.

"The officers . . . the representatives of the nobility in the army" — these scraps of sentences reached our ears — "an end has been put to centuries of injustice . . . I expect sacrifices from the nobility . . . the loyal nobility will gather round the throne" . . . and so on. Enthusiastic hurrahs resounded amongst the officers as he ended.

We ran rather than marched back on our way to the corps, — hurrying to be in time for the Italian opera, of which the last performance in the season was to be given that afternoon ; some manifestation was sure to take place then. Our military attire was flung off with great haste, and several of us dashed, lightfooted, to the sixth-story gallery. The house was crowded.

During the first entr'acte the smoking-room of the opera filled with excited young men, who all talked to one another, whether acquainted or not. We planned at once to return to the hall, and to sing, with the whole public in a mass choir, the hymn "God Save the Tsar."

However, sounds of music reached our ears, and we all hurried back to the hall. The band of the opera was already playing the hymn, which was drowned immediately in enthusiastic hurrahs coming from all parts of the hall. I saw Bavéri, the conductor of the band, waving his stick, but not a sound could be heard from the powerful band. Then Bavéri stopped, but the hurrahs continued. I saw the stick waved again in the air; I saw the fiddle-bows moving, and musicians blowing the brass instruments, but again the sound of voices overwhelmed the band. Bavéri began conducting the hymn once more, and it was only by the end of that third repetition that isolated sounds of the brass instruments pierced through the clamor of human voices.

The same enthusiasm was in the streets. Crowds of peasants and educated men stood in front of the palace, shouting hurrahs, and the Tsar could not appear without being followed by demonstrative crowds running after his carriage. Hérzen was right when, two years later, as Alexander was drowning the Polish insurrection in blood, and "Muravióff the Hanger" was strangling it on the scaffold, he wrote, "Alexander Nikoláevich, why did you not die on that day? Your name would have been transmitted in history as that of a hero."

Where were the uprisings which had been predicted by the champions of slavery? Conditions more indefinite than those which had been created by the Polozhénie (the emancipation law) could not have been invented. If anything could have provoked revolts, it was precisely the perplexing vagueness of the conditions created by the new law. And yet, except in two places where there were insurrections, and a very few other spots where small disturbances entirely due to misunderstandings and immediately appeased took place, Russia remained quiet, — more quiet than ever. With their usual good sense, the peasants had understood that serfdom was done away with, that "freedom had come," and they accepted the conditions imposed upon them, although these conditions were very heavy.

I was in Nikólskoye in August, 1861, and again in the summer of 1862, and I was struck with the quiet, intelligent way in which the peasants had accepted the new conditions. They knew perfectly well how difficult it would be to pay the redemption tax for the land, which was in reality an indemnity to the nobles in lieu of the obligations of serfdom. But they so much valued the abolition of their personal enslavement that they accepted the ruinous charges — not without murmuring, but as a hard necessity — the moment that personal freedom was obtained. For the first months they kept two holidays a week, saying that it was a sin to work on Friday ; but when the summer came they resumed work with even more energy than before.

When I saw our Nikólskoye peasants, fifteen months after the liberation, I could not but admire them. Their inborn good nature and softness remained with them, but all traces of servility had disappeared. They talked to their masters as equals talk to equals, as if they never had stood in different relations. Besides, such men came out from among them as could make a stand for their rights. The Polozhénie was a large and difficult book, which it took me a good deal of time to understand; but when Vasíli Ivánoff, the elder of Nikólskoye, came one day to ask me to explain to him some obscurity in it, I saw that he, who was not even a fluent reader, had admirably found his way amongst the intricacies of the chapters and paragraphs of the law.

The "household people " — that is, the servants — came

out the worst of all.   They got no land, and would hardly
have known what to do with it if they had.   They got
freedom, and nothing besides.   In our neighborhood nearly
all of them left their masters ; none, for example, remained
in the household of my father.   They went in search of
positions elsewhere, and a number of them found employment at once with the merchant class, who were proud of
having the coachman of Prince So and So, or the cook of
General So and So.   Those who knew a trade found work
in the towns : for instance, my father's band remained a
band, and made a good living at Kalúga, retaining amiable
relations with us.   But those who had no trade had hard
times before them ; and yet, the majority preferred to live
anyhow, rather than remain with their old masters.

As to the landlords, while the larger ones made all
possible efforts at St. Petersburg to reintroduce the old
conditions under one name or another (they succeeded in
doing so to some extent under Alexander III.), by far the
greater number submitted to the abolition of serfdom as to
a sort of necessary calamity.   The young generation gave
to Russia that remarkable staff of " peace mediators " and
justices of the peace who contributed so much to the peaceful issue of the emancipation.   As to the old generation,
most of them had already discounted the considerable sums
of money they were to receive from the peasants for the
land which was granted to the liberated serfs, and which
was valued much above its market price ; they schemed as
to how they would squander that money in the restaurants
of the capitals, or at the green tables in gambling.   And
they did squander it, almost all of them, as soon as they
got it.

For many landlords, the liberation of the serfs was an
excellent money transaction.   Thus, land which my father,
in anticipation of the emancipation, sold in parcels at the
rate of eleven rubles the Russian acre, was now estimated at

forty rubles in the peasants' allotments, — that is, three and a half times above its market value, — and this was the rule in all our neighborhood; while in my father's Tambóv estate, on the prairies, the *mir* — that is, the village community — rented all his land for twelve years, at a price which represented twice as much as he used to get from that land by cultivating it with servile labor.

Eleven years after that memorable time I went to the Tambóv estate, which I had inherited from my father. I stayed there for a few weeks, and on the evening of my departure our village priest — an intelligent man of independent opinions, such as one meets occasionally in our southern provinces — went out for a walk round the village. The sunset was glorious; a balmy air came from the prairies. He found a middle-aged peasant — Antón Savélieff — sitting on a small eminence outside the village and reading a book of psalms. The peasant hardly knew how to spell, in Old Slavonic, and often he would read a book from the last page, turning the pages backward; it was the process of reading which he liked most, and then a word would strike him, and its repetition pleased him. He was reading now a psalm of which each verse began with the word "rejoice."

"What are you reading?" he was asked.

"Well, father, I will tell you," was his reply. "Fourteen years ago the old prince came here. It was in the winter. I had just returned home, almost frozen. A snowstorm was raging. I had scarcely begun undressing, when we heard a knock at the window: it was the elder, who was shouting, 'Go to the prince! He wants you!' We all — my wife and our children — were thunderstruck. 'What can he want of you?' my wife cried, in alarm. I signed myself with the cross and went; the snowstorm almost blinded me as I crossed the bridge. Well, it ended all

right.   The old prince was taking his afternoon sleep, and
when he woke up he asked me if I knew plastering work,
and only told me, 'Come to-morrow to repair the plaster in
that room.'   So I went home quite happy, and when I came
to the bridge I found my wife standing there.   She had
stood there all the time in the snowstorm, with the baby in
her arms, waiting for me.   'What has happened, Savélich?'
she cried.   'Well,' I said, 'no harm; he only asked me
to make some repairs.'   That, father, was under the old
prince.   And now, the young prince came here the other
day.   I went to see him, and found him in the garden, at
the tea table, in the shadow of the house; you, father, sat
with him, and the elder of the canton, with his mayor's
chain upon his breast.   'Will you have tea, Savélich?' he
asks me.   'Take a chair.   Petr Grigórieff,' — he says that
to the old one, — 'give us one more chair.'   And Petr
Grigórieff — you know what a terror for us he was when he
was the manager of the old prince — brought the chair, and
we all sat round the tea table, talking, and he poured out
tea for all of us.   Well, now, father, the evening is so
beautiful, the balm comes from the prairies, and I sit and
read, 'Rejoice!   Rejoice!'"

This is what the abolition of serfdom meant for the
peasants.

IX

In June, 1861, I was nominated sergeant of the corps of pages. Some of our officers, I must say, did not like the idea of it, saying that there would be no "discipline" with me acting as a sergeant; but it could not be helped; it was usually the first pupil of the upper form who was nominated sergeant, and I had been at the top of our form for several years in succession. This appointment was considered very enviable, not only because the sergeant occupied a privileged position in the school and was treated like an officer, but especially because he was also the page de chambre of the Emperor for the time being; and to be personally known to the Emperor was of course considered as a stepping-stone to further distinctions. The most important point to me was, however, that it freed me from all the drudgery of the inner service of the school, which fell on the pages de chambre, and that I should have for my studies a separate room, where I could isolate myself from the bustle of the school. True, there was also an important drawback to it: I had always found it tedious to pace up and down, many times a day, the whole length of our rooms, and used therefore to run the distance full speed, which was severely prohibited; and now I should have to walk very solemnly, with the service-book under my arm, instead of running! A consultation was even held among a few friends of mine upon this serious matter, and it was decided that from time to time I could still find opportunities to take my favorite runs; as to my relations with all the others, it depended upon myself to put them on a new comrade-like footing, and this I did.

The pages de chambre had to be at the palace frequently, in attendance at the great and small levees, the balls, the receptions, the gala dinners, and so on. During Christmas, New Year, and Easter weeks we were summoned to the palace almost every day, and sometimes twice a day. Moreover, in my military capacity of sergeant I had to report to the Emperor every Sunday, at the parade in the riding-school, that "all was well at the company of the corps of pages," even when one third of the school was ill of some contagious disease. "Shall I not report to-day that all is not quite well?" I asked the colonel on this occasion. "God bless you," was his reply, "you ought only to say so if there were an insurrection!"

Court life has undoubtedly much that is picturesque about it. With its elegant refinement of manners, — superficial though it may be, — its strict etiquette, and its brilliant surroundings, it is certainly meant to be impressive. A great levee is a fine pageant, and even the simple reception of a few ladies by the Empress becomes quite different from a common call, when it takes place in a richly decorated drawing-room of the palace, — the guests ushered by chamberlains in gold-embroidered uniforms, the hostess followed by brilliantly dressed pages and a suite of ladies, and everything conducted with striking solemnity. To be an actor in the court ceremonies, in attendance upon the chief personages, offered something more than the mere interest of curiosity for a boy of my age. Besides, I then looked upon Alexander II. as a sort of hero; a man who attached no importance to the court ceremonies, but who, at this period of his reign, began his working day at six in the morning, and was engaged in a hard struggle with a powerful reactionary party in order to carry through a series of reforms, in which the abolition of serfdom was only the first step.

But gradually, as I saw more of the spectacular side of court life, and caught now and then a glimpse of what was

going on behind the scenes, I realized not only the futility
of these shows and the things they were intended to conceal,
but also that these small things so much absorbed the court
as to prevent consideration of matters of far greater importance. The realities were often lost in the acting. And
then from Alexander II. himself slowly faded the aureole
with which my imagination had surrounded him; so that
by the end of the year, even if at the outset I had cherished
some illusions as to useful activity in the spheres nearest to
the palace, I should have retained none.

On every important holiday, as also on the birthdays
and name days of the Emperor and Empress, on the coronation day, and on other similar occasions, a great levee
was held at the palace. Thousands of generals and officers
of all ranks, down to that of captain, as well as the high
functionaries of the civil service, were arranged in lines in
the immense halls of the palace, to bow at the passage of
the Emperor and his family, as they solemnly proceeded
to the church. All the members of the imperial family
came on those days to the palace, meeting together in a
drawing-room, and merrily chatting till the moment arrived
for putting on the mask of solemnity. Then the column
was formed. The Emperor, giving his hand to the Empress, opened the march. He was followed by his page
de chambre, and he in turn by the general aide-de-camp,
the aide-de-camp on duty that day, and the minister of the
imperial household; while the Empress, or rather the immense train of her dress, was attended by her two pages
de chambre, who had to support the train at the turnings
and to spread it out again in all its beauty. The heir
apparent, who was a young man of eighteen, and all the
other grand dukes and duchesses came next, in the order
of their right of succession to the throne, — each of the
grand duchesses followed by her page de chambre; then
there was a long procession of the ladies in attendance, old

and young, all wearing the so-called Russian costume, —
that is, an evening dress which was supposed to resemble
the costume worn by the women of Old Russia.

As the procession passed, I could see how each of the
eldest military and civil functionaries, before making his
bow, would try to catch the eye of the Emperor, and if he
had his bow acknowledged by a smiling look of the Tsar,
or by a hardly perceptible nod of the head, or perchance
by a word or two, he would look round upon his neighbors,
full of pride, in the expectation of their congratulations.

From the church the procession returned in the same
way, and then every one hurried back to his own affairs.
Apart from a few devotees and some young ladies, not one
in ten present at these levees regarded them otherwise than
as a tedious duty.

Twice or thrice during the winter great balls were given
at the palace, and thousands of people were invited to
them.   After the Emperor had opened the dances with a
polonaise, full liberty was left to every one to enjoy the
time as he liked.   There was plenty of room in the immense brightly illuminated halls, where young girls were
easily lost to the watchful eyes of their parents and aunts,
and many thoroughly enjoyed the dances and the supper,
during which the young people managed to be left to themselves.

My duties at these balls were rather difficult.   Alexander II. did not dance, nor did he sit down, but he moved
all the time amongst his guests, his page de chambre having to follow him at a distance, so as to be within easy
call, and yet not inconveniently near.   This combination of
presence with absence was not easy to attain, nor did the
Emperor require it: he would have preferred to be left
entirely to himself; but such was the tradition, and he had
to submit to it.   The worst was when he entered a dense
crowd of ladies who stood round the circle in which the

grand dukes danced, and slowly circulated among them. It was not at all easy to make a way through this living garden, which opened to give passage to the Emperor, but closed in immediately behind him. Instead of dancing themselves, hundreds of ladies and girls stood there, closely packed, each in the expectation that one of the grand dukes would perhaps notice her and invite her to dance a waltz or a polka. Such was the influence of the court upon St. Petersburg society that if one of the grand dukes cast his eye upon a girl, her parents would do all in their power to make their child fall madly in love with the great personage, even though they knew well that no marriage could result from it, — the Russian grand dukes not being allowed to marry " subjects " of the Tsar. The conversations which I once heard in a " respectable " family, connected with the court, after the heir apparent had danced twice or thrice with a girl of seventeen, and the hopes which were expressed by her parents surpassed all that I could possibly have imagined.

Every time that we were at the palace we had lunch or dinner there, and the footmen would whisper to us bits of news from the scandalous chronicle of the place, whether we cared for it or not. They knew everything that was going on in the different palaces, — that was their domain. For truth's sake, I must say that during the year which I speak of, that sort of chronicle was not as rich in events as it became in the seventies. The brothers of the Tsar were only recently married, and his sons were all very young. But the relations of the Emperor himself with the Princess X., whom Turguéneff has so admirably depicted in "Smoke" under the name of Irène, were even more freely spoken of by the servants than by St. Petersburg society. One day, however, when we entered the room where we used to dress, we were told, "The X. has to-day got her dismissal, — a complete one this time." Half an hour later, we saw the lady in question coming to assist at mass, with eyes swollen from weeping, and swallowing her tears during the mass, while the other ladies managed so to stand at a distance from her as to put her in evidence. The footmen were already informed about the incident, and commented upon it in their own way. There was something truly repulsive in the talk of these men, who the day before would have crouched down before the same lady.

The system of espionage which is exercised in the palace, especially around the Emperor himself, would seem almost incredible to the uninitiated. The following incident will give some idea of it. A few years later, one of the grand dukes received a severe lesson from a St. Petersburg gentleman. The latter had forbidden the grand duke his house, but, returning home unexpectedly, he found him in his drawing-room, and rushed upon him with his lifted stick. The young man dashed down the staircase, and was already jumping into his carriage, when the pursuer caught him, and dealt him a blow with his stick. The policeman who stood at the door saw the adventure and ran to report it to the chief of the police, General Trépoff, who, in his turn, jumped into his carriage and hastened to the Emperor, to be the first to report the "sad incident." Alexander II. summoned the grand duke and had a talk with him. A couple of days later, an old functionary who belonged to the Third Section of the Emperor's Chancery, — that is, to the state police, — and who was a friend at the house of one of my comrades, related the whole conversation. "The Emperor," he informed us, "was very angry, and said to the grand duke in conclusion, 'You should know better how to manage your little affairs.'" He was asked, of course, how he could know anything about a private conversation, but the reply was very characteristic: "The

words and the opinions of his Majesty must be known
to our department. How otherwise could such a delicate
institution as the state police be managed? Be sure that
the Emperor is the most closely watched person in all St.
Petersburg."

There was no boasting in these words. Every minister,
every governor-general, before entering the Emperor's study
with his reports, had a talk with the private valet of the
Emperor, to know what was the mood of the master that
day; and, according to that mood, he either laid before him
some knotty affair, or let it lie at the bottom of his portfolio
in hope of a more lucky day. The governor-general of East
Siberia, when he came to St. Petersburg, always sent his
private aide-de-camp with a handsome gift to the private
valet of the Emperor. "There are days," he used to say,
"when the Emperor would get into a rage, and order a
searching inquest upon every one and myself, if I should
lay before him on such a day certain reports; whereas there
are other days when all will go off quite smoothly. A
precious man that valet is." To know from day to day the
frame of mind of the Emperor was a substantial part of the
art of retaining a high position, — an art which later on
Count Shuváloff and General Trépoff understood to perfection; also Count Ignátieff, who, I suppose from what I saw
of him, possessed that art even without the help of the
valet.

At the beginning of my service I felt a great admiration
for Alexander II., the liberator of the serfs. Imagination
often carries a boy beyond the realities of the moment, and
my frame of mind at that time was such that if an attempt
had been made in my presence upon the Tsar, I should have
covered him with my body. One day, at the beginning of
January, 1862, I saw him leave the procession and rapidly
walk alone toward the halls where parts of all the regiments

of the St. Petersburg garrison were aligned for a parade. This parade usually took place outdoors, but this year, on account of the frost, it was held indoors, and Alexander II., who generally galloped at full speed in front of the troops at the reviews, had now to march in front of the regiments. I knew that my court duties ended as soon as the Emperor appeared in his capacity of military commander of the troops, and that I had to follow him to this spot, but no further. However, on looking round, I saw that he was quite alone. The two aides-de-camp had disappeared, and there was with him not a single man of his suite. "I will not leave him alone!" I said to myself, and followed him.

Whether Alexander II. was in a great hurry that day, or had other reasons to wish that the review should be over as soon as possible, I cannot say, but he dashed in front of the troops, and marched along their rows at such a speed, making such big and rapid steps, — he was very tall, — that I had the greatest difficulty in following him at my most rapid pace, and in places had almost to run in order to keep close behind him. He hurried as if running away from a danger. His excitement communicated itself to me, and every moment I was ready to jump in front of him, regretting only that I had on my ordnance sword and not my own sword, with a Toledo blade, which pierced copper and was a far better weapon. It was only after he had passed in front of the last battalion that he slackened his pace, and, on entering another hall, looked round, to meet my eyes glittering with the excitement of that mad march. The younger aide-de camp was running at full speed, two halls behind. I was prepared to get a severe scolding, instead of which Alexander II. said to me, perhaps betraying his own inner thoughts: "You here? Brave boy!" and as he slowly walked away, he turned into space that problematic, absent-minded gaze, which I had begun often to notice.

Such was then the frame of my mind. However, various

small incidents, as well as the reactionary character which the policy of Alexander II. was decidedly taking, instilled more and more doubts into my heart. Every year, on January 6, a half Christian and half pagan ceremony of sanctifying the waters is performed in Russia. It is also performed at the palace. A pavilion is built on the Nevá River, opposite the palace, and the imperial family, headed by the clergy, proceed from the palace, across the superb quay, to the pavilion, where a Te Deum is sung and the cross is plunged into the water of the river. Thousands of people stand on the quay and on the ice of the Nevá to witness the ceremony from a distance. All have to stand bareheaded during the service. This year, as the frost was rather sharp, an old general had put on a wig, and in the hurry of drawing on his cape, his wig had been dislodged and now lay across his head, without his noticing it. The Grand Duke Constantine, having caught sight of it, laughed the whole time the Te Deum was being sung, with the younger grand dukes, looking in the direction of the un-happy general, who smiled stupidly without knowing why he was the cause of so much hilarity. Constantine finally whispered to the Emperor, who also looked at the general and laughed.

A few minutes later, as the procession once more crossed the quay, on its way back to the palace, an old peasant, bareheaded too, pushed himself through the double hedge of soldiers who lined the path of the procession, and fell on his knees just at the feet of the Emperor, holding out a petition, and crying with tears in his eyes, " Father, defend us ! " Ages of oppression of the Russian peasantry was in this exclamation; but Alexander II., who a few minutes before laughed during the church-service at a wig lying the wrong way, now passed by the peasant without taking the slightest notice of him. I was close behind him, and only saw in him a shudder of fear at the sudden appearance of the peasant, after which he went on without deigning even to cast a glance on the human figure at his feet. I looked round. The aides-de-camp were not there; the Grand Duke Constantine, who followed, took no more notice of the peasant than his brother did; there was nobody even to take the petition, so that I took it, although I knew that I should get a scolding for doing so. It was not my business to receive petitions, but I remembered what it must have cost the peasant before he could make his way to the capital, and then through the lines of police and soldiers who surrounded the procession. Like all peasants who hand petitions to the Tsar, he was going to be put under arrest, for no one knows how long.

On the day of the emancipation of the serfs, Alexander II. was worshiped at St. Petersburg; but it is most remarkable that, apart from that moment of general enthusiasm, he had not the love of the city. His brother Nicholas — no one could say why — was at least very popular among the small tradespeople and the cabmen; but neither Alexander II., nor his brother Constantine, the leader of the reform party, nor his third brother, Mikhael, had won the hearts of any class of people in St. Petersburg. Alexander II. had retained too much of the despotic character of his father, which pierced now and then through his usually good-natured manners. He easily lost his temper, and often treated his courtiers in the most contemptuous way. He was not what one would describe as a truly reliable man, either in his policy or in his personal sympathies, and he was vindictive. I doubt whether he was sincerely attached to any one. Some of the men in his nearest surroundings were of the worst description, — Count Adlerberg, for instance, who made him pay over and over again his enormous debts, and others renowned for their colossal thefts. From the beginning of 1862 he commenced to

show himself capable of reviving the worst practices of his
father's reign.   It was known that he still wanted to carry
through a series of important reforms in the judicial organization and in the army; that the terrible corporal punishments were about to be abolished, and that a sort of local
self-government, and perhaps a constitution of some sort,
would be granted.   But the slightest disturbance was repressed under his orders with a stern severity : he took each
movement as a personal offense, so that at any moment
one might expect from him the most reactionary measures.
The disorders which broke out at the universities of St.
Petersburg, Moscow, and Kazán, in October, 1861, were
repressed with an ever increasing strictness.   The University of St. Petersburg was closed, and although free courses
were opened by most of the professors at the Town Hall, they
were also soon closed, and some of the best professors left
the university.   Immediately after the abolition of serfdom,
a great movement began for the opening of Sunday-schools;
they were opened everywhere by private persons and corporations, — all the teachers being volunteers, — and the
peasants and workers, old and young, flocked to these
schools.   Officers, students, even a few pages, became
teachers ; and such excellent methods were worked out that
(Russian having a phonetic spelling) we succeeded in teaching a peasant to read in nine or ten lessons.   But suddenly all
Sunday-schools, in which the mass of the peasantry would
have learned to read in a few years, without any expenditure
by the state, were closed.   In Poland, where a series of patriotic manifestations had begun, the Cossacks were sent out to
disperse the crowds with their whips, and to arrest hundreds
of people in the churches with their usual brutality.   Men
were shot in the streets of Warsaw by the end of 1861, and
for the suppression of the few peasant insurrections which
broke out, the horrible flogging through the double line of
soldiers — that favorite punishment of Nicholas I. — was

applied. The despot that Alexander II. became in the years 1870–81 was foreshadowed in 1862.

Of all the imperial family, undoubtedly the most sympathetic was the Empress Marie Alexándrovna. She was sincere, and when she said something pleasant, she meant it. The way in which she once thanked me for a little courtesy (it was after her reception of the ambassador of the United States, who had just come to St. Petersburg) deeply impressed me: it was not the way of a lady spoiled by courtesies, as an empress is supposed to be. She certainly was not happy in her home life; nor was she liked by the ladies of the court, who found her too severe, and could not understand why she should take so much to heart the *étourderies* of her husband. It is now known that she played a by no means unimportant part in bringing about the abolition of serfdom. But at that time her influence in this direction seems to have been little known, the Grand Duke Constantine and the Grand Duchess Hélène Pávlovna, who was the main support of Nicholas Milútin at the court, being considered the two leaders of the reform party in the palace spheres. The Empress was better known for the decisive part she had taken in the creation of girls' gymnasia (high schools), which received from the outset a high standard of organization and a truly democratic character. Her friendly relations with Ushínsky, a great pedagogist, saved him from sharing the fate of all men of mark of that time, — that is, exile.

Being very well educated herself, Marie Alexándrovna did her best to give a good education to her eldest son. The best men in all branches of knowledge were sought as teachers, and she even invited for that purpose Kavélin, although she knew well his friendly relations with Hérzen. When he mentioned to her that friendship, she replied that she had no grudge against Hérzen, except for his violent language about the Empress dowager.

The heir apparent was extremely handsome, — perhaps, even too femininely handsome. He was not proud in the least, and during the levees he used to chatter in the most comrade-like way with the pages de chambre. (I even remember, at the reception of the diplomatic corps on New Year's Day, trying to make him appreciate the simplicity of the uniform of the ambassador of the United States as compared with the parrot-colored uniforms of the other ambassadors.) However, those who knew him well described him as profoundly egoistic, a man absolutely incapable of contracting an attachment to any one. This feature was prominent in him, even more than it was in his father. As to his education, all the pains taken by his mother were of no avail. In August, 1861, his examinations, which were made in the presence of his father, proved to be a dead failure, and I remember Alexander II., at a parade of which the heir apparent was the commander, and during which he made some mistake, loudly shouting out, so that every one would hear it, " Even that you could not learn ! " He died, as is known, at the age of twenty-two, from some disease of the spinal cord.

His brother, Alexander, who became the heir apparent in 1865, and later on was Alexander III., was a decided contrast to Nicholas Alexándrovich. He reminded me so much of Paul I., by his face, his figure, and his contemplation of his own grandeur, that I used to say, " If he ever reigns, he will be another Paul I. in the Gátchina palace, and will have the same end as his great-grandfather had at the hands of his own courtiers." He obstinately refused to learn. It was rumored that Alexander II., having had so many difficulties with his brother Constantine, who was better educated than himself, adopted the policy of concentrating all his attention on the heir apparent, and neglecting the education of his other sons ; however, I doubt if such was the case : Alexander Alexándrovich must have been averse to any education from childhood; in fact, his spelling, which I saw in the telegrams he addressed to his bride at Copenhagen, was unimaginably bad. I cannot render here his Russian spelling, but in French he wrote, "*Ecri* à oncle à propos parade . . . les nouvelles sont *mauvaisent*," and so on.

He is said to have improved in his manners toward the end of his life, but in 1870, and also much later, he was a true descendant of Paul I. I knew at St. Petersburg an officer, of Swedish origin (from Finland), who had been sent to the United States to order rifles for the Russian army. On his return he had to report about his mission to Alexander Alexándrovich, who had been appointed to superintend the re-arming of the army. During this interview, the Tsarevich, giving full vent to his violent temper, began to scold the officer, who probably replied with dignity, whereupon the prince fell into a real fit of rage, insulting the officer in bad language. The officer, who belonged to that type of self-respecting but very loyal men who are frequently met with amongst the Swedish nobility in Russia, left at once, and wrote a letter in which he asked the heir apparent to apologize within twenty-four hours, adding that if the apology did not come, he would shoot himself. It was a sort of Japanese duel. Alexander Alexándrovich sent no excuses, and the officer kept his word. I saw him at the house of a warm friend of mine, his intimate friend, when he was expecting every minute to receive the apology. Next morning he was dead. The Tsar was very angry with his son, and ordered him to follow the hearse of the officer to the grave. But even this terrible lesson did not cure the young man of his Románoff haughtiness and impetuosity.

PART THIRD

SIBERIA

I

In the middle of May, 1862, a few weeks before our promotion, I was told one day by the captain to make up the final list of the regiments which each of us intended to join. We had the choice of all the regiments of the Guard, which we could enter with the first officer's grade, and of the Army with the third grade of lieutenant. I took a list of our form and went the rounds of my comrades. Every one knew well the regiment he was going to join, most of them already wearing in the garden the officer's cap of that regiment.

"Her Majesty's Cuirassiers," "The Body Guard Preobrazhénsky," "The Horse Guards," were the replies which I inscribed.

"But you, Kropótkin? The artillery? The Cossacks?" I was asked on all sides. I could not stand these questions, and at last, asking a comrade to complete the list, I went to my room to think once more over my final decision.

That I should not enter a regiment of the Guard, and give my life to parades and court balls, I had settled long ago. My dream was to enter the university, — to study, to live the student's life. That meant, of course, to break entirely with my father, whose ambitions were quite different, and to rely for my living upon what I might earn by means of lessons. Thousands of Russian students live in that way, and such a life did not frighten me in the least. But how should I get over the first steps in that life ? In a few weeks I should have to leave the school, to don my own clothes, to have my own lodging, and I saw no possibility of providing even the little money which would be required for the most modest start. Then, failing the university, I had been often thinking of late that I could enter the artillery academy. That would free me for two years from the drudgery of military service, and, besides the military sciences, I could study mathematics and physics. But the wind of reaction was blowing, and the officers in the academies had been treated during the previous winter as if they were schoolboys; in two academies they had revolted, and in one of them they had left in a body.

My thoughts turned more and more toward Siberia. The Amúr region had recently been annexed by Russia; I had read all about that Mississippi of the East, the mountains it pierces, the subtropical vegetation of its tributary, the Usurí, and my thoughts went further, — to the tropical regions which Humboldt had described, and to the great generalizations of Ritter, which I delighted to read. Besides, I reasoned, there is in Siberia an immense field for the application of the great reforms which have been made or are coming : the workers must be few there, and I shall find a field of action to my tastes. The worst was that I should have to separate from my brother Alexander; but he had been compelled to leave the University of Moscow after the last disorders, and in a year or two, I guessed (and guessed rightly), in one way or another we should be together. There remained only the choice of the regiment in the Amúr region. The Usurí attracted me most; but, alas! there was on the Usurí only one regiment of infantry Cossacks. A Cossack not on horseback, — that was too bad for the boy that I still was, and I settled upon "the mounted Cossacks of the Amúr."

This I wrote on the list, to the great consternation of all

my comrades. "It is so far," they said, while my friend Daúroff, seizing the Officers' Handbook, read out of it, to the horror of all present: "Uniform, black, with a plain red collar without braids; fur bonnet made of dog's fur or any other fur; trousers, gray."

"Only look at that uniform!" he exclaimed. "Bother the cap! — you can wear one of wolf or bear fur; but think only of the trousers! Gray, like a soldier of the Train!" The consternation reached its climax after that reading.

I joked as best I could, and took the list to the captain.

"Kropótkin must always have his joke!" he cried. "Did I not tell you that the list must be sent to the grand duke to-day?"

Astonishment and pity were depicted on his face when I told him that the list really stated my intention.

However, next day, my resolution almost gave way when I saw how Klasóvsky took my decision. He had hoped to see me in the university, and had given me lessons in Latin and Greek for that purpose; and I did not dare to tell him what really prevented me from entering the university: I knew that if I told him the truth, he would offer to share with me the little that he had.

Then my father telegraphed to the director that he forbade my going to Siberia; and the matter was reported to the grand duke, who was the chief of the military schools. I was called before his assistant, and talked about the vegetation of the Amúr and like things, because I had strong reasons for believing that if I said I wanted to go to the university, and could not afford it, a bursary would be offered to me by some one of the imperial family, — an offer which by all means I wished to avoid.

It is impossible to say how all this would have ended, but an event of much importance — the great fire at St

Petersburg — brought about in an indirect way a solution of my difficulties.

On the Monday after Trinity — the day of the Holy Ghost, which was that year on May 26, Old Style — a terrible fire broke out in the so-called Apráxin Dvor. The Apráxin Dvor was an immense space, more than half a mile square, which was entirely covered with small shops, — mere shanties of wood, — where all sorts of second and third hand goods were sold. Old furniture and bedding, second-hand dresses and books, poured in from every quarter of the city, and were stored in the small shanties, in the passages between them, and even on their roofs. This accumulation of inflammable materials had at its back the Ministry of the Interior and its archives, where all the documents concerning the liberation of the serfs were kept; and in the front of it, which was lined by a row of shops built of stone, was the state Bank. A narrow lane, also bordered with stone shops, separated the Apráxin Dvor from a wing of the Corps of Pages, which was occupied by grocery and oil shops in its lower story, and had the apartments of the officers in its upper story. Almost opposite the Ministry of the Interior, on the other side of a canal, there were extensive timber yards. This labyrinth of small shanties and the timber yards opposite took fire almost at the same moment, at four o'clock in the afternoon.

If there had been wind on that day, half the city would have perished in the flames, including the Bank, several Ministries, the Gostínoi Dvor (another great block of shops on the Nevsky Prospekt), the Corps of Pages, and the National Library.

I was that afternoon at the Corps, dining at the house of one of our officers, and we dashed to the spot as soon as we saw from the windows the first clouds of smoke rising in our immediate neighborhood. The sight was terrific. Like an immense snake, rattling and whistling, the fire threw itself in all directions, right and left, enveloped the shanties, and suddenly rose in a huge column, darting out its whistling tongues to lick up more shanties with their contents. Whirlwinds of smoke and fire were formed; and when the whirls of burning feathers from the bedding shops began to sweep about the space, it became impossible to remain any longer inside the burning market. The whole had to be abandoned.

The authorities had entirely lost their heads. There was not, at that time, a single steam fire engine in St. Petersburg, and it was workmen who suggested bringing one from the iron works of Kólpino, situated twenty miles by rail from the capital. When the engine reached the railway station, it was the people who dragged it to the conflagration. Of its four lines of hose, one was damaged by an unknown hand, and the other three were directed upon the Ministry of the Interior.

The grand dukes came to the spot and went away again. Late in the evening, when the Bank was out of danger, the Emperor also made his appearance, and said, what every one knew already, that the Corps of Pages was now the key of the battle, and must be saved by all means. It was evident that if the Corps had taken fire, the National Library and half of the Nevsky Prospekt would have gone.

It was the crowd, the people, who did everything to prevent the fire from spreading further and further. There was a moment when the Bank was seriously menaced. The goods cleared from the shops opposite were thrown into the Sadóvaya street, and lay in great heaps upon the walls of the left wing of the Bank. The articles which covered the street itself continually took fire, but the people, roasting there in an almost unbearable heat, prevented the flames from being communicated to the piles of goods on the other side. They swore at all the authorities, seeing that there was not a pump on the spot. "What are they all doing at the Ministry of the Interior, when the Bank and the Foundlings' House are going to take fire? They have all lost their heads!" "Where is the chief of police that he cannot send a fire brigade to the Bank?" they said. I knew the chief, General Annenkoff, personally, as I had met him once or twice at our sub-inspector's house, where he came with his brother, the well-known literary critic, and I volunteered to find him. I found him, indeed, walking aimlessly in a street; and when I reported to him the state of affairs, incredible though it may seem, it was to me, a boy, that he gave the order to move one of the fire brigades from the Ministry to the Bank. I exclaimed, of course, that the men would never listen to me, and I asked for a written order; but General Annenkoff had not, or pretended not to have, a scrap of paper, so that I requested one of our officers, L. L. Gosse, to come with me to transmit the order. We at last prevailed upon the captain of one fire brigade — who swore at all the world and at his chiefs — to move his men to the Bank.

The Ministry itself was not on fire; it was the archives which were burning, and many boys, chiefly cadets and pages, together with a number of clerks, carried bundles of papers out of the burning building and loaded them into cabs. Often a bundle would fall out, and the wind, taking possession of its leaves, would strew them about the square. Through the smoke a sinister fire could be seen raging in the timber yards on the other side of the canal.

The narrow lane which separated the Corps of Pages from the Apráxin Dvor was in a deplorable state. The shops which lined it were full of brimstone, oil, turpentine, and the like, and immense tongues of fire of many hues, thrown out by explosions, licked the roofs of the wing of the Corps, which bordered the lane on its other side.   The windows and the pilasters under the roof began already to smoulder, while the pages and some cadets, after having cleared the lodgings, pumped water through a small fire engine, which received at long intervals scanty supplies from old-fashioned barrels which had to be filled with ladles.   A couple of firemen who stood on the hot roof continually shouted out, " Water ! Water !" in tones which were simply heart-rending.   I could not stand these cries, and I rushed into the Sadóvaya street, where by sheer force I compelled the driver of one of the barrels belonging to a police fire-brigade to enter our yard, and to supply our pump with water.   But when I attempted to do the same once more, I met with an absolute refusal from the driver. " I shall be court-martialed," he said, " if I obey you." On all sides my comrades urged me, " Go and find somebody, — the chief of the police, the grand duke, any one, — and tell them that without water we shall have to abandon the Corps to the fire."   " Ought we not to report to our director ? " somebody would remark.   " Bother the whole lot ! you won't find them with a lantern.   Go and do it yourself."

I went once more in search of General Annenkoff, and was at last told that he must be in the yard of the Bank. Several officers stood there around a general in whom I recognized the governor-general of St. Petersburg, Prince Suvóroff.   The gate, however, was locked, and a Bank official who stood at it refused to let me in.   I insisted, menaced, and finally was admitted.   Then I went straight to Prince Suvóroff, who was writing a note on the shoulder of his aide-de-camp.

When I reported to him the state of affairs, his first question was, " Who has sent you ? "   " Nobody — the comrades," was my reply.   " So you say the Corps will soon be on fire ? "   " Yes."   He started at once, and, seizing in the street an empty hatbox, covered his head with it, and ran full speed to the lane.   Empty barrels, straw, wooden boxes, and the like covered the lane, between the flames of the oil shops on the one side and the buildings of our Corps, of which the window frames and the pilasters were smouldering, on the other side.   Prince Suvóroff acted resolutely.   "There is a company of soldiers in your garden," he said to me : "take a detachment and clear that lane — at once.   A hose from the steam engine will be brought here immediately.   Keep it playing.   I trust it to you personally."

It was not easy to move the soldiers out of our garden. They had cleared the barrels and boxes of their contents, and with their pockets full of coffee, and with conical lumps of sugar concealed in their *képis*, they were enjoying the warm night under the trees, cracking nuts.   No one cared to move till an officer interfered.   The lane was cleared, and the pump kept going.   The comrades were delighted, and every twenty minutes we relieved the men who directed the jet of water, standing by their side in a terrible scorching heat.

About three or four in the morning it was evident that bounds had been put to the fire ; the danger of its spreading to the Corps was over, and after having quenched our thirst with half a dozen glasses of tea, in a small "white inn" which happened to be open, we fell, half dead from fatigue, on the first bed that we found unoccupied in the hospital of the Corps.

Next morning I woke up early and went to see the site of the conflagration.   On my return to the Corps I met the Grand Duke Mikhael, whom I accompanied, as was my duty, on his round.   The pages, with their faces quite black from the smoke, with swollen eyes and inflamed lids, some of them with their hair burned, raised their heads from the pillows.   It was hard to recognize them.   They were proud, though, of feeling that they had not been merely "white hands," and had worked as hard as any one else.

This visit of the grand duke settled my difficulties. He asked me why I conceived that fancy of going to the Amúr, — whether I had friends there, whether the governor-general knew me; and learning that I had no relatives in Siberia, and knew nobody there, he exclaimed, "But how are you going, then ? They may send you to a lonely Cossack village. What will you do there ? I had better write about you to the governor-general, to recommend you."

After such an offer I was sure that my father's objections would be removed, — and so it proved. I was free to go to Siberia.

This great conflagration became a turning-point not only in the policy of Alexander II., but also in the history of Russia for that part of the century. That it was not a mere accident was self-evident. Trinity and the day of the Holy Ghost are great holidays in Russia, and there was nobody inside the market except a few watchmen; besides, the Apráxin market and the timber yards took fire at the same time, and the conflagration at St. Petersburg was followed by similar disasters in several provincial towns. The fire was lit by somebody, but by whom ? This question remains unanswered to the present time.

Katkóff, the ex-Whig, who was inspired with personal hatred of Hérzen, and especially of Bakúnin, with whom he had once to fight a duel, on the very day after the fire accused the Poles and the Russian revolutionists of being the cause of it ; and that opinion prevailed at St. Petersburg and at Moscow.

Poland was preparing then for the revolution which broke out in the following January, and the secret revolutionary

government had concluded an alliance with the London
refugees; it had its men in the very heart of the St. Petersburg administration.   Only a short time after the conflagration occurred, the lord lieutenant of Poland, Count
Lüders, was shot at by a Russian officer; and when the
Grand Duke Constantine was nominated in his place (with
the intention, it was said, of making Poland a separate
kingdom for Constantine), he also was immediately shot at,
on June 26.   Similar attempts were made in August against
the Marquis Wielepólsky, the Polish leader of the pro-
Russian Union party.   Napoleon III. maintained among
the Poles the hope of an armed intervention in favor of
their independence.   In such conditions, judging from the
ordinary narrow military standpoint, to destroy the Bank of
Russia and several Ministries, and to spread a panic in the
capital, might have been considered a good plan of warfare;
but there never was the slightest scrap of evidence forthcoming to support this hypothesis.

On the other side, the advanced parties in Russia saw
that no hope could any longer be placed in Alexander's
reformatory initiative : he was clearly drifting into the reactionary camp.   To men of forethought it was evident that
the liberation of the serfs, under the conditions of redemption which were imposed upon them, meant their certain
ruin, and revolutionary proclamations were issued in May,
at St. Petersburg, calling the people and the army to a
general revolt, while the educated classes were asked to in
sist upon the necessity of a national convention.   Under
such circumstances, to disorganize the machine of the government might have entered into the plans of some revolutionists.

Finally, the indefinite character of the emancipation had
produced a great deal of fermentation among the peasants,
who constitute a considerable part of the population in all
Russian cities; and through all the history of Russia, every

time such a fermentation has begun, it has resulted in anonymous letters foretelling fires, and eventually in incendiarism.

It was possible that the idea of setting the Apráxin market on fire might occur to isolated men in the revolutionary camp, but neither the most searching inquiries nor the wholesale arrests which began all over Russia and Poland immediately after the fire revealed the slightest indication that such was really the case. If anything of the sort had been found, the reactionary party would have made capital out of it. Many reminiscences and volumes of correspondence from those times have since been published, but they contain no hint whatever in support of this suspicion.

On the contrary, when similar conflagrations broke out in several towns on the Vólga, and especially at Sarátoff, and when Zhdánoff, a member of the Senate, was sent by the Tsar to make a searching inquiry, he returned with the firm conviction that the conflagration at Sarátoff was the work of the reactionary party. There was among that party a general belief that it would be possible to induce Alexander II. to postpone the final abolition of serfdom, which was to take place on February 19, 1863. They knew the weakness of his character, and immediately after the great fire at St. Petersburg, they began a violent campaign for postponement, and for the revision of the emancipation law in its practical applications. It was rumored in well-informed legal circles that Senator Zhdánoff was in fact returning with positive proofs of the culpability of the reactionaries at Sarátoff; but he died on his way back, his portfolio disappeared, and it has never been found.

Be it as it may, the Apráxin fire had the most deplorable consequences. After it Alexander II. surrendered to the reactionaries, and — what was still worse — the public opinion of that part of society at St. Petersburg, and especially at Moscow, which carried most weight with the government suddenly threw off its liberal garb, and turned against not only the more advanced section of the reform party, but even against its moderate wing. A few days after the conflagration, I went on Sunday to see my cousin, the aide-de-camp of the Emperor, in whose apartment I had often seen the Horse Guard officers in sympathy with Chernyshévsky; my cousin himself had been up till then an assiduous reader of " The Contemporary " (the organ of the advanced reform party). Now he brought several numbers of "The Contemporary," and, putting them on the table I was sitting at, said to me, " Well, now, after *this* I will have no more of that incendiary stuff; enough of it," — and these words expressed the opinion of " all St. Petersburg." It became improper to talk of reforms. The whole atmosphere was laden with a reactionary spirit. " The Contemporary " and other similar reviews were suppressed; the Sunday-schools were prohibited under any form; wholesale arrests began. The capital was placed under a state of siege.

A fortnight later, on June 13 (25), the time which we pages and cadets had so long looked for came at last. The Emperor gave us a sort of military examination in all kinds of evolutions, — during which we commanded the companies, and I paraded on a horse before the battalion, — and we were promoted to be officers.

When the parade was over, Alexander II. loudly called out, "The promoted officers to me!" and we gathered round him. He remained on horseback.

Here I saw him in a quite new light. The man who the next year appeared in the rôle of a bloodthirsty and vindictive suppressor of the insurrection in Poland rose now, full size, before my eyes, in the speech he addressed to us.

He began in a quiet tone. " I congratulate you : you

are officers." He spoke about military duty and loyalty
as they are usually spoken of on such occasions. "But if
any one of you," he went on, distinctly shouting out every
word, his face suddenly contorted with anger,—"but if any
one of you — which God preserve you from — should under
any circumstances prove disloyal to the Tsar, the throne,
and the fatherland, take heed of what I say, — he will
be treated with all the se-ve-ri-ty of the laws, without the
slightest com-mi-se-ra-tion!"

His voice failed; his face was peevish, full of that expression of blind rage which I saw in my childhood on the faces
of landlords when they threatened their serfs "to skin them
under the rods." He violently spurred his horse, and rode
out of our circle. Next morning, the 14th of June, by
his orders, three officers were shot at Módlin in Poland, and
one soldier, Szur by name, was killed under the rods.

"Reaction, full speed backwards," I said to myself, as
we made our way back to the Corps.

I saw Alexander II. once more before leaving St. Petersburg. Some days after our promotion, all the newly appointed officers were at the palace, to be presented to him.
My more than modest uniform, with its prominent gray
trousers, attracted universal attention, and every moment I
had to satisfy the curiosity of officers of all ranks, who
came to ask me what was the uniform that I wore. The
Amúr Cossacks being then the youngest regiment of the
Russian army, I stood somewhere near the end of the hundreds of officers who were present. Alexander II. found
me, and asked, "So you go to Siberia? Did your father
consent to it, after all?" I answered in the affirmative.
"Are you not afraid to go so far?" I warmly replied,
"No, I want to work. There must be so much to do in
Siberia to apply the great reforms which are going to be
made." He looked straight at me; he became pensive; at

last he said, "Well, go; one can be useful everywhere;" and his face took on such an expression of fatigue, such a character of complete surrender, that I thought at once, "He is a used-up man; he is going to give it all up."

St. Petersburg had assumed a gloomy aspect. Soldiers marched in the streets, Cossack patrols rode round the palace, the fortress was filled with prisoners. Wherever I went I saw the same thing, — the triumph of the reaction. I left St. Petersburg without regret.

I went every day to the Cossack administration to ask them to make haste and deliver me my papers, and as soon as they were ready, I hurried to Moscow to join my brother Alexander.

II

THE five years that I spent in Siberia were for me a genuine education in life and human character. I was brought into contact with men of all descriptions: the best and the worst; those who stood at the top of society and those who vegetated at the very bottom, — the tramps and the so-called incorrigible criminals. I had ample opportunities to watch the ways and habits of the peasants in their daily life, and still more opportunities to appreciate how little the state administration could give to them, even if it was animated by the very best intentions. Finally, my extensive journeys, during which I traveled over fifty thousand miles in carts, on board steamers, in boats, but chiefly on horseback, had a wonderful effect in strengthening my health. They also taught me how little man really needs as soon as he comes out of the enchanted circle of conventional civilization. With a few pounds of bread and a few ounces of tea in a leather bag, a kettle and a hatchet hanging at the side of the saddle, and under the saddle a blanket, to be spread at the camp-fire upon a bed of freshly cut spruce twigs, a man feels wonderfully independent, even amidst unknown mountains thickly clothed with woods, or capped with snow. A book might be written about this part of my life, but I must rapidly glide over it here, there being so much more to say about the later periods.

Siberia is not the frozen land buried in snow and peopled with exiles only, that it is imagined to be, even by many Russians. In its southern parts it is as rich in natural productions as are the southern parts of Canada, which it resembles so much in its physical aspects; and beside half a million of natives, it has a population of more than four millions of Russians. The southern parts of West Siberia are as thoroughly Russian as the provinces to the north of Moscow. In 1862 the upper administration of Siberia was far more enlightened and far better all round than that of any province of Russia proper. For several years the post of governor-general of East Siberia had been occupied by a remarkable personage, Count N. N. Muravióff, who annexed the Amúr region to Russia. He was very intelligent, very active, extremely amiable, and desirous to work for the good of the country. Like all men of action of the governmental school, he was a despot at the bottom of his heart; but he held advanced opinions, and a democratic republic would not have quite satisfied him. He had succeeded to a great extent in getting rid of the old staff of civil service officials, who considered Siberia a camp to be plundered, and he had gathered around him a number of young officials, quite honest, and many of them animated by the same excellent intentions as himself. In his own study, the young officers, with the exile Bakúnin among them (he escaped from Siberia in the autumn of 1861), discussed the chances of creating the United States of Siberia, federated across the Pacific Ocean with the United States of America.

When I came to Irkútsk, the capital of East Siberia, the wave of reaction which I saw rising at St. Petersburg had not yet reached these distant dominions. I was very well received by the young governor-general, Korsákoff, who had just succeeded Muravióff, and he told me that he was delighted to have about him men of liberal opinions. As to the commander of the general staff, Kúkel, — a young general not yet thirty-five years old, whose personal aide-de-camp I became, — he at once took me to a room in his house, where I found, together with the best Russian reviews, complete collections of the London revolutionary editions of Hérzen. We were soon warm friends.

General Kúkel temporarily occupied at that time the post of governor of Transbaikália, and a few weeks later we crossed the beautiful Lake Baikál and went further east, to the little town of Chitá, the capital of the province. There I had to give myself, heart and soul, without loss of time, to the great reforms which were then under discussion. The St. Petersburg ministries had applied to the local authorities, asking them to work out schemes of complete reform in the administration of the provinces, the organiza- tion of the police, the tribunals, the prisons, the system of exile, the self-government of the townships, — all on broadly liberal bases laid down by the Emperor in his manifestoes.

Kúkel, supported by an intelligent and practical man, Colonel Pedashénko, and a couple of well-meaning civil service officials, worked all day long, and often a good deal of the night. I became the secretary of two committees, — for the reform of the prisons and the whole system of exile, and for preparing a scheme of municipal self-government, — and I set to work with all the enthusiasm of a youth of nineteen years. I read much about the historical devel- opment of these institutions in Russia and their present condition abroad, excellent works and papers dealing with these subjects having been published by the ministries of the interior and of justice; but what we did in Transbaiká- lia was by no means merely theoretical. I discussed first the general outlines, and subsequently every point of detail, with practical men, well acquainted with the real needs and the local possibilities; and for that purpose I met a considerable number of men both in town and in the pro- vince. Then the conclusions we arrived at were re-dis- cussed with Kúkel and Pedashénko; and when I had put the results into a preliminary shape, every point was again very thoroughly thrashed out in the committees. One of these committees, for preparing the municipal government scheme, was composed of citizens of Chitá, elected by all the population, as freely as they might have been elected in the United States. In short, our work was very serious; and even now, looking back at it through the perspective of so many years, I can say in full confidence that if municipal self-government had been granted then, in the modest shape which we gave to it, the towns of Siberia would be very different from what they are. But nothing came of it all, as will presently be seen.

There was no lack of other incidental occupations. Money had to be found for the support of charitable institutions; an economic description of the province had to be written in connection with a local agricultural exhibition; or some serious inquiry had to be made. "It is a great epoch we live in; work, my dear friend; remember that you are the secretary of all existing and future committees," Kúkel would sometimes say to me, — and I worked with doubled energy.

An example or two will show with what results. There was in our province a " district chief " — that is, a police officer invested with very wide and indeterminate rights — who was simply a disgrace. He robbed the peasants and flogged them right and left, — even women, which was against the law; and when a criminal affair fell into his hands, it might lie there for months, men being kept in the meantime in prison till they gave him a bribe. Kúkel would have dismissed this man long before, but the governor-general did not like the idea of it, because he had strong protectors at St. Petersburg. After much hesitation, it was decided at last that I should go to make an investigation on the spot, and collect evidence against the man. This was not by any means easy, because the peasants, terrorized by him, and well knowing an old Russian saying, " God is far away, while your chief is your next-door neighbor," did not

dare to testify. Even the woman he had flogged was afraid
at first to make a written statement. It was only after I
had stayed a fortnight with the peasants, and had won their
confidence, that the misdeeds of their chief could be brought
to light. I collected crushing evidence, and the district
chief was dismissed. We congratulated ourselves on having
got rid of such a pest. What was, however, our astonishment when, a few months later, we learned that this same
man had been nominated to a higher post in Kamchátka!
There he could plunder the natives free of any control, and
so he did. A few years later he returned to St. Petersburg
a rich man. The articles he occasionally contributes now
to the reactionary press are, as one might expect, full of high
" patriotic " spirit.

The wave of reaction, as I have already said, had not
then reached Siberia, and the political exiles continued to
be treated with all possible leniency, as in Muravióff's time.
When, in 1861, the poet Mikháiloff was condemned to hard
labor for a revolutionary proclamation which he had issued,
and was sent to Siberia, the governor of the first Siberian
town on his way, Tobólsk, gave a dinner in his honor, in
which all the officials took part. In Transbaikália he was
not kept at hard labor, but was allowed officially to stay in
the hospital prison of a small mining village. His health
being very poor, — he was dying from consumption, and did
actually die a few months later, — General Kúkel gave him
permission to stay in the house of his brother, a mining
engineer, who had rented a gold mine from the Crown on
his own account. Unofficially that was well known all over
Siberia. But one day we learned from Irkútsk that, in
consequence of a secret denunciation, the general of the
gendarmes (state police) was on his way to Chitá, to make
a strict inquiry into the affair. An aide-de-camp of the
governor-general brought us the news. I was dispatched in
great haste to warn Mikháiloff, and to tell him that he must

return at once to the hospital prison, while the general of the gendarmes was kept at Chitá. As that gentleman found himself every night the winner of considerable sums of money at the green table in Kúkel's house, he soon decided not to exchange this pleasant pastime for a long journey to the mines in a temperature which was then a dozen degrees below the freezing-point of mercury, and eventually went back to Irkútsk, quite satisfied with his lucrative mission.

The storm, however, was coming nearer and nearer, and it swept everything before it soon after the insurrection broke out in Poland.

III

In January, 1863, Poland rose against Russian rule. Insurrectionary bands were formed, and a war began which lasted for full eighteen months. The London refugees had implored the Polish revolutionary committees to postpone the movement. They foresaw that it would be crushed, and would put an end to the reform period in Russia. But it could not be helped. The repression of the nationalist manifestations which took place at Warsaw in 1861, and the cruel, quite unprovoked executions which followed, exasperated the Poles. The die was cast.

Never before had the Polish cause so many sympathizers in Russia as at that time. I do not speak of the revolutionists; but even among the more moderate elements of Russian society it was thought, and was openly said, that it would be a benefit for Russia to have in Poland a friendly neighbor instead of a hostile subject. Poland will never lose her national character, it is too strongly developed; she has, and will have, her own literature, her own art and industry. Russia can keep her in servitude only by means of sheer force and oppression, — a condition of things which has hitherto favored, and necessarily will favor, oppression in Russia herself. Even the peaceful Slavophiles were of that opinion; and while I was at school, St. Petersburg society greeted with full approval the "dream" which the Slavophile Iván Aksákoff had the courage to print in his paper, "The Day." His dream was that the Russian troops had evacuated Poland, and he discussed the excellent results which would follow.

When the revolution of 1863 broke out, several Russian

officers refused to march against the Poles, while others openly took their part, and died either on the scaffold or on the battlefield. Funds for the insurrection were collected all over Russia, — quite openly in Siberia, — and in the Russian universities the students equipped those of their comrades who were going to join the revolutionists.

Then, amidst this effervescence, the news spread over Russia that, during the night of January 10, bands of insurgents had fallen upon the soldiers who were cantoned in the villages, and had murdered them in their beds, although on the very eve of that day the relations of the troops with the Poles seemed to be quite friendly. There was some exaggeration in the report, but unfortunately there was also truth in it, and the impression it produced in Russia was most disastrous. The old antipathies between the two nations, so akin in their origins, but so different in their national characters, woke once more.

Gradually the bad feeling faded away to some extent. The gallant fight of the always brave sons of Poland, and the indomitable energy with which they resisted a formidable army, won sympathy for that heroic nation. But it became known that the Polish revolutionary committee, in its demand for the reëstablishment of Poland with its old frontiers, included the Little Russian or Ukraínian provinces, the Greek Orthodox population of which hated its Polish rulers, and more than once in the course of the last three centuries had slaughtered them wholesale. Moreover, Napoleon III. began to menace Russia with a new war, — a vain menace, which did more harm to the Poles than all other things put together. And finally, the radical elements of Russia saw with regret that now the purely nationalist elements of Poland had got the upper hand, the revolutionary government did not care in the least to grant the land to the serfs, — a blunder of which the Russian government did not fail to take advantage, in order to appear in the position of protector of the peasants against their Polish landlords.

When the revolution broke out in Poland, it was generally believed in Russia that it would take a democratic, republican turn ; and that the liberation of the serfs on a broad democratic basis would be the first thing which a revolutionary government, fighting for the independence of the country, would accomplish.

The emancipation law, as it had been enacted at St. Petersburg in 1861, provided ample opportunity for such a course of action. The personal obligations of the serfs to their owners came to an end only on the 19th of February, 1863. Then, a very slow process had to be gone through in order to obtain a sort of agreement between the landlords and the serfs as to the size and the location of the land allotments which were to be given to the liberated serfs. The yearly payments for these allotments (disproportionally high) were fixed by law at so much per acre; but the peasants had also to pay an additional sum for their homesteads, and of this sum the maximum only had been fixed by the statute, — it having been thought that the landlords might be induced to forego that additional payment, or to be satisfied with only a part of it. As to the so-called " redemption " of the land, — in which case the government undertook to pay the landlord its full value in state bonds, and the peasants, receiving the land, had to pay in return, for forty-nine years, six per cent. on that sum as interest and annuities, — not only were these payments extravagant and ruinous for the peasants, but no time was fixed for the redemption. It was left to the will of the landlord, and in an immense number of cases the redemption arrangements had not even been entered upon, twenty years after the emancipation.

Under such conditions a revolutionary government had

ample opportunity for immensely improving upon the Russian law. It was bound to accomplish an act of justice towards the serfs — whose condition in Poland was as bad as, and often worse than in Russia itself — by granting them better and more definite terms of emancipation. But nothing of the sort was done. The purely nationalist party and the aristocratic party having obtained the upper hand in the movement, this fundamentally important matter was left out of sight. This made it easy for the Russian government to win the peasants to its side.

Full advantage was taken of this mistake when Nicholas Milútin was sent to Poland by Alexander II. with the mission of liberating the peasants in the way he intended doing it in Russia, — whether the landlords were ruined in consequence or not. "Go to Poland; apply there your Red programme against the Polish landlords," said Alexander II. to him; and Milútin, together with Prince Cherkássky and many others, really did their best to take the land from the landlords and give good-sized allotments to the peasants.

I once met one of the Russian functionaries who went to Poland under Milútin and Prince Cherkássky. "We had full liberty," he said to me, "to turn over the land to the peasants. My usual plan was to go and to convoke the peasants' assembly. 'Tell me first,' I would say, 'what land do you hold at this moment?' They would point it out to me. 'Is this all the land you ever held?' I would then ask. 'Surely not,' they would reply with one voice. 'Years ago these meadows were ours; this wood was once in our possession; these fields, too,' they would say. I would let them go on talking all over and then would ask: 'Now, which of you can certify under oath that this land or that land has ever been held by you?' Of course there would be nobody forthcoming, — it was all too long ago. At last, some old man would be thrust out from the crowd, the rest saying: 'He knows all about it; he can

swear to it.'   The old man would begin a long story about
what he knew in his youth, or had heard from his father,
but I would cut the story short. . . . 'State on oath what
you know to have been held by the *gmína* (the village
community), and the land is yours.'   And as soon as he
took the oath — one could trust that oath implicitly — I
wrote out the papers and declared to the assembly : ' Now,
this land is yours.   You stand no longer under any obligations whatever to your late masters: you are simply their
neighbors; all you will have to do is to pay the redemption
tax, so much every year, to the government.   Your homesteads go with the land : you get them free.' "

One can imagine the effect which such a policy had upon
the peasants.   A cousin of mine, Petr Nikoláevich Kropótkin, a brother of the aide-de-camp whom I have mentioned, was in Poland or in Lithuania with his regiment of
uhlans of the guard.   The revolution was so serious that
even the regiments of the guard had been sent from St.
Petersburg against it, and it is now known that when
Mikhael Muravióff was sent to Lithuania and came to take
leave of the Empress Marie, she said to him : " Save at
least Lithuania for Russia ! "   Poland was regarded as lost.

" The armed bands of the revolutionists held the country," my cousin said to me, " and we were powerless to
defeat them, or even to find them.   Small bands over and
over again attacked our smaller detachments, and as they
fought admirably, and knew the country, and found support
in the population, they often had the best of the skirmishes.
We were thus compelled to march in large columns only.
We would cross a region, marching through the woods,
without finding any trace of the bands; but when we
marched back again, we learned that bands had reappeared
in our rear; that they had levied the patriotic tax in the
country ; and if some peasant had rendered himself useful
in any way to our troops, we found him hanged on a tree

by the revolutionary bands. So it went on for months, with no chance of improvement, until Milútin and Cherkássky came and freed the peasants, giving them the land. Then — all was over. The peasants sided with us; they helped us to capture the bands, and the insurrection came to an end."

I often spoke with the Polish exiles in Siberia upon this subject, and some of them understood the mistake that had been made. A revolution, from its very outset, must be an act of justice towards "the downtrodden and the oppressed," not a promise of such reparation later on; otherwise it is sure to fail. Unfortunately, it often happens that the leaders are so much absorbed with mere questions of military tactics that they forget the main thing. For revolutionists not to succeed in proving to the masses that a new era has really begun for them is to insure the certain failure of their cause.

The disastrous consequences for Poland of this revolution are known; they belong to the domain of history. How many thousand men perished in battle, how many hundreds were hanged, and how many scores of thousands were transported to various provinces of Russia and Siberia is not yet fully known. But even the official figures which were printed in Russia a few years ago show that in the Lithuanian provinces alone — not to speak of Poland proper — that terrible man, Mikhael Muravióff, to whom the Russian government has just erected a monument at Wílno, hanged by his own authority 128 Poles, and transported to Russia and Siberia 9423 men and women. Official lists, also published in Russia, give 18,672 men and women exiled to Siberia from Poland, of whom 10,407 were sent to East Siberia. I remember that the governor-general of East Siberia mentioned to me the same number, about 11,000 persons, sent to hard labor or exile in his

domains.   I saw them there, and witnessed their sufferings.
Altogether, something like 60,000 or 70,000 persons, if not
more, were torn out of Poland and transported to different
provinces of Russia, to the Urals, to Caucasus, and to
Siberia.

For Russia the consequences were equally disastrous.
The Polish insurrection was the definitive close of the reform period.   True, the law of provincial self-government
(*Zémstvos*) and the reform of the law courts were promul-
gated in 1864 and 1866; but both were ready in 1862, and,
moreover, at the last moment Alexander II. gave preference
to the scheme of self-government which had been prepared
by the reactionary party of Valúeff, as against the scheme
that had been prepared by Nicholas Milútin; and immediately after the promulgation of both reforms, their importance was reduced, and in some cases destroyed, by the
enactment of a number of by-laws.

Worst of all, public opinion itself took a further step
backward.   The hero of the hour was Katkóff, the leader
of the serfdom party, who appeared now as a Russian
" patriot," and carried with him most of the St. Petersburg
and Moscow society.   After that time, those who dared
to speak of reforms were at once classed by Katkóff as
" traitors to Russia."

The wave of reaction soon reached our remote province.
One day in March a paper was brought by a special messenger from Irkútsk.   It intimated to General Kúkel that he
was at once to leave the post of governor of Transbaikália
and go to Irkútsk, waiting there for further orders, and that
he was not to reassume the post of commander of the
general staff.

Why ? What did that mean ?   There was not a word of
explanation.   Even the governor-general, a personal friend
of Kúkel, had not run the risk of adding a single word to

the mysterious order. Did it mean that Kúkel was going to be taken between two gendarmes to St. Petersburg, and immured in that huge stone coffin, the fortress of St. Peter and St. Paul? All was possible. Later on we learned that such was indeed the intention; and so it would have been done but for the energetic intervention of Count Nicholas Muravióff, "the conqueror of the Amúr," who personally implored the Tsar that Kúkel should be spared that fate.

Our parting with Kúkel and his charming family was like a funeral. My heart was very heavy. I not only lost in him a dear personal friend, but I felt also that this parting was the burial of a whole epoch, full of long-cherished hopes, — "full of illusions," as it became the fashion to say.

So it was. A new governor came, — a good-natured, "leave-me-in-peace" man. With renewed energy, seeing that there was no time to lose, I completed our plans for the reform of the system of exile and municipal self-government. The governor made a few objections here and there for formality's sake, but finally signed the schemes, and they were sent to headquarters. But at St. Petersburg reforms were no longer wanted. There our projects lie buried still, with hundreds of similar ones from all parts of Russia. A few "improved" prisons, even more terrible than the old unimproved ones, have been built in the capitals, to be shown during prison congresses to distinguished foreigners; but the remainder, and the whole system of exile, were found by George Kennan in 1886 in exactly the same state in which I left them in 1862. Only now, after thirty-five years have passed away, the authorities are introducing the reformed tribunals and a parody of self-government in Siberia, and committees have been nominated again to inquire into the system of exile.

When Kennan came back to London from his journey to

Siberia, he managed, on the very next day after his arrival in London, to hunt up Stepniák, Tchaykóvsky, myself, and another Russian refugee. In the evening we all met at Kennan's room in a small hotel near Charing Cross. We saw him for the first time, and having no excess of confidence in enterprising Englishmen who had previously undertaken to learn all about the Siberian prisons without even learning a word of Russian, we began to cross-examine Kennan. To our astonishment, he not only spoke excellent Russian, but he knew everything worth knowing about Siberia. One or another of us had been acquainted with the greater proportion of all political exiles in Siberia, and we besieged Kennan with questions: "Where is So and So? Is he married? Is he happy in his marriage? Does he still keep fresh in spirit?" We were soon satisfied that Kennan knew all about every one of them.

When this questioning was over, and we were preparing to leave, I asked, "Do you know, Mr. Kennan, if they have built a watchtower for the fire brigade at Chitá?" Stepniák looked at me, as if to reproach me for abusing Kennan's goodwill. Kennan, however, began to laugh, and I soon joined him. And with much laughter we tossed each other questions and answers: "Why, do you know about that?" "And you too?" "Built?" "Yes, double estimates!" and so on, till at last Stepniák interfered, and in his most severely good-natured way objected: "Tell us at least what you are laughing about." Whereupon Kennan told the story of that watchtower which his readers must remember. In 1859 the Chitá people wanted to build a watchtower, and collected the money for it; but their estimates had to be sent to St. Petersburg. So they went to the ministry of the interior; but when they came back, two years later, duly approved, all the prices for timber and work had gone up in that rising young town. This was in 1862, while I was at Chitá. New estimates were made and sent to St.

Petersburg, and the story was repeated for full twenty-five years, till at last the Chitá people, losing patience, put in their estimates prices nearly double the real ones. These fantastic estimates were solemnly considered at St. Petersburg, and approved. This is how Chitá got its watchtower.

It has often been said that Alexander II. committed a great fault, and brought about his own ruin, by raising so many hopes which later on he did not satisfy. It is seen from what I have just said — and the story of little Chitá was the story of all Russia — that he did worse than that. It was not merely that he raised hopes. Yielding for a moment to the current of public opinion around him, he induced men all over Russia to set to work, to issue from the domain of mere hopes and dreams, and to touch with the finger the reforms that were required. He made them realize what could be done immediately, and how easy it was to do it; he induced them to sacrifice whatever of their ideals could not be immediately realized, and to demand only what was practically possible at the time. And when they had framed their ideas, and had shaped them into laws which merely required his signature to become realities, then he refused that signature. No reactionist could raise, or ever has raised, his voice to assert that what was left — the unreformed tribunals, the absence of municipal self-government, or the system of exile — was good and was worth maintaining: no one has dared to say that. And yet, owing to the fear of doing anything, all was left as it was; for thirty-five years those who ventured to mention the necessity of a change were treated as "suspects;" and institutions unanimously recognized as bad were permitted to continue in existence only that nothing more might be heard of that abhorred word "reform."

IV

Seeing that there was nothing more to be done at Chitá in the way of reforms, I gladly accepted the offer to visit the Amúr that same summer of 1863.

The immense domain on the left (northern) bank of the Amúr, and along the Pacific coast as far south as the bay of Peter the Great (Vladivostók), had been annexed to Russia by Count Muravióff, almost against the will of the St. Petersburg authorities and certainly without much help from them. When he conceived the bold plan of taking possession of the great river whose southern position and fertile lands had for the last two hundred years always attracted the Siberians; and when, on the eve of the opening of Japan to Europe, he decided to take for Russia a strong position on the Pacific coast, and to join hands with the United States, he had almost everybody against him at St. Petersburg: the ministry of war, which had no men to dispose of; the ministry of finance, which had no money for annexations; and especially the ministry of foreign affairs, always guided by its preoccupation of avoiding "diplomatic complications." Muravióff had thus to act on his own responsibility, and to rely upon the scanty means which thinly populated Eastern Siberia could afford for this grand enterprise. Moreover, everything had to be done in a hurry, in order to oppose the "accomplished fact" to the protests of the West European diplomatists, which would certainly be raised.

A nominal occupation would have been of no avail, and the idea was to have on the whole length of the great river and of its southern tributary, the Usurí, — full 2500

miles, — a chain of self-supporting settlements, and thus
to establish a regular communication between Siberia and
the Pacific coast.   Men were wanted for these settlements,
and as the scanty population of East Siberia could not
supply them, Muravióff was forced to unusual measures.
Released convicts who, after having served their time, had
become serfs to the imperial mines, were freed and organized as Transbaikálian Cossacks, part of whom were settled
along the Amúr and the Usurí, forming two new Cossack
communities.   Then Muravióff obtained the release of
a thousand hard-labor convicts (mostly robbers and mur-
derers), who were to be settled as free men on the lower
Amúr.   He came himself to see them off, and as they were
going to leave, addressed them on the beach: "Go, my
children, be free there, cultivate the land, make it Russian
soil, start a new life," and so on.   The Russian peasant
women nearly always, of their own free will, follow their
husbands, if the latter happen to be sent to hard labor in
Siberia, and many of the would-be colonists had thus their
families with them.   But those who had none ventured
to remark to Muravióff: "What is agriculture without a
wife!   We ought to be married."   Whereupon Muravióff
ordered the release of all the hard-labor convict women of the
place — about a hundred — and offered them their choice
of the men.   But there was little time to lose; the
high water in the river was rapidly going down, the rafts
had to start, and Muravióff, asking the people to stand in
pairs on the beach, blessed them, saying: "I marry you,
children.   Be kind to each other; you men, don't ill-treat
your wives, — and be happy."

I saw these settlers some six years after that scene.
Their villages were poor, the land they had been settled
on having had to be cleared from under virgin forests;
but, all things considered, their settlements were not a
failure; and the Muravióff marriages were not less happy

than marriages are on the average. That excellent, intelligent man, Innocentus, bishop of the Amúr, afterward recognized these marriages, as well as the children that were born, as quite legal, and had them inscribed on the church registers.

Muraviöff was less successful, however, with another batch of men that he added to the population of East Siberia. In his penury of men, he had accepted a couple of thousand soldiers from the punishment battalions. They were incorporated as "adopted sons" in the families of the Cossacks, or were settled in joint households in the villages of the Siberians. But ten or twenty years of barrack life under the horrid discipline of Nicholas I.'s time surely were not a preparation for an agricultural life. The "sons" deserted their adopted fathers, and constituted the floating population of the towns, living from hand to mouth on occasional jobs, spending chiefly in drink what they earned, and then waiting as care-free as birds for new jobs to turn up.

The motley crowd of Transbaikálian Cossacks, of ex-convicts, and "sons" — all settled in a hurry, and often in a haphazard way, along the banks of the Amúr — certainly did not attain prosperity, especially in the lower parts of the river and on the Usurí, where almost every square yard of land had to be won from a virgin sub-tropical forest, and where deluges of rain brought by the monsoons in July, inundations on a gigantic scale, millions of migrating birds, and the like, continually destroyed the crops, finally reducing whole populations to sheer despair and apathy.

Considerable supplies of salt, flour, cured meat, and so on had therefore to be shipped every year, to support both the regular troops and the settlements on the lower Amúr, and for that purpose some hundred and fifty barges were yearly built at Chitá and floated with the early spring high water down the Ingodá, the Shílka, and the Amúr.

The whole flotilla was divided into detachments of from twenty to thirty barges, which were placed under the orders of a number of Cossack and civil-service officers. Most of these did not know much about navigation, but they could be trusted, at least, not to steal the provisions and then report them as lost. I was nominated assistant to the chief of all that flotilla, — let me name him, — Major Maróvsky.

My first experiences in my new capacity of navigator were not entirely successful. It so happened that I had to proceed with a few barges as rapidly as possible to a certain point on the Amúr, and there to hand over my vessels. For that purpose I had to hire men from among those very "sons" whom I have already mentioned. None of them had ever had any experience in river navigation; nor had I. On the morning of our start my crew had to be collected from the public houses of the place, most of them being so drunk at that early hour that they had to be bathed in the river to bring them back to their senses. When we were afloat, I had to teach them everything that was to be done. Still, things went pretty well during the day; the barges, carried along by a swift current, floated down the river, and my crew, inexperienced though they were, had no interest in throwing their vessels upon the shore: that would have required special exertion. But when dusk came, and it was time to bring our huge, heavily laden barges to the shore and fasten them for the night, one of them, which was far ahead of the one that carried me, was stopped only when it was fast upon a rock, at the foot of a tremendously high, insurmountable cliff. There it stood immovable, while the level of the river, temporarily swollen by rains, was rapidly going down. My ten men evidently could not move it. I rowed down to the next village to ask assistance from the Cossacks, and at the same time dispatched a messenger to a friend, a Cossack officer who was staying some twenty miles away, and who had had experience in such things.

The morning came ; a hundred Cossacks — men and women — had come to my aid, but there was no means whatever of connecting the barge with the shore, in order to unload it, so deep was the water under the cliff. And, as soon as we attempted to push it off the rock, its bottom was broken in, and the water freely entered, sweeping away the flour and salt which formed the cargo. To my great horror I perceived numbers of small fish entering through the hole and swimming about in the barge, and I stood there helpless, without knowing what to do next.   There is a very simple and effective remedy for such emergencies.   A sack of flour is forced into the hole, to the shape of which it soon adapts itself, while the outer crust of paste which is formed in the sack prevents water from penetrating through the flour; but none of us knew this at the time.

Happily for me, a few minutes later a barge was sighted coming down the river towards us.   The appearance of the swan which carried Lohengrin was not greeted with more enthusiasm by the despairing Elsa than that clumsy vessel was greeted by me.   The haze which covered the beautiful Shílka at that early hour in the morning added even more to the poetry of the vision.   It was my friend, the Cossack officer, who had realized by my description that no human force could drag my barge off the rock, — that it was lost, — and was bringing an empty barge which by chance was at hand, to take away the cargo of my doomed craft.

Now the hole was stopped, the water was pumped out, the cargo was transferred to the new barge, and next morning I could continue my journey.   This little experience was of great profit to me, and I soon reached my destination on the Amúr without further adventures worth mentioning.   Every night we found some stretch of steep but relatively low shore where to stop with the barges, and our fires were soon lighted on the bank of the swift and clear river, amidst the most beautiful mountain scenery. In daytime, one could hardly imagine a more pleasant journey than on board a barge, which floats leisurely down, without any of the noise of the steamer; one or two strokes being occasionally given with its immense stern sweep to keep it in the main current. For the lover of nature, the lower part of the Shílka and the upper part of the Amúr, where one sees a most beautiful, wide, and swift river flowing amidst mountains rising in steep, wooded cliffs a couple of thousand feet above the water, offer some of the most delightful scenes in the world. But these same cliffs make communication along the shore on horseback, by way of a narrow trail, extremely difficult. I learned this that very autumn at my own expense. In East Siberia the seven last stations along the Shílka (about 120 miles) were known as the Seven Mortal Sins. This stretch of the Trans-Siberian railway — if it is ever built — will cost unimaginable sums of money; much more than the stretch of the Canadian Pacific line in the Rocky Mountains, in the cañon of the Fraser River, has cost.

After I had delivered my barges, I made about a thousand miles down the Amúr in one of the post boats which are used on the river. The stern of the boat was covered in, and in the bow was a box filled with earth upon which a fire was kept to cook the food. My crew consisted of three men. We had to make haste, and therefore used to row in turns all day long, while at night the boat was left to float with the current, and I kept the watch for three or four hours to maintain the boat in the middle of the river, and to prevent it from being drawn into some side channel. These watches — the full moon shining above and the dark hills reflected in the river — were beautiful beyond

description.   My rowers were taken from the aforemen-
tioned "sons;" they were three tramps, who had the reputation of being incorrigible thieves and robbers; — and I carried with me a heavy sack full of banknotes, silver, and
copper.   In Western Europe such a journey, on a lonely
river, would have been considered risky ; not so in East
Siberia.   I made it without even having so much as an old
pistol, and I found my three tramps excellent company.
Only, as we approached Blagovéschensk, they became restless.   " Khánshina " (the Chinese brandy) " is cheap there,"
they reasoned, with deep sighs.   " We are sure to get into
trouble !   It 's cheap, and it knocks you over in no time,
from want of being used to it ! "   I offered to leave the
money which was due to them with a friend who would
see them off with the first steamer.   " That would not
help us," they replied mournfully.   " Somebody will offer
a glass, — it 's cheap, — and a glass knocks you over ! "
they persisted in saying.   They were really perplexed, and
when, a few months later, I returned through the town,
I learned that one of "my sons," as people called them
in town, had really got into trouble.   When he had sold
the last pair of boots to get the poisonous drink, he had
committed some theft and had been locked up.   My friend
finally obtained his release and shipped him back.

Only those who have seen the Amúr, or know the Mississippi or the Yang-tze-kiang, can imagine what an immense
river the Amúr becomes after it has joined the Sungarí, and
can realize what tremendous waves roll over its bed if the
weather is stormy.   When the rainy season, due to the monsoons, comes in July, the Sungarí, the Usurí, and the Amúr
are swollen by unimaginable quantities of water ; thousands
of low islands usually covered with willow thickets are
inundated or washed away, and the width of the river at-
tains in places two, three, and even five miles ; water rushes

into the side channels and the lakes which spread in the
low lands along the main channel; and when a fresh
wind blows from an easterly quarter, against the current,
tremendous waves, even higher than those which one sees
in the estuary of the St. Lawrence, roll up both the main
river and the side channels. Still worse is it when a
typhoon blows from the Chinese Sea and spreads over the
Amúr region.

We experienced such a typhoon. I was then on board
a large decked boat, with Major Maróvsky, whom I joined
at Blagovéschensk. He had rigged his boat so that she
would sail close to the wind, and when the storm began we
managed to bring our boat to the sheltered side of the
river, and to find refuge in a small tributary. There we
stayed for two days, while the storm raged with such fury
that, when I ventured for a few hundred yards into the
surrounding forest, I had to retreat on account of the number of immense trees which the wind was blowing down
around me. We began to feel very uneasy for our barges.
It was evident that if they had been afloat that morning,
they never would have been able to reach the sheltered
side of the river, but must have been driven by the storm
to the bank exposed to the full rage of the wind, and there
destroyed. A disaster was almost certain.

We sailed out as soon as the fury of the storm had
abated. We knew that we ought soon to overtake two detachments of barges; but we sailed one day, two days, and
found no trace of them. My friend Maróvsky lost both
sleep and appetite, and looked as if he had just had a serious illness. He sat whole days on the deck, motionless,
murmuring: "All is lost, all is lost." The villages are
few and far between on this part of the Amúr, and nobody
could give us any information. A new storm came on, and
finally, reaching a village at daybreak, we learned that no
barges had passed, but that quantities of wreckage had been

seen floating down the river during the previous day. It
was evident that at least forty barges, which carried a cargo
of about two thousand tons, must have been lost. It meant
a certain famine next spring on the lower Amúr if no supplies were brought in time, for it was late in the season,
navigation would soon come to a close, and there was then
no telegraph along the river.

We held a council, and decided that Maróvsky should sail
as quickly as possible to the mouth of the Amúr. Some
purchases of grain might perhaps be made in Japan before
the close of navigation. Meanwhile I was to go with all
possible speed up the river, to determine the losses, and do
my best to cover the two thousand miles up the Amúr and
the Shílka, — in boats, on horseback, or on board steamer if
I met one. The sooner I could warn the Chitá authorities,
and dispatch any amount of provisions available, the better
it would be. Perhaps part of them would this same
autumn reach the upper Amúr, whence it would be easier
to ship them in the early spring to the low lands. If only
a few weeks or even days could be saved, it might make an
immense difference in case of a famine.

I began my two thousand miles' journey in a row-boat,
changing rowers at each village, every twenty miles or so.
It was very slow progress, but there might be no steamer
coming up the river for a fortnight, and in the meantime I
could reach the places where the barges were wrecked, and
see if any of the provisions had been saved. Then, at the
mouth of the Usurí (Khabaróvsk) I might secure a steamer.
The boats which I found at the villages were miserable, and
the weather was very stormy. We kept along the shore, of
course, but we had to cross some branches of the Amúr, of
considerable width, and the waves driven by the high wind
continually threatened to swamp our little craft. One day
we had to cross a branch of the river nearly half a mile
wide. Choppy waves rose like mountains as they rolled up

that branch. My rowers, two peasants, were seized with terror; their faces were white as paper; their blue lips trembled; they murmured prayers. But a boy of fifteen, who held the rudder, calmly kept a watchful eye upon the waves. He glided between them as they seemed to sink around us for a moment, but when he saw them rising to a menacing height in front of us, he gave a slight turn to the boat and steadied it across the waves. The boat shipped water from each wave, and I bailed it out with an old ladle, noting at times that it accumulated more rapidly than I could throw it out. There was a moment, when the boat shipped two such big waves, that at a sign from one of the trembling rowers I unfastened the heavy sack, full of copper and silver, that I carried across my shoulder. . . . For several days in succession we had such crossings. I never forced the men to cross, but they themselves, knowing why I had to hurry, would decide at a given moment that an attempt must be made. "There are not seven deaths in one's life, and one cannot be avoided," they would say, and, signing themselves with the cross, they would seize the oars and pull over.

I soon reached the place where the main destruction of our barges had taken place. Forty-four of them had been wrecked by the storm. Unloading had been impossible, and very little of the cargo had been saved. Two thousand tons of flour had been destroyed. With this news I continued my journey.

A few days later, a steamer slowly creeping up the river overtook me, and when I boarded her, the passengers told me that the captain had drunk himself into a delirium and jumped overboard. He was saved, however, and was now lying ill in his cabin. They asked me to take command of the steamer, and I had to consent; but soon I found to my great astonishment that everything went on by itself in such an excellent routine way that, though I paraded all day on the bridge, I had almost nothing to do. Apart from a few minutes of real responsibility, when the steamer had to be brought to the landing-places, where we took wood for fuel, and saying a word or two now and then to encourage the stokers to start as soon as the dawn permitted us faintly to distinguish the outlines of the shores, matters took care of themselves. A pilot who would have been able to interpret the map would have managed as well.

Traveling by steamer and a great deal on horseback, I reached at last Transbaikália. The idea of a famine that might break out next spring on the lower Amúr oppressed me all the time. I found that on the Shílka the small steamer did not progress up the swift river rapidly enough; so I abandoned it and rode with a Cossack a couple of hundred miles up the Argúñ, along one of the wildest mountain tracks in Siberia, never stopping to light our camp-fire until midnight had overtaken us in the woods. Even the ten or twenty hours that I might gain by this exertion were not to be despised, for every day brought nearer the close of navigation; ice was already forming on the river at night. At last I met the Governor of Transbaikália and my friend Colonel Pedashénko on the Shílka, at the convict settlement of Kará, and the latter took in hand the care of shipping immediately all available provisions. As for me, I left immediately to report all about the matter at Irkútsk.

People at Irkútsk wondered that I had managed to make this long journey so rapidly; but I was quite worn out. However, I recuperated by sleeping, for a week's time, such a number of hours every day that I should be ashamed to mention it now.

"Have you taken enough rest?" the governor-general asked me, a week or so after my arrival. "Could you start to-morrow for St. Petersburg, as a courier, to report there yourself upon the loss of the barges?"

It meant to cover in twenty days — not one day more —

another distance of 3200 miles between Irkútsk and Nízni Nóvgorod, where I could take the railway to St. Petersburg; to gallop day and night in post carts, which had to be changed at every station, because no carriage would stand such a journey full speed over the frozen roads.   But to see my brother Alexander was too great an attraction for me not to accept the offer, and I started the next night.   When I reached the low lands of West Siberia and the Urals, the journey really became a torture.   There were days when the wheels of the carts would be broken in the frozen ruts at every successive station.   The rivers were freezing, and I had to cross the Ob in a boat amidst floating ice, which threatened at every moment to crush our small craft.   When I reached the Tom River, on which the floating ice had just frozen together during the preceding night, the peasants refused for some time to take me over, asking me to give them " a receipt."

" What sort of receipt do you want ? "

" Well, you write on a paper : ' I, the undersigned, hereby testify that I was drowned by the will of God, and through no fault of the peasants,' and you give us that paper."

" With pleasure — on the other shore."

At last they took me over.   A boy — a brave, bright boy whom I had selected in the crowd — headed the procession, testing the strength of the ice with a pole; I followed him, carrying my dispatch box on my shoulders, and we two were attached to long lines, which five peasants held, following us at a distance, — one of them carrying a bundle of straw, to be thrown on the ice where it did not seem strong enough.

Finally I reached Moscow, where my brother met me at the station, and thence we proceeded at once to St. Petersburg.

Youth is a grand thing.   After such a journey, which

lasted twenty-four days and nights, arriving early in the
morning at St. Petersburg, I went the same day to deliver
my dispatches, and did not fail also to call upon an aunt,
or rather upon a cousin of mine. She was radiant. "We
have a dancing party to-night. Will you come?" she said.
Of course I would! And not only come, but dance until
an early hour of the morning.

When I reached St. Petersburg and saw the authorities,
I understood why I had been sent to make the report.
Nobody would believe the possibility of such a destruction
of the barges. "Have you been on the spot?" "Did you
see the destruction with your own eyes?" "Are you perfectly sure that 'they' have not simply stolen the provisions, and shown you the wreck of some barges?" Such
were the questions I had to answer.

The high functionaries who stood at the head of Siberian
affairs at St. Petersburg were simply charming in their
innocent ignorance of Siberia. "*Mais, mon cher,*" one of
them said to me, — he always spoke French, — "how *is* it
possible that forty barges should be destroyed on the Nevá
without any one rushing to save them?" "The Nevá!"
I exclaimed, "put three — four Nevás side by side and you
will have the lower Amúr!"

"Is it really as big as that?" And two minutes later
he was chatting, in excellent French, about all sorts of
things. "When did you last see Schwartz, the painter?
Is not his 'Ivan the Terrible' a wonderful picture? Do
you know why they were going to arrest Kúkel?" and he
told me all about a letter that had been addressed to him,
asking his support for the Polish insurrection. "Do you
know that Chernyshévsky has been arrested? He is now
in the fortress."

"What for? What has he done?" I asked.

"Nothing in particular, nothing! But, *mon cher*, you

know, — State considerations! . . . Such a clever man, awfully clever! And such an influence he has upon the youth. You understand that a government cannot tolerate that: that's impossible! *intolérable, mon cher, dans un Etat bien ordonné !* "

Count Ignátieff asked no such questions: he knew the Amúr very well, — and he knew St. Petersburg, too. Amidst all sorts of jokes and witty remarks about Siberia, which he made with an astounding vivacity, he said to me, "It is a very lucky thing that you were there on the spot and saw the wrecks. And 'they' were clever to send you with the report. Well done! At first nobody wanted to believe about the barges. 'Some new swindling,' it was thought. But now people say that you were well known as a page, and you have only been a few months in Siberia; so you would not shelter the people there, if it were swindling; they trust in you."

The Minister of War, Dmítri Milútin, was the only man high in the administration at St. Petersburg who took the matter seriously. He asked me many questions: all to the point. He mastered the subject at once, and all our conversation went on in short sentences, without hurry, but without any waste of words. "The coast settlements to be supplied from the sea, you mean? The remainder only from Chitá? Quite right. But if a storm happens next year, — will there be the same destruction once more?" "No, if there are two small tugs to convoy the barges." "Will it do?" "Yes; with one tug the loss would not have been half so heavy." "Very probably. Write to me, please; state all you have said; quite plainly — no formalities."

V

I DID not stay long at St. Petersburg, but returned to Irkútsk the same winter. My brother was going to join me there in a few months: he was accepted as an officer of the Irkútsk Cossacks.

Traveling across Siberia in the winter is supposed to be a terrible experience; but, all things considered, it is on the whole more comfortable than at any other season of the year. The snow-covered roads are excellent, and although the cold is intense, one can stand it well enough. Lying full length in the sledge, as every one does in Siberia, wrapped in fur blankets, fur inside and fur outside, one does not suffer much from the cold, even when the temperature is forty or sixty degrees below zero, Fahrenheit. Traveling in courier fashion, — that is, rapidly changing horses at each station and stopping only once a day for one hour to take a meal, — I reached Irkútsk nineteen days after leaving St. Petersburg. Two hundred miles a day is the normal speed in such cases, and I remember having covered the last 660 miles of my journey in seventy hours. The frost was not severe then, the roads were in an excellent condition, the drivers were kept in good spirits by a free allowance of silver coins, and the team of three small and light horses seemed to enjoy running swiftly over hill and vale, across rivers frozen as hard as steel, and through forests glistening in their silver attire under the rays of the sun.

I was now appointed attaché to the Governor-General of East Siberia for Cossack affairs, and had to reside at Irkútsk; but there was nothing in particular to do. To let everything go on according to the established routine, with no more reference to changes, — such was the watchword that came now from St. Petersburg. I therefore gladly accepted the proposal to undertake geographical exploration in Manchuria.

If one casts a glance on a map of Asia, one sees that the Russian frontier which runs in Siberia, broadly speaking, along the fiftieth degree of latitude, suddenly bends in Transbaikália to the north. It follows for three hundred miles the Argún River; then, on reaching the Amúr, it turns southeastward, the town of Blagovéschensk, which was the capital of the Amúr land, being situated again in about the same latitude of fifty degrees. Between the southeastern corner of Transbaikália (New Tsurukháitu) and Blagovéschensk on the Amúr, the distance west to east is only five hundred miles; but along the Argún and the Amúr it is over a thousand miles, and moreover communication along the Argún, which is not navigable, is extremely difficult. In its lower parts there is nothing but a mountain track of the wildest description.

Transbaikália is very rich in cattle, and the Cossacks who occupy its southeastern corner and are wealthy cattle-breeders wanted to establish a direct communication with the middle Amúr, which would be a good market for their cattle. They used to trade with the Mongols, and they had heard from them that it would not be difficult to reach the Amúr, traveling eastward across the Great Khingán. Going straight towards the east, they were told, one would fall in with an old Chinese route which crosses the Khingán and leads to the Manchurian town of Merghén (on the Nónni River, a tributary to the Sungarí), whence there is an excellent road to the middle Amúr.

I was offered the leadership of a trading caravan which the Cossacks intended to organize in order to find that route, and I accepted it with enthusiasm. No European had ever visited that region; and a Russian topographer who went that way a few years before was killed. Only two Jesuits, in the times of the Emperor Kan-si, had penetrated from the south as far as Merghén, and had determined its latitude. All the immense region to the north of it, five hundred miles wide, and seven hundred miles deep, was totally, absolutely unknown. I consulted all the available sources about this region. Nobody, not even the Chinese geographers, knew anything about it. Besides, the very fact of connecting the middle Amúr with Transbaikália had its importance, and Tsurukháitu is now going to be the head of the Trans-Manchuria Railway. We were thus the pioneers of that great enterprise.

There was, however, one difficulty. The treaty with China granted to the Russians free trade with the "Empire of China, and Mongolia." Manchuria was not mentioned in it, and could as well be excluded as included in the treaty. The Chinese frontier authorities interpreted it one way, and the Russians the other way. Moreover, only trade being mentioned, an officer would not be allowed to enter Manchuria. I had thus to go as a trader; so I bought at Irkútsk various goods and went disguised as a merchant. The governor-general delivered me a passport 'To the Irkútsk second guild merchant, Petr Alexéiev, and his companions;' and he warned me that if the Chinese authorities arrested me and took me to Pekin, and thence across the Góbi to the Russian frontier, — in a cage, on a camel's back, was their way of conveying prisoners across Mongolia, — I must not betray him by naming myself. I accepted, of course, all the conditions, the temptation to visit a country which no European had ever seen being too great for an explorer to resist.

It would not have been easy to conceal my identity while I was in Transbaikália. The Cossacks are an extremely inquisitive people, — real Mongols, — and as soon

as a stranger comes to their villages, while treating him
with the greatest hospitality, the master of the house where
he stays subjects him to a formal interrogatory.

"A tedious journey, I suppose," he begins; "a long
way from Chitá, is it not? And then, perhaps, longer
still for one who comes from some place beyond Chitá.
Maybe from Irkútsk? Trading there, I believe. Many
tradesmen come this way. You are going also to Ner-
chínsk, are you not? Yes, people are often married at
your age: and you, too, must have left a family, I suppose. Many children? Not all boys, I should say?"
And so on for quite half an hour.

The local commander of the Cossacks, Captain Buxhövden, knew his people, and consequently we had taken
our precautions. At Chitá and at Irkútsk we often had
had amateur theatricals, playing by preference dramas of
Ostróvsky, in which the scene of action is nearly always
amongst the merchant classes. I played several times in
such dramas, and found so great pleasure in acting that
I even wrote on one occasion to my brother an enthusiastic letter confessing to him my passionate desire to abandon my military career and to go on the stage. I played
mostly young merchants, and had acquired sufficiently well
their ways of talking and gesticulating and tea-drinking
from the saucer, — I learned those ways in my Nikólskoye
experiences, — and now I had a good opportunity to act it
all out in reality for useful purposes.

"Take your seat, Petr Alexéievich," Captain Buxhövden
would say to me when the boiling tea urn, throwing out
clouds of steam, was placed on the table.

"Thank you; we will stay here," I would reply, sitting
on the edge of a chair at a distance, and beginning to drink
my tea in true Moscow merchant fashion, Buxhövden
meanwhile nearly exploding with laughter, as I blew upon
my saucer with "staring eyes" and bit off in a special way

microscopic particles from a small lump of sugar which was to serve for half a dozen cups.

We knew that the Cossacks would soon make out the truth about me, but the important thing was to win a few days, and to cross the frontier while my identity was still undiscovered. I must have played my part pretty well, for the Cossacks treated me like a petty merchant. In one village an old woman beckoned to me as I passed, and asked, "Are there more people coming behind you on the road, my dear?"

"None, grandmother, that we heard of."

"They said a prince, Rapótsky, was going to come. Is he coming?"

"Oh, I see. You are right, grandmother. His highness intended to go, too, from Irkútsk. But how can 'they'? Such a journey! Not suitable for them. So they remained where they were."

"Of course, how can he!"

To be brief, we crossed the frontier unmolested. We were eleven Cossacks, one Tungus, and myself, all on horseback. We had with us about forty horses for sale and two carts, — one of which, two-wheeled, belonged to me, and contained the cloth, the velveteen, the gold braid, and so on, which I had taken in my capacity of merchant. I attended to my cart and my horses entirely myself, while we chose one of the Cossacks to be the "elder" of our caravan. He had to manage all the diplomatic talk with the Chinese authorities. All the Cossacks spoke Mongolian, and the Tungus understood Manchurian. The Cossacks of the caravan knew of course who I was, — one of them knew me at Irkútsk, — but they never betrayed that knowledge, understanding that the success of the expedition depended upon it. I wore a long blue cotton dress, like all the others, and the Chinese paid no attention to me, so that, unnoticed by them, I could make the compass survey of the route. On the first day, when all sorts of Chinese soldiers hung about us, in the hope of getting a glass of whiskey, I had often to cast only a furtive glance at my compass, and to jot down the bearings and the distances inside of my pocket, without taking my paper out. We had with us no arms whatever. Only our Tungus, who was going to be married, had taken his matchlock gun and used it to hunt fallow deer, bringing us meat for supper, and securing furs with which to pay for his future wife.

When there was no more whiskey to be obtained from us, the Chinese soldiers left us alone. So we went straight eastward, finding our way as best we could across hill and dale, and after a four or five days' march we actually fell in with the Chinese track which would take us across the Khingán to Merghén.

To our astonishment, we found that the crossing of the great ridge, which looked so black and terrible on the maps, was very easy. We overtook on the road an old Chinese functionary, miserably wretched, traveling in a two-wheeled cart. For the last two days the road was up-hill, and the country bore testimony to its high altitude. The ground became marshy, and the road muddy; the grass was very poor, and the trees grew thin, undeveloped, often crippled, and covered with lichens. Mountains bare of forests rose to right and left, and we were thinking already of the difficulties we should experience in crossing the ridge, when we saw the old Chinese functionary alighting from his cart before an *obó*, — that is, a heap of stones and branches of trees to which bundles of horsehair and small rags had been attached. He drew several hairs out of the mane of his horse, and attached them to the branches. "What is that?" we asked. "The obó; the waters before us flow now to the Amúr." "Is that all of the Khingán?" "It's all! No more mountains to cross until we reach the Amúr, only hills!"

Quite a commotion spread in our caravan. "The rivers flow to the Amúr, the Amúr!" shouted the Cossacks to one another. All their lives they had heard the old Cossacks talking about the great river where the vine grows wild, where the prairies extend for hundreds of miles and could give wealth to millions of men ; then, after the Amúr had been annexed to Russia, they heard of the long journey to it, the difficulties of the first settlers, and the prosperity of their relatives settled in the upper Amúr ; and now we had found the short way to them! We had before us a steep slope, the road leading downwards in zigzags to a small river which pierced its way through a choppy sea of mountains, and led to the Amúr. No more obstacles lay between us and the great river. A traveler will imagine my delight at this unexpected geographical discovery. As to the Cossacks, they hastened to dismount and to attach in their turn bundles of hair taken from their horses to the branches thrown on the obó. The Siberians in general have a sort of awe of the gods of the heathens. They do not think much of them, but these gods, they say, are wicked creatures, bent on mischief, and it is never good to be on bad terms with them. It is far better to bribe them with small tokens of respect.

"Look, here is a strange tree ; it must be an oak," they exclaimed, as we descended the steep slope. The oak´does not grow in Siberia at all, and is not found until the eastern slope of the high plateau has been reached. "Look, nut trees!" they exclaimed next. "And what tree is that ? " they said, seeing a lime-tree, or some other trees which do not grow in Russia, and which I knew as part of the Manchurian flora. The northerners, who for many years had dreamed of warmer lands, and now saw them, were delighted. Lying upon the ground covered with rich grass, they caressed it with their eyes, — they would have kissed it. Now they burned with the desire to reach the

Amúr as soon as possible. And when, a fortnight later, we stopped at our last camp-fire within twenty miles of the river, they grew impatient like children. They began to saddle their horses shortly after midnight, and made me start long before daybreak ; and when at last from an eminence we caught a sight of the mighty stream, the eyes of these unimpressionable Siberians, generally devoid of poetical feeling, gleamed with a poet's ardor as they looked upon the blue waters of the majestic Amúr. It was evident that, sooner or later, with or without the support, or even against the wish, of the Russian government, both banks of this river, a desert now but rich with possibilities, as well as the immense unpopulated stretches of North Manchuria, would be invaded by Russian settlers, just as the shores of the Mississippi were colonized by the Canadian *voyageurs.*

In the meantime, the old half-blind Chinese functionary with whom we had crossed the Khingán, having donned his blue coat and official hat with a glass button on its top, declared to us next morning that he would not let us go further. Our "elder" had received him and his clerk in our tent, and the old man, repeating what the clerk whispered to him, raised all sorts of objections to our further progress. He wanted us to camp on the spot while he should send our pass to Pekin to get orders, — which we absolutely refused to do. Then he sought to quarrel with our passport.

"What sort of a passport is that ? " he said, looking with disdain at our pass, which was written in a few lines on a plain sheet of foolscap paper, in Russian and Mongolian, and had a simple sealing-wax seal. " You may have written it yourselves and sealed it with a copper," he remarked. " Look at my pass : this is worth something ; " and he unrolled before us a sheet of paper, two feet long, covered with Chinese characters.

I sat quietly aside during this conference packing some-

thing in my box, when a sheet of the " Moscow Gazette "
fell under my hand. The "Gazette," being the property
of the Moscow University, had an eagle printed on its
title-heading. "Show him this," I said to our elder. He
unfolded the immense sheet and pointed out the eagle.
"That pass was to show to you," our elder said, "but this
is what we have for ourselves." "Why, is it all written
about you?" the old man asked, with terror. "All about
us," our elder replied, without even a twinkle in his eyes.

The old man — a true functionary — looked quite dum-
founded at seeing such a proficiency of writing. He examined every one of us, nodding with his head. But the
clerk was still whispering something to his chief, who
finally declared that he would not let us continue the
journey.

"Enough of talking," I said to the elder; "give the
order to saddle the horses." The Cossacks were of the
same opinion, and in no time our caravan started, bidding
good-by to the old functionary, and promising him to report
that short of resorting to violence— which he was not able
to do — he had done all in his power to prevent us from
entering Manchuria, and that it was our fault if we went
nevertheless.

A few days later we were at Merghén, where we traded a
little, and soon reached the Chinese town Aigún on the
right bank of the Amúr, and the Russian town of Blagovéschensk on the left bank. We had discovered the direct
route and many interesting things besides : the border-ridge
character of the Great Khingán, the ease with which it can
be crossed, the tertiary volcanoes of the Uyún Kholdontsí
region which had so long been a puzzle in geographical literature, and so on. I cannot say that I was a sharp tradesman, for at Merghén I persisted (in broken Chinese) in
asking thirty-five rubles for a watch, when the Chinese

buyer had already offered me forty-five; but the Cossacks traded all right.   They sold all their horses very well, and when my horses, my goods, and the like were sold by the Cossacks, it appeared that the expedition had cost the government the modest sum of twenty-two rubles,—eleven dollars.

VI

ALL this summer I traveled on the Amúr. I went as far as its mouth, or rather its estuary, — Nikoláevsk, — to join the governor-general, whom I accompanied in a steamer up the Usurí; and after that, in the autumn, I made a still more interesting journey up the Sungarí, to the very heart of Manchuria, as far as Ghirín (or Kirín, according to the southern pronunciation).

Many rivers in Asia are made by the junction of two equally important streams, so that it is difficult for the geographer to say which of the two is the main one, and which is a tributary. The Ingodá and the Onón join to make the Shílka; the Shílka and the Argúñ join to make the Amúr; and the Amúr joins the Sungarí to form that mighty stream which flows northeastward and enters the Pacific in the inhospitable latitudes of the Tartar strait.

Up to the year 1864, the great river of Manchuria remained very little known. All information about it dated from the times of the Jesuits, and that was scanty. Now that a revival in the exploration of Mongolia and Manchuria was going to take place, and the fear of China which had hitherto been entertained in Russia appeared to be exaggerated, all of us younger people pressed upon the governor-general the necessity of exploring the Sungarí. To have next door to the Amúr an immense region, almost as little known as an African desert, seemed to us provoking. Suddenly General Korsákoff decided to send a steamer up the Sungarí, under the pretext of carrying some message of friendship to the governor-general of the Ghirín province. A Russian consul from Urgá had to carry the message. A doctor, an astronomer, and myself, all under the command of a Colonel Chernyáeff, were sent upon the expedition in a tiny steamer, Usurí, which took in tow a barge with coal. Twenty-five soldiers, whose rifles were carefully concealed in the coal, went with us, on the barge.

All was organized very hurriedly, and there was no accommodation on the small steamer to receive such a numerous company; but we were all full of enthusiasm, and huddled as best we could in the tiny cabins. One of us had to sleep on a table, and when we started we found that there were not even knives and forks for all of us, — not to speak of other necessaries. One of us resorted to his penknife at dinner time, and my Chinese knife with two sticks, serving as a fork, was a welcome addition to our equipment.

It was not an easy task to go up the Sungarí. The great river in its lower parts, where it flows through the same low lands as the Amúr, is very shallow, and although our steamer drew only three feet, we often could not find a channel deep enough for us. There were days when we advanced but some forty miles, and scraped as many times the sandy bottom of the river with our keel; over and over again a rowboat was sent out to find the necessary depth. But our young captain had made up his mind that he would reach Ghirín that autumn, and we progressed every day. As we ascended higher and higher, we found the river more and more beautiful, and more and more easy of navigation; and when we had passed the sandy deserts at its junction with its sister river, the Nónni, progress became easy and pleasant. In a few weeks we thus reached the capital of that province of Manchuria. An excellent map of the river was made by the topographers. There was no time to spare, unfortunately, and so we very seldom landed in any village or town. The villages along the banks of the river are few and far between, and on its lower parts we found only low lands, which are inundated every year;

higher up we sailed for a hundred miles amidst sand dunes; and it was only when we reached the upper Sungarí and began to approach Ghirín, that we found a dense population.

If our aim had been to establish friendly relations with Manchuria, and not simply to learn what the Sungarí is, our expedition might well have been considered a dead failure. The Manchurian authorities had it fresh in their memories how, eight years before, the " visit " of Muravióff ended in the annexation of the Amúr and the Usurí, and they could not but look with suspicion on this new and uncalled-for visitation. The twenty-five rifles concealed in the coal, which had been duly reported to the Chinese authorities before we left, still more provoked their suspicions; and when our steamer cast her anchor in front of the populous city of Ghirín, we found all its merchants armed with rusty swords from some old arsenal. We were not prevented, however, from walking in the streets, but all shops were closed as soon as we landed, and the merchants were not allowed to sell anything. Some provisions were sent to us on board the steamer as a gift, but no money was taken in return.

The autumn was rapidly coming to its end, the frosts had begun already, and we had to hurry back, as we could not winter on the Sungarí. In short, we saw Ghirín, but spoke to no one but the two interpreters who came every morning on board our steamer. Our aim, however, was fulfilled: we had ascertained that the river is navigable, and an excellent map of it was made, from its mouth to Ghirín, with the aid of which we were able to steam on our return journey at full speed without any accident. At one time our steamer ran upon a sandbank. But the Ghirín officials, desirous above all things that we should not be compelled to winter on the river, sent two hundred Chinese, who aided us in getting off. When I jumped into the water, and, taking a stick, began to sing our river-song, "Dubí-

Aet. 22

P. Kropotkin

nushka," which helps all present to give a sudden push at the same moment, the Chinese enjoyed immensely the fun of it, and after several such pushes the steamer was soon afloat. The most cordial relations were established between ourselves and the Chinese by this little adventure. I mean, of course, the people, who seemed to dislike very much their arrogant Manchurian officials.

We called at several Chinese villages, peopled with exiles from the Celestial Empire, and were received in the most cordial way. One evening especially impressed itself on my memory. We came to a picturesque little village as night was already falling. Some of us landed, and I went alone through the village. A thick crowd of about a hundred Chinese soon surrounded me, and although I knew not a word of their tongue, and they knew as little of mine, we chatted in the most amicable way by mimicry, and we understood one another. To pat one on the shoulders in sign of friendship is decidedly international language. To offer one another tobacco and to be offered a light is again an international expression of friendship. One thing interested them, — why had I, though young, a beard? They wear none before they are sixty. And when I told them by signs that in case I should have nothing to eat I might eat it, the joke was transmitted from one to the other through the whole crowd. They roared with laughter, and began to pat me even more caressingly on the shoulders; they took me about, showing me their houses; every one offered me his pipe, and the whole crowd accompanied me as a friend to the steamer. I must say that there was not one single *boshkó* (policeman) in that village. In other villages our soldiers and myself always made friends with the Chinese, but as soon as a boshkó appeared, all was spoiled. In return, one should have seen what "faces" they used to make at the boshkó behind his back! They evidently hated this representative of authority.

This expedition has since been forgotten. The astronomer Th. Usóltzeff and I published reports about it in the
Memoirs of the Siberian Geographical Society; but a few
years later a terrible conflagration at Irkútsk destroyed all
the copies left of the Memoirs, as well as the original map
of the Sungarí; and it was only last year, when work upon
the Trans-Manchurian Railway was beginning, that Russian
geographers unearthed our reports, and found that the great
river had been explored five-and-thirty years ago by our
expedition.

VII

As there was nothing more to be done in the direction of reform, I tried to do what seemed to be possible under the existing circumstances, — only to become convinced of the absolute uselessness of such efforts. In my new capacity of attaché to the governor-general for Cossack affairs, I made, for instance, a most thorough investigation of the economical conditions of the Usurí Cossacks, whose crops used to be lost every year, so that the government had every winter to feed them in order to save them from famine. When I returned from the Usurí with my report, I received congratulations on all sides, I was promoted, I got special rewards. All the measures I recommended were accepted, and special grants of money were given for aiding the emigration of some and for supplying cattle to others, as I had suggested. But the practical realization of the measures went into the hands of some old drunkard, who would squander the money and pitilessly flog the unfortunate Cossacks for the purpose of converting them into good agriculturalists. And thus it went on in all directions, beginning with the Winter Palace at St. Petersburg, and ending with the Usurí and Kamchátka.

The higher administration of Siberia was influenced by excellent intentions, and I can only repeat that, everything considered, it was far better, far more enlightened, and far more interested in the welfare of the country than the administration of any other province of Russia. But it was an administration, — a branch of the tree which had its root at St. Petersburg, and that was quite sufficient to paralyze all its excellent intentions, and to make it interfere with all beginnings of local spontaneous life and progress. Whatever was started for the good of the country by local men was looked at with distrust, and was immediately paralyzed by hosts of difficulties which came, not so much from the bad intentions of men, — men, as a rule, are better than institutions, — but simply because they belonged to a pyramidal, centralized administration. The very fact of its being a government which had its source in a distant capital caused it to look upon everything from the point of view of a functionary of the government who thinks, first of all, about what his superiors will say, and how this or that will appear in the administrative machinery, and not of the interests of the country.

Gradually I turned my energy more and more toward scientific exploration. In 1865 I explored the western Sayáns, where I got a new glimpse into the structure of the Siberian highlands, and came upon another important volcanic region on the Chinese frontier; and finally, next year, I undertook a long journey to discover a direct communication between the gold mines of the Yakútsk province (on the Vitím and the Olókma) and Transbaikália. For several years (1860–64) the members of the Siberian expedition had tried to find such a passage, and had endeavored to cross the series of very wild stony parallel ridges which separate these mines from Transbaikália; but when they reached that region, coming from the south, and saw before them these dreary mountains spreading for hundreds of miles northward, all of them, save one who was killed by natives, returned southward. It was evident that, in order to be successful, the expedition must move from the north to the south, — from the dreary and unknown wilderness to the warmer and populated regions. It also happened that while I was preparing for the expedition, I was shown a map which a native had traced with his knife on a piece of bark. This little map — a splendid example, by the way,

of the usefulness of the geometrical sense in the lowest
stages of civilization, and one which would consequently
interest A. R. Wallace — so struck me by its seeming truth
to nature that I fully trusted to it, and began my journey,
following the indications of the map. In company with a
young and promising naturalist, Polakóff, and a topographer, I went first down the Léna to the northern gold
mines. There we equipped our expedition, taking provisions for three months, and started southward. An old
Yakút hunter, who twenty years before had once followed the
passage indicated on the Tungus map, undertook to act for us
as guide, and to cross the mountain region, — full 250 miles
wide, — following the river valleys and gorges indicated by
the knife of the Tungus on the birch-bark map. He really
accomplished this wonderful feat, although there was no
track of any sort to follow, and all the valleys that one sees
from the top of a mountain pass, all equally filled with
woods, seem, to the unpracticed eye, to be absolutely alike.

This time the passage was found. For three months
we wandered in the almost totally uninhabited mountain
deserts and over the marshy plateau, till at last we reached
our destination, Chitá. I am told that this passage is now
of value for bringing cattle from the south to the gold
mines; as for me, the journey helped me immensely afterward in finding the key to the structure of the mountains
and plateaus of Siberia, — but I am not writing a book of
travel, and must stop.

The years that I spent in Siberia taught me many lessons
which I could hardly have learned elsewhere. I soon
realized the absolute impossibility of doing anything really
useful for the mass of the people by means of the administrative machinery. With this illusion I parted forever.
Then I began to understand not only men and human
character, but also the inner springs of the life of human

society. The constructive work of the unknown masses, which so seldom finds any mention in books, and the importance of that constructive work in the growth of forms of society, fully appeared before my eyes. To witness, for instance, the ways in which the communities of Dukhobórtsy (brothers of those who are now going to settle in Canada, and who find such a hearty support in the United States) migrated to the Amúr region, to see the immense advantages which they got from their semi-communistic brotherly organization, and to realize what a wonderful success their colonization was, amidst all the failures of state colonization, was learning something which cannot be learned from books. Again, to live with natives, to see at work all the complex forms of social organization which they have elaborated far away from the influence of any civilization, was, as it were, to store up floods of light which illuminated my subsequent reading. The part which the unknown masses play in the accomplishment of all important historical events, and even in war, became evident to me from direct observation, and I came to hold ideas similar to those which Tolstoy expresses concerning the leaders and the masses in his monumental work, "War and Peace."

Having been brought up in a serf-owner's family, I entered active life, like all young men of my time, with a great deal of confidence in the necessity of commanding, ordering, scolding, punishing, and the like. But when, at an early stage, I had to manage serious enterprises and to deal with men, and when each mistake would lead at once to heavy consequences, I began to appreciate the difference between acting on the principle of command and discipline and acting on the principle of common understanding. The former works admirably in a military parade, but it is worth nothing where real life is concerned, and the aim can be achieved only through the severe effort of many converging wills. Although I did not then formulate my observations

in terms borrowed from party struggles, I may say now ...
I lost in Siberia whatever faith in state discipline I had
cherished before. I was prepared to become an anarchist.

From the age of nineteen to twenty-five I had to work out
important schemes of reform, to deal with hundreds of men
on the Amúr, to prepare and to make risky expeditions with
ridiculously small means, and so on; and if all these things
ended more or less successfully, I account for it only by the
fact that I soon understood that in serious work commanding and discipline are of little avail. Men of initiative are
required everywhere; but once the impulse has been given,
the enterprise must be conducted, especially in Russia, not
in military fashion, but in a sort of communal way, by
means of common understanding. I wish that all framers of
plans of state discipline could pass through the school of
real life before they begin to frame their state Utopias. We
should then hear far less than at present of schemes of
military and pyramidal organization of society.

With all that, life in Siberia became less and less attractive to me, although my brother Alexander had joined me
in 1864 at Irkútsk, where he commanded a squadron of
Cossacks. We were happy to be together; we read a great
deal, and discussed all the philosophical, scientific, and
sociological questions of the day; but we both longed after
intellectual life, and there was none in Siberia. The
occasional passage through Irkútsk of Raphael Pumpelly or
of Adolph Bastian — the only two men of science who
visited our capital during my stay there — was quite an
event for both of us. The scientific and especially the
political life of Western Europe, of which we heard through
the papers, attracted us, and the return to Russia was the
subject to which we continually came back in our conversations. Finally, the insurrection of the Polish exiles in
1866 opened our eyes to the false position we both occupied
as officers of the Russian army.

VIII

I WAS far away, in the Vitím mountains, when the Polish exiles, who were employed in excavating a new road in the cliffs round Lake Baikál, made a desperate attempt to break their chains, and to force their way to China across Mongolia. Troops were sent out against them, and a Russian officer — whom I will call Pótaloff — was killed by the insurgents. I heard of it on my return to Irkútsk, where some fifty Poles were to be tried by court-martial. The sittings of courts-martial being open in Russia, I followed this, taking detailed notes of the proceedings, which I sent to a St. Petersburg paper, and which were published in full, to the great dissatisfaction of the governor-general.

Eleven thousand Poles, men and women, had been transported to East Siberia alone, in consequence of the insurrection of 1863. They were chiefly students, artists, ex-officers, nobles, and especially skilled artisans from the intelligent and highly developed workers' population of Warsaw and other towns. A great number of them were kept at hard labor, while the remainder were settled all over the country, in villages where they could find no work whatever, and lived in a state of semi-starvation. Those who were at hard labor worked either at Chitá, building the barges for the Amúr, — these were the happiest, — or in iron works of the Crown, or in salt works. I saw some of the latter, on the Léna, standing half-naked in a shanty, around an immense cauldron filled with salt-brine, and mixing the thick, boiling brine with long shovels, in an infernal temperature, while the gates of the shanty were wide open, to make a strong current of glacial air. After two years of such work these martyrs were sure to die from consumption.

Afterward, a considerable number of Polish exiles were employed as navvies building a road along the southern coast of Lake Baikál. This narrow Alpine lake, four hundred miles long, surrounded by beautiful mountains rising three to five thousand feet above its level, cuts off Transbaikália and the Amúr from Irkútsk. In winter it may be crossed upon the ice, and in summer there are steamers; but for six weeks in the spring and another six weeks in the autumn the only way to reach Chitá and Kyákhta (for Pekin) from Irkútsk is to travel on horseback a long, circuitous route, across mountains 7000 to 8000 feet in altitude. I once traveled along this track, greatly enjoying the scenery of the mountains, which were snow-clad in May, but otherwise the journey was really awful. To climb eight miles only, to the top of the main pass, Khamár-dabán, it took me the whole day from three in the morning till eight at night. Our horses continually fell through the thawing snow, plunging with their riders many times a day into the icy water which flowed underneath the snow crust. It was decided accordingly to build a permanent road along the southern coast of the lake, blasting out a passage in the steep, almost vertical cliffs which rise along the shore, and spanning with bridges a hundred wild torrents that furiously rush from the mountains into the lake. Polish exiles were employed at this hard work.

Several batches of Russian political exiles had been sent during the last century to Siberia, but with the submissiveness to fate which is characteristic of the Russians, they never revolted; they allowed themselves to be killed inch by inch without ever attempting to free themselves. The Poles, on the contrary, — to their honor be it said, — were never so submissive as that, and this time they broke

into open revolt. It was evident that they had no chance
of success, but they revolted nevertheless. They had before
them the great lake, and behind them a girdle of absolutely
impracticable mountains, beyond which spread the wilder-
nesses of North Mongolia; but they conceived the idea of
disarming the soldiers who guarded them, forging those
terrible weapons of the Polish insurrections, — scythes
fastened as pikes on long poles, — and making their way
across the mountains and across Mongolia, towards China,
where they would find English ships to take them. One
day the news came to Irkútsk that part of those Poles
who were at work on the Baikál road had disarmed a dozen
soldiers and broken out into revolt. Eighty soldiers were
all that could be dispatched against them from Irkútsk;
crossing the Baikál in a steamer, they went to meet the
insurgents on the other side of the lake.

The winter of 1866 had been unusually dull at Irkútsk.
In the Siberian capital there is no such distinction between
the different classes as one sees in Russian provincial towns,
and Irkútsk "society," composed of numerous officers and
officials, together with the wives and daughters of local
traders and even clergymen, met during the winter, every
Thursday, at the Assembly rooms. This winter, however,
there was no "go" in the evening parties. Amateur theatricals, too, were not successful; and gambling, which usually flourished on a grand scale at Irkútsk, only dragged
along; a serious want of money was felt among the officials, and even the arrival of several mining officers was
not signalized by the heaps of banknotes with which these
privileged gentlemen commonly enlivened the knights of
the green tables. The season was decidedly dull, — just
the season for starting spiritualistic experiences with talking tables and talkative spirits. A gentleman who had
been the pet of Irkútsk society the previous winter for the
tales from popular life which he recited with great talent,

seeing that interest in himself and his tales was failing, took now to spiritualism as a new amusement. He was clever, and in a week's time all Irkútsk society was mad over talking spirits. A new life was infused into those who did not know how to kill time. Talking tables appeared in every drawing-room, and love-making went hand in hand with spirit rapping. Lieutenant Pótaloff took it all in deadly earnest, — talking tables and love. Perhaps he was less fortunate with the latter than with the tables; at any rate, when the news of the Polish insurrection came, he asked to be sent to the spot with the eighty soldiers. He hoped to return with a halo of military glory.

"I go against the Poles," he wrote in his diary; "it would be so interesting to be slightly wounded!"

He was killed. He rode on horseback by the side of the colonel who commanded the soldiers, when "the battle with the insurgents" — the glowing description of which may be found in the annals of the general staff — began. The soldiers were slowly advancing along the road when they met some fifty Poles, five or six of whom were armed with rifles and the remainder with sticks and scythes. The Poles occupied the forest and from time to time fired their guns. The file of soldiers returned the fire. Pótaloff twice asked the permission of the colonel to dismount and dash into the forest. The colonel very angrily ordered him to stay where he was. Notwithstanding this, the next moment the lieutenant had disappeared. Several shots resounded in the wood in succession, followed by wild cries; the soldiers rushed that way, and found the lieutenant bleeding on the grass. The Poles fired their last shots and surrendered; the battle was over, and Pótaloff was dead. He had rushed, revolver in hand, into the thicket, where he found several Poles armed with scythes. He fired upon them all his shots, in a haphazard way, wounding one of them, whereupon the others rushed upon him with their scythes.

At the other end of the road, on this side of the lake, two Russian officers behaved in the most abominable way towards the Poles who were building the same road, but took no part in the insurrection. One of the two officers rushed into their tent, swearing and firing his revolver at the peaceful exiles, two of whom he badly wounded.

Now, the logic of the Siberian military authorities was that as a Russian officer had been killed, several Poles must be executed. The court-martial condemned five of them to death: Szaramówicz, a pianist, a fine looking man of thirty, who was the leader of the insurrection; Celínski, a man of sixty, who had once been an officer in the Russian army; and three others whose names I do not remember.

The governor-general telegraphed to St. Petersburg asking permission to reprieve the condemned insurgents; but no answer came. He had promised us not to execute them, but after having waited several days for the reply, he ordered the sentence to be carried out in secrecy, early in the morning. The reply from St. Petersburg came four weeks later, by post: the governor was left to act "according to the best of his understanding." In the mean time five brave men had been shot.

The insurrection, people said, was foolish. And yet this brave handful of insurgents had obtained something. The news of it reached Europe. The executions, the brutalities of the two officers, which became known through the proceedings of the court, produced a commotion in Austria, and Austria interfered in favor of the Galicians who had taken part in the revolution of 1863 and had been sent to Siberia. Soon after the insurrection, the fate of the Polish exiles in Siberia was substantially bettered, and they owed it to the insurgents, — to those five brave men who were shot at Irkútsk, and those who had taken arms by their side.

For my brother and myself this insurrection was a great

lesson. We realized what it meant to belong in any way to the army. I was far away, but my brother was at Irkútsk, and his squadron was dispatched against the insurgents. Happily, the commander of the regiment to which my brother belonged knew him well, and, under some pretext, he ordered another officer to take command of the mobilized part of the squadron. Otherwise, Alexander, of course, would have refused to march. If I had been at Irkútsk, I should have done the same.

We decided then to leave the military service and to return to Russia. This was not an easy matter, especially as Alexander had married in Siberia; but at last all was arranged, and early in 1867 we were on our way to St. Petersburg.

PART FOURTH

ST. PETERSBURG; FIRST JOURNEY TO WESTERN EUROPE

I

EARLY in the autumn of 1867 my brother and I, with his family, were settled at St. Petersburg. I entered the university, and sat on the benches among young men, almost boys, much younger than myself. What I so longed for five years before was accomplished, — I could study; and, acting upon the idea that a thorough training in mathematics is the only solid basis for all subsequent work and thought, I joined the physico-mathematical faculty in its mathematical section. My brother entered the military academy for jurisprudence, whilst I entirely gave up military service, to the great dissatisfaction of my father, who hated the very sight of a civilian dress. We both had now to rely entirely upon ourselves.

Study at the university and scientific work absorbed all my time for the next five years. A student of the mathematical faculty has, of course, very much to do, but my previous studies in higher mathematics permitted me to devote part of my time to geography; and, moreover, I had not lost in Siberia the habit of hard work.

The report of my last expedition was in print; but in the meantime a vast problem rose before me. The journeys that I had made in Siberia had convinced me that the mountains which at that time were drawn on the maps of Northern Asia were mostly fantastic, and gave no idea whatever of the structure of the country. The great plateaus which are so prominent a feature of Asia were not even suspected by those who drew the maps. Instead of them, several great ridges, such as, for instance, the eastern portion of the Stanovói, which used to be drawn on the maps as a black worm creeping eastward, had grown up in the topographic bureaus, contrary to the indications and even to the sketches of such explorers as L. Schwartz. These ridges have no existence in nature. The heads of the rivers which flow toward the Arctic Ocean on the one side, and toward the Pacific on the other, lie intermingled on the surface of a vast plateau ; they rise in the same marshes. But, in the European topographer's imagination, the highest mountain ridges must run along the chief water-partings, and the topographers had drawn there the highest Alps, of which there is no trace in reality. Many such imaginary mountains were made to intersect the maps of Northern Asia in all directions.

To discover the true leading principles in the disposition of the mountains of Asia — the harmony of mountain formation — now became a question which for years absorbed my attention. For a considerable time the old maps, and still more the generalizations of Alexander von Humboldt, who, after a long study of Chinese sources, had covered Asia with a network of mountains running along the meridians and parallels, hampered me in my researches, until at last I saw that even Humboldt's generalizations, stimulating though they had been, did not agree with the facts.

Beginning, then, with the beginning, in a purely inductive way, I collected all the barometrical observations of previous travelers, and from them calculated hundreds of altitudes ; I marked on a large scale map all geological and physical observations that had been made by different travelers, — the facts, not the hypotheses ; and I tried to find out what structural lines would answer best to the observed realities. This preparatory work took me more than two years; and then followed months of intense thought, in order to find out what all the bewildering chaos of scattered observations meant, until one day, all of a sudden, the whole became clear and comprehensible, as if it were illuminated with a flash of light. The main structural lines of Asia are *not* north and south, or west and east; they are from the southwest to the northeast, — just as, in the Rocky Mountains and the plateaus of America, the lines are northwest to southeast; only secondary ridges shoot out northwest. Moreover, the mountains of Asia are not bundles of independent ridges, like the Alps, but are subordinated to an immense plateau, an old continent which once pointed toward Behring Strait. High border ridges have towered up along its fringes, and in the course of ages, terraces, formed by later sediments, have emerged from the sea, thus adding on both sides to the width of that primitive backbone of Asia.

There are not many joys in human life equal to the joy of the sudden birth of a generalization, illuminating the mind after a long period of patient research. What has seemed for years so chaotic, so contradictory, and so problematic takes at once its proper position within an harmonious whole. Out of a wild confusion of facts and from behind the fog of guesses, — contradicted almost as soon as they are born, — a stately picture makes its appearance, like an Alpine chain suddenly emerging in all its grandeur from the mists which concealed it the moment before, glittering under the rays of the sun in all its simplicity and variety, in all its mightiness and beauty. And when the generalization is put to a test, by applying it to hundreds of separate facts which had seemed to be hopelessly contradictory the moment before, each of them assumes its due position, increasing the impressiveness of the picture, accentuating some characteristic outline, or adding an unsuspected detail full of meaning. The generalization gains in strength and extent; its foundations grow in width and solidity; while in the distance, through the far-off mist on the horizon, the eye detects the outlines of new and still wider generalizations.

He who has once in his life experienced this joy of scientific creation will never forget it; he will be longing to renew it; and he cannot but feel with pain that this sort of happiness is the lot of so few of us, while so many could also live through it, — on a small or on a grand scale, — if scientific methods and leisure were not limited to a handful of men.

This work I consider my chief contribution to science. My first intention was to produce a bulky volume, in which the new ideas about the mountains and plateaus of Northern Asia should be supported by a detailed examination of each separate region; but in 1873, when I saw that I should soon be arrested, I only prepared a map which embodied my views and wrote an explanatory paper. Both were published by the Geographical Society, under the supervision of my brother, while I was already in the fortress of St. Peter and St. Paul. Petermann, who was then preparing a map of Asia, and knew my preliminary work, adopted my scheme for his map, and it has been accepted since by most cartographers. The map of Asia, as it is now understood, explains, I believe, the main physical features of the great continent, as well as the distribution of its climates, faunas, and floras, and even its history. It reveals, also, as I was able to see during my last journey to America, striking analogies between the structure and the geological growth of the two continents of the northern hemisphere. Very few cartographers could say now whence all these changes in the map of Asia have come; but in science it is better that new ideas should make their way independently of any name attached to them. The errors, which are unavoidable in a first generalization, are easier to rectify.

II

At the same time I worked a great deal for the Russian Geographical Society in my capacity of secretary to its section of physical geography.

Great interest was taken then in the exploration of Turkestan and the Pamírs. Syévertsoff had just returned after several years of travel. A great zoölogist, a gifted geographer, and one of the most intelligent men I ever came across, he, like so many Russians, disliked writing. When he had made an oral communication at a meeting of the society, he could not be induced to write anything beyond revising the reports of his communication, so that all that has been published over his signature is very far from doing full justice to the real value of the observations and the generalizations he had made. This reluctance to put down in writing the results of thought and observation is unfortunately not uncommon in Russia. The remarks on the orography of Turkestan, on the geographical distribution of plants and animals, on the part played by hybrids in the production of new species of birds, and so on, which I have heard Syévertsoff make, and the observations on the importance of mutual support in the progressive development of species which I have found just mentioned in a couple of lines in some report of a meeting, — these bore the stamp of more than ordinary talent and originality; but he did not possess the exuberant force of exposition in an appropriately beautiful form which might have made of him one of the most prominent men of science of our time.

Miklúkho-Makláy, well known in Australia, which to

wards the end of his life became the country of his adoption, belonged to the same order of men : the men who have had so much more to say than they have said in print. He was a tiny, nervous man, always suffering from malaria, who had just returned from the coasts of the Red Sea when I made his acquaintance. A follower of Haeckel, he had worked a great deal upon the marine invertebrates in their natural surroundings. The Geographical Society managed next to get him taken on board a Russian man-of-war to some unknown part of the coast of New Guinea, where he wanted to study the most primitive savages. Accompanied by one sailor only, he was left on this inhospitable shore, the inhabitants of which had the reputation of terrible cannibals. A hut was built for the two Crusoes, and they lived eighteen months or more near a native village on excellent terms with the natives. Always to be straightforward towards them, and never to deceive them, — not even in the most trifling matters, not even for scientific purposes, — was the point on which he was most scrupulous. When he was traveling some time later in the Malayan archipelago, he had with him a native who had entered into his service on the express condition of never being photographed. The natives, as every one knows, consider that something is taken out of them when their likeness is taken by photography. One day when the native was fast asleep, Makláy, who was collecting anthropological materials, confessed that he was awfully tempted to photograph his native, the more so as he was a typical representative of his tribe and would never have known that he had been photographed. But he remembered his agreement and refrained. When he left New Guinea, the natives made him promise to return ; and a few years later, although he was severely ill, he kept his word and did return. This remarkable man has, however, published only an infinitesimal part of the truly invaluable observations he made.

Fédchenko, who had made extensive zoölogical observations in Turkestan, — in company with his wife, Olga Fédchenko, also a naturalist, — was, as we used to say, a "West European." He worked hard to bring out in an elaborated form the results of his observations; but he was, unfortunately, killed in climbing a mountain in Switzerland. Glowing with youthful ardor after his journeys in the Turkestan highlands, and full of confidence in his own powers, he undertook an ascent without proper guides, and perished in a snowstorm. His wife, happily, completed the publication of his "Travels" after his death, and I believe she has now a son who continues the work of his father and mother.

I also saw a great deal of Prjeválsky, or rather Przewálski, as his Polish name ought to be spelled, although he himself preferred to appear as a "Russian patriot." He was a passionate hunter, and the enthusiasm with which he made his explorations of Central Asia was almost as much the result of his desire to hunt all sorts of difficult game, — bucks, wild camels, wild horses, and so on, — as of his desire to discover lands, new and difficult to approach. When he was induced to speak of his discoveries, he would soon interrupt his modest descriptions with an enthusiastic exclamation: "But what game there! What hunting!" And he would describe enthusiastically how he crept such and such a distance to approach a wild horse within shooting range. No sooner was he back at St. Petersburg than he planned a new expedition, and parsimoniously laying aside all his money, tried to increase it by stock exchange operations for that purpose. He was the type of a traveler in his strong physique, and in his capacity for living for years the rough life of a mountain hunter. He delighted in leading such a life. He made his first journey with only three comrades, and always kept on excellent terms with the natives. However, as his subsequent expeditions took on more of a military character, he began unfortunately to rely more upon the force of his armed escort than upon peaceful intercourse with the natives, and I heard it said in well-informed quarters that even if he had not died at the very start of his Tibet expedition, — so admirably and peacefully conducted after his death by his companions, Pyevtsóff, Roboróvsky, and Kozlóff, — he very probably would not have returned alive.

There was considerable activity at that time in the Geographical Society, and many were the geographical questions in which our section, and consequently its secretary, took a lively interest. Most of them were too technical to be mentioned in this place, but I must allude to the awakening of interest in the Russian settlements, the fisheries, and the trade in the Russian portion of the Arctic Ocean, which took place in these years. A Siberian merchant and gold miner, Sídoroff, made the most persevering efforts to awaken that interest. He foresaw that with a little aid in the shape of naval schools, the exploration of the White Sea, and so on, the Russian fisheries and Russian navigation could be largely developed. But that little, unfortunately, had to be done entirely through St. Petersburg; and the ruling powers of that courtly, bureaucratic, literary, artistic, and cosmopolitan city could not be moved to take an interest in anything provincial. Poor Sídoroff was simply ridiculed for his efforts. Interest in our far north had to be enforced upon the Russian Geographical Society from abroad.

In the years 1869–71 the bold Norwegian seal-hunters had quite unexpectedly opened the Kara Sea to navigation. To our extreme astonishment, we learned one day at the society that that sea, which lies between the island of Nóvaya Zemlyá and the Siberian coast, and which we used confidently to describe in our writings as "an ice cellar permanently stocked with ice," had been entered by a num-

ber of small Norwegian schooners and crossed by them in
all directions. Even the wintering place of the famous
Dutchman Barentz, which we believed to be concealed
forever from the eyes of man by ice fields hundreds of
years old, had been visited by these adventurous Norse-
men.

"Exceptional seasons and an exceptional state of the ice"
was what our old navigators said. But to a few of us it
was quite evident that, with their small schooners and their
small crews, the bold Norwegian hunters, who feel at
home amidst the ice, had ventured to pierce the floating ice
which usually bars the way to the Kara Sea, while the
commanders of government ships, hampered by the respon-
sibilities of the naval service, had never risked doing so.

A general interest in arctic exploration was awakened by
these discoveries. In fact, it was the seal-hunters who
opened the new era of arctic enthusiasm which culminated
in Nordenskjöld's circumnavigation of Asia, in the permanent establishment of the northeastern passage to Siberia,
in Peary's discovery of North Greenland, and in Nansen's
Fram expedition. Our Russian Geographical Society also
began to move, and a committee was appointed to prepare
the scheme of a Russian arctic expedition, and to indicate
the scientific work that could be done by it. Specialists
undertook to write each of the special scientific chapters of
this report; but, as often happens, a few chapters only, on
botany, geology, and meteorology, were ready in time,
and the secretary of the committee — that is, myself — had
to write the remainder. Several subjects, such as marine
zoölogy, the tides, pendulum observations, and terrestrial
magnetism, were quite new to me; but the amount of work
which a healthy man can accomplish in a short time, if he
strains all his forces and goes straight to the root of the
subject, no one would suppose beforehand, — and so my
report was ready.

It concluded by advocating a great arctic expedition, which would awaken in Russia a permanent interest in arctic questions and arctic navigation, and in the meantime a reconnoitring expedition on board a schooner chartered in Norway with its captain, pushing north or northeast of Nóvaya Zemlyá. This expedition, we suggested, might also try to reach, or at least to sight, an unknown land which must be situated at no great distance from Nóvaya Zemlyá. The probable existence of such a land had been indicated by an officer of the Russian navy, Baron Schilling, in an excellent but little known paper on the currents in the Arctic Ocean. When I read this paper, as also Lütke's journey to Nóvaya Zemlyá, and made myself acquainted with the general conditions of this part of the Arctic Ocean, I saw at once that the supposition must be correct. There must be a land to the northwest of Nóvaya Zemlyá, and it must reach a higher latitude than Spitzbergen. The steady position of the ice at the west of Nóvaya Zemlyá, the mud and stones on it, and various other smaller indications confirmed the hypothesis. Besides, if such a land were not located there, the ice current which flows westward from the meridian of Behring Strait to Greenland (the current of the Fram's drift) would, as Baron Schilling had truly remarked, reach the North Cape and cover the coasts of Laponia with masses of ice, just as it covers the northern extremity of Greenland. The warm current alone — a feeble continuation of the Gulf Stream — could not have prevented the accumulation of ice on the coasts of Northern Europe. This land, as is known, was discovered a couple of years later by the Austrian expedition, and named Franz Josef Land.

The arctic report had a quite unexpected result for me. I was offered the leadership of the reconnoitring expedition, on board a Norwegian schooner chartered for the purpose. I replied, of course, that I had never been to sea; but I was told that by combining the experience of a Carlsen or a Johansen with the initiative of a man of science, something valuable could be done; and I would have accepted, had not the ministry of finance at this juncture interposed with its veto. It replied that the exchequer could not grant the three or four thousand pounds which would be required for the expedition. Since that time Russia has taken no part in the exploration of the arctic seas. The land which we distinguished through the subpolar mists was discovered by Payer and Weyprecht, and the archipelagoes which must exist to the northeast of Nóvaya Zemlyá — I am even more firmly persuaded of it now than I was then — remain undiscovered.

Instead of joining an arctic expedition, I was sent out by the Geographical Society for a modest tour in Finland and Sweden, to explore the glacial deposits; and that journey drifted me in a quite different direction.

The Russian Academy of Sciences sent out that summer two of its members — the old geologist General Helmersen and Frederick Schmidt, the indefatigable explorer of Siberia — to study the structure of those long ridges of drift which are known as *åsar* in Sweden and Finland, and as *eskers, kames,* and so on, in the British Isles. The Geographical Society sent me to Finland for the same purpose. We visited, all three, the beautiful ridge of Pungahárju and then separated. I worked hard during the summer. I traveled a great deal in Finland, and crossed over to Sweden, where I spent many happy hours in the company of A. Nordenskjöld. As early as then — 1871 — he mentioned to me his schemes for reaching the mouths of the Siberian rivers, and even the Behring Strait, by the northern route. Returning to Finland I continued my researches till late in the autumn, and collected a mass of most interesting observations relative to the glaciation of the country. But I also thought a great deal during this journey about social matters, and these thoughts had a decisive influence upon my subsequent development.

All sorts of valuable materials relative to the geography of Russia passed through my hands in the Geographical Society, and the idea gradually came to me of writing an exhaustive physical geography of that immense part of the world. My intention was to give a thorough geographical description of the country, basing it upon the main lines of the surface structure, which I began to disentangle for European Russia; and to sketch, in that description, the different forms of economic life which ought to prevail in different physical regions. Take, for instance, the wide prairies of Southern Russia, so often visited by droughts and failure of crops. These droughts and failures must not be treated as accidental calamities: they are as much a natural feature of that region as its position on a southern slope, its fertility, and the rest; and the whole of the economic life of the southern prairies ought to be organized in prevision of the unavoidable recurrence of periodical droughts. Each region of the Russian Empire ought to be treated in the same scientific way, just as Karl Ritter has treated parts of Asia in his beautiful monographs.

But such a work would have required plenty of time and full freedom for the writer, and I often thought how helpful to this end it would be were I to occupy some day the position of secretary to the Geographical Society. Now, in the autumn of 1871, as I was working in Finland, slowly moving on foot toward the seacoast along the newly built railway, and closely watching the spot where the first unmistakable traces of the former extension of the post-glacial sea would appear, I received a telegram from the Geographical Society: "The council begs you to accept the position of secretary to the Society." At the same time

the outgoing secretary strongly urged me to accept the proposal.

My hopes were realized. But in the meantime other
thoughts and other longings had pervaded my mind. I
seriously thought over the reply, and wired, " Most cordial
thanks, but cannot accept."

III

It often happens that men pull in a certain political, social, or familiar harness simply because they never have time to ask themselves whether the position they stand in and the work they accomplish are right; whether their occupations really suit their inner desires and capacities, and give them the satisfaction which every one has the right to expect from his work. Active men are especially liable to find themselves in such a position. Every day brings with it a fresh batch of work, and a man throws himself into his bed late at night without having completed what he had expected to do; then in the morning he hurries to the unfinished task of the previous day. Life goes, and there is no time left to think, no time to consider the direction that one's life is taking. So it was with me.

But now, during my journey in Finland, I had leisure. When I was crossing in a Finnish two-wheeled *karria* some plain which offered no interest to the geologist, or when I was walking, hammer on shoulder, from one gravel-pit to another, I could think; and amidst the undoubtedly interesting geological work I was carrying on, one idea, which appealed far more strongly to my inner self than geology, persistently worked in my mind.

I saw what an immense amount of labor the Finnish peasant spends in clearing the land and in breaking up the hard boulder-clay, and I said to myself: "I will write the physical geography of this part of Russia, and tell the peasant the best means of cultivating this soil. Here an American stump-extractor would be invaluable; there certain methods of manuring would be indicated by science.

. . . But what is the use of talking to this peasant about American machines, when he has barely enough bread to live upon from one crop to the next; when the rent which he has to pay for that boulder-clay grows heavier and heavier in proportion to his success in improving the soil? He gnaws at his hard-as-a-stone rye-flour cake which he bakes twice a year; he has with it a morsel of fearfully salted cod and a drink of skimmed milk. How dare I talk to him of American machines, when all that he can raise must be sold to pay rent and taxes? He needs me to live with him, to help him to become the owner or the free occupier of that land. Then he will read books with profit, but not now."

And my thoughts wandered from Finland to our Nikóls-koye peasants, whom I had lately seen. Now they are free, and they value freedom very much. But they have no meadows. In one way or another, the landlords have got all the meadows for themselves. When I was a child, the Savókhins used to send out six horses for night pasture, the Tolkachóffs had seven. Now, these families have only three horses each; other families, which formerly had three horses, have only one, or none. What can be done with one miserable horse? No meadows, no horses, no manure! How can I talk to them of grass-sowing? They are already ruined, — poor as Lazarus, — and in a few years they will be made still poorer by a foolish taxation. How happy they were when I told them that my father gave them permission to mow the grass in the small open spaces in his Kóstino forest! "Your Nikólskoye peasants are *ferocious* for work," — that is the common saying about them in our neighborhood; but the arable land, which our stepmother has taken out of their allotments in virtue of the "law of minimum," — that diabolic clause introduced by the serf-owners when they were allowed to revise the emancipation law, — is now a forest of thistles, and the "ferocious" workers are not allowed to till it. And the same sort of thing goes on throughout all Russia. Even at that time it was evident, and official commissioners gave warning of it, that the first serious failure of crops in Middle Russia would result in a terrible famine, — and famine came, in 1876, in 1884, in 1891, in 1895, and again in 1898.

Science is an excellent thing. I knew its joys and valued them, — perhaps more than many of my colleagues did. Even now, as I was looking on the lakes and the hillocks of Finland, new and beautiful generalizations arose before my eyes. I saw in a remote past, at the very dawn of mankind, the ice accumulating from year to year in the northern archipelagoes, over Scandinavia and Finland. An immense growth of ice invaded the north of Europe and slowly spread as far as its middle portions. Life dwindled in that part of the northern hemisphere, and, wretchedly poor, uncertain, it fled further and further south before the icy breath which came from that immense frozen mass. Man — miserable, weak, ignorant — had every difficulty in maintaining a precarious existence. Ages passed away, till the melting of the ice began, and with it came the lake period, when countless lakes were formed in the cavities, and a wretched subpolar vegetation began timidly to invade the unfathomable marshes with which every lake was surrounded. Another series of ages passed before an extremely slow process of drying up set in, and vegetation began its slow invasion from the south. And now we are fully in the period of a rapid desiccation, accompanied by the formation of dry prairies and steppes, and man has to find out the means to put a check to that desiccation to which Central Asia already has fallen a victim, and which menaces Southeastern Europe.

Belief in an ice-cap reaching Middle Europe was at that time rank heresy; but before my eyes a grand picture was rising, and I wanted to draw it, with the thousands of details I saw in it; to use it as a key to the present distri-

bution of floras and faunas; to open new horizons for geology
and physical geography.

But what right had I to these highest joys, when all
around me was nothing but misery and struggle for a mouldy
bit of bread; when whatsoever I should spend to enable
me to live in that world of higher emotions must needs be
taken from the very mouths of those who grew the wheat
and had not bread enough for their children? From somebody's mouth it must be taken, because the aggregate production of mankind remains still so low.

Knowledge is an immense power. Man must know.
But we already know much! What if that knowledge —
and only that — should become the possession of all?
Would not science itself progress in leaps, and cause mankind to make strides in production, invention, and social
creation, of which we are hardly in a condition now to
measure the speed?

The masses want to know: they are willing to learn;
they *can* learn. There, on the crest of that immense
moraine which runs between the lakes, as if giants had
heaped it up in a hurry to connect the two shores, there
stands a Finnish peasant plunged in contemplation of the
beautiful lakes, studded with islands, which lie before him.
Not one of these peasants, poor and downtrodden though
they may be, will pass this spot without stopping to admire
the scene. Or there, on the shore of a lake, stands another peasant, and sings something so beautiful that the
best musician would envy him his melody, for its feeling
and its meditative power. Both deeply feel, both meditate,
both think; they are ready to widen their knowledge, —
only give it to them, only give them the means of getting
leisure.

This is the direction in which, and these are the kind of
people for whom, I must work. All those sonorous phrases

about making mankind progress, while at the same time the progress-makers stand aloof from those whom they pretend to push onwards, are mere sophisms made up by minds anxious to shake off a fretting contradiction.

So I sent my negative reply to the Geographical Society.

IV

St. Petersburg had changed greatly from what it was when I left it in 1862. "Oh, yes, you knew the St. Petersburg of Chernyshévsky," the poet Máikoff remarked to me once. True, I knew the St. Petersburg of which Chernyshévsky was the favorite. But how shall I describe the city which I found on my return? Perhaps as the St. Petersburg of the *cafés chantants*, of the music halls, if the words "all St. Petersburg" ought really to mean the upper circles of society which took their keynote from the court.

At the court, and in its circles, liberal ideas were in sorely bad repute. All prominent men of the sixties, even such moderates as Count Nicholas Muravióff and Nicholas Milútin, were treated as suspects. Only Dmítri Milútin, the minister of war, was kept by Alexander II. at his post, because the reform which he had to accomplish in the army required many years for its realization. All other active men of the reform period had been brushed aside.

I spoke once with a high dignitary of the ministry for foreign affairs. He sharply criticised another high functionary, and I remarked in the latter's defense, "Still, there is this to be said for him, that he never accepted service under Nicholas I." "And now he is in service under the reign of Shuváloff and Trépoff!" was the reply, which so correctly described the situation that I could say nothing more.

General Shuváloff, the chief of the state police, and General Trépoff, the chief of the St. Petersburg police, were indeed the real rulers of Russia. Alexander II. was their executive, their tool. And they ruled by fear. Trépoff had so frightened Alexander by the spectre of a revolution which was going to break out at St. Petersburg, that if the omnipotent chief of the police was a few minutes late in appearing with his daily report at the palace, the Emperor would ask, " Is everything quiet at St. Petersburg ? "

Shortly after Alexander had given an " entire dismissal " to Princess X., he conceived a warm friendship for General Fleury, the aide-de-camp of Napoleon III., that sinister man who was the soul of the *coup d'état* of December 2, 1852. They were continually seen together, and Fleury once informed the Parisians of the great honor which was bestowed upon him by the Russian Tsar. As the latter was riding along the Nevsky Prospekt, he saw Fleury, and asked him to mount into his carriage, an *égoïste*, which had a seat only twelve inches wide, for a single person ; and the French general recounted at length how the Tsar and he, holding fast to each other, had to leave half of their bodies hanging in the air on account of the narrowness of the seat. It is enough to name this new friend, fresh from Compiègne, to suggest what the friendship meant.

Shuváloff took every advantage of the present state of mind of his master. He prepared one reactionary measure after another, and when Alexander showed reluctance to sign any one of them, Shuváloff would speak of the coming revolution and the fate of Louis XVI., and, " for the salvation of the dynasty," would implore him to sign the new additions to the laws of repression. For all that, sadness and remorse would from time to time besiege Alexander. He would fall into a gloomy melancholy, and speak in a sad tone of the brilliant beginning of his reign, and of the reactionary character which it was taking. Then Shuváloff would organize a bear hunt. Hunters, merry courtiers, and carriages full of ballet girls would go to the forests of Nóvgorod. A couple of bears would be killed by Alexander II., who was a good shot, and used to let the animals approach within a few yards of his rifle; and there, in the excitement of the hunting festivities, Shuváloff would obtain his master's signature to any scheme of repression or robbery in the interest of his clients, which he had concocted.

Alexander II. certainly was not a rank-and-file man, but two different men lived in him, both strongly developed, struggling with each other; and this inner struggle became more and more violent as he advanced in age. He could be charming in his behavior, and the next moment display sheer brutality. He was possessed of a calm, reasoned courage in the face of a real danger, but he lived in constant fear of dangers which existed in his brain only. He assuredly was not a coward; he would meet a bear face to face; on one occasion, when the animal was not killed outright by his first bullet, and the man who stood behind him with a lance, rushing forward, was knocked down by the bear, the Tsar came to his rescue, and killed the bear close to the muzzle of his gun (I know this from the man himself); yet he was haunted all his life by the fears of his own imagination and of an uneasy conscience. He was very kind in his manner toward his friends, but that kindness existed side by side with the terrible cold-blooded cruelty — a seventeenth century cruelty — which he displayed in crushing the Polish insurrection, and later on in 1880, when similar measures were taken to put down the revolt of the Russian youth; a cruelty of which no one would have thought him capable. He thus lived a double life, and at the period of which I am speaking, he merrily signed the most reactionary decrees, and afterward became despondent about them. Toward the end of his life this inner struggle, as will be seen later on, became still stronger, and assumed an almost tragical character.

In 1872 Shuváloff was nominated ambassador to England, but his friend General Potápoff continued the same policy till the beginning of the Turkish war in 1877. During all this time, the most scandalous plundering of the state exchequer, as also of the crown lands, the estates confiscated in Lithuania after the insurrection, the Bashkír lands in Orenbúrg, and so on, was proceeding on a grand scale. Several such affairs were subsequently brought to light and judged publicly by the Senate acting as a high court of justice, after Potápoff, who became insane, and Trépoff had been dismissed, and their rivals at the palace wanted to show them to Alexander II. in their true light. In one of these judicial inquiries it came out that a friend of Potápoff had most shamelessly robbed the peasants of a Lithuanian estate of their lands, and afterward, empowered by his friends at the ministry of the interior, he had caused the peasants, who sought redress, to be imprisoned, subjected to wholesale flogging, and shot down by the troops. This was one of the most revolting stories of the kind even in the annals of Russia, which teem with similar robberies up to the present time. It was only after Véra Zasúlich had shot at Trépoff and wounded him (to avenge his having ordered one of the political prisoners to be flogged in prison) that the thefts of Potápoff and his clients became widely known and he was dismissed. Thinking that he was going to die, Trépoff wrote his will, from which it became known that this man, who made the Tsar believe that he died poor, even though he had occupied for years the lucrative post of chief of the St. Petersburg police, left in reality to his heirs a considerable fortune. Some courtiers reported it to Alexander II. Trépoff lost his credit, and it was then that a few of the robberies of the Shuváloff-Potápoff-and-Trépoff party were brought before the Senate.

The pillage which went on in all the ministries, especially in connection with the railways and all sorts of industrial enterprises, was really enormous. Immense fortunes were made at that time. The navy, as Alexander II. himself said to one of his sons, was "in the pockets of So-and-So." The cost of the railways, guaranteed by the state, was simply fabulous. As to commercial enterprises, it was openly known that none could be launched unless a specified percentage of the dividends was promised to different functionaries in the several ministries. A friend of mine, who intended to start some enterprise at St. Petersburg, was frankly told at the ministry of the interior that he would have to pay twenty-five per cent. of the net profits to a certain person, fifteen per cent. to one man at the ministry of finances, ten per cent. to another man in the same ministry, and five per cent. to a fourth person. The bargains were made without concealment, and Alexander II. knew it. His own remarks, written on the reports of the comptroller-general, bear testimony to this. But he saw in the thieves his protectors from the revolution, and kept them until their robberies became an open scandal.

The young grand dukes, with the exception of the heir apparent, afterward Alexander III., who always was a good and thrifty *paterfamilias*, followed the example of the head of the family. The orgies which one of them used to arrange in a small restaurant on the Nevsky Prospekt were so degradingly notorious that one night the chief of the police had to interfere, and warned the owner of the restaurant that he would be marched to Siberia if he ever again let his "grand duke's room" to the grand duke. "Imagine my perplexity," this man said to me, on one occasion, when he was showing me that room, the walls and ceiling of which were upholstered with thick satin cushions. "On the one side I had to offend a member of the imperial family, who could do with me what he liked, and on the other side General Trépoff menaced me with Siberia! Of course, I obeyed the general; he is, as you know, omnipotent now." Another grand duke became conspicuous for ways belonging to the domain of psychopathy; and a third was exiled to Turkestan, after he had stolen the diamonds of his mother.

The Empress Marie Alexándrovna, abandoned by her husband, and probably horrified at the turn which court life was taking, became more and more a devotee, and soon she was entirely in the hands of the palace priest, a representative of a quite new type in the Russian Church, — the Jesuitic. This new genus of well-combed, depraved, and Jesuitic clergy made rapid progress at that time; already they were working hard and with success to become a power in the state, and to lay hands on the schools.

It has been proved over and over again that the village clergy in Russia are so much taken up by their functions — performing baptisms and marriages, administering communion to the dying, and so on — that they cannot pay due attention to the schools; even when the priest is paid for giving the Scripture lesson at a village school, he usually passes that lesson to some one else, as he has no time to attend to it himself. Nevertheless, the higher clergy, exploiting the hatred of Alexander II. toward the so-called revolutionary spirit, began their campaign for laying their hands upon the schools. " No schools unless clerical ones " became their motto. All Russia wanted education, but even the ridiculously small sum of four million dollars included every year in the state budget for primary schools used *not* to be spent by the ministry of public instruction, while nearly as much was given to the Synod as an aid for establishing schools under the village clergy, — schools most of which existed, and now exist, on paper only.

All Russia wanted technical education, but the ministry opened only classical gymnasia, because formidable courses of Latin and Greek were considered the best means of preventing the pupils from reading and thinking. In these gymnasia, only two or three per cent. of the pupils suc-

ceeded in completing an eight years' course, — all boys
promising to become something and to show some independence of thought being carefully sifted out before they could
reach the last form ; and all sorts of measures were taken
to *reduce* the number of pupils.   Education was considered
as a sort of luxury, for the few only.   At the same time
the ministry of education was engaged in a continuous,
passionate struggle against all private persons and all institutions — district and county councils, municipalities, and
the like — which endeavored to open teachers' seminaries
or technical schools, or even simple primary schools.   Technical education — in a country which was so much in want
of engineers, educated agriculturists, and geologists — was
treated as equivalent to revolutionism.   It was prohibited,
prosecuted ; so that up to the present time, every autumn,
something like two or three thousand young men are refused
admission to the higher technical schools from mere lack of
vacancies.   A feeling of despair took possession of all those
who wished to do anything useful in public life ; while the
peasantry were ruined at an appalling rate by over-taxation,
and by "beating out" of them the arrears of the taxes by
means of semi-military executions, which ruined them forever.   Only those governors of the provinces were in favor
at the capital who managed to beat out the taxes in the
most severe way.

Such was the official St. Petersburg.   Such was the influence it exercised upon Russia.

V

WHEN we were leaving Siberia, we often talked, my brother and I, of the intellectual life which we should find
at St. Petersburg, and of the interesting acquaintances we
should make in the literary circles. We made such acquaintances, indeed, both among the radicals and among the
moderate Slavophiles; but I must confess that they were
rather disappointing. We found plenty of excellent men,
— Russia is full of excellent men, — but they did not
quite correspond to our ideal of political writers. The best
writers — Chernyshévsky, Mikháiloff, Lavróff — were in
exile, or were kept in the fortress of St. Peter and St. Paul,
like Písareff. Others, taking a gloomy view of the situation, had changed their ideas, and were now leaning toward
a sort of paternal absolutism; while the greater number,
though holding still to their beliefs, had become so cautious
in expressing them that their prudence was almost equal
to desertion.

At the height of the reform period nearly every one in
the advanced literary circles had had some relations either
with Hérzen or with Turguéneff and his friends, or with
the Great Russian or the Land and Freedom secret societies which had had at that period an ephemeral existence.
Now, these same men were only the more anxious to bury
their former sympathies as deep as possible, so as to appear
above political suspicion.

One or two of the liberal reviews which were tolerated
at that time, owing chiefly to the superior diplomatic talents
of their editors, contained excellent material, showing the
ever growing misery and the desperate conditions of the

great mass of the peasants, and making clear enough the obstacles that were put in the way of every progressive worker. The amount of such facts was enough to drive one to despair. But no one dared to suggest any remedy, or to hint at any field of action, at any outcome from a position which was represented as hopeless. Some writers still cherished the hope that Alexander II. would once more assume the character of reformer; but with the majority the fear of seeing their reviews suppressed, and both editors and contributors marched " to some more or less remote part of the empire," dominated all other feelings. Fear and hope equally paralyzed them.

The more radical they had been ten years before, the greater were their fears. My brother and I were very well received in one or two literary circles, and we went occasionally to their friendly gatherings; but the moment the conversation began to lose its frivolous character, or my brother, who had a great talent for raising serious questions, directed it toward home affairs, or toward the state of France, where Napoleon III. was hastening to his fall in 1870, some sort of interruption was sure to occur. " What do you think, gentlemen, of the latest performance of ' La Belle Hélène ' ? " or " What is your opinion of that cured fish ? " was loudly asked by one of the elder guests, — and the conversation was brought to an end.

Outside the literary circles, things were even worse. In the sixties, Russia, and especially St. Petersburg, was full of men of advanced opinions, who seemed ready at that time to make any sacrifices for their ideas. " What has become of them ? " I asked myself. I looked up some of them; but, " Prudence, young man ! " was all they had to say. "Iron is stronger than straw," or " One cannot break a stone wall with his forehead," and similar proverbs, unfortunately too numerous in the Russian language, constituted now their code of practical philosophy. " We have done something in our life : ask no more from us ; " or " Have patience : this sort of thing will not last," they told us, while we, the youth, were ready to resume the struggle, to act, to risk, to sacrifice everything, if necessary, and only asked them to give us advice, some guidance, and some intellectual support.

Turguéneff has depicted in "Smoke" some of the ex-reformers from the upper layers of society, and his picture is disheartening. But it is especially in the heart-rending novels and sketches of Madame Kohanóvsky, who wrote under the pseudonym of " V. Krestóvskiy " (she must not be confounded with another novel-writer, Vsévolod Krestóvskiy), that one can follow the many aspects which the degradation of the " liberals of the sixties " took at that time. " The joy of living " — perhaps the joy of having survived — became their goddess, as soon as the nameless crowd which ten years before made the force of the reform movement refused to hear any more of " all that sentimentalism." They hastened to enjoy the riches which poured into the hands of " practical " men.

Many new ways to fortune had been opened since serfdom had been abolished, and the crowd rushed with eagerness into these channels. Railways were feverishly built in Russia ; to the lately opened private banks the landlords went in numbers to mortgage their estates ; the newly established private notaries and lawyers at the courts were in possession of large incomes ; the shareholders' companies multiplied with an appalling rapidity and the promoters flourished. A class of men who formerly would have lived in the country on the modest income of a small estate cultivated by a hundred serfs, or on the still more modest salary of a functionary in a law court, now made fortunes, or had such yearly incomes as in the times of serfdom were possible only for the land magnates.

The very tastes of " society " sunk lower and lower. The

Italian opera, formerly a forum for radical demonstrations, was now deserted; the Russian opera, timidly asserting the rights of its great composers, was frequented by a few enthusiasts only.   Both were found "tedious," and the cream of St. Petersburg society crowded to a vulgar theatre where the second-rate stars of the Paris small theatres won easy laurels from their Horse Guard admirers, or went to see "La Belle Hélène," which was played on the Russian stage, while our great dramatists were forgotten.   Offenbach's music reigned supreme.

It must be said that the political atmosphere was such that the best men had reasons, or had at least weighty excuses, for keeping quiet.   After Karakózoff had shot at Alexander II. in April, 1866, the state police had become omnipotent.   Every one suspected of "radicalism," no matter what he had done or what he had not done, had to live under the fear of being arrested any night, for the sympathy he might have shown to some one involved in this or that political affair, or for an innocent letter intercepted in a midnight search, or simply for his "dangerous" opinions; and arrest for political reasons might mean anything: years of seclusion in the fortress of St. Peter and St. Paul, transportation to Siberia, or even torture in the casemates of the fortress.

This movement of the circles of Karakózoff remains up to this date very imperfectly known, even in Russia.   I was at that time in Siberia, and know of it only by hearsay.   It appears, however, that two different currents combined in it.   One of them was the beginning of that great movement "toward the people," which later took on such formidable dimensions; while the other current was mainly political. Groups of young men, some of whom were on the road to become brilliant university professors, or men of mark as historians and ethnographers, had come together about 1864, with the intention of carrying to the people education and knowledge in spite of the opposition of the government. They went as mere artisans to great industrial towns, and started there coöperative associations, as well as informal schools, hoping that by the exercise of much tact and patience they might be able to educate the people, and thus to create the first centres from which better and higher conceptions would gradually radiate amongst the masses. Their zeal was great; considerable fortunes were brought into the service of the cause; and I am inclined to think that, compared with all similar movements which took place later on, this one stood perhaps on the most practical basis. Its initiators certainly were very near to the working-people.

On the other side, with some of the members of these circles — Karakózoff, Ishútin, and their nearest friends — the movement took a political direction. During the years from 1862 to 1866 the policy of Alexander II. had assumed a decidedly reactionary character; he had surrounded himself with men of the most reactionary type, taking them as his nearest advisers; the very reforms which made the glory of the beginning of his reign were now wrecked wholesale by means of by-laws and ministerial circulars; a return to manorial justice and serfdom in a disguised form was openly expected in the old camp; while no one could hope at that time that the main reform — the abolition of serfdom — could withstand the assaults directed against it from the Winter Palace itself. All this must have brought Karakózoff and his friends to the idea that a further continuance of Alexander II.'s reign would be a menace even to the little that had been won; that Russia would have to return to the horrors of Nicholas I., if Alexander continued to rule. Great hopes were felt at the same time — this is "an often repeated story, but always new"— as to the liberal inclinations of the heir to the throne and his uncle Constantine. I must also say that before 1866 such fears and such con-

siderations were not unfrequently expressed in much higher
circles than those with which Karakózoff seems to have been
in contact. At any rate, Karakózoff shot at Alexander II.
one day, as he was coming out of the summer garden to take
his carriage.   The shot missed, and Karakózoff was arrested
on the spot.

Katkóff, the leader of the Moscow reactionary party, and
a great master for extracting pecuniary profits out of every
political disturbance, at once accused of complicity with
Karakózoff all radicals and liberals, — which was certainly
untrue, — and insinuated in his paper, making all Moscow believe it, that Karakózoff was a mere instrument in
the hands of the Grand Duke Constantine, the leader of
the reform party in the highest circles.   One can imagine
to what an extent the two rulers, Shuváloff and Trépoff,
exploited these accusations, and the consequent fears of
Alexander II.

Mikhael Muravióff, who had won during the Polish insurrection his nickname " the hangman," received orders to
make a most searching inquiry, and to discover by every
possible means the plot which was supposed to exist. He
made arrests in all classes of society, ordered hundreds of
searches, and boasted that he " would find the means to
render the prisoners more talkative."   He certainly was not
the man to recoil even before torture, — and public opinion
in St. Petersburg was almost unanimous in saying that
Karakózoff was tortured to obtain avowals, but made none.

State secrets are well kept in fortresses, especially in that
huge mass of stone opposite the Winter Palace, which has
seen so many horrors, only in recent times disclosed by historians.   It still keeps Muravióff's secrets. However, the
following may perhaps throw some light on this matter.

In 1866 I was in Siberia.   One of our Siberian officers,
who traveled from Russia to Irkútsk toward the end of that
year, met at a post station two gendarmes.   They had ac-

companied to Siberia a functionary exiled for theft, and were now returning home. Our Irkútsk officer, who was a very amiable man, finding the gendarmes at the tea table on a cold winter night, joined them and chatted with them, while the horses were being changed. One of the men knew Karakózoff.

"He was cunning, he was," he said. "When he was in the fortress, we were ordered, two of us, — we were relieved every two hours, — not to let him sleep. So we kept him sitting on a small stool, and as soon as he began to doze, we shook him to keep him awake. . . . What will you ? — we were ordered to do so! . . . Well, see how cunning he was : he would sit with crossed legs, swinging one of his legs to make us believe that he was awake, and himself, in the meantime, would get a nap, continuing to swing his leg. But we soon made it out and told those who relieved us, so that he was shaken and waked up every few minutes, whether he swung his leg or not." "And how long did that last ?" my friend asked. "Oh, many days, — more than one week."

The naïve character of this description is in itself a proof of veracity : it could not have been invented ; and that Karakózoff was tortured to this degree may be taken for granted.

When Karakózoff was hanged, one of my comrades from the corps of pages was present at the execution with his regiment of cuirassiers. "When he was taken out of the fortress," my comrade told me, " sitting on the high platform of the cart which was jolting on the rough glacis of the fortress, my first impression was that they were bringing out an india-rubber doll to be hanged ; that Karakózoff was already dead. Imagine that the head, the hands, the whole body were absolutely loose, as if there were no bones in the body, or as if the bones had all been broken. It was a terrible thing to see, and to think what it meant.

However, when two soldiers took him down from the cart, I saw that he moved his legs and made strenuous endeavors to walk by himself and to ascend the steps of the scaffold. So it was not a doll, nor could he have been in a swoon. All the officers were very much puzzled at the circumstance and could not explain it." When, however, I suggested to my comrade that perhaps Karakózoff had been tortured, the color came into his face and he replied, " So we all thought."

Absence of sleep for weeks would alone be sufficient to explain the state in which that morally very strong man was at the time of the execution. I may add that I am absolutely certain that — at least in one case — drugs were administered to a prisoner in the fortress, namely, Adrián Saburoff, in 1879. Did Muravióff limit the torture to this only? Was he prevented from going any further, or not? I do not know. But this much I know : that I often heard from high officials at St. Petersburg that torture had been resorted to in this case.

Muravióff had promised to root out all radical elements in St. Petersburg, and all those who had had in any degree a radical past now lived under the fear of falling into the despot's clutches. Above all, they kept aloof from the younger people, from fear of being involved with them in some perilous political associations. In this way a chasm was opened not only between the "fathers" and the "sons," as Turguéneff described it in his novel, — not only between the two generations, but also between all men who had passed the age of thirty and those who were in their early twenties. Russian youth stood consequently in the position not only of having to fight in their fathers the defenders of serfdom, but of being left entirely to themselves by their elder brothers, who were unwilling to join them in their leanings toward Socialism, and were

afraid to give them support even in their struggle for
more political freedom. Was there ever before in history,
I ask myself, a youthful band engaging in a fight against
so formidable a foe, so deserted by fathers and even by
elder brothers, although those young men had merely taken
to heart, and had tried to realize in life, the intellectual inheritance of these same fathers and brothers? Was there
ever a struggle undertaken in more tragical conditions than
these?

VI

THE only bright point which I saw in the life of St. Petersburg was the movement which was going on amongst the youth of both sexes. Various currents joined to produce the mighty agitation which soon took an underground and revolutionary character, and engrossed the attention of Russia for the next fifteen years. I shall speak of it in a subsequent chapter; but I must mention in this place the movement which was carried on, quite openly, by our women for obtaining access to higher education. St. Petersburg was at that time its main centre.

Every afternoon the young wife of my brother, on her return from the women's pedagogical courses which she followed, had something new to tell us about the animation which prevailed there. Schemes were laid for opening a medical academy and universities for women; debates upon schools or upon different methods of education were organized in connection with the courses, and hundreds of women took a passionate interest in these questions, discussing them over and over again in private. Societies of translators, publishers, printers, and bookbinders were started in order that work might be provided for the poorest members of the sisterhood who flocked to St. Petersburg, ready to do any sort of work, only to live in the hope that they, too, would some day have their share of higher education. A vigorous, exuberant life reigned in those feminine centres, in striking contrast to what I met elsewhere.

Since the government had shown its determined intention not to admit women to the existing universities, they had directed all their efforts toward opening universities of their own. They were told at the ministry of education that the girls who had passed through the girls' gymnasia (the high schools) were not prepared to follow university lectures. "Very well," they replied, "permit us to open intermediate courses, preparatory to the university, and impose upon us any programme you like. We ask no grants from the state. Only give us the permission, and it will be done." Of course, the permission was not given.

Then they started private courses and drawing-room lectures in all parts of St. Petersburg. Many university professors, in sympathy with the new movement, volunteered to give lectures. Poor men themselves, they warned the organizers that any mention of remuneration would be taken as a personal offense. Natural science excursions used to be made every summer in the neighborhood of St. Petersburg, under the guidance of university professors, and women constituted the bulk of the excursionists. In the courses for midwives they forced the professors to treat each subject in a far more exhaustive way than was required by the programme, or to open additional courses. They took advantage of every possibility, of every breach in the fortress, to storm it. They gained admission to the anatomical laboratory of old Dr. Gruber, and by their admirable work they won this enthusiast of anatomy entirely to their side. If they learned that a professor had no objection to letting them work in his laboratory on Sundays and at night on week days, they took advantage of the opportunity.

At last, notwithstanding all the opposition of the ministry, they opened the intermediate courses, only giving them the name of pedagogical courses. Was it possible, indeed, to forbid future mothers studying the methods of education? But as the methods of teaching botany or mathematics could not be taught in the abstract, botany, mathematics, and the rest were soon introduced into the curriculum of the pedagogical courses, which became preparatory for the university.

Step by step the women thus widened their rights.   As soon as it became known that at some German university a certain professor might open his lecture-room to a few women, they knocked at his door and were admitted.   They studied law and history at Heidelberg, and mathematics at Berlin ; at Zürich, more than a hundred girls and women worked at the university and the polytechnicum.   There they won something more valuable than the degree of Doctor of Medicine ; they won the esteem of the most learned professors, who expressed it publicly several times. When I came to Zürich in 1872, and became acquainted with some of the students, I was astonished to see quite young girls, who were studying at the polytechnicum, solving intricate problems of the theory of heat, with the aid of the differential calculus, as easily as if they had had years of mathematical training.   One of the Russian girls who studied mathematics under Weierstrass at Berlin, Sophie Kovalévsky, became a mathematician of high repute, and was invited to a professorship at Stockholm; she was, I believe, the first woman in our century to hold a professorship in a university for men.   She was so young that in Sweden no one wanted to call her by anything but her diminutive name of Sónya.

In spite of the open hatred of Alexander II. for educated women, — when he met in his walks a girl wearing spectacles and a round Garibaldian cap, he began to tremble, thinking that she must be a nihilist bent on shooting at him ; in spite of the bitter opposition of the state police, who represented every woman student as a revolutionist; in spite of the thunders and the vile accusations which Katkóff directed against the whole of the movement in almost every number of his venomous gazette, the women succeeded, in the teeth of the government, in opening a series of educational institutions. When several of them had obtained medical degrees abroad, they forced the government, in 1872, to let them open a medical academy with their own private means. And when the Russian women were recalled by their government from Zürich, to prevent their intercourse with the revolutionist refugees, they forced the government to let them open in Russia four universities of their own, which soon had nearly a thousand pupils. It seems almost incredible, but it is a fact that notwithstanding all the prosecutions which the Women's Medical Academy had to live through, and its temporary closure, there are now in Russia more than six hundred and seventy women practicing as physicians.

It was certainly a grand movement, astounding in its success and instructive in a high degree. Above all, it was through the unlimited devotion of a mass of women in all possible capacities that they gained their successes. They had already worked as sisters of charity during the Crimean war; as organizers of schools later on; as the most devoted schoolmistresses in the villages; as educated midwives and doctors' assistants amongst the peasants. They went afterward as nurses and doctors in the fever-stricken hospitals during the Turkish war of 1878, and won the admiration of the military commanders and of Alexander II. himself. I know two ladies, both very eagerly "wanted" by the state police, who served as nurses during the war, under assumed names which were guaranteed by false passports; one of them, the greater "criminal" of the two, who had taken a prominent part in my escape, was even appointed head nurse of a large hospital for wounded soldiers, while her friend nearly died from typhoid fever. In short, women took any position, no matter how low in the social scale, and no matter what privations it involved, if only they could be in any way useful to the people; not a few of them, but hundreds and thousands. They have *conquered* their rights in the true sense of the word.

Another feature of this movement was that in it the chasm between the two generations — the older and the younger sisters — did not exist ; or, at least, it was bridged over to a great extent. Those who were the leaders of the movement from its origin never broke the link which connected them with their younger sisters, even though the latter were far more advanced in their ideals than the older women were.

They pursued their aims in the higher spheres ; they kept strictly aloof from any political agitation ; but they never committed the fault of forgetting that their true force was in the masses of younger women, of whom a great number finally joined the radical or revolutionary circles. These leaders were correctness itself, — I considered them too correct ; but they did not break with those younger students who went about as typical nihilists, with short-cropped hair, disdaining crinoline, and betraying their democratic spirit in all their behavior. The leaders did not mix with them, and occasionally there was friction, but they never repudiated them, — a great thing, I believe, in those times of madly raging prosecutions.

They seemed to say to the younger and more democratic people : " We shall wear our velvet dresses and chignons, because we have to deal with fools who see in a velvet dress and a chignon the tokens of ' political reliability ; ' but you, girls, remain free in your tastes and inclinations." When the women who studied at Zürich were ordered by the Russian government to return, these correct ladies did not turn against the rebels. They simply said to the government : " You don't like it ? Well, then, open women's universities at home ; otherwise our girls will go abroad in still greater numbers, and of course will enter into relations with the political refugees." When they were reproached with breeding revolutionists, and were menaced with the closing of their academy and universities, they retorted, "Yes, many students become revolutionists; but is that a reason for closing all universities?" How few political leaders have the moral courage not to turn against the more advanced wing of their own party!

The real secret of their wise and fully successful attitude was that none of the women who were the soul of that movement were mere "feminists," desirous to get their share of the privileged positions in society and the state. Far from that. The sympathies of most of them went with the masses. I remember the lively part which Miss Stásova, the veteran leader of the agitation, took in the Sunday schools in 1861, the friendships she and her friends made among the factory girls, the interest they manifested in the hard life of these girls outside the school, the fights they fought against their greedy employers. I recall the keen interest which the women showed, at their pedagogical courses, in the village schools, and in the work of those few who, like Baron Korff, were permitted for some time to do something in that direction, and the social spirit which permeated those courses. The rights they strove for — both the leaders and the great bulk of the women — were not only the individual right to higher instruction, but much more, far more, the right to be useful workers among the people, the masses. This is why they succeeded to such an extent.

VII

FOR the last few years the health of my father had been going from bad to worse, and when my brother Alexander and I came to see him, in the spring of 1871, we were told by the doctors that with the first frosts of autumn he would be gone. He had continued to live in the old style, in the Stáraya Konúshennaya, but around him everything in this aristocratic quarter had changed. The rich serf-owners, who once were so prominent there, had gone. After having spent in a reckless way the redemption money which they had received at the emancipation of the serfs, and after having mortgaged and remortgaged their estates in the new land banks which preyed upon their helplessness, they had withdrawn at last to the country or to provincial towns, there to sink into oblivion. Their houses had been taken by "the intruders,"—rich merchants, railway builders, and the like,—while in nearly every one of the old families which remained in the Old Equerries' Quarter a young life struggled to assert its rights upon the ruins of the old one. A couple of retired generals, who cursed the new ways, and relieved their griefs by predicting for Russia a certain and speedy ruin under the new order, or some relative occasionally dropping in, were all the company my father had now. Out of our many relatives, numbering nearly a score of families at Moscow alone in my childhood, two families only had remained in the capital, and these had joined the current of the new life, the mothers discussing with their girls and boys such matters as schools for the people and women's universities. My father looked upon them with contempt. My stepmother and my younger sister, Pauline, who had not changed, did their best to comfort him; but they themselves felt strange in their unwonted surroundings.

My father had always been unkind and most unjust toward my brother Alexander, but Alexander was utterly incapable of holding a grudge against any one. When he entered our father's sick-room, with the deep, kind look of his large blue eyes and with a smile revealing his infinite kindness, and when he immediately found out what could be done to render the sufferer more comfortable in his sick-chair, and did it as naturally as if he had left the sick-room only an hour before, my father was simply bewildered; he stared at him without being able to understand. Our visit brought life into the dull, gloomy house; the nursing became brighter; my stepmother, Pauline, the servants themselves, grew more animated, and my father felt the change.

One thing worried him, however. He had expected to see us come as repentant sons, imploring his support. But when he tried to direct conversation into that channel, we stopped him with such a cheerful " Don't bother about that; we get on very nicely," that he was still more bewildered. He looked for a scene in the old style, — his sons begging pardon — and money; perhaps he even regretted for a moment that this did not happen; but he regarded us with a greater esteem. We were all three affected at parting. He seemed almost to dread returning to his gloomy loneliness amidst the wreckage of a system he had lived to maintain. But Alexander had to go back to his service, and I was leaving for Finland.

When I was called home again from Finland, I hurried to Moscow, to find the burial ceremony just beginning, in that same old red church where my father had been baptized, and where the last prayers had been said over his mother. As the funeral procession passed along the streets, of which every house was so familiar to me in my child-hood, I noticed that the houses had changed little, but I knew that in all of them a new life had begun.

In the house which had formerly belonged to my father's mother and then to Princess Mírski, and which now was the property of General N——, an old inhabitant of the quarter, the only daughter of the family maintained for a couple of years a painful struggle against her good-natured but obstinate parents, who worshiped her, but would not allow her to study at the university courses which had been opened for ladies at Moscow. At last she was allowed to join these courses, but was taken to them in an elegant carriage, under the close supervision of her mother, who courageously sat for hours on the benches amongst the students, by the side of her beloved daughter; and yet, notwithstanding all this care and watchfulness, a couple of years later the daughter joined the revolutionary party, was arrested, and spent one year in the fortress of St. Peter and St. Paul.

In the house opposite, the despotic heads of the family, Count and Countess Z——, were in a bitter struggle against their two daughters, who were sick of the idle and useless existence their parents forced them to lead, and wanted to join those other girls who, free and happy, flocked to the university courses. The struggle lasted for years; the parents did not yield in this case, and the result was that the elder girl ended her life by poisoning herself, whereupon her younger sister was allowed to follow her own inclinations.

In the house next door, which had been our family residence for a year, when I entered it with Tchaykóvsky to hold in it the first secret meeting of a circle which we founded at Moscow, I at once recognized the rooms which had been so familiar to me in such a different atmosphere in my childhood. It now belonged to the family of Nathalie Armfeld,—that highly sympathetic Kará "convict," whom George Kennan has so touchingly described in his book on Siberia. And in a house within a stone's throw of that in which my father had died, and only a few months after his death, I received Stepniák, clothed as a peasant, he having escaped from a country village where he had been arrested for spreading socialist ideas among the peasants.

Such were the changes which the Old Equerries' Quarter had undergone within the last fifteen years. The last stronghold of the old nobility was now invaded by the new spirit.

VIII

THE next year, early in the spring, I made my first journey to Western Europe. In crossing the Russian frontier, I experienced what every Russian feels on leaving his mother country. So long as the train runs on Russian ground, through the thinly populated northwestern provinces, one has the feeling of crossing a desert. Hundreds of miles are covered with low growths which hardly deserve the name of forests. Here and there the eye discovers a small, miserably poor village buried in the snow, or an impracticable, muddy, narrow, and winding village road. Then everything — scenery and surroundings — changes all of a sudden, as soon as the train enters Prussia, with its clean-looking villages and farms, its gardens, and its paved roads; and the sense of contrast grows stronger and stronger as one penetrates further into Germany. Even dull Berlin seemed animated, after our Russian towns.

And the contrast of climate! Two days before, I had left St. Petersburg thickly covered with snow, and now, in middle Germany, I walked without an overcoat along the railway platform, in warm sunshine, admiring the budding flowers. Then came the Rhine, and further on Switzerland bathed in the rays of a bright sun, with its small, clean hotels, where breakfast was served out of doors, in view of the snow-clad mountains. I never before had realized so vividly what Russia's northern position meant, and how the history of the Russian nation had been influenced by the fact that the main centres of its life had to develop in high latitudes, as far north as the shores of the Gulf of Finland. Only then I fully understood the uncontrollable attraction which southern lands have exercised on the Russians, the colossal efforts which they have made to reach the Black Sea, and the steady pressure of the Siberian colonists southward, further into Manchuria.

At that time Zürich was full of Russian students, both women and men. The famous Oberstrass, near the Polytechnic, was a corner of Russia, where the Russian language prevailed over all others. The students lived as most Russian students do, especially the women; that is, upon very little. Tea and bread, some milk, and a thin slice of meat cooked over a spirit lamp, amidst animated discussions of the latest news from the socialistic world or the last book read, — that was their regular fare. Those who had more money than was needed for such a mode of living gave it for the common cause, — the library, the Russian review which was going to be published, the support of the Swiss labor papers. As to their dress, the most parsimonious economy reigned in that direction. Púshkin has written in a well-known verse, "What hat may not suit a girl of sixteen?" Our girls at Zürich seemed defiantly to throw this question at the population of the old Zwinglian city: "Can there be a simplicity in dress which does not become a girl, when she is young, intelligent, and full of energy?"

With all this, the busy little community worked harder than any other students have ever worked since there were universities in existence, and the Zürich professors were never tired of showing the progress accomplished by the women at the university, as an example to the male students.

For many years I had longed to learn all about the International Workingmen's Association. Russian papers mentioned it pretty frequently in their columns, but they were not allowed to speak of its principles or of what it was doing. I felt that it must be a great movement, full of consequences, but I could not grasp its aims and tendencies. Now that I was in Switzerland, I determined to satisfy my longings.

The association was then at the height of its development. Great hopes had been awakened in the years 1840–48 in the hearts of European workers. Only now we begin to realize what a formidable amount of socialist literature was circulated in those years by socialists of all denominations, — Christian socialists, state socialists, Fourierists, Saint-Simonists, Owenites, and so on; and only now we begin to understand the depth of this movement, as we discover how much of what our generation has considered the product of contemporary thought was already developed and said — often with great penetration — during those years. The republicans understood then under the name of " republic " a quite different thing from the democratic organization of capitalist rule which now goes under that name. When they spoke of the United States of Europe, they understood the brotherhood of workers, the weapons of war transformed into tools, and those tools used by all members of society for the benefit of all, — " the iron returned to the laborer," as Pierre Dupont said in one of his songs. They meant not only the reign of equality as regards criminal law and political rights, but particularly economic equality. The nationalists themselves saw in their dreams Young Italy, Young Germany, and Young Hungary taking the lead in far-reaching agrarian and economic reforms.

The defeat of the June insurrection at Paris, of Hungary by the armies of Nicholas I., and of Italy by the French and the Austrians, and the fearful reaction, political and intellectual, which followed everywhere in Europe, totally destroyed that movement. Its literature, its achievements, its very principles of economic revolution and universal brotherhood, were simply forgotten, lost, during the next twenty years.

However, one idea had survived, — the idea of an international brotherhood of all workers, which a few French emigrants continued to preach in the United States, and the followers of Robert Owen in England. The understanding which was reached by some English workers and a few French workers' delegates to the London International Exhibition of 1862 became the starting-point for a formidable movement, which soon spread all over Europe, and included several million workers. The hopes which had been dormant for twenty years were awakened once more, when the workers were called upon to unite, "without distinction of creed, sex, nationality, race, or color," to proclaim that "the emancipation of the workers must be their own work," and to throw the weight of a strong, united, international organization into the evolution of mankind, — not in the name of love and charity, but in the name of justice, of the force that belongs to a body of men moved by a reasoned consciousness of their own aims and aspirations.

Two strikes at Paris, in 1868 and 1869, more or less helped by small contributions sent from abroad, especially from England, insignificant though they were in themselves, and the prosecutions which the French imperial government directed against the International, became the origin of an immense movement in which the solidarity of the workers of all nations was proclaimed in the face of the rivalries of the states. The idea of an international union of all trades, and of a struggle against capital with the aid of international support, carried away the most indifferent of the workers. The movement spread like wildfire in France, Italy, and Spain, bringing to the front a great number of intelligent, active, and devoted workers, and attracting to it a few decidedly superior men and women from the wealthier educated classes. A force, never before suspected to exist, grew stronger every day in Europe; and if the movement had not been arrested in its growth by the Franco-German war, great things would probably have happened in Europe, deeply modifying the aspects of our civilization, and undoubtedly accelerating human progress; but the crushing victory of the Germans brought about abnormal conditions; it stopped for a quarter of a century the normal development of France, and threw all Europe into the period of militarism in which we are living at the present time.

All sorts of partial solutions of the great social question had currency at that time among the workers: coöperation, productive associations supported by the state, people's banks, gratuitous credit, and so on. Each of these solutions was brought before the "sections" of the association, and then before the local, regional, national, and international congresses, and eagerly discussed. Every annual congress of the association marked a new step in advance, in the development of ideas about the great social problem which stands before our generation and calls for a solution. The amount of intelligent things which were said at these congresses, and of scientifically correct, deeply thought over ideas which were circulated, — all being the results of the *collective* thought of the workers, — has never yet been sufficiently appreciated; but there is no exaggeration in saying that all schemes of social reconstruction which are now in vogue under the name of "scientific socialism" or "anarchism" had their origin in the discussions and reports of the different congresses of the International Association. The few educated men who joined the movement have only put into a theoretical shape the criticisms and the aspirations which were expressed in the sections, and subsequently in the congresses, by the workers themselves.

The war of 1870–71 had hampered the development of the association, but had not stopped it. In all the industrial centres of Switzerland numerous and animated sec-

tions of the International existed, and thousands of workers
flocked to their meetings, at which war was declared upon
the existing system of private ownership of land and factories, and the near end of the capitalist system was proclaimed. Local congresses were held in various parts of
the country, and at each of these gatherings the most ardu-
ous and difficult problems of the present social organization
were discussed, with a knowledge of the matter and a depth
of conception which alarmed the middle classes even more
than did the numbers of adherents who joined the sections,
or groups, of the International. The jealousies and prejudices which had hitherto existed in Switzerland between
the privileged trades (the watchmakers and the jewelers)
and the rougher trades (weavers, and so on), and which had
prevented joint action in labor disputes, were disappearing.
The workers asserted with increasing emphasis that, of all
the divisions which exist in modern society, by far the most
important is that between the owners of capital and those
who come into the world penniless, and are doomed to remain producers of wealth for the favored few.

Italy, especially middle and northern Italy, was honeycombed with groups and sections of the International; and
in these the Italian unity so long struggled for was declared
a mere illusion. The workers were called upon to make
their own revolution, — to take the land for the peasants
and the factories for the workers themselves, and to abolish
the oppressive centralized organization of the state, whose
historical mission always was to protect and to maintain
the exploitation of man by man.

In Spain, similar organizations covered Catalonia, Valen-
cia, and Andalusia; they were supported by, and united
with, the powerful labor unions of Barcelona, which had
already introduced the eight hours' day in the building
trades. The International had no less than eighty thousand regularly paying Spanish members; it embodied all

the active and thinking elements of the population ; and by its distinct refusal to meddle with the political intrigues during 1871–72 it had drawn to itself in a very high degree the sympathies of the masses.   The proceedings of its provincial and national congresses, and the manifestoes which they issued, were models of a severe logical criticism of the existing conditions, as well as admirably lucid statements of the workers' ideals.

In Belgium, Holland, and even in Portugal, the same movement was spreading, and it had already brought into the association the great mass and the best elements of the Belgian coal miners and weavers.   In England, the always conservative trade unions had also joined the movement, at least in principle, and, without committing themselves to socialism, were ready to support their Continental brethren in direct struggles against capital, especially in strikes.   In Germany, the socialists had concluded a union with the rather numerous followers of Lassalle, and the first foundations of a social democratic party had been laid.   Austria and Hungary followed in the same track ; and although no international organization was possible at that time in France, after the defeat of the Commune and the reaction which followed (Draconic laws having been enacted against the adherents of the association), every one was persuaded, nevertheless, that this period of reaction would not last, and that France would soon join the association again and take the lead in it.

When I came to Zürich, I joined one of the local sections of the International Workingmen's Association.   I also asked my Russian friends where I could learn more about the great movement which was going on in other countries.   "Read," was their reply, and my sister-in-law, who was then studying at Zürich, brought me large numbers of books and collections of newspapers for the last two years.   I spent days and nights in reading, and received a deep impression which nothing will efface; the flood of new thoughts awakened is associated in my mind with a tiny clean room in the Oberstrass, commanding from a window a view of the blue lake, with the mountains beyond it, where the Swiss fought for their independence, and the high spires of the old town, — that scene of so many religious struggles.

Socialistic literature has never been rich in books. It is written for workers, for whom one penny is money, and its main force lies in its small pamphlets and its newspapers. Moreover, he who seeks for information about socialism finds in books little of what he requires most. They contain the theories or the scientific arguments in favor of socialist aspirations, but they give no idea how the workers accept socialist ideals, and how the latter could be put into practice. There remains nothing but to take collections of papers and read them all through, — the news as well as the leading articles, the former perhaps even more than the latter. Quite a new world of social relations and methods of thought and action is revealed by this reading, which gives an insight into what cannot be found anywhere else, — namely, the depth and the moral force of the movement, the degree to which men are imbued with the new theories, their readiness to carry them out in their daily life and to suffer for them. All discussions about the impracticability of socialism and the necessary slowness of evolution are of little value, because the speed of evolution can only be judged from a close knowledge of the human beings of whose evolution we are speaking. What estimate of a sum can be made without knowing its components ?

The more I read, the more I saw that there was before me a new world, unknown to me, and totally unknown to the learned makers of sociological theories, — a world that I could know only by living in the Workingmen's Association and by meeting the workers in their every-day life. I decided, accordingly, to spend a couple of months in such a life. My Russian friends encouraged me, and after a few days' stay at Zürich I left for Geneva, which was then a great centre of the international movement.

The place where the Geneva sections used to meet was the spacious Masonic Temple Unique. More than two thousand men could come together in its large hall, at the general meetings, while every evening all sorts of committee and section meetings took place in the side rooms, or classes in history, physics, engineering, and so on were held. Free instruction was given there to the workers by the few, very few, middle-class men who had joined the movement, mainly French refugees of the Paris Commune. It was a people's university as well as a people's forum.

One of the chief leaders of the movement at the Temple Unique was a Russian, Nicholas Ootin, — a bright, clever, and active man; and the real soul of it was a most sympathetic Russian lady, who was known far and wide amongst the workers as Madame Olga. She was the working force in all the committees. Both Ootin and Madame Olga received me cordially, made me acquainted with all the men of mark in the sections of the different trades, and invited me to be present at the committee meetings. So I went, but I preferred being with the workers themselves. Taking a glass of sour wine at one of the tables in the hall, I used to sit there every evening amid the workers, and soon became friendly with several of them, especially with a stone-mason from Alsace, who had left France after the insurrection of the Commune. He had children, just about the age of the two whom my brother had so suddenly lost a few months before, and through the children I was soon on good terms with the family and their friends. I could thus follow the movement from the inside, and know the workers' view of it.

The workers had built all their hopes on the international movement. Young and old flocked to the Temple Unique after their long day's work, to get hold of the scraps of instruction which they could obtain there, or to listen to the speakers who promised them a grand future, based upon the common possession of all that man requires for the production of wealth, and upon a brotherhood of men, without distinction of caste, race, or nationality. All hoped that a great social revolution, peaceful or not, would soon come and totally change the economic conditions. No one desired class war, but all said that if the ruling classes rendered it unavoidable through their blind obstinacy, the war must be fought, provided it would bring with it well-being and liberty to the downtrodden masses.

One must have lived among the workers at that time to realize the effect which the sudden growth of the association had upon their minds,—the trust they put in it, the love with which they spoke of it, the sacrifices they made for it. Every day, week after week and year after year, thousands of workers gave their time and their money, even went hungry, in order to support the life of each group, to secure the appearance of the papers, to defray the expenses of the congresses, to support the comrades who had suffered for the association, — nay, even to be present at the meetings and the manifestations. Another thing that impressed me deeply was the elevating influence which the International exercised. Most of the Paris Internationalists were almost total abstainers from drink, and all had abandoned smoking. "Why should I nurture in myself that weakness?" they said. The mean, the trivial disappeared to leave room for the grand, the elevating inspirations.

Outsiders never realize the sacrifices which are made by the workers in order to keep their labor movements alive. No small amount of moral courage was required to join openly a section of the International Association, and to

face the discontent of the master and a probable dismissal
at the first opportunity, with the long months out of work
which usually followed.   But even under the best circumstances, belonging to a trade union, or to any advanced
party, requires a series of uninterrupted sacrifices.   Even
a few pence given for the common cause represent a burden
on the meagre budget of the European worker, and many
pence had to be disbursed every week.   Frequent attendance at the meetings means a sacrifice, too.   For us it may
be a pleasure to spend a couple of hours at a meeting, but
for men whose working day begins at five or six in the
morning those hours have to be stolen from necessary rest.

I felt this devotion as a standing reproach.   I saw how
eager the workers were to gain instruction, and despairingly
few were those who volunteered to aid them.   I saw how
much the toiling masses needed to be helped by men possessed of education and leisure, in their endeavors to spread
and to develop the organization ; but few were those who
came to assist without the intention of making political
capital out of this very helplessness of the people !   More
and more I began to feel that I was bound to cast in my
lot with them.   Stepniák says, in his "Career of a Nihilist,"
that every revolutionist has had a moment in his life when
some circumstance, maybe unimportant in itself, has brought
him to pronounce his oath of giving himself to the cause of
revolution.   I know that moment; I lived through it after
one of the meetings at the Temple Unique, when I felt
more acutely than ever before how cowardly are the educated men who hesitate to put their education, their knowledge, their energy, at the service of those who are so much
in need of that education and that energy.   "Here are
men," I said to myself, "who are conscious of their servitude, who work to get rid of it ; but where are the helpers ?
Where are those who will come to serve the masses — not
to utilize them for their own ambitions ? "

Gradually, however, some doubts began to creep into my mind as to the soundness of the agitation which was carried on at the Temple Unique. One night, a well-known Geneva lawyer, Monsieur A., came to the meeting, and stated that if he had not hitherto joined the association, it was because he had first to settle his own business affairs; having now succeeded in that direction, he came to join the labor movement. I felt shocked at this cynical avowal, and when I communicated my reflections to my stone-mason friend, he explained to me that this gentleman, having been defeated at the previous election, when he sought the support of the radical party, now hoped to be elected by the support of the labor vote. "We accept their services for the present," my friend concluded, "but when the revolution comes, our first move will be to throw all of them overboard."

Then came a great meeting, hastily convoked, to protest, as it was said, against "the calumnies" of the "Journal de Genève." This organ of the moneyed classes of Geneva had ventured to suggest that mischief was brewing at the Temple Unique, and that the building trades were going once more to make a general strike, such as they had made in 1869. The leaders at the Temple Unique called the meeting. Thousands of workers filled the hall, and Ootin asked them to pass a resolution, the wording of which seemed to me very strange, — an indignant protest was expressed in it against the inoffensive suggestion that the workers were going to strike. "Why should this suggestion be described as a calumny?" I asked myself. "Is it then a crime to strike?" Ootin concluded a hurried speech with the words, "If you agree, citizens, to this resolution, I will send it at once to the press." He was going to leave the platform, when somebody in the hall suggested that discussion would not be out of place; and then the representatives of all branches of the building trades stood up in succession, saying that the wages had lately been so low that they could hardly live upon them; that with the opening of the spring there was plenty of work in view, of which they intended to take advantage to increase their wages; and that if an increase were refused they intended to begin a general strike.

I was furious, and next day hotly reproached Ootin for his behavior. "As a leader," I told him, "you were bound to know that a strike had really been spoken of." In my innocence I did not suspect the real motives of the leaders, and it was Ootin himself who made me understand that a strike at that time would be disastrous for the election of the lawyer, Monsieur A.

I could not reconcile this wire-pulling by the leaders with the burning speeches I had heard them pronounce from the platform. I felt disheartened, and spoke to Ootin of my intention to make myself acquainted with the other section of the International Association at Geneva, which was known as the Bakúnists; the name "anarchist" was not much in use then. Ootin gave me at once a word of introduction to another Russian, Nicholas Joukóvsky, who belonged to that section, and, looking straight into my face, he added, with a sigh, "Well, you won't return to us; you will remain with them." He had guessed right.

IX

I WENT first to Neuchâtel, and then spent a week or so among the watchmakers in the Jura Mountains. I thus made my first acquaintance with that famous Jura Federation which for the next few years played an important part in the development of socialism, introducing into it the no-government, or anarchist, tendency.

In 1872 the Jura Federation was becoming a rebel against the authority of the general council of the International Workingmen's Association. The association was essentially a workingmen's movement, the workers understanding it as such and not as a political party. In east Belgium, for instance, they had introduced into the statutes a clause in virtue of which no one could be a member of a section unless employed in a manual trade; even foremen were excluded.

The workers were, moreover, federalist in principle. Each nation, each separate region, and even each local section had to be left free to develop on its own lines. But the middle-class revolutionists of the old school who had entered the International, imbued as they were with the notions of the centralized, pyramidal secret organizations of earlier times, had introduced the same notions into the Workingmen's Association. Beside the federal and national councils, a general council was nominated at London, to act as a sort of intermediary between the councils of the different nations. Marx and Engels were its leading spirits. It soon appeared, however, that the mere fact of having such a central body became a source of substantial inconvenience. The general council was not satisfied with playing the part of a correspondence bureau; it strove to govern the movement, to approve or to censure the action of the local federations and sections, and even of individual members. When the Commune insurrection began in Paris, — and "the leaders had only to follow," without being able to say whereto they would be led within the next twenty-four hours, — the general council insisted upon directing the insurrection from London. It required daily reports about the events, gave orders, favored this and hampered that, and thus put in evidence the disadvantage of having a governing body, even within the association. The disadvantage became still more evident when, at a secret conference held in 1871, the general council, supported by a few delegates, decided to direct the forces of the association toward electoral agitation. It set people thinking about the evils of any government, however democratic its origin. This was the first spark of anarchism. The Jura Federation became the centre of opposition to the general council.

The separation between leaders and workers which I had noticed at Geneva in the Temple Unique did not exist in the Jura Mountains. There were a number of men who were more intelligent, and especially more active than the others; but that was all. James Guillaume, one of the most intelligent and broadly educated men I ever met, was a proof-reader and the manager of a small printing-office. His earnings in this capacity were so small that he had to give his nights to translating novels from German into French, for which he was paid eight francs — one dollar and sixty cents — for sixteen pages !

When I came to Neuchâtel, he told me that unfortunately he could not give even as much as a couple of hours for a friendly chat. The printing-office was just issuing that afternoon the first number of a local paper, and in addition to his usual duties of proof-reader and co-editor, he had to write the addresses of a thousand persons to whom the first three numbers were to be sent, and to put on the wrappers himself.

I offered to aid him in writing the addresses, but that was not practicable because they were either kept in memory, or written on scraps of paper in an unreadable hand. " Well, then," said I, " I will come in the afternoon to the office and put on the wrappers, and you will give me the time which you may thus save."

We understood each other. Guillaume warmly shook my hand, and that was the beginning of a standing friendship. We spent all the afternoon in the office, he writing the addresses, I fastening the wrappers, and a French communard, who was a compositor, chatting with us all the while as he rapidly set up a novel, intermingling his conversation with the sentences which he was putting in type and which he read aloud.

" The fight in the streets," he would say, " became very sharp " . . . " Dear Mary, I love you " . . . " The workers were furious and fought like lions at Montmartre " . . . "and he fell on his knees before her " . . . "and that lasted for four days. We knew that Gallifet was shooting all prisoners, — the more terrible still was the fight," — and so on he went, rapidly lifting the type from the case.

It was late in the evening when Guillaume took off his working blouse, and we went out for a friendly chat for a couple of hours ; then he had to resume his work as editor of the " Bulletin " of the Jura Federation.

At Neuchâtel I also made the acquaintance of Malon. He was born in a village, and in his childhood he was a shepherd. Later on, he came to Paris, learned there a trade, — basket-making, — and, like the bookbinder Varlin and the carpenter Pindy, with whom he was associated in the International, had come to be widely known as one of the leaders of the Association when it was prosecuted in 1869 by Napoleon III. All three had quite won the hearts of the Paris workers, and when the Commune insurrection broke out, they were elected members of the Council of the Commune, each receiving a large vote. Malon was also mayor of one of the Paris *arrondissements*. Now, in Switzerland, he earned his living as a basket-maker. He had rented for a few coppers a month a small open shed, out of town, on the slope of a hill, from which he enjoyed, while at work, an extensive view of the lake of Neuchâtel. At night he wrote letters, a book on the Commune, short articles for the labor papers, and thus he became a writer.

Every day I went to see him, and to hear what the broad-faced, laborious, slightly poetical, quiet, and most good-hearted communard had to tell me about the insurrection in which he took a prominent part, and which he had just described in a book, "The Third Defeat of the French Proletariat."

One morning, as I had climbed the hill and reached his shed, he met me, quite radiant, with the words: "Do you know, Pindy is alive! Here is a letter from him: he is in Switzerland." Nothing had been heard of Pindy since he was seen last on the 25th or 26th of May at the Tuileries, and he was supposed to be dead, while in reality he had remained in concealment in Paris. And while Malon's fingers continued to ply the wickers and to shape them into an elegant basket, he told me in his quiet voice, which only slightly trembled at times, how many men had been shot by the Versailles troops on the supposition that they were Pindy, Varlin, himself, or some other leader. He told me what he knew of the deaths of Varlin — the bookbinder, whom the Paris workers worshiped — and old Delécluze, who did not want to survive that new defeat, and many others; and he related the horrors which he had witnessed during that carnival of blood with which the wealthy classes of Paris celebrated their return to the capital, and then the spirit of retaliation which took hold of a crowd of people, led by Raoul Rigault, which executed the hostages of the Commune.

His lips quivered when he spoke of the heroism of the children; and he quite broke down when he told me the story of that boy whom the Versailles troops were about to shoot, and who asked the officer's permission to hand first a silver watch, which he had on, to his mother, who lived close by. The officer, yielding to an impulse of pity, let the boy go, probably hoping that he would never return. But a quarter of an hour later the boy came back, and, taking his place amidst the corpses at the wall, said: "I am ready." Twelve bullets put an end to his young life.

I think I never suffered so much as when I read that terrible book, "Le Livre Rouge de la Justice Rurale," which contained nothing but extracts from the letters of the "Standard," "Daily Telegraph," and "Times" correspondents, written from Paris during the last days of May, 1871, relating the horrors committed by the Versailles army, under Gallifet, with a few quotations from the Paris "Figaro," imbued with a bloodthirsty spirit toward the insurgents. I was seized with a profound despair of mankind as I read these pages, and I should have retained that despair, had I not seen afterward, in those of the defeated party who had lived through all these horrors, that absence of hatred, that confidence in the final triumph of their ideas, that calm though sad gaze directed toward the future, and that readiness to forget the nightmare of the past, which struck one in Malon, and, in fact, in nearly all the refugees of the Commune whom I met at Geneva, — and which I still see in Louise Michel, Lefrançais, Elisée Reclus, and other friends.

From Neuchâtel I went to Sonvilliers. In a little valley in the Jura hills there is a succession of small towns and

villages, of which the French-speaking population was at
that time entirely employed in the various branches of
watchmaking; whole families used to work in small workshops.   In one of them I found another leader, Adhémar
Schwitzguébel, with whom, also, I afterward became very
closely connected.   He sat among a dozen young men who
were engraving lids of gold and silver watches.   I was
asked to take a seat on a bench, or table, and soon we were
all engaged in a lively conversation upon socialism, government or no government, and the coming congresses.

In the evening a heavy snowstorm raged ; it blinded us
and froze the blood in our veins, as we struggled to the
next village.   But, notwithstanding the storm, about fifty
watchmakers, chiefly old people, came from the neighboring
towns and villages, — some of them as far as seven miles
distant, — to join a small informal meeting that was called
for that evening.

The very organization of the watch trade, which permits
men to know one another thoroughly and to work in their
own houses, where they are free to talk, explains why the
level of intellectual development in this population is higher
than that of workers who spend all their life from early
childhood in the factories.   There is more independence
and more originality among the petty trades' workers.   But
the absence of a division between the leaders and the masses
in the Jura Federation was also the reason why there was
not a question upon which every member of the federation
would not strive to form his own independent opinion.
Here I saw that the workers were not a mass that was
being led and made subservient to the political ends of a few
men; their leaders were simply their more active comrades, —
initiators rather than leaders.   The clearness of insight, the
soundness of judgment, the capacity for disentangling complex social questions, which I noticed amongst these workers, especially the middle-aged ones, deeply impressed me;

and I am firmly persuaded that if the Jura Federation has played a prominent part in the development of socialism, it is not only on account of the importance of the no-government and federalist ideas of which it was the champion, but also on account of the expression which was given to these ideas by the good sense of the Jura watchmakers. Without their aid, these conceptions might have remained mere abstractions for a long time.

The theoretical aspects of anarchism, as they were then beginning to be expressed in the Jura Federation, especially by Bakúnin; the criticisms of state socialism — the fear of an economic despotism, far more dangerous than the merely political despotism — which I heard formulated there; and the revolutionary character of the agitation, appealed strongly to 'my mind. But the equalitarian relations which I found in the Jura Mountains, the independence of thought and expression which I saw developing in the workers, and their unlimited devotion to the cause appealed far more strongly to my feelings; and when I came away from the mountains, after a week's stay with the watchmakers, my views upon socialism were settled. I was an anarchist.

A subsequent journey to Belgium, where I could compare once more the centralized political agitation at Brussels with the economic and independent agitation that was going on amongst the clothiers at Verviers, only strengthened my views. These clothiers were one of the most sympathetic populations that I have ever met with in Western Europe.

X

BAKÚNIN was at that time at Locarno. I did not see him, and now regret it very much, because he was dead when I returned four years later to Switzerland. It was he who had helped the Jura friends to clear up their ideas and to formulate their aspirations; he who had inspired them with his powerful, burning, irresistible revolutionary enthusiasm. As soon as he saw that a small newspaper, which Guillaume began to edit in the Jura hills (at Locle) was sounding a new note of independent thought in the socialist movement, he came to Locle, talked for whole days and whole nights also to his new friends about the historical necessity of a new move in the direction of anarchy; he wrote for that paper a series of profound and brilliant articles on the historical progress of mankind towards freedom; he infused enthusiasm into his new friends, and he created that centre of propaganda, from which anarchism spread later on to other parts of Europe.

After he had moved to Locarno, — whence he started a similar movement in Italy, and, through his sympathetic and gifted emissary, Fanelli, also in Spain, — the work that he had begun in the Jura hills was continued independently by the Jurassians themselves. The name of "Michel" often recurred in their conversations, — not, however, as that of an absent chief whose opinions were law, but as that of a personal friend of whom every one spoke with love, in a spirit of comradeship. What struck me most was that Bakúnin's influence was felt much less as the influence of an intellectual authority than as the influence of a moral personality. In conversations about

anarchism, or about the attitude of the federation, I never
heard it said, "Bakúnin says so," or "Bakúnin thinks so," as
if it settled the question. His writings and his sayings were
not regarded as laws, — as is unfortunately often the case in
political parties. In all such matters, in which intellect is
the supreme judge, every one in discussion used his own
arguments. Their general drift and tenor might have been
suggested by Bakúnin, or Bakúnin might have borrowed
them from his Jura friends; at any rate, in each individual the arguments retained their own individual character.
I only once heard Bakúnin's name invoked as an authority
in itself, and that impressed me so deeply that I even now
remember the spot where the conversation took place and
all the surroundings. Some young men were indulging in
talk that was not very respectful toward the other sex,
when one of the women who were present put a sudden
stop to it by exclaiming : " Pity that Michel is not here :
he would put you in your place ! " The colossal figure of
the revolutionist who had given up everything for the sake
of the revolution, and lived for it alone, borrowing from
his conception of it the highest and the purest views of
life, continued to inspire them.

I returned from this journey with distinct sociological
ideas which I have retained since, doing my best to develop
them in more and more definite, concrete forms.

There was, however, one point which I did not accept
without having given to it a great deal of thinking and
many hours of my nights. I clearly saw that the immense
change which would deliver everything that is necessary
for life and production into the hands of society — be it the
Folk State of the social democrats or the unions of freely
associated groups, which the anarchists advocate — would
imply a revolution far more profound than any of the revolutions which history had on record. Moreover, in such

a revolution the workers would have against them, not the rotten generation of aristocrats against whom the French peasants and republicans had to fight in the last century, — and even that fight was a desperate one, — but the middle classes, which are far more powerful, intellectually and physically, and have at their service all the potent machinery of the modern state. However, I soon noticed that no revolution, whether peaceful or violent, had ever taken place without the new ideals having deeply penetrated into the very class whose economical and political privileges were to be assailed. I had witnessed the abolition of serfdom in Russia, and I knew that if a consciousness of the injustice of their privileges had not spread widely within the serf-owners' class itself (as a consequence of the previous evolution and revolutions accomplished in Western Europe), the emancipation of the serfs would never have been accomplished as easily as it was accomplisned in 1861. And I saw that the idea of emancipating the workers from the present wage-system was making headway amongst the middle classes themselves. The most ardent defenders of the present economical conditions had already abandoned the idea of *right* in defending their present privileges, — questions as to the *opportuneness* of such a change having already taken its place. They did not deny the desirability of some such change, they only asked whether the new economical organization advocated by the socialists would really be better than the present one; whether a society in which the workers would have a dominant voice would be able to manage production better than the individual capitalists actuated by mere considerations of self-interest manage it at the present time.

Besides, I began gradually to understand that revolutions — that is, periods of accelerated rapid evolution and rapid changes — are as much in the nature of human society as the slow evolution which incessantly goes on now among the civilized races of mankind. And each time that such a period of accelerated evolution and reconstruction on a grand scale begins, civil war is liable to break out on a small or large scale. The question is, then, not so much how to avoid revolutions, as how to attain the greatest results with the most limited amount of civil war, the smallest number of victims, and a minimum of mutual embitterment. For that end there is only one means; namely, that the oppressed part of society should obtain the clearest possible conception of what they intend to achieve, and how, and that they should be imbued with the enthusiasm which is necessary for that achievement; in that case they will be sure to attach to their cause the best and the freshest intellectual forces of the privileged class.

The Commune of Paris was a terrible example of an outbreak with insufficiently determined ideals. When the workers became, in March, 1871, the masters of the great city, they did not attack the property rights vested in the middle classes. On the contrary, they took these rights under their protection. The leaders of the Commune covered the National Bank with their bodies, and notwithstanding the crisis which had paralyzed industry and the consequent absence of earnings for a mass of workers, they protected the rights of the owners of the factories, the trade establishments, and the dwelling-houses at Paris with their decrees. However, when the movement was crushed, no account was taken by the middle classes of the modesty of the communalistic claims of the insurgents. Having lived for two months in fear that the workers would make an assault upon their property rights, the rich men of France took upon them just the same revenge as if they had made the assault in reality. Nearly thirty thousand of them were slaughtered, as is known, — not in battle, but after they had lost the battle. If they had taken steps towards the socialization of property, the revenge could not have been more terrible.

If, then, — my conclusion was, — there are periods in human development when a conflict is unavoidable, and civil war breaks out quite independently of the will of particular individuals, — let, at least, these conflicts take place, not on the ground of vague aspirations, but upon definite issues; not upon secondary points, the insignificance of which does not diminish the violence of the conflict, but upon broad ideas which inspire men by the grandness of the horizon which they bring into view.   In this last case the conflict itself will depend much less upon the efficacy of firearms and guns than upon the force of the creative genius which will be brought into action in the work of reconstruction of Society.   It will depend chiefly upon the constructive forces of Society taking for the moment a free course; upon the inspirations being of a higher standard and so winning more sympathy even from those who, as a class, are opposed to the change.   The conflict, being thus engaged on larger issues, will purify the social atmosphere itself, and the numbers of victims on both sides will certainly be much smaller than if the fight is over matters of secondary importance in which the lower instincts of men find a free play.

With these ideas I returned to Russia.

XI

DURING my journey I had bought a number of books and collections of socialist newspapers. In Russia, such books were "unconditionally prohibited" by censorship; and some of the collections of newspapers and reports of international congresses could not be bought for any amount of money, even in Belgium. "Shall I part with them, while my brother and my friends would be so glad to have them at St. Petersburg?" I asked myself; and I decided that by all means I must get them into Russia.

I returned to St. Petersburg via Vienna and Warsaw. Thousands of Jews live by smuggling on the Polish frontier, and I thought that if I could succeed in discovering only one of them, my books would be carried in safety across the border. However, to alight at a small railway station near the frontier, while every other passenger went on, and to hunt there for smugglers, would hardly have been reasonable; so I took a side branch of the railway and went to Cracow. "The capital of old Poland is near to the frontier," I thought, "and I shall find there some Jew who will lead me to the men I seek."

I reached the once renowned and brilliant city in the evening, and early next morning went out from the hotel on my search. To my bewilderment I saw, however, at every street corner and wherever I turned my eyes in the otherwise deserted market-place, a Jew, wearing the traditional long dress and locks of his forefathers, and watching there for some Polish nobleman or tradesman who might send him on an errand and pay him a few coppers for the service. I wanted to find *one* Jew; and now there were

too many of them. Whom should I approach? I made
the round of the town, and then, in my despair, I decided
to accost the Jew who stood at the entrance gate of my
hotel, — an immense old palace, of which, in former days,
every hall was filled with elegant crowds of gayly dressed
dancers, but which now fulfilled the more prosaic function
of giving food and shelter to a few occasional travelers. I
explained to the man my desire of smuggling into Russia a
rather heavy bundle of books and newspapers.

"Very easily done, sir," he replied. "I will just bring
to you the representative of the Universal Company for the
International Exchange of (let me say) Rags and Bones.
They carry on the largest smuggling business in the world,
and he is sure to oblige you." Half an hour later he really
returned with the representative of the company, — a most
elegant young man, who spoke in perfection Russian, German, and Polish.

He looked at my bundle, weighed it with his hands, and
asked what sort of books were in it.

"All severely prohibited by Russian censorship: that is
why they must be smuggled in."

"Books," he said, "are not exactly in our line of trade;
our business lies in costly silks. If I were going to pay my
men by weight, according to our silk tariff, I should have
to ask you a quite extravagant price. And then, to tell
the truth, I don't much like meddling with books. The
slightest mishap, and 'they' would make of it a political
affair, and then it would cost the Universal Rags and Bones
Company a tremendous sum of money to get clear of it."

I probably looked very sad, for the elegant young man
who represented the Universal Rags and Bones Company
immediately added: "Don't be troubled. He [the hotel
commissionnaire] will arrange it for you in some other
way."

"Oh, yes. There are scores of ways to arrange such a

trifle, to oblige the gentleman," jovially remarked the commissionnaire, as he left me.

In an hour's time he came back with another young man.
This one took the bundle, put it by the side of the door,
and said: "It's all right. If you leave to-morrow, you
shall have your books at such a station in Russia," and he
explained to me how it would be managed.

" How much will it cost ? " I asked.

" How much are you disposed to pay ? " was the reply.

I emptied my purse on the table, and said : " That much
for my journey. The remainder is yours. I will travel
third class ! "

" Wai, wai, wai ! " exclaimed both men at once. " What
are you saying, sir ?   Such a gentleman travel third class !
Never !   No, no, no, that won't do. . . . Five dollars will
do for us, and then one dollar or so for the commissionnaire,
if you are agreeable to it, — just as much as you like.   We
are not highway robbers, but honest tradesmen." And
they bluntly refused to take more money.

I had often heard of the honesty of the Jewish smugglers
on the frontier; but I had never expected to have such
a proof of it.   Later on, when our circle imported many
books from abroad, or still later, when so many revolutionists and refugees crossed the frontier in entering or leaving
Russia, there was not a case in which the smugglers betrayed any one, or took advantage of circumstances to exact
an exorbitant price for their services.

Next day I left Cracow; and at the designated Russian
station a porter approached my compartment, and, speaking
loudly, so as to be heard by the gendarme who was walking
along the platform, said to me, " Here is the bag your highness left the other day," and handed me my precious parcel.

I was so pleased to have it that I did not even stop at
Warsaw, but continued my journey directly to St. Petersburg, to show my trophies to my brother.

XII

A FORMIDABLE movement was developing in the meantime amongst the educated youth of Russia. Serfdom was
abolished. But quite a network of habits and customs of
domestic slavery, of utter disregard of human individuality,
of despotism on the part of the fathers, and of hypocritical
submission on that of the wives, the sons, and the daughters, had developed during the two hundred and fifty years
that serfdom had existed. Everywhere in Europe, at the
beginning of this century, there was a great deal of domestic
despotism, — the writings of Thackeray and Dickens bear
ample testimony to it; but nowhere else had that tyranny
attained such a luxurious development as in Russia. All
Russian life, in the family, in the relations between commander and subordinate, military chief and soldier, employer
and employee, bore the stamp of it. Quite a world of customs and manners of thinking, of prejudices and moral
cowardice, of habits bred by a lazy existence, had grown up.
Even the best men of the time paid a large tribute to these
products of the serfdom period.

Law could have no grip upon these things. Only a vigorous social movement, which would attack the very roots
of the evil, could reform the habits and customs of every-
day life; and in Russia this movement — this revolt of the
individual — took a far more powerful character, and became far more sweeping in its criticisms, than anywhere in
Western Europe or America. "Nihilism" was the name
that Turguéneff gave it in his epoch-making novel, "Fathers
and Sons."

The movement is misunderstood in Western Europe. In

the press, for example, nihilism is continually confused with terrorism. The revolutionary disturbance which broke out in Russia toward the close of the reign of Alexander II., and ended in the tragical death of the Tsar, is constantly described as nihilism. This is, however, a mistake. To confuse nihilism with terrorism is as wrong as to confuse a philosophical movement like stoicism or positivism with a political movement such as, for example, republicanism. Terrorism was called into existence by certain special conditions of the political struggle at a given historical moment. It has lived, and has died. It may revive and die out again. But nihilism has impressed its stamp upon the whole of the life of the educated classes of Russia, and that stamp will be retained for many years to come. It is nihilism, divested of some of its rougher aspects, — which were unavoidable in a young movement of that sort, — which gives now to the life of a great portion of the educated classes of Russia a certain peculiar character which we Russians regret not to find in the life of Western Europe. It is nihilism, again, in its various manifestations, which gives to many of our writers that remarkable sincerity, that habit of "thinking aloud," which astounds Western European readers.

First of all, the nihilist declared war upon what may be described as "the conventional lies of civilized mankind." Absolute sincerity was his distinctive feature, and in the name of that sincerity he gave up, and asked others to give up, those superstitions, prejudices, habits, and customs which their own reason could not justify. He refused to bend before any authority except that of reason, and in the analysis of every social institution or habit he revolted against any sort of more or less masked sophism.

He broke, of course, with the superstitions of his fathers, and in his philosophical conceptions he was a positivist, an agnostic, a Spencerian evolutionist, or a scientific materialist;

and while he never attacked the simple, sincere religious belief which is a psychological necessity of feeling, he bitterly fought against the hypocrisy that leads people to assume the outward mask of a religion which they repeatedly throw aside as useless ballast.

The life of civilized people is full of little conventional lies. Persons who hate each other, meeting in the street, make their faces radiant with a happy smile; the nihilist remained unmoved, and smiled only for those whom he was really glad to meet. All those forms of outward politeness which are mere hypocrisy were equally repugnant to him, and he assumed a certain external roughness as a protest against the smooth amiability of his fathers. He saw them wildly talking as idealist sentimentalists, and at the same time acting as real barbarians toward their wives, their children, and their serfs; and he rose in revolt against that sort of sentimentalism which, after all, so nicely accommodated itself to the anything but ideal conditions of Russian life. Art was involved in the same sweeping negation. Continual talk about beauty, the ideal, art for art's sake, æsthetics, and the like, so willingly indulged in, — while every object of art was bought with money exacted from starving peasants or from underpaid workers, and the so-called "worship of the beautiful" was but a mask to cover the most commonplace dissoluteness, — inspired him with disgust, and the criticisms of art which Tolstóy, one of the greatest artists of the century, has now so powerfully formulated, the nihilist expressed in the sweeping assertion, "A pair of boots is more important than all your Madonnas and all your refined talk about Shakespeare."

Marriage without love, and familiarity without friendship, were equally repudiated. The nihilist girl, compelled by her parents to be a doll in a Doll's House, and to marry for property's sake, preferred to abandon her house and her silk dresses. She put on a black woolen dress of the plainest description, cut off her hair, and went to a high school, in order to win there her personal independence. The woman who saw that her marriage was no longer a marriage, that neither love nor friendship connected those who were legally considered husband and wife, preferred to break a bond which retained none of its essential features. Accordingly she often went with her children to face poverty, preferring loneliness and misery to a life which, under conventional conditions, would have given a perpetual lie to her best self.

The nihilist carried his love of sincerity even into the minutest details of every-day life. He discarded the conventional forms of society talk, and expressed his opinions in a blunt and terse way, even with a certain affectation of outward roughness.

In Irkútsk we used to meet once a week in a club and have some dancing. I was for a time a regular visitor at these soirées, but afterwards, having to work, I abandoned them. One night, when I had not made my appearance for several weeks, a young friend of mine was asked by one of the ladies why I did not appear any more at their gatherings. " He takes a ride now when he wants exercise," was the rather rough reply of my friend. " But he might come and spend a couple of hours with us, without dancing," one of the ladies ventured to say. "What would he do here ? " retorted my nihilist friend ; " talk with you about fashions and furbelows ? He has had enough of that nonsense." " But he sees Miss So-and-So occasionally," timidly remarked one of the young ladies present. " Yes, but she is a studious girl," bluntly replied my friend ; " he helps her with her German." I must add that this undoubtedly rough rebuke had its effect, for most of the Irkútsk girls soon began to besiege my brother, my friend, and myself with questions as to what we should advise them to read or to study.

With the same frankness the nihilist spoke to his acquaintances, telling them that all their talk about "this poor people" was sheer hypocrisy so long as they lived upon the underpaid work of these people whom they commiserated at their ease as they chatted together in richly decorated rooms; and with the same frankness a nihilist would declare to a high functionary that the latter cared not a straw for the welfare of those whom he ruled, but was simply a thief, and so on.

With a certain austerity the nihilist would rebuke the wou.an who indulged in small talk and prided herself on her "womanly" manners and elaborate toilette. He would bluntly say to a pretty young person : "How is it that you are not ashamed to talk this nonsense and to wear that chignon of false hair ? " In a woman he wanted to find a comrade, a human personality, — not a doll or a "muslin girl," — and he absolutely refused to join in those petty tokens of politeness with which men surround those whom they like so much to consider as "the weaker sex." When a lady entered a room a nihilist did not jump from his seat to offer it to her, unless he saw that she looked tired and there was no other seat in the room. He behaved towards her as he would have behaved towards a comrade of his own sex; but if a lady — who might have been a total stranger to him — manifested the desire to learn something which he knew and she did not, he would walk every night to the far end of a large city to help her.

Two great Russian novelists, Turguéneff and Goncharóff, have tried to represent this new type in their novels. Goncharóff, in " Precipice," taking a real but unrepresentative individual of this class, made a caricature of nihilism. Turguéneff was too good an artist, and had himself conceived too much admiration for the new type, to let himself be drawn into caricature painting; but even his nihilist, Bazároff, did not satisfy us. We found him too harsh, especially in his relations with his old parents, and, above all, we reproached him with his seeming neglect of his duties as a citizen. Russian youth could not be satisfied with the merely negative attitude of Turguéneff's hero. Nihilism, with its affirmation of the rights of the individual and its negation of all hypocrisy, was but a first step toward a higher type of men and women, who are equally free, but live for a great cause. In the nihilists of Chernyshévsky, as they are depicted in his far less artistic novel, "What is to be Done?" they saw better portraits of themselves.

"It is bitter, the bread that has been made by slaves," our poet Nekrásoff wrote. The young generation actually refused to eat that bread, and to enjoy the riches that had been accumulated in their fathers' houses by means of servile labor, whether the laborers were actual serfs or slaves of the present industrial system.

All Russia read with astonishment, in the indictment which was produced at the court against Karakózoff and his friends, that these young men, owners of considerable fortunes, used to live three or four in the same room, never spending more than five dollars apiece a month for all their needs, and giving at the same time their fortunes for starting coöperative associations, coöperative workshops (where they themselves worked), and the like. Five years later, thousands and thousands of the Russian youth — the best part of it — were doing the same. Their watchword was, "V naród!" (To the people; be the people.) During the years 1860–65, in nearly every wealthy family a bitter struggle was going on between the fathers, who wanted to maintain the old traditions, and the sons and daughters, who defended their right to dispose of their lives according to their own ideals. Young men left the military service, the counter, the shop, and flocked to the university towns. Girls, bred in the most aristocratic families, rushed penniless to St. Petersburg, Moscow, and Kíeff, eager to learn a profession which would free them from the domestic yoke, and some day, perhaps, also from the possible yoke of a husband. After hard and bitter struggles, many of them won that personal freedom. Now they wanted to utilize it, not for their own personal enjoyment, but for carrying to the people the knowledge that had emancipated them.

In every town of Russia, in every quarter of St. Petersburg, small groups were formed for self-improvement and self-education; the works of the philosophers, the writings of the economists, the historical researches of the young Russian historical school, were carefully read in these circles, and the reading was followed by endless discussions. The aim of all that reading and discussion was to solve the great question which rose before them. In what way could they be useful to the masses? Gradually, they came to the idea that the only way was to settle amongst the people, and to live the people's life. Young men went into the villages as doctors, doctors' helpers, teachers, village scribes, even as agricultural laborers, blacksmiths, woodcutters, and so on, and tried to live there in close contact with the peasants. Girls passed teachers' examinations, learned midwifery or nursing, and went by the hundred into the villages, devoting themselves entirely to the poorest part of the population.

These people went without any ideal of social reconstruction in their mind, or any thought of revolution. They simply wanted to teach the mass of the peasants to read, to instruct them in other things, to give them medical help, and in any way to aid in raising them from their darkness and misery, and to learn at the same time what were *their* popular ideals of a better social life.

When I returned from Switzerland, I found this movement in full swing.

XIII

I HASTENED to share with my friends my impressions of the International Workingmen's Association and my books. At the university I had no friends, properly speaking; I was older than most of my companions, and among young people a difference of a few years is always an obstacle to complete comradeship. It must also be said that since the new rules of admission to the university had been introduced in 1861, the best of the young men — the most developed and the most independent in thought — were sifted out of the gymnasia, and did not gain admittance to the university. Consequently, the majority of my comrades were good boys, laborious, but taking no interest in anything besides the examinations. I was friendly with only one of them: let me call him Dmítri Kelnitz. He was born in South Russia, and although his name was German, he hardly spoke German, and his face was South Russian rather than Teutonic. He was very intelligent, had read a great deal, and had seriously thought over what he had read. He loved science and deeply respected it, but, like many of us, he soon came to the conclusion that to follow the career of a scientific man meant to join the camp of the Philistines, and that there was plenty of other and more urgent work that he could do. He attended the university lectures for two years, and then abandoned them, giving himself entirely to social work. He lived anyhow; I even doubt if he had a permanent lodging. Sometimes he would come to me and ask, "Have you some paper?" and having taken a supply of it, he would sit at the corner of a table for an hour or two, diligently making a translation. The little that he earned in this way was more than sufficient to satisfy all his limited wants. Then he would hurry to a distant part of the town to see a comrade or to help a needy friend; or he would cross St. Petersburg on foot, to a remote suburb, in order to obtain free admission to a college for some boy in whom the comrades were interested. He was undoubtedly a gifted man. In Western Europe a man far less gifted would have worked his way to a position of political or socialist leadership. No such thought ever entered the brain of Kelnitz. To lead men was by no means his ambition, and there was no work too insignificant for him to do. This trait, however, was not distinctive of him alone; all those who had lived some years in the students' circles of those times were possessed of it to a high degree.

Soon after my return Kelnitz invited me to join a circle which was known amongst the youth as "the Circle of Tchaykóvsky." Under this name it played an important part in the history of the social movement in Russia, and under this name it will go down to history. "Its members," Kelnitz said to me, "have hitherto been mostly constitutionalists; but they are excellent men, with minds open to any honest idea; they have plenty of friends all over Russia, and you will see later on what you can do." I already knew Tchaykóvsky, and a few other members of this circle. Tchaykóvsky had won my heart at our first meeting, and our friendship has remained unshaken for twenty-seven years.

The beginning of this circle was a very small group of young men and women, — one of whom was Sophie Peróvskaya, — who had united for purposes of self-education and self-improvement. Tchaykóvsky was of their number. In 1869 Necháieff had tried to start a secret revolutionary organization among the youth imbued with the beforementioned desire of working among the people, and to secure this end he resorted to the ways of old conspirators, without recoiling even before deceit when he wanted to force his associates to follow his lead. Such methods could have no success in Russia, and very soon his society broke down. All the members were arrested, and some of the best and purest of the Russian youth went to Siberia before they had done anything. The circle of self-education of which I am speaking was constituted in opposition to the methods of Nechaieff. The few friends had judged, quite correctly, that a morally developed individuality must be the foundation of every organization, whatever political character it may take afterward, and whatever programme of action it may adopt in the course of future events. This was why the Circle of Tchaykóvsky, gradually widening its programme, spread so extensively in Russia, achieved such important results, and later on, when the ferocious prosecutions of the government created a revolutionary struggle, produced that remarkable set of men and women who fell in the terrible contest they waged against autocracy.

At that time, however, — that is, in 1872, — the circle had nothing revolutionary in it. If it had remained a mere circle of self-improvement, it would soon have petrified, like a monastery. But the members found a suitable work. They began to spread good books. They bought the works of Lassalle, Bervi (on the condition of the laboring classes in Russia), Marx, Russian historical works, and so on, — whole editions, — and distributed them among students in the provinces. In a few years there was not a town of importance in "thirty-eight provinces of the Russian Empire," to use official language, where this circle did not have a group of comrades engaged in the spreading of that sort of literature. Gradually, following the general drift of the times, and stimulated by the news which came from Western Europe about the rapid growth of the labor movement, the circle became more and more a centre of socialistic propaganda among the educated youth, and a natural intermediary between members of provincial circles; and then, one day, the ice between students and workers was broken, and direct relations were established with working-people at St. Petersburg and in some of the provinces. It was at that juncture that I joined the circle, in the spring of 1872.

All secret societies are fiercely prosecuted in Russia, and the Western reader will perhaps expect from me a description of my initiation and of the oath of allegiance which I took. I must disappoint him, because there was nothing of the sort, and could not be; we should have been the first to laugh at such ceremonies, and Kelnitz would not have missed the opportunity of putting in one of his sarcastic remarks, which would have killed any ritual. There was not even a statute. The circle accepted as members only persons who were well known and had been tested in various circumstances, and of whom it was felt that they could be trusted absolutely. Before a new member was received, his character was discussed with the frankness and seriousness which were characteristic of the nihilist. The slightest token of insincerity or conceit would have barred the way to admission. The circle did not care to make a show of numbers, and had no tendency to concentrate in its hands all the activity that was going on amongst the youth, or to include in one organization the scores of different circles which existed in the capitals and the provinces. With most of them friendly relations were maintained; they were helped, and they helped us, when necessity arose, but no assault was made on their autonomy.

The circle preferred to remain a closely united group of friends; and never did I meet elsewhere such a collection of morally superior men and women as the score of persons whose acquaintance I made at the first meeting of the Circle of Tchaykóvsky. I still feel proud of having been received into that family.

XIV

WHEN I joined the Circle of Tchaykóvsky, I found its members hotly discussing the direction to be given to their activity. Some were in favor of continuing to carry on radical and socialistic propaganda among the educated youth; but others thought that the sole aim of this work should be to prepare men who would be capable of arousing the great inert laboring masses, and that their chief activity ought to be among the peasants and workmen in the towns. In all the circles and groups which were formed at that time by the hundred, at St. Petersburg and in the provinces, the same discussions went on; and everywhere the second programme prevailed over the first.

If our youth had merely taken to socialism in the abstract, they might have felt satisfied with a simple declaration of socialist principles, including as a distant aim " the communistic possession of the instruments of production,"— and in the meantime they might have carried on some sort of political agitation. Many middle-class socialist politicians in Western Europe and America really take this course. But our youth had been drawn to socialism in quite another way. They were not theorists about socialism, but had become socialists by living no better than the workers live, by making no distinction between " mine and thine " in their circles, and by refusing to enjoy for their own satisfaction the riches they had inherited from their fathers. They had done with regard to capitalism what Tolstóy urges should be done with regard to war, when he calls upon the people, instead of criticising war and continuing to wear the military uniform, to refuse, each one

for himself, to be a soldier and to bear arms.   In this
same way our Russian youth, each one for himself or herself, refused to take personal advantage of the revenues of
their fathers.   It was, of course, necessary that they should
identify themselves with the people.   Thousands and thousands of young men and women had already left their
houses, and now they tried to live in the villages and the
industrial towns in all possible capacities.   This was not an
organized movement : it was one of those mass movements
which occur at certain periods of sudden awakening of
human conscience.   Now that small organized groups were
formed, ready to try a systematic effort for spreading ideas
of freedom and revolt in Russia, they were forced to carry
on that propaganda among the masses of the peasants and
of the workers in the towns.   Various writers have tried to
explain this movement "to the people" by influences from
abroad: "foreign agitators are everywhere," was a favorite
explanation.   It is certainly true that our youth listened to
the mighty voice of Bakúnin, and that the agitation of the
International Workingmen's Association had a fascinating
effect upon us.   But the movement had a far deeper origin :
it began before "foreign agitators" had spoken to the Russian youth, and even before the International Association
had been founded.   It was beginning in the groups of
Karakózoff in 1866 ; Turguéneff saw it coming, and already
in 1859 faintly indicated it.   I did my best to promote that
movement in the Circle of Tchaykóvsky; but I was only
working with the tide which was infinitely more powerful
than any individual efforts.

We often spoke, of course, of the necessity of a political
agitation against our absolute government.   We saw already
that the mass of the peasants were being driven to unavoidable and irremediable ruin by foolish taxation, and by still
more foolish selling off of their cattle to cover the arrears of
taxes.   We "visionaries" saw coming that complete ruin

of a whole population which by this time, alas, has been accomplished to an appalling extent in Central Russia, and is confessed by the government itself. We knew how, in every direction, Russia was being plundered in a most scandalous manner. We knew, and we learned more every day, of the lawlessness of the functionaries, and the almost incredible bestiality of many among them. We heard continually of friends whose houses were raided at night by the police, who disappeared in prisons, and who — we ascertained later on — had been transported without judgment to hamlets in some remote province of Russia. We felt, therefore, the necessity of a political struggle against this terrible power, which was crushing the best intellectual forces of the nation. But we saw no possible ground, legal or semi-legal, for such a struggle.

Our elder brothers did not want our socialistic aspirations, and we could not part with them. Nay, even if some of us had done so, it would have been of no avail. The young generation, as a whole, were treated as "suspects," and the elder generation feared to have anything to do with them. Every young man of democratic tastes, every young woman following a course of higher education, was a suspect in the eyes of the state police, and was denounced by Katkóff as an enemy of the state. Cropped hair and blue spectacles worn by a girl, a Scotch plaid worn in winter by a student, instead of an overcoat, which were evidences of nihilist simplicity and democracy, were denounced as tokens of "political unreliability." If any student's lodging came to be frequently visited by other students, it was periodically invaded by the state police and searched. So common were the night raids in certain students' lodgings that Kelnitz once said, in his mildly humorous way, to the police officer who was searching the rooms : " Why should you go through all our books, each time you come to make a search ? You might as well have a list of them, and then come once a month to see if they are all on the shelves; and you might, from time to time, add the titles of the new ones." The slightest suspicion of political unreliability was sufficient ground upon which to take a young man from a high school, to imprison him for several months, and finally to send him to some remote province of the Uráls, — "for an undetermined term," as they used to say in their bureaucratic slang. Even at the time when the Circle of Tchaykóvsky did nothing but distribute books, all of which had been printed with the censor's approval, Tchaykóvsky was twice arrested and kept some four or six months in prison; on the second occasion at a critical time of his career as a chemist. His researches had recently been published in the "Bulletin of the Academy of Sciences," and he had come up for his final university examinations. He was released at last, because the police could not discover sufficient evidence against him to warrant his transportation to the Uráls! "But if we arrest you once more," he was told, "we shall send you to Siberia." In fact, it was a favorite dream of Alexander II. to have somewhere in the steppes a special town, guarded night and day by patrols of Cossacks, where all suspected young people could be sent, so as to make of them a city of ten or twenty thousand inhabitants. Only the menace which such a city might some day offer prevented him from carrying out this truly Asiatic scheme.

One of our members, an officer, had belonged to a group of young men whose ambition was to serve in the provincial *Zémstvos* (district and county councils). They regarded work in this direction as a high mission, and prepared themselves for it by serious studies of the economical conditions of Central Russia. Many young people cherished for a time the same hopes; but all these hopes vanished at the first contact with the actual government machinery.

Having granted a very limited form of self-government to certain provinces of Russia, the government immediately directed all its efforts to reducing that reform to nothing by depriving it of all its meaning and vitality. The provincial "self-government" had to content itself with the mere function of state officials who would collect additional local taxes and spend them for the local needs of the state. Every attempt of the county councils to take the initiative in any improvement — schools, teachers' colleges, sanitary measures, agricultural improvements, etc. — was met by the central government with suspicion, with hostility, — and denounced by the "Moscow Gazette" as "separatism," as the creation of "a state within the state," as rebellion against autocracy.

If any one were to tell the true history, for example, of the teachers' college of Tver, or of any similar undertaking of a Zémstvo in those years, with all the petty persecutions, the prohibitions, the suspensions, and what not with which the institution was harassed, no West European, and especially no American reader, would believe it. He would throw the book aside, saying, "It cannot be true; it is too stupid to be true." And yet it was so. Whole groups of the elected representatives of several Zémstvos were deprived of their functions, ordered to leave their province and their estates, or were simply exiled, for having dared to petition the Emperor in the most loyal manner concerning such rights as belonged to the Zémstvos by law. "The elected members of the provincial councils must be simple ministerial functionaries, and obey the minister of the interior:" such was the theory of the St. Petersburg government. As to the less prominent people, — teachers, doctors, and the like, in the service of the local councils, — they were removed and exiled by the state police in twenty-four hours, without further ceremony than an order of the omnipotent Third Section of the imperial chancelry. No

longer ago than last year, a lady whose husband is a rich
landowner and occupies a prominent position in one of the
Zémstvos, and who is herself interested in education, invited eight schoolmasters to her birthday party. "Poor
men," she said to herself, "they never have the opportunity
of seeing any one but the peasants." The day after the
party, the village policeman called at the mansion and insisted upon having the names of the eight teachers, in order
to report them to the police authorities. The lady refused
to give the names. "Very well," he replied, "I will find
them out, nevertheless, and make my report. Teachers
must not come together, and I am bound to report if they
do." The high position of the lady sheltered the teachers,
in this case; but if they had met in the lodgings of one of
their own number, they would have received a visit from
the state police, and half of them would have been dismissed by the ministry of education; and if, moreover, an
angry word had escaped from one of them during the police
raid, he or she would have been sent to some province of
the Uráls. This is what happens to-day, thirty-three years
after the opening of the county and district councils; but it
was far worse in the seventies. What sort of basis for a
political struggle could such institutions offer?

When I inherited from my father his Tambóv estate, I
thought very seriously for a time of settling on that estate,
and devoting my energy to work in the local Zémstvo.
Some peasants and the poorer priests of the neighborhood
asked me to do so. As for myself, I should have been
content with anything I could do, no matter how small
it might be, if only it would help to raise the intellectual
level and the well-being of the peasants. But one day,
when several of my advisers were together, I asked them:
"Supposing I were to try to start a school, an experimental farm, a coöperative enterprise, and, at the same time,
also took upon myself the defense of that peasant from our

village who has lately been wronged, — would the authorities let me do it?" "Never!" was the unanimous reply.

An old gray-haired priest, a man who was held in great esteem in our neighborhood, came to me, a few days later, with two influential dissenting leaders, and said: "Talk with these two men. If you can manage it, go with them and, Bible in hand, preach to the peasants. . . . Well, you know what to preach. . . . No police in the world will find you, if they conceal you. . . . There's nothing to be done besides; that's what I, an old man, advise you."

I told them frankly why I could not assume the part of Wiclif. But the old man was right. A movement similar to that of the Lollards is rapidly growing now amongst the Russian peasants. Such tortures as have been inflicted on the peace-loving Dukhobórs, and such raids upon the peasant dissenters in South Russia as were made in 1897, when children were kidnapped so that they might be educated in orthodox monasteries, will only give to that movement a force that it could not have attained five-and-twenty years ago.

As the question of agitation for a constitution was continually being raised in our discussions, I once proposed to our circle to take it up seriously, and to choose an appropriate plan of action. I was always of the opinion that when the circle decided anything unanimously, each member ought to put aside his personal feeling and give all his strength to the task. "If you decide to agitate for a constitution," I said, "this is my plan: I will separate myself from you, for appearance' sake, and maintain relations with only one member of the circle, — for instance, Tchaykóv-sky, — through whom I shall be kept informed how you succeed in your work, and can communicate to you in a general way what I am doing. My work will be among the courtiers and the higher functionaries. I have among them many acquaintances, and know a number of persons who are disgusted with the present conditions. I will bring them together and unite them, if possible, into a sort of organization; and then, some day, there is sure to be an opportunity to direct all these forces toward compelling Alexander II. to give Russia a constitution. There certainly will come a time when all these people, feeling that they are compromised, will in their own interest take a decisive step. If it is necessary, some of us, who have been officers, might be very helpful in extending the propaganda amongst the officers in the army; but this action must be quite separate from yours, though parallel with it. I have seriously thought of it. I know what connections I have and who can be trusted, and I believe some of the discontented already look upon me as a possible centre for some action of this sort. This course is not the one I should take of my own choice; but if you think that it is best, I will give myself to it with might and main."

The circle did not accept that proposal. Knowing one another as well as they did, my comrades probably thought that if I went in this direction I should cease to be true to myself. For my own personal happiness, for my own personal life, I cannot feel too grateful now that my proposal was not accepted. I should have gone in a direction which was not the one dictated by my own nature, and I should not have found in it the personal happiness which I have found in other paths. But when, six or seven years later, the terrorists were engaged in their terrible struggle against Alexander II., I regretted that there had not been somebody else to do the sort of work I had proposed to do in the higher circles at St. Petersburg. With some understanding there beforehand, and with the ramifications which such an understanding probably would have taken all over the empire, the holocausts of victims would not have been made in vain. At any rate, the underground work of the executive committee ought by all means to have been supported by a parallel agitation at the Winter Palace.

Over and over again the necessity of a political effort thus came under discussion in our little group, with no result. The apathy and the indifference of the wealthier classes were hopeless, and the irritation among the persecuted youth had not yet been brought to that high pitch which ended, six years later, in the struggle of the terrorists under the executive committee. Nay, — and this is one of the most tragical ironies of history, — it was the same youth whom Alexander II., in his blind fear and fury, ordered to be sent by the hundred to hard labor and condemned to slow death in exile; it was the same youth who protected him in 1871–78. The very teachings of the socialist circles were such as to prevent the repetition of a Karakózoff attempt on the Tsar's life. "Prepare in Russia a great socialist mass movement amongst the workers and the peasants," was the watchword in those times. "Don't trouble about the Tsar and his counselors. If such a movement begins, if the peasants join in the mass movement to claim the land and to abolish the serfdom redemption taxes, the imperial power will be the first to seek support in the moneyed classes and the landlords and to convoke a Parliament, — just as the peasant insurrection in France, in 1789, compelled the royal power to convoke the National Assembly ; so it will be in Russia."

But there was more than that. Separate men and groups, seeing that the reign of Alexander II. was hopelessly doomed to sink deeper and deeper in reaction, and entertaining at the same time vague hopes as to the supposed "liberalism" of the heir apparent, — all young heirs to thrones are supposed to be liberal, — persistently reverted to the idea that the example of Karakózoff ought to be followed.　The organized circles, however, strenuously opposed such an idea, and urged their comrades not to resort to that course of action.　I may now divulge the following fact which has never before been made public.　When a young man came to St. Petersburg from one of the southern provinces with the firm intention of killing Alexander II., and some members of the Tchaykóvsky circle learned of his plan, they not only applied all the weight of their arguments to dissuade the young man, but, when he would not be dissuaded, they informed him that they would keep a watch over him and prevent him by force from making any such attempt.　Knowing well how loosely guarded the Winter Palace was at that time, I can positively say that they saved the life of Alexander II.　So firmly were the youth opposed at that time to the war in which later, when the cup of their sufferings was filled to overflowing, they took part.

XV

THE two years that I worked with the Circle of Tchaykóvsky, before I was arrested, left a deep impression upon all my subsequent life and thought. During these two years it was life under high pressure, — that exuberance of life when one feels at every moment the full throbbing of all the fibres of the inner self, and when life is really worth living. I was in a family of men and women so closely united by their common object, and so broadly and delicately humane in their mutual relations, that I cannot now recall a single moment of even temporary friction marring the life of our circle. Those who have had any experience of political agitation will appreciate the value of this statement.

Before abandoning entirely my scientific career, I considered myself bound to complete the report of my journey to Finland for the Geographical Society, as well as some other work that I had in hand for the same society; and my new friends were the first to confirm me in that decision. It would not be fair, they said, to do otherwise. Consequently, I worked hard to finish my geographical and geological books.

Meetings of our circle were frequent, and I never missed them. We used to meet then in a suburban part of St. Petersburg, in a small house of which Sophie Peróvskaya, under the assumed name and the fabricated passport of an artisan's wife, was the supposed tenant. She was born of a very aristocratic family, and her father had been for some time the military governor of St. Petersburg; but, with the approval of her mother, who adored her, she had left her home to join a high school, and with the three sisters Korníloff — daughters of a rich manufacturer — she had founded that little circle of self-education which later on became our circle. Now, in the capacity of an artisan's wife, in her cotton dress and men's boots, her head covered with a cotton kerchief, as she carried on her shoulders her two pails of water from the Nevá, no one would have recognized in her the girl who a few years before shone in one of the most fashionable drawing-rooms of the capital. She was a general favorite, and every one of us, on entering the house, had a specially friendly smile for her, — even when she, making a point of honor of keeping the house relatively clean, quarreled with us about the dirt which we, dressed in peasant top-boots and sheepskins, brought in, after walking the muddy streets of the suburbs. She tried then to give to her girlish, innocent, and very intelligent little face the most severe expression possible to it. In her moral conceptions she was a "rigorist," but not in the least of the sermon-preaching type. When she was dissatisfied with some one's conduct, she would cast a severe glance at him from beneath her brows; but in that glance one saw her open-minded, generous nature, which understood all that is human. On one point only she was inexorable. "A women's man," she once said, speaking of some one, and the expression and the manner in which she said it, without interrupting her work, are engraved forever in my memory.

Peróvskaya was a "popularist" to the very bottom of her heart, and at the same time a revolutionist, a fighter of the truest steel. She had no need to embellish the workers and the peasants with imaginary virtues, in order to love them and to work for them. She took them as they were, and said to me once: "We have begun a great thing. Two generations, perhaps, will succumb in the task, and yet it must be done." None of the women of our circle

would have given way before the certainty of death on the
scaffold. Each would have looked death straight in the
face. But none of them, at that stage of our propaganda,
thought of such a fate. Peróvskaya's well-known portrait
is exceptionally good; it records so well her earnest courage,
her bright intelligence, and her loving nature. The letter
she wrote to her mother a few hours before she went to the
scaffold is one of the best expressions of a loving soul that
a woman's heart ever dictated.

The following incident will show what the other women
of our circle were. One night, Kupreyánoff and I went to
Varvara B., to whom we had to make an urgent communication. It was past midnight, but, seeing a light in her
window, we went upstairs. She sat in her tiny room, at a
table, copying a programme of our circle. We knew how
resolute she was, and the idea came to us to make one of
those stupid jokes which men sometimes think funny.
"B.," I said, "we came to fetch you: we are going to try
a rather mad attempt to liberate our friends from the fortress." She asked not one question. She quietly laid
down her pen, rose from the chair, and said only, "Let us
go." She spoke in so simple, so unaffected a voice that I
felt at once how foolishly I had acted, and told her the
truth. She dropped back into her chair, with tears in her
eyes, and in a despairing voice asked: "It was only a joke?
Why do you make *such* jokes?" I fully realized then the
cruelty of what I had done.

Another general favorite in our circle was Serghéi Krav-
chínsky, who became so well known, both in England and
in the United States, under the name of Stepniák. He was
often called "the Baby," so unconcerned was he about his
own security; but this carelessness about himself was merely
the result of a complete absence of fear, which, after all, is
often the best policy for one who is hunted by the police.

He soon became well known for his propaganda in the circles of workers, under his real Christian name of Serghéi, and consequently was very much wanted by the police; notwithstanding that, he took no precautions whatever to conceal himself, and I remember that one day he was severely scolded at one of our meetings for what was described as a gross imprudence. Being late for the meeting, as he often was, and having a long distance to cover in order to reach our house, he, dressed as a peasant in his sheepskin, ran the whole length of a great main thoroughfare at full speed in the middle of the street. "How could you do it?" he was reproachfully asked. "You might have aroused suspicion and have been arrested as a common thief." But I wish that every one had been as cautious as he was in affairs where other people could be compromised.

We made our first intimate acquaintance over Stanley's book, "How I Discovered Livingstone." One night our meeting had lasted till twelve, and as we were about to leave, one of the Korníloffs entered with a book in her hand, and asked who among us could undertake to translate by the next morning at eight o'clock sixteen printed pages of Stanley's book. I looked at the size of the pages, and said that if somebody would help me, the work could be done during the night. Serghéi volunteered, and by four o'clock the sixteen pages were done. We read to each other our translations, one of us following the English text; then we emptied a jar of Russian porridge which had been left on the table for us, and went out together to return home. We became close friends from that night.

I have always liked people capable of working, and doing their work properly. So Serghéi's translation and his capacity of working rapidly had already influenced me in his favor. But when I came to know more of him, I felt real love for his honest, frank nature, for his youthful energy and good sense, for his superior intelligence, simplicity, and truthfulness, and for his courage and tenacity. He had read and thought a great deal, and upon the revolutionary character of the struggle which he had undertaken, it appeared we had similar views. He was ten years younger than I was, and perhaps did not quite realize what a hard contest the coming revolution would be. He told us later on, with much humor, how he once worked among the peasants in the country. "One day," he said, "I was walking along the road with a comrade, when we were overtaken by a peasant in a sleigh. I began to tell the peasant that he must not pay taxes, that the functionaries plunder the people, and I tried to convince him by quotations from the Bible that they must revolt. The peasant whipped up his horse, but we followed rapidly; he made his horse trot, and we began to trot behind him; all the time I continued to talk to him about taxes and revolt. Finally he made his horse gallop; but the animal was not worth much, — an underfed peasant pony, — so my comrade and I did not fall behind, but kept up our propaganda till we were quite out of breath."

For some time Serghéi stayed in Kazán, and I had to correspond with him. He always hated writing letters in cipher, so I proposed a means of correspondence which had often been used before in conspiracies. You write an ordinary letter about all sorts of things, but in this letter it is only certain words — let us say every fifth word — which has a sense. You write, for instance : "Excuse my hurried letter. Come to-night to see me; to-morrow I shall go away to my sister. My brother Nicholas is worse; it was late to perform an operation." Reading each fifth word, you find, "Come to-morrow to Nicholas, late." We had to write letters of six or seven pages to transmit one page of information, and we had to cultivate our imagination in order to fill the letters with all sorts of things by way of introducing the words that were required. Serghéi, from whom it was impossible to obtain a cipher letter, took to this kind of correspondence, and used to send me letters containing stories with thrilling incidents and dramatic endings. He said to me afterward that this correspondence helped to develop his literary talent. When one has talent, everything contributes to its development.

In January or February, 1874, I was at Moscow, in one of the houses in which I had spent my childhood. Early in the morning I was told that a peasant desired to see me. I went out and found it was Serghéi, who had just escaped from Tver. He was strongly built, and he and another ex-officer, Rogachóff, endowed with equal physical force, went traveling about the country as lumber sawyers. The work was very hard, especially for inexperienced hands, but both of them liked it; and no one would have thought to look for disguised officers in these two strong sawyers. They wandered in this capacity for about a fortnight without arousing suspicion, and made revolutionary propaganda right and left without fear. Sometimes Serghéi, who knew the New Testament almost by heart, spoke to the peasants as a religious preacher, proving to them by quotations from the Bible that they ought to start a revolution. Sometimes he formed his arguments of quotations from the economists. The peasants listened to the two men as to real apostles, took them from one house to another, and refused to be paid for food. In a fortnight they had produced quite a stir in a number of villages. Their fame was spreading far and wide. The peasants, young and old, began to whisper to one another in the barns about the "delegates;" they began to speak out more loudly than they usually did that the land would soon be taken from the landlords, who would receive pensions from the Tsar. The younger people became more aggressive toward the police officers, saying: "Wait a little; our turn will soon come; you Herods will not rule long now." But the fame of the sawyers reached the ears of one of the police authorities, and they were arrested. An order was given to take them to the next police official, ten miles away.

They were taken under the guard of several peasants, and on their way had to pass through a village which was holding its festival. "Prisoners ? All right ! Come on here, my uncle," said the peasants, who were all drinking in honor of the occasion. They were kept nearly the whole day in that village, the peasants taking them from one house to another, and treating them to home-made beer. The guards did not have to be asked twice. They drank, and insisted that the prisoners should drink, too. "Happily," Serghéi said, "they passed round the beer in such large wooden bowls that I could put my mouth to the rim of the bowl as if I were drinking, but no one could see how much beer I had imbibed." The guards were all drunk toward night, and preferred not to appear in this state before the police officer, so they decided to stay in the village till morning. Serghéi kept talking to them; and all listened to him, regretting that such a good man had been caught. As they were going to sleep, a young peasant whispered to Serghéi, "When I go to shut the gate, I will leave it unbolted." Serghéi and his comrade understood the hint, and as soon as all fell asleep, they went out into the street. They started at a fast pace, and at five o'clock in the morning were twenty miles away from the village, at a small railway station, where they took the first train, and went to Moscow. Serghéi remained there, and later, when all of us at St. Petersburg had been arrested, the Moscow circle, under his and Voinarálsky's inspiration, became the main centre of the agitation.

Here and there, small groups of propagandists had settled in towns and villages in various capacities. Blacksmiths' shops and small farms had been started, and young men of the wealthier classes worked in the shops or on the farms, to be in daily contact with the toiling masses. At Moscow, a number of young girls, of rich families, who had studied at the Zürich University and had started a separate organization, went even so far as to enter cotton factories, where they worked from fourteen to sixteen hours a day, and lived in the factory barracks the miserable life of the Russian factory girls. It was a grand movement, in which, at the lowest estimate, from two to three thousand persons took an active part, while twice or thrice as many sympathizers and supporters helped the active vanguard in various ways. With a good half of that army our St. Petersburg circle was in regular correspondence, — always, of course, in cipher.

The literature which could be published in Russia under a rigorous censorship — the faintest hint of socialism being prohibited — was soon found insufficient, and we started a printing-office of our own abroad. Pamphlets for the workers and the peasants had to be written, and our small "literary committee," of which I was a member, had its hands full of work. Serghéi wrote two such pamphlets, one in the Lamennais style and another containing an exposition of socialism in a fairy tale, and both had a wide circulation. The books and pamphlets which were printed abroad were smuggled into Russia by thousands, stored at certain spots, and sent out to the local circles, which distributed them amongst the peasants and the workers. All this required a vast organization as well as much traveling about, and a colossal correspondence, particularly for protecting our helpers and our bookstores from the police. We had special ciphers for different provincial circles, and often, after six or seven hours had been passed in discussing all details, the women, who did not trust to our accuracy in the cipher correspondence, spent all the night in covering sheets of paper with cabalistic figures and fractions.

The utmost cordiality always prevailed at our meetings. Chairmen and all sorts of formalism are so utterly repugnant to the Russian mind that we had none; and although our debates were sometimes extremely hot, especially when "programme questions" were under discussion, we always managed very well without resorting to Western formalities. An absolute sincerity, a general desire to settle the difficulties for the best, and a frankly expressed contempt for all that in the least degree approached theatrical affectation were quite sufficient. If any one of us had ventured to attempt oratorical effects by a speech, friendly jokes would have shown him at once that speech-making was out of place. Often we had to take our meals during these meetings, and they invariably consisted of rye bread, with cucumbers, a bit of cheese, and plenty of weak tea to quench the thirst. Not that money was lacking; there was always enough, and yet there was never too much to cover the steadily growing expenses for printing, transportation of books, concealing friends wanted by the police, and starting new enterprises.

At St. Petersburg, it was not long before we had wide acquaintance amongst the workers. Serdukóff, a young man of splendid education, had made a number of friends amongst the engineers, most of them employed in a state factory of the artillery department, and he had organized a circle of about thirty members, which used to meet for reading and discussion. The engineers are pretty well paid at St. Petersburg, and those who were not married were fairly well off. They soon became quite familiar with the current radical and socialist literature, — Buckle, Lassalle, Mill, Draper, Spielhagen, were familiar names to them; and in their aspect these engineers differed little from students. When Kelnitz, Serghéi, and I joined the circle, we frequently visited their group, and gave them informal lectures upon all sorts of things. Our hopes, however, that these young men would grow into ardent propagandists amidst less privileged classes of workers were not fully realized.   In a free country they would have been the habitual speakers at public meetings; but, like the privileged workers of the watch trade in Geneva, they treated the mass of the factory hands with a sort of contempt, and were in no haste to become martyrs to the socialist cause. It was only after they had been arrested and kept three or four years in prison for having dared to *think* as socialists, and had sounded the full depth of Russian absolutism, that several of them developed into ardent propagandists, chiefly of a political revolution.

My sympathies went especially toward the weavers and the workers in the cotton factories.   There are many thousands of them at St. Petersburg, who work there during the winter, and return for the three summer months to their native villages to cultivate the land.   Half peasants and half town workers, they had generally retained the social spirit of the Russian villager.   The movement spread like wildfire among them.   We had to restrain the zeal of our new friends; otherwise they would have brought to our lodgings hundreds at a time, young and old.   Most of them lived in small associations, or *artéls*, ten or twelve persons hiring a common apartment and taking their meals together, each one paying every month his share of the general expenses.   It was to these lodgings that we used to go, and the weavers soon brought us in contact with other artéls, of stone-masons, carpenters, and the like.   In some of these artéls Serghéi, Kelnitz, and two more of our friends were quite at home, and spent whole nights talking about socialism.   Besides, we had in different parts of St. Petersburg special apartments, kept by some of our people, to which ten or twelve workers would come every night, to learn reading and writing, and after that to have a talk.

From time to time one of us went to the native villages of our town friends, and spent a couple of weeks in almost open propaganda amongst the peasants.

Of course, all of us who had to deal with this class of workers had to dress like the workers themselves; that is, to wear the peasant garb. The gap between the peasants and the educated people is so great in Russia, and contact between them is so rare, that not only does the appearance in a village of a man who wears the town dress awaken general attention, but even in town, if one whose talk and dress reveal that he is not a worker is seen to go about with workers, the suspicion of the police is aroused at once. "Why should he go about with 'low people,' if he has not a bad intention?" Often, after a dinner in a rich mansion, or even in the Winter Palace, where I went frequently to see a friend, I took a cab, hurried to a poor student's lodging in a remote suburb, exchanged my fine clothes for a cotton shirt, peasant top-boots, and a sheepskin, and, joking with peasants on the way, went to meet my worker friends in some slum. I told them what I had seen of the labor movement abroad. They listened eagerly; they lost not a word of what was said; and then came the question, "What can we do in Russia?" "Agitate, organize," was our reply; "there is no royal road;" and we read them a popular story of the French Revolution, an adaptation of Erckmann-Chatrian's admirable "Histoire d'un Paysan." Every one admired M. Chovel, who went as a propagandist through the villages, distributing prohibited books, and all burned to follow in his footsteps. "Speak to others," we said; "bring men together; and when we become more numerous, we shall see what we can attain." They fully understood, and we had only to moderate their zeal.

Amongst them I passed my happiest hours. New Year's Day of 1874, the last I spent in Russia at liberty, is especially memorable to me. The previous evening I had been in a choice company. Inspiring, noble words were spoken that night about the citizen's duties, the well-being of the country, and the like. But underneath all the thrilling speeches one note sounded : How could each of the speakers preserve his own personal well-being ? Yet no one had the courage to say, frankly and openly, that he was ready to do only that which would not endanger his own dovecote. Sophisms — no end of sophisms — about the slowness of evolution, the inertia of the lower classes, the uselessness of sacrifice, were uttered to justify the unspoken words, all intermingled with assurances of each one's willingness to make sacrifices. I returned home, seized suddenly with profound sadness amid all this talk.

Next morning I went to one of our weavers' meetings. It took place in an underground dark room. I was dressed as a peasant, and was lost in the crowd of other sheepskins. My comrade, who was known to the workers, simply introduced me : " Borodín, a friend." " Tell us, Borodín," he said, " what you have seen abroad." And I spoke of the labor movement in Western Europe, its struggles, its difficulties, and its hopes.

The audience consisted mostly of middle-aged people. They were intensely interested. They asked me questions, all to the point, about the minute details of the workingmen's unions, the aims of the International Association and its chances of success. And then came questions about what could be done in Russia and the prospects of our propaganda. I never minimized the dangers of our agitation, and frankly said what I thought. " *We* shall probably be sent to Siberia, one of these days ; and you — part of you — will be kept long months in prison for having listened to us." This gloomy prospect did not frighten them. " After all, there are men in Siberia, too, — not bears only." " Where men are living others can live." " The devil is not so terrible as they paint him." "If you are afraid of wolves, never go into the wood," they said, as we parted. And when, afterward, several of them were arrested, they nearly all behaved bravely, sheltering us and betraying no one.

XVI

DURING the two years of which I am now speaking many arrests were made, both at St. Petersburg and in the provinces. Not a month passed without our losing some one, or learning that members of this or that provincial group had disappeared. Toward the end of 1873 the arrests became more and more frequent. In November one of our main settlements in a suburb of St. Petersburg was raided by the police. We lost Peróvskaya and three other friends, and all our relations with the workers in this suburb had to be suspended. We founded a new settlement, further away from the town, but it had soon to be abandoned. The police became very vigilant, and the appearance of a student in the workmen's quarters was noticed at once; spies circulated among the workers, who were watched closely. Dmítri Kelnitz, Serghéi, and myself, in our sheepskins and with our peasant looks, passed unnoticed, and continued to visit the haunted ground. But Dmítri and Serghéi, whose names had acquired a wide notoriety in the workmen's quarters, were eagerly wanted by the police; and if they had been found accidentally during a nocturnal raid at a friend's lodgings, they would have been arrested at once. There were periods when Dmítri had to hunt every day for a place where he could spend the night in relative safety. "Can I spend the night with you?" he would ask, entering some comrade's room at ten o'clock. "Impossible! my lodgings have been closely watched lately. Better go to N." "I have just come from him, and he says spies swarm his neighborhood." "Then go to M.; he is a great friend of mine and above suspicion. But it is far from here, and you must take a cab. Here is the money." But on principle Dmítri would not take a cab, and would walk to the other end of the town to find a refuge, or at last go to a friend whose rooms might be searched at any moment.

Early in January, 1874, another settlement, our main stronghold for propaganda amongst the weavers, was lost. Some of our best propagandists disappeared behind the gates of the mysterious Third Section. Our circle became narrower, general meetings were increasingly difficult, and we made strenuous efforts to form new circles of young men who might continue our work when we should all be arrested. Tchaykóvsky was in the south, and we forced Dmítri and Serghéi to leave St. Petersburg, — actually forced them, imperiously ordering them to leave. Only five or six of us remained to transact all the business of our circle. I intended, as soon as I should have delivered my report to the Geographical Society, to go to the southwest of Russia, and there to start a sort of land league, similar to the league which became so powerful in Ireland at the end of the seventies.

After two months of relative quiet, we learned in the middle of March that nearly all the circle of the engineers had been arrested, and with them a young man named Nízovkin, an ex-student, who unfortunately had their confidence, and, we were sure, would soon try to clear himself by telling all he knew about us. Besides Dmítri and Serghéi he knew Serdukóff, the founder of the circle, and myself, and he would certainly name us as soon as he was pressed with questions. A few days later, two weavers — most unreliable fellows, who had even embezzled some money from their comrades, and who knew me under the name of Borodín — were arrested. These two would surely set the police at once upon the track of Borodín, the man dressed as a peasant, who spoke at the weavers' meetings. Within

a week's time all the members of our circle, excepting Serdukóff and myself, were arrested.

There was nothing left us but to fly from St. Petersburg: this was exactly what we did not want to do. All
our immense organization for printing pamphlets abroad
and for smuggling them into Russia; all the network of
circles, farms, and country settlements with which we were
in correspondence in nearly forty (out of fifty) provinces
of European Russia, and which had been slowly built up
during the last two years; and finally, our workers' groups
at St. Petersburg and our four different centres for propaganda amongst workers of the capital, — how could we
abandon all these without having found men to maintain
our relations and correspondence? Serdukóff and I decided to admit to our circle two new members, and to
transfer the business to them. We met every evening in
different parts of the town, and as we never kept any addresses or names in writing, — the smuggling addresses alone
had been deposited in a secure place, in cipher, — we had
to teach our new members hundreds of names and addresses
and a dozen ciphers, repeating them over and over, until
our friends had learned them by heart. Every evening we
went over the whole map of Russia in this way, dwelling
especially on its western frontier, which was studded with
men and women engaged in receiving books from the smugglers, and on the eastern provinces, where we had our main
settlements. Then, always in disguise, we had to take the
new members to our sympathizers in the town, and introduce
them to those workers who had not yet been arrested.

The thing to be done in such a case was to disappear from
one's apartments, and to reappear somewhere else under an
assumed name. Serdukóff had abandoned his lodging, but,
having no passport, he concealed himself in the houses of
friends. I ought to have done the same, but a strange circumstance prevented me. I had just finished my report

upon the glacial formations in Finland and Russia, and this report had to be read at a meeting of the Geographical Society. The invitations were already issued, but it happened that on the appointed day the two geological societies of St. Petersburg had a joint meeting, and they asked the Geographical Society to postpone the reading of my report for a week. It was known that I would present certain ideas about the extension of the ice cap as far as Middle Russia, and our geologists, with the exception of my friend and teacher, Friedrich Schmidt, considered this a speculation of too far-reaching character, and wanted to have it thoroughly discussed. For one week more, consequently, I could not go away.

Strangers prowled about my house and called upon me under all sorts of fantastical pretexts : one of them wanted to buy a forest on my Tambóv estate, which was situated in absolutely treeless prairies. I noticed in my street — the fashionable Morskáya — one of the two arrested weavers whom I have mentioned, and thus learned that my house was watched. Yet I had to act as if nothing extraordinary had happened, because I was to appear at the meeting of the Geographical Society the following Friday night.

The meeting came. The discussions were very animated, and one point, at least, was won. It was recognized that all old theories concerning the diluvial period in Russia were totally baseless, and that a new departure must be made in the investigation of the whole question. I had the satisfaction of hearing our leading geologist, Barbot-de-Marny, say, "Ice cap or not, we must acknowledge, gentlemen, that all we have hitherto said about the action of floating ice had no foundation whatever in actual exploration." And I was proposed at that meeting to be nominated president of the physical geography section, while I was asking myself whether I should not spend that very night in the prison of the Third Section.

It would have been best not to return at all to my apartment, but I was broken down with fatigue, after the
exertion of the last few days, and went home. There was
no police raid during that night. I looked through the
heaps of my papers, destroyed everything that might be
compromising for any one, packed all my things, and prepared to leave. I knew that my apartment was watched,
but I hoped that the police would not pay me a visit before
late in the night, and that at dusk I could slip out of the
house without being noticed. Dusk came, and, as I was
starting, one of the servant girls said to me, " You had
better go by the service staircase." I understood what she
meant, and went quickly down the staircase and out of the
house. One cab only stood at the gate ; I jumped into it.
The driver took me to the great Nevsky Prospekt. There
was no pursuit at first, and I thought myself safe ; but presently I noticed another cab running full speed after us ; our
horse was delayed somehow, and the other cab passed ours.

To my astonishment, I saw in it one of the two arrested
weavers, accompanied by some one else. He waved his
hand as if he had something to tell me. I told my cabman
to stop. "Perhaps," I thought, " he has been released
from arrest, and has an important communication to make to
me." But as soon as we stopped, the man who was with
the weaver — he was a detective — shouted loudly, " Mr.
Borodín, Prince Kropótkin, I arrest you ! " He made a
signal to the policemen, of whom there are hosts along the
main thoroughfare of St. Petersburg, and at the same time
jumped into my cab and showed me a paper which bore the
stamp of the St. Petersburg police. "I have an order to
take you before the governor-general for an explanation,"
he said. Resistance was impossible, — a couple of policemen were already close by, — and I told my cabman to turn
round and drive to the governor-general's house. The
weaver remained in his cab and followed us.

It was now evident that the police had hesitated for ten days to arrest me, because they were not sure that Borodín and I were the same person. My response to the weaver's call had settled their doubts.

It so happened that just as I was leaving my house a young man came from Moscow, bringing me a letter from a friend, Voinarálsky, and another from Dmítri addressed to our friend Polakóff. The former announced the establishment of a secret printing-office at Moscow, and was full of cheerful news concerning the activity in that city. I read it and destroyed it. As the second letter contained nothing but innocent friendly chat, I took it with me. Now that I was arrested, I thought it would be better to destroy it, and, asking the detective to show me his paper again, I took advantage of the time that he was fumbling in his pocket to drop the letter on the pavement without his noticing it. However, as we reached the governor-general's house the weaver handed it to the detective, saying, "I saw the gentleman drop this letter on the pavement, so I picked it up."

Now came tedious hours of waiting for the representativ) of the judicial authorities, the procureur or public prosu cutor. This functionary plays the part of a straw mar, who is paraded by the state police during their searches : he gives an aspect of legality to their proceedings. It was many hours before that gentleman was found and brought to perform his functions as a sham representative of Justice. I was taken back to my house, and a most thorough search of all my papers was made; this lasted till three in the morning, but did not reveal a scrap of paper that could tell against me or any one else.

From my house I was taken to the Third Section, that omnipotent institution which has ruled in Russia from the beginning of the reign of Nicholas I. down to the present time, — a true " state in the state." It began under Peter

I. in the Secret Department, where the adversaries of the founder of the Russian military empire were subject to the most abominable tortures, under which they expired; it was continued in the Secret Chancelry during the reigns of the Empresses, when the Torture Chamber of the powerful Minich inspired all Russia with terror; and it received its present organization from the iron despot, Nicholas I., who attached to it the corps of gendarmes, — the chief of the gendarmes becoming a person far more dreaded in the Russian Empire than the Emperor himself.

In every province of Russia, in every populous town, nay, at every railway station, there are gendarmes who report directly to their own generals or colonels, who in turn correspond with the chief of the gendarmes; and the latter, seeing the Emperor every day, reports to him what he finds necessary to report. All functionaries of the empire are under gendarme supervision; it is the duty of the generals and colonels to keep an eye upon the public and private life of every subject of the Tsar, — even upon the governors of the provinces, the ministers, and the grand dukes. The Emperor himself is under their close watch, and as they are well informed of the petty chronicle of the palace, and know every step that the Emperor takes outside his palace, the chief of the gendarmes becomes, so to speak, a confidant of the most intimate affairs of the rulers of Russia.

At this period of the reign of Alexander II. the Third Section was absolutely all-powerful. The gendarme colonels made searches by the thousand without troubling themselves in the least about the existence of laws and law courts in Russia. They arrested whom they liked, kept people imprisoned as long as they pleased, and transported hundreds to Northeast Russia or Siberia according to the fancy of general or colonel; the signature of the minister of the interior was a mere formality, because he had no control over them and no knowledge of their doings.

It was four o'clock in the morning when my examination began. "You are accused," I was solemnly told, "of having belonged to a secret society which has for its object the overthrow of the existing form of government, and of conspiracy against the sacred person of his Imperial Majesty. Are you guilty of this crime?"

"Till I am brought before a court where I can speak publicly, I will give you no replies whatever."

"Write," the procureur dictated to a scribe: "'Does not acknowledge himself guilty.' Still," he continued, after a pause, "I must ask you certain questions. Do you know a person of the name of Nikolái Tchaykóvsky?"

"If you persist in your questions, then write 'No' to any question whatsoever that you are pleased to ask me."

"But if we ask you whether you know, for instance, Mr. Polakóff, whom you spoke about awhile ago?"

"The moment *you* ask me such a question, don't hesitate: write 'No.' And if you ask me whether I know my brother, or my sister, or my stepmother, write 'No.' You will not receive from me another reply: because if I answered 'Yes' with regard to any person, you would at once plan some evil against him, making a raid or something worse, and saying next that I named him."

A long list of questions was read, to which I patiently replied each time, "Write 'No.'" That lasted for an hour, during which I learned that all who had been arrested, with the exception of the two weavers, had behaved very well. The weavers knew only that I had twice met a dozen workers, and the gendarmes knew nothing about our circle.

"What are you doing, prince?" a gendarme officer said, as he took me to my cell. "Your refusal to answer questions will be made a terrible weapon against you."

"It is my right, is it not?"

"Yes, but — you know. . . . I hope you will find this

room comfortable. It has been kept warm since your arrest."

I found it quite comfortable, and fell sound asleep. I was waked the next morning by a gendarme, who brought me the morning tea. He was soon followed by somebody else, who whispered to me in the most unconcerned way, "Here's a scrap of paper and a pencil : write your letter." It was a sympathizer, whom I knew by name; he used to transmit our correspondence with the prisoners of the Third Section.

From all sides I heard knocks on the walls, following in rapid succession. It was the prisoners communicating with one another by means of light taps ; but, being a newcomer, I could make nothing out of the noise, which seemed to come from all parts of the building at once.

One thing worried me. During the search in my house, I overheard the procureur whispering to the gendarme officer about going to make a search at the apartment of my friend Polakóff, to whom the letter of Dmítri was addressed. Polakóff was a young student, a very gifted zoölogist and botanist, with whom I had made my Vitím expedition in Siberia. He was born of a poor Cossack family on the frontier of Mongolia, and, after having surmounted all sorts of difficulties, he had come to St. Petersburg, entered the university, where he had won the reputation of a most promising zoölogist, and was then passing his final examinations. We had been great friends since our long journey, and had even lived together for a time at St. Petersburg, but he took no interest in my political activity.

I spoke of him to the procureur. "I give you my word of honor," I said, "that Polakóff has never taken part in any political affair. To-morrow he has to pass an examination, and you will spoil forever the scientific career of a young man who has gone through great hardships, and has struggled for years against all sorts of obstacles, to attain his present position. I know that you do not much care for it, but he is looked upon at the university as one of the future glories of Russian science."

The search was made, nevertheless, but a respite of three days was given for the examinations. A little later I was called before the procureur, who triumphantly showed me an envelope addressed in my handwriting, and in it a note, also in my handwriting, which said, "Please take this packet to V. E., and ask that it be kept until demand in due form is made." The person to whom the note was addressed was not mentioned in the note. "This letter," the procureur said, "was found at Mr. Polakóff's; and now, prince, his fate is in your hands. If you tell me who V. E. is, Mr. Polakóff will be released; but if you refuse to do so, he will be kept as long as he does not make up his mind to give us the name of that person."

Looking at the envelope, which was addressed in black chalk, and the letter, which was written in common lead pencil, I immediately remembered the circumstances under which the two had been written. "I am positive," I exclaimed at once, "that the note and the envelope were not found together! It is *you* who have put the letter in the envelope."

The procureur blushed. "Would you have me believe," I continued, "that you, a practical man, did not notice that the two were written with different pencils? And now you are trying to make people think that the two belong to each other! Well, sir, then I tell you that the letter was not to Polakóff."

He hesitated for some time, but then, regaining his audacity, he said, "Polakóff has admitted that this letter of yours was written to him."

Now I knew he was lying. Polakóff would have admitted

everything concerning himself; but he would have preferred to be marched to Siberia rather than to involve another person. So, looking straight in the face of the procureur, I replied, "No, sir, he has *never* said that, and you know perfectly well that your words are not true."

He became furious, or pretended to be so. "Well, then," he said, "if you wait here a moment, I will bring you Polakóff's written statement to that effect. He is in the next room under examination."

"Ready to wait as long as you like."

I sat on a sofa, smoking countless cigarettes. The statement did not come, and never came.

Of course there was no such statement. I met Polakóff in 1878 at Geneva, whence we made a delightful excursion to the Aletsch glacier. I need not say that his answers were what I expected them to be: he denied having any knowledge of the letter or of the person the letters V. E. represented. Scores of books used to be taken from me to him, and back to me, and the letter was found in a book, while the envelope was discovered in the pocket of an old coat. He was kept several weeks under arrest, and then released, owing to the intervention of his scientific friends. V. E. was not molested, and delivered my papers in due time.

I was not taken back to my cell, but half an hour later the procureur came in, accompanied by a gendarme officer. "Our examination," he announced to me, "is now terminated; you will be removed to another place."

Later on, each time I saw him I teased him with the question: "And what about Polakóff's statement?"

A four-wheeled cab stood at the gate. I was asked to enter it, and a stout gendarme officer, of Circassian origin, sat by my side. I spoke to him, but he only snored. The cab crossed the Chain Bridge, then passed the parade grounds and ran along the canals, as if avoiding the more

frequented thoroughfares. "Are we going to the Litóvskiy prison ? " I asked the officer, as I knew that many of
my comrades were already there. He made no reply.
The system of absolute silence which was maintained toward me for the next two years began in this four-wheeled
cab; but when we went rolling over the Palace Bridge, I
understood that I was on the way to the fortress of St.
Peter and St. Paul.

I admired the beautiful river, knowing that I should not
soon see it again. The sun was going down. Thick gray
clouds were hanging in the west above the Gulf of Finland,
while light clouds floated over my head, showing here and
there patches of blue sky. Then the carriage turned to
the left and entered a dark arched passage, the gate of the
fortress.

"Now I shall have to remain here for a couple of years,"
I remarked to the officer.

"No, why so long ? " replied the Circassian, who now
that we were within the fortress had regained the power of
speech. "Your affair is almost terminated, and may be
brought into court in a fortnight."

"My affair," I replied, " is very simple; but before
bringing me to a court you will try to arrest all the socialists in Russia, and they are many, very many ; in two years
you will not have done." I did not then realize how prophetic my remark was.

The carriage stopped at the door of the military commander of the fortress, and we entered his reception hall. General Korsákoff, a thin old man, came in, with a peevish
expression on his face. The officer spoke to him in a subdued voice, and the old man answered, "All right," looking at him with a sort of scorn, and then turned his eyes
toward me. It was evident that he was not at all pleased
to receive a new inmate, and that he felt slightly ashamed
of his rôle ; but he seemed to add, " I am a soldier, and

only do my duty." Presently we got into the carriage
again, but soon stopped before another gate, where we were
kept a long time until a detachment of soldiers opened it
from the inside. Proceeding on foot through narrow passages we came to a third iron gate, opening into a dark
arched passage, from which we entered a small room where
darkness and dampness prevailed.

Several non-commissioned officers of the fortress troops
moved noiselessly about in their soft felt boots, without
speaking a word, while the governor signed the Circassian's
book acknowledging the reception of a new prisoner. I was
required to take off all my clothes, and to put on the prison
dress,—a green flannel dressing-gown, immense woolen
stockings of an incredible thickness, and boat-shaped yellow
slippers, so big that I could hardly keep them on my feet
when I tried to walk. I always hated dressing-gowns and
slippers, and the thick stockings inspired me with disgust.
I had to take off even a silk undergarment, which in the
damp fortress it would have been especially desirable to
retain, but that could not be allowed. I naturally began
to protest and to make a noise about this, and after an hour
or so it was restored to me by order of General Korsákoff.

Then I was taken through a dark passage, where I saw
armed sentries walking about, and was put into a cell. A
heavy oak door was shut behind me, a key turned in the
lock, and I was alone in a half-dark room.

PART FIFTH

THE FORTRESS; THE ESCAPE

I

This was, then, the terrible fortress where so much of the true strength of Russia had perished during the last two centuries, and the very name of which is uttered in St. Petersburg in a hushed voice.

Here Peter I. tortured his son Alexis and killed him with his own hand; here the Princess Tarakánova was kept in a cell which filled with water during an inundation, — the rats climbing upon her to save themselves from drowning; here the terrible Minich tortured his enemies, and Catherine II. buried alive those who objected to her having murdered her husband. And from the times of Peter I. for a hundred and seventy years, the annals of this mass of stone which rises from the Nevá in front of the Winter Palace were annals of murder and torture, of men buried alive, condemned to a slow death, or driven to insanity in the loneliness of the dark and damp dungeons.

Here the Decembrists, who were the first to unfurl in Russia the banner of republican rule and the abolition of serfdom, underwent their first experiences of martyrdom, and traces of them may still be found in the Russian Bastille. Here were imprisoned the poets Ryléeff and Shevchénko, Dostoévsky, Bakúnin, Chernyshévsky, Písareff, and so many others of our best contemporary writers. Here Karakózoff was tortured and hanged.

Here, somewhere in the Alexis ravelin, is still kept Necháieff, who was given up to Russia by Switzerland as a common-law criminal, but is treated as a dangerous political prisoner, and will never again see the light.   In the same ravelin are also two or three men whom, rumor says, Alexander II., because of what they knew, and others must not know, about some palace mystery, ordered imprisoned for life.   One of them, adorned with a long gray beard, was lately seen by an acquaintance of mine in the mysterious fortress.

All these shadows rose before my imagination.   But my thoughts fixed especially on Bakúnin, who, though he had been shut up in an Austrian fortress, after 1848, for two years, chained to the wall, and then handed over to Nicholas I., who kept him in the fortress for six years longer, yet came out, when the Iron Tsar's death released him, fresher and fuller of vigor than his comrades who had remained at liberty.   "He has lived it through," I said to myself, "and I must, too : I will *not* succumb here !"

My first movement was to approach the window, which was placed so high that I could hardly reach it with my lifted hand.   It was a long, low opening, cut in a wall five feet thick, and protected by an iron grating and a double iron window frame.   At a distance of a dozen yards from this window I saw the outer wall of the fortress, of immense thickness, on the top of which I could make out a gray sentry box.   Only by looking upward could I perceive a bit of the sky.

I made a minute inspection of the room where I had now to spend no one could say how many years.   From the position of the high chimney of the Mint I guessed that I was in the southwestern corner of the fortress, in a bastion overlooking the Nevá.   The building in which I was incarcerated, however, was not the bastion itself, but what is called in a fortification a *réduit ;* that is, an inner two-storied pentagonal piece of masonry which rises a little higher than the walls of the bastion, and is meant to contain two tiers of guns. This room of mine was a casemate destined for a big gun, and the window was an embrasure. The rays of the sun could never penetrate it; even in summer they were lost in the thickness of the wall. The room held an iron bed, a small oak table, and an oak stool. The floor was covered with painted felt, and the walls with yellow paper. However, in order to deaden sounds, the paper was not put on the wall itself; it was pasted upon canvas, and behind the canvas I discovered a wire grating, back of which was a layer of felt; only beyond the felt could I reach the stone wall. At the inner side of the room there was a washstand, and a thick oak door in which I made out a locked opening, for passing food through, and a little slit, protected by glass and by a shutter from the outside: this was the "Judas," through which the prisoner could be spied upon at every moment. The sentry who stood in the passage frequently lifted the shutter and looked inside, — his boots squeaking as he crept toward the door. I tried to speak to him; then the eye which I could see through the slit assumed an expression of terror and the shutter was immediately let down, only to be furtively opened a minute or two later; but I could not get a word of response from the sentry.

Absolute silence reigned all round. I dragged my stool to the window and looked upon the little bit of sky that I could see; I tried to catch any sound from the Nevá or from the town on the opposite side of the river, but I could not. This dead silence began to oppress me, and I tried to sing, softly at first, and louder and louder afterwards.

"Have I then to say farewell to love forever?" I caught myself singing from my favorite opera, Glínka's "Ruslán and Ludmíla." . . .

"Sir, do not sing, please," a bass voice said through the food-window in my door.

"I *will* sing."

" You must not."

" I will sing nevertheless."

Then came the governor, who tried to persuade me that I must not sing, as it would have to be reported to the commander of the fortress, and so on.

" But my throat will become blocked and my lungs become useless if I do not speak and cannot sing," I tried to argue.

" Better try to sing in a lower tone, more or less to yourself," said the old governor in a supplicatory manner.

But all this was useless. A few days later I had lost all desire to sing. I tried to do it on principle, but it was of no avail.

" The main thing," I said to myself, " is to preserve my physical vigor. I *will* not fall ill. Let me imagine myself compelled to spend a couple of years in a hut in the far north, during an arctic expedition. I will take plenty of exercise, practice gymnastics, and not let myself be broken down by my surroundings. Ten steps from one corner to the other is already something. If I repeat them one hundred and fifty times, I shall have walked one verst " (two thirds of a mile). I determined to walk every day seven versts, — about five miles : two versts in the morning, two before dinner, two after dinner, and one before going to sleep. " If I put on the table ten cigarettes, and move one of them each time that I pass the table, I shall easily count the three hundred times that I must walk up and down. I must walk rapidly, but turn slowly in the corner to avoid becoming giddy, and turn each time a different way. Then, twice a day I shall practice gymnastics with my heavy stool." I lifted it by one leg, holding it at arm's length. I turned it like a wheel, and soon learned to throw it from one hand to the other, over my head, behind my back, and across my legs.

A few hours after I had been brought into the prison the

governor came to offer me some books, and among them was
an old acquaintance and friend of mine, the first volume of
George Lewes's "Physiology," in a Russian translation; but
the second volume, which I especially wanted to read again,
was missing.   I asked, of course, to have paper, pen, and
ink, but was absolutely refused.   Pen and ink are never
allowed in the fortress, unless special permission is obtained
from the Emperor himself.   I suffered very much from this
forced inactivity, and began to compose in my imagination
a series of novels for popular reading, taken from Russian
history, — something like Eugène Sue's "Mystères du
Peuple."   I made up the plot, the descriptions, the dialogues, and tried to commit the whole to memory from the
beginning to the end.   One can easily imagine how exhaust-
ing such a work would have been if I had had to continue
it for more than two or three months.

But my brother Alexander obtained pen and ink for me.
One day I was asked to enter a four-wheeled cab, in company with the same speechless Georgian gendarme officer of
whom I have spoken before.   I was taken to the Third
Section, where I was allowed an interview with my brother,
in the presence of two gendarme officers.

Alexander was at Zürich when I was arrested.   From
early youth he had longed to go abroad, where men think
as they like, read what they like, and openly express their
thoughts.   Russian life was hateful to him.   Veracity —
absolute veracity — and the most open-hearted frankness
were the dominating features of his character.   He could
not bear deceit or even conceit in any form.   The absence
of free speech in Russia, the Russian readiness to submit
to oppression, the veiled words to which our writers resort,
were utterly repulsive to his frank and open nature.   Soon
after my return from Western Europe he removed to Switzerland, and decided to settle there.   After he had lost his
two children — one from cholera in a few hours, and the

other from consumption — St. Petersburg became doubly repugnant to him.

My brother did not take part in our work of agitation. He did not believe in the possibility of a popular uprising, and he conceived a revolution only as the action of a representative body, like the National Assembly of France in 1789. As for the socialist agitation, he knew it only by means of public meetings and public speeches, — not as the secret, minute work of personal propaganda which we were carrying on. In England he would have sided with John Bright or with the Chartists. If he had been in Paris during the uprising of June, 1848, he would surely have fought with the last handful of workers behind the last barricade; but in the preparatory period he would have followed Louis Blanc or Ledru Rollin.

In Switzerland he settled at Zürich, and his sympathies went with the moderate wing of the International. Socialist on principle, he carried out his principles in his most frugal and laborious mode of living, toiling on passionately at his great scientific work, — the main purpose of his life, — a work which was to be a nineteenth-century counterpart to the famous "Tableau de la Nature" of the Encyclopædists. He soon became a close personal friend of the old refugee Colonel P. L. Lavróff, with whom he had very much in common in his Kantian philosophical views.

When he learned about my arrest, Alexander immediately left everything, — the work of his life, the life itself of freedom which was as necessary for him as free air is necessary for a bird, — and returned to St. Petersburg, which he disliked, only to help me through my imprisonment.

We were both very much affected at this interview. My brother was extremely excited. He hated the very sight of the blue uniforms of the gendarmes, — those executioners of all independent thought in Russia, — and expressed his feeling frankly in their presence. As for me, the sight of him at St. Petersburg filled me with the most dismal apprehensions. I was happy to see his honest face, his eyes full of love, and to hear that I should see them once a month; and yet I wished him hundreds of miles away from that place to which he came free that day, but to which he would inevitably be brought some night under an escort of gendarmes. "Why did you come into the lion's den? Go back at once!" my whole inner self cried; and yet I knew that he would remain as long as I was in prison.

He understood better than any one else that inactivity would kill me, and had already made application to obtain for me permission to resume work. The Geographical Society wanted me to finish my book on the glacial period, and my brother turned the whole scientific world in St. Petersburg upside down to move it to support his application. The Academy of Sciences was interested in the matter; and finally, two or three months after my imprisonment, the governor entered my cell and announced to me that I was permitted by the Emperor to complete my report to the Geographical Society, and that I should be allowed pen and ink for that purpose. "Till sunset only," he added. Sunset, at St. Petersburg, is at three in the afternoon, in winter time; but that could not be helped. "Till sunset" were the words used by Alexander II. when he granted the permission.

II

So I could work!

I could hardly express now the immensity of relief I then felt at being enabled to resume writing. I would have consented to live on nothing but bread and water, in the dampest of cellars, if only permitted to work.

I was, however, the only prisoner to whom writing materials were allowed. Several of my comrades spent three years and more in confinement before the famous trial of "the hundred and ninety-three" took place, and all they had was a slate. Of course, even the slate was welcome in that dreary loneliness, and they used it to write exercises in the languages they were learning, or to work out mathematical problems; but what was jotted down on the slate could last only a few hours.

My prison life now took on a more regular character. There was something immediate to live for. At nine in the morning I had already made the first three hundred pacings across my cell, and was waiting for my pencils and pens to be delivered to me. The work which I had prepared for the Geographical Society contained, beside a report of my explorations in Finland, a discussion of the bases upon which the glacial hypothesis ought to rest. Now, knowing that I had plenty of time before me, I decided to rewrite and enlarge that part of my work. The Academy of Sciences put its admirable library at my service, and a corner of my cell soon filled up with books and maps, including the whole of the Swedish Geological Survey publications, a nearly complete collection of reports of all arctic travels, and whole sets of the Quarterly Journal of the

London Geological Society. My book grew in the fortress to the size of two large volumes. The first of them was printed by my brother and Polakóff (in the Geographical Society's Memoirs) ; while the second, not quite finished, remained in the hands of the Third Section when I ran away. The manuscript was found only in 1895, and given to the Russian Geographical Society, by whom it was forwarded to me in London.

At five in the afternoon, — at three in the winter, — as soon as the tiny lamp was brought in, my pencils and pens were taken away, and I had to stop work. Then I used to read, mostly books of history. Quite a library had been formed in the fortress by the generations of political prisoners who had been confined there. I was allowed to add to the library a number of staple works on Russian history, and with the books which were brought to me by my relatives I was enabled to read almost every work and collection of acts and documents bearing on the Moscow period of the history of Russia. I relished, in reading, not only the Russian annals, especially the admirable annals of the democratic mediæval republic of Pskov, — the best, perhaps, in Europe for the history of that type of mediæval cities, — but all sorts of dry documents, and even the Lives of the Saints, which occasionally contain facts of the real life of the masses which cannot be found elsewhere. I also read during this time a great number of novels, and even arranged for myself a treat on Christmas Eve. My relatives managed to send me then the Christmas stories of Dickens, and I spent the festival laughing and crying over those beautiful creations of the great novelist.

III

THE worst was the silence, as of the grave, which reigned about me. In vain I knocked on the walls and struck the floor with my foot, listening for the faintest sound in reply. None was to be heard. One month passed, then two, three, fifteen months, but there was no reply to my knocks. We were only six then, scattered among thirty-six casemates, — all my arrested comrades being kept in the Litóvskiy Zámok prison. When the non-commissioned officer entered my cell to take me out for a walk, and I asked him, "What kind of weather have we? Does it rain?" he cast a furtive side glance at me, and without saying a word promptly retired behind the door, where a sentry and another non-commissioned officer kept watch upon him. The only living being from whom I could hear even a few words was the governor, who came to my cell every morning to say "good-morning" and ask whether I wanted to buy tobacco or paper. I tried to engage him in conversation; but he also cast furtive glances at the non-commissioned officers who stood in the half-opened door, as if to say, "You see, I am watched, too." Only the pigeons were not afraid to hold intercourse with me. Every morning and afternoon they came to my window to receive their food through the grating.

There were no sounds whatever except the squeak of the sentry's boots, the hardly perceptible noise of the shutter of the Judas, and the ringing of the bells on the fortress cathedral. They rang a "Lord save me" ("Góspodi pomílui") every quarter of an hour, — one, two, three, four times. Then, each hour, the big bell struck slowly, with long intervals between successive strokes. A lugu-brious canticle followed, chimed by the bells, which at every sudden change of temperature went out of tune, making at such times a horrible cacophony which sounded like the ringing of bells at a burial. At the gloomy hour of mid-night, the canticle, moreover, was followed by the discord-ant notes of a "God save the Tsar." The ringing lasted a full quarter of an hour; and no sooner had it come to an end than a new "Lord save me" announced to the sleep-less prisoner that a quarter of an hour of his uselessly spent life had gone in the meantime, and that many quarters of an hour, and hours, and days, and months of the same vege-tative life would pass, before his keepers, or maybe death, would release him.

Every morning I was taken out for a half-hour's walk in the prison yard. This yard was a small pentagon with a narrow pavement round it, and a little building — the bath house — in the middle. But I liked those walks.

The need of new impressions is so great in prison that, when I walked in our narrow yard, I always kept my eyes fixed upon the high gilt spire of the fortress cathedral. This was the only thing in my surroundings which changed its aspect, and I liked to see it glittering like pure gold when the sun shone from a clear blue sky, or assuming a fairy aspect when a light bluish haze lay upon the town, or becoming steel gray when dark clouds obscured the sky.

During these walks I occasionally saw the daughter of the governor, a girl of eighteen or nineteen, as she came out from her father's apartment and had to walk a few steps in our yard in order to reach the entrance gate, the only issue from the building. She always hurried along, with her eyes cast down, as if she felt ashamed of being the daughter of a jailer. Her younger brother, on the con-trary, a cadet whom I also saw once or twice in the yard, always looked straight in my face with such a frank ex-

pression of sympathy that I was struck with it and even
mentioned it to some one after my release. Four or five
years later, when he was already an officer, he was exiled
to Siberia. He had joined the revolutionary party, and
must have helped, I suppose, to carry on correspondence
with prisoners in the fortress.

Winter is gloomy at St. Petersburg for those who cannot
be out in the brightly lighted streets. It was still gloomier,
of course, in a casemate. But dampness was even worse
than darkness. The casemates are so damp that in order
to drive away moisture they must be overheated, and I felt
almost suffocated; but when at last I obtained my request,
that the temperature should be kept lower than before, the
outer wall became dripping with moisture, and the paper
was as if a pail of water had been poured upon it every
day, — the consequence being that I suffered a great deal
from rheumatism.

With all that I was cheerful, continuing to write and to
draw maps in the darkness, sharpening my lead pencils
with a broken piece of glass which I had managed to get
hold of in the yard; I faithfully walked my five miles a
day in the cell, and performed gymnastic feats with my
oak stool. Time went on. But then sorrow crept into
my cell and nearly broke me down. My brother Alexander
was arrested.

Toward the end of December, 1874, I was allowed an
interview with him and our sister Hélène, in the fortress,
in the presence of a gendarme officer. Interviews, granted
at long intervals, always bring both the prisoner and his
relatives into a state of excitement. One sees beloved faces
and hears beloved voices, knowing that the vision will last
but a few moments; one feels so near to the other, and yet
so far off, as there can be no intimate conversation before a
stranger, an enemy and a spy. Besides, my brother and

sister felt anxious for my health, upon which the dark, gloomy winter days and the dampness had already marked their first effects. We parted with heavy hearts.

A week after that interview I received, instead of an expected letter from my brother concerning the printing of my book, a short note from Polakóff. He informed me that henceforward he would read the proofs, and that I should have to address to him everything relative to the printing. From the very tone of the note I understood at once that something must be wrong with my brother. If it were only illness, Polakóff would have mentioned it. Days of fearful anxiety came upon me. Alexander must have been arrested, and I must have been the cause of it! Life suddenly ceased to have any meaning for me. My walks, my gymnastics, my work, lost interest. All the day long I went ceaselessly up and down my cell, thinking of nothing but Alexander's arrest. For me, an unmarried man, imprisonment was only personal inconvenience; but he was married, he passionately loved his wife, and they now had a boy, upon whom they had concentrated all the love that they had felt for their first two children.

Worst of all was the incertitude. What could he have done? For what reason had he been arrested? What were they going to do with him? Weeks passed; my anxiety became deeper and deeper; but there was no news, till at last I heard in a roundabout way that he had been arrested for a letter written to P. L. Lavróff.

I learned the details much later. After his last interview with me he wrote to his old friend, who at that time was editing a Russian socialist review, " Forward," in London. He mentioned in this letter his fears about my health; he spoke of the many arrests which were then being made in Russia; and he freely expressed his hatred of the despotic rule. The letter was intercepted at the post-office by the Third Section, and they came on Christmas Eve to search his apartments. They carried out their search in an even more brutal manner than usual. After midnight half a dozen men made an irruption into his flat, and turned everything upside down. The very walls were examined; the sick child was taken out of its bed, that the bedding and the mattresses might be inspected. They found nothing, — there was nothing to find.

My brother very much resented this search. With his customary frankness, he said to the gendarme officer who conducted it : "Against you, captain, I have no grievance. You have received little education, and you hardly understand what you are doing. But you, sir," he continued, turning towards the procureur, "you know what part you are playing in these proceedings. You have received a university education. You know the law, and you know that you are trampling all law, such as it is, under your feet, and covering the lawlessness of these men by your presence; you are simply — a scoundrel!"

They swore hatred against him. They kept him imprisoned in the Third Section till May. My brother's child — a charming boy, whom illness had rendered still more affectionate and intelligent — was dying from consumption. The doctors said he had only a few days more to live. Alexander, who had never asked any favor of his enemies, asked them this time to permit him to see his child for the last time. He begged to be allowed to go home for one hour, upon his word of honor to return, or to be taken there under escort. They refused. They could not deny themselves that vengeance.

The child died, and its mother was thrown once more into a state bordering on insanity when my brother was told that he was to be transported to East Siberia, to a small town, Minusínsk. He would travel in a cart between two gendarmes, and his wife might follow later, but could not travel with him.

"Tell me, at least, what is my crime," he demanded; but there was no accusation of any sort against him beyond the letter. This transportation appeared so arbitrary, so much an act of mere revenge on the part of the Third Section, that none of our relatives could believe that the exile would last more than a few months. My brother lodged a complaint with the minister of the interior. The reply was that the minister could not interfere with the will of the chief of the gendarmes. Another complaint was lodged with the Senate. It was of no avail.

A couple of years later our sister Hélène, acting on her own initiative, wrote a petition to the Tsar. Our cousin Dmítri, governor-general of Khárkoff, aide-de-camp of the Emperor, and a favorite at the court, also deeply incensed at this treatment by the Third Section, handed the petition personally to the Tsar, and in so-doing added a few words in support of it. But the vindictiveness of the Románoffs was a family trait strongly developed in Alexander II. He wrote upon the petition, "Pust posidít" (Let him remain some time more). My brother stayed in Siberia twelve years, and never returned to Russia.

IV

THE countless arrests which were made in the summer of 1874, and the serious turn which was given by the police to the prosecution of our circle, produced a deep change in the opinions of Russian youth. Up to that time the prevailing idea had been to pick out among the workers, and eventually the peasants, a number of men who should be prepared to become socialistic agitators. But the factories were now flooded with spies, and it was evident that, do what they might, both propagandists and workers would very soon be arrested and hidden forever in Siberia. Then began a great movement "to the people" in a new form, when several hundred young men and women, disregarding all precautions hitherto taken, rushed to the country, and, traveling through the towns and villages, incited the masses to revolution, almost openly distributing pamphlets, songs, and proclamations. In our circles this summer received the name of "the mad summer."

The gendarmes lost their heads. They had not hands enough to make the arrest nor eyes enough to trace the steps of every propagandist. Yet not less than fifteen hundred persons were arrested during this hunt, and half of them were kept in prison for years.

One day in the summer of 1875, in the cell that was next to mine, I distinctly heard the light steps of heeled boots, and a few minutes later I caught fragments of a conversation. A feminine voice spoke from the cell, and a deep bass voice — evidently that of the sentry — grunted something in reply. Then I recognized the sound of the colonel's spurs, his rapid steps, his swearing at the sentry, and the click of the key in the lock. He said something, and a feminine voice loudly replied : " We did not talk. I only asked him to call the non-commissioned officer." Then the door was locked, and I heard the colonel swearing in whispers at the sentry.

So I was alone no more. I had a lady neighbor, who at once broke down the severe discipline which had hitherto reigned amongst the soldiers. From that day the walls of the fortress, which had been mute during the last fifteen months, became animated. From all sides I heard knocks with the foot on the floor : one, two, three, four, . . . eleven knocks, twenty-four knocks, fifteen knocks; then an interruption, followed by three knocks and a long succession of thirty-three knocks. Over and over again these knocks were repeated in the same succession, until the neighbor would guess at last that they were meant for " Kto vy ? " (Who are you ?) the letter *v* being the third letter in our alphabet. Thereupon conversation was soon established, and usually was conducted in the abridged alphabet ; that is, the alphabet being divided into six rows of five letters, each letter is marked by its row and its place in the row.

I discovered with great pleasure that I had at my left my friend Serdukóff, with whom I could soon talk about everything, especially when we used our cipher. But intercourse with men brought its sufferings as well as its joys. Underneath me was lodged a peasant, whom Serdukóff knew. He talked to him by means of knocks ; and even against my will, often unconsciously during my work, I followed their conversations. I also spoke to him. Now, if solitary confinement without any sort of work is hard for educated men, it is infinitely harder for a peasant who is accustomed to physical work, and not at all wont to spend years in reading. Our peasant friend felt quite miserable, and having been kept for nearly two years in another prison before he was brought to the fortress, — his crime was that he had listened to socialists, — he was already broken down. Soon I began to notice, to my terror, that from time to time his mind wandered. Gradually his thoughts grew more and more confused, and we two perceived, step by step, day by day, evidences that his reason was failing, until his talk became at last that of a lunatic. Frightful noises and wild cries came next from the lower story; our neighbor was mad, but was still kept for several months in the casemate before he was removed to an asylum, from which he never emerged. To witness the destruction of a man's mind, under such conditions, was terrible. I am sure it must have contributed to increase the nervous irritability of my good and true friend Serdukóff. When, after four years of imprisonment, he was acquitted by the court and released, he shot himself.

One day I received a quite unexpected visit. The Grand Duke Nicholas, brother of Alexander II., who was inspecting the fortress, entered my cell, followed only by his aide-de-camp. The door was shut behind him. He rapidly approached me, saying, " Good-day, Kropótkin." He knew me personally, and spoke in a familiar, good-natured tone, as to an old acquaintance. "How is it possible, Kropótkin, that you, a page de chambre, a sergeant of the corps of pages, should be mixed up in this business, and now be here in this horrible casemate ? "

"Every one has his own opinions," was my reply.

"Opinions ! So your opinions were that you must stir up a revolution ? "

What was I to reply ? Yes ? Then the construction which would be put upon my answer would be that I, who had refused to give any answers to the gendarmes, " avowed everything " before the brother of the Tsar. His tone was that of a commander of a military school when trying to obtain "avowals" from a cadet. Yet I could not say No: it would have been a lie. I did not know what to say, and stood without saying anything.

"You see! You feel ashamed of it now" —

This remark angered me, and I at once said in a rather sharp way, "I have given my replies to the examining magistrate, and have nothing to add."

"But understand, Kropótkin, please," he said then, in the most familiar tone, "that I don't speak to you as an examining magistrate. I speak quite as a private person, — quite as a private man," he repeated, lowering his voice.

Thoughts went whirling in my head. To play the part of Marquis Posa? To tell the Emperor through the grand duke of the desolation of Russia, the ruin of the peasantry, the arbitrariness of the officials, the terrible famines in prospect? To say that we wanted to help the peasants out of their desperate condition, to make them raise their heads, and by all this try to influence Alexander II.? These thoughts followed one another in rapid succession, till at last I said to myself: "Never! Nonsense! They know all that. They are enemies of the nation, and such talk would not change them."

I replied that he always remained an official person, and that I could not look upon him as a private man.

He then began to ask me indifferent questions. "Was it not in Siberia, with the Decembrists, that you began to entertain such ideas?"

"No; I knew only one Decembrist, and with him I had no talks worth speaking of."

"Was it then at St. Petersburg that you got them?"

"I was always the same."

"Why! Were you such in the corps of pages?" he asked me with terror.

"In the corps I was a boy, and what is indefinite in boyhood grows definite in manhood."

He asked me some other similar questions, and as he spoke I distinctly saw what he was driving at. He was trying to obtain avowals, and my imagination vividly pictured him saying to his brother : " All these examining magistrates are imbeciles. He gave them no replies, but I talked to him ten minutes, and he told me everything." That began to annoy me; and when he said to me something to this effect, " How could you have anything to do with all these people, — peasants and people with no names ? " — I sharply turned upon him and said, " I have told you already that I have given my replies to the examining magistrate." Then he abruptly left the cell.

Later, the soldiers of the guard made quite a legend of that visit. The person who came in a carriage to carry me away at the time of my escape wore a military cap, and, having sandy whiskers, bore a faint resemblance to the Grand Duke Nicholas. So a tradition grew up amongst the soldiers of the St. Petersburg garrison that it was the grand duke himself who came to rescue me and kidnapped me. Thus are legends created even in times of newspapers and biographical dictionaries.

V

Two years had passed. Several of my comrades had died, several had become insane, but nothing was heard yet of our case coming before a court.

My health gave way before the end of the second year. The oak stool now seemed heavy in my hand, and the five miles became an endless distance. As there were about sixty of us in the fortress, and the winter days were short, we were taken out for a walk in the yard for twenty minutes only every third day. I did my best to maintain my energy, but the "arctic wintering" without an interruption in the summer got the better of me. I had brought back from my Siberian journeys slight symptoms of scurvy; now, in the darkness and dampness of the casemate, they developed more distinctly; that scourge of the prisons had got hold of me.

In March or April, 1876, we were at last told that the Third Section had completed the preliminary inquest. The "case" had been transmitted to the judicial authorities, and consequently we were removed to a prison attached to the court of justice, — the house of detention.

It was an immense show prison, recently built on the model of the French and Belgian prisons, consisting of four stories of small cells, each of which had a window overlooking an inner yard and a door opening on an iron balcony; the balconies of the several stories were connected by iron staircases.

For most of my comrades the transfer to this prison was a great relief. There was much more life in it than in the fortress; more opportunity for correspondence, for seeing one's relatives, and for mutual intercourse. Tapping on the walls continued all day long undisturbed, and I was able in this way to relate to a young neighbor the history of the Paris Commune from the beginning to the end. It took, however, a whole week's tapping.

As to my health, it grew even worse than it had lately been in the fortress. I could not bear the close atmosphere of the tiny cell, which measured only four steps from one corner to another, and where, as soon as the steampipes were set to work, the temperature changed from a glacial cold to an unbearable heat. Having to turn so often, I became giddy after a few minutes' walk, and ten minutes of outdoor exercise, in the corner of a yard inclosed between high brick walls, did not refresh me in the least. As to the prison doctor, who did not want to hear the word "scurvy" pronounced "in his prison," the less said of him the better.

I was allowed to receive food from home, it so happening that one of my relatives, married to a lawyer, lived a few doors from the court. But my digestion had become so bad that I was soon able to eat nothing but a small piece of bread and one or two eggs a day. My strength rapidly failed, and the general opinion was that I should not live more than a few months. When climbing the staircase which led to my cell in the second story, I had to stop two or three times to rest, and I remember an elderly soldier from the escort once commiserating me and saying, "Poor man, you won't live till the end of the summer."

My relatives now became very much alarmed. My sister Hélène tried to obtain my release on bail, but the procureur, Shúbin, replied to her, with a sardonic smile, "If you bring me a doctor's certificate that he will die in ten days, I will release him." He had the satisfaction of seeing my sister fall into a chair and sob aloud in his presence. She succeeded, however, in gaining her request that I should

be visited by a good physician, — the chief doctor of the
military hospital of the St. Petersburg garrison. He was
a bright, intelligent, aged general, who examined me in the
most scrupulous manner, and concluded that I had no organic
disease, but was suffering simply from a want of oxidation
of the blood. "Air is all that you want," he said. Then
he stood a few moments in hesitation, and added in a decided manner, "No use talking, you cannot remain here;
you must be transferred."

Some ten days later I was transferred to the military
hospital, which is situated on the outskirts of St. Petersburg, and has a special small prison for the officers and
soldiers who fall ill when they are under trial. Two of
my comrades had already been removed to this hospital
prison, when it was certain that they would soon die of
consumption.

In the hospital I began at once to recover. I was given
a spacious room on the ground floor, close by the room of
the military guard. It had an immense grated window
looking south, which opened on a small boulevard with two
rows of trees; and beyond the boulevard there was a wide
space where two hundred carpenters were engaged in building wooden shanties for typhoid patients. Every evening
they gave an hour or so to singing in chorus, — such a
chorus as is formed only in large carpenters' artéls. A sentry marched up and down the boulevard, his box standing
opposite my room.

My window was kept open all the day, and I battened
in the rays of the sun, which I had missed for such a long
time. I breathed the balmy air of May with a full chest,
and my health improved rapidly, — too rapidly, I began to
think. I was soon able to digest light food, gained strength,
and resumed my work with renewed energy. Seeing no
way in which I could finish the second volume of my work,

I wrote a résumé of it, which was printed in the first volume.

In the fortress I had heard from a comrade who had been in the hospital prison that it would not be hard for me to escape from it, and I made my presence there known to my friends. However, escape proved far more difficult than I had been led to believe. A stricter supervision than had ever before been heard of was exercised over me. The sentry in the passage was placed at my door, and I was never let out of my room. The hospital soldiers and the officers of the guard who occasionally entered it seemed to be afraid to stay more than a minute or two.

Various plans were made by my friends to liberate me, — some of them very amusing. I was, for instance, to file through the iron bars of my window. Then, on a rainy night, when the sentry on the boulevard was dozing in his box, two friends were to creep up from behind and over- turn the box, so that it would fall upon the sentry and catch him like a mouse in a trap, without hurting him. In the meantime, I was to jump out of the window. But a better solution came in an unexpected way.

" Ask to be let out for a walk," one of the soldiers whis- pered to me one day. I did so. The doctor supported my demand, and every afternoon, at four, I was allowed to take an hour's walk in the prison yard. I had to keep on the green flannel dressing-gown which is worn by the hospital patients, but my boots, my vest, and my trousers were delivered to me every day.

I shall never forget my first walk. When I was taken out, I saw before me a yard full three hundred paces long and more than two hundred paces wide, all covered with grass. The gate was open, and through it I could see the street, the immense hospital opposite, and the people who passed by. I stopped on the doorsteps of the prison, unable for a moment to move when I saw that yard and that gate.

At one end of the yard stood the prison, — a narrow building, about one hundred and fifty paces long, — at each end of which was a sentry box. The two sentries paced up and down in front of the building, and had tramped out a footpath in the green. Along this footpath I was told to walk, and the two sentries continued to walk up and down, — so that I was never more than ten or fifteen paces from the one or the other. Three hospital soldiers took their seats on the doorsteps.

At the opposite end of this spacious yard wood for fuel was being unloaded from a dozen carts, and piled up along the wall by a dozen peasants. The whole yard was inclosed by a high fence made of thick boards. Its gate was open to let the carts in and out.

This open gate fascinated me. "I must not stare at it," I said to myself; and yet I looked at it all the time. As soon as I was taken back to my cell I wrote to my friends to communicate to them the welcome news. "I feel well-nigh unable to use the cipher," I wrote with a tremulous hand, tracing almost illegible signs instead of figures. "This nearness of liberty makes me tremble as if I were in a fever. They took me out to-day in the yard; its gate was open, and no sentry near it. Through this unguarded gate I will run out; my sentries will not catch me," — and I gave the plan of the escape. "A lady is to come in an open carriage to the hospital. She is to alight, and the carriage to wait for her in the street, some fifty paces from the gate. When I am taken out, at four, I shall walk for a while with my hat in my hand, and somebody who passes by the gate will take it as the signal that all is right within the prison. Then you must return a signal: 'The street is clear.' Without it I shall not start; once beyond the gate I must not be recaptured. Light or sound only can be used for your signal. The coachman may send a flash of light, — the sun's rays reflected from his lacquered hat

upon the main hospital building; or, still better, the sound of
a song continued as long as the street is clear; unless you
can occupy the little gray bungalow which I see from the
yard, and signal to me from its window. The sentry will run
after me like a dog after a hare, describing a curve, while I
run in a straight line, and I *will* keep five or ten paces in
advance of him. In the street, I shall spring into the carriage and we shall gallop away. If the sentry shoots —
well, that cannot be helped; it lies beyond our foresight;
and then, against a certain death in prison, the thing is
well worth the risk."

Counter proposals were made, but that plan was ultimately
adopted. The matter was taken in hand by our circle;
people who never had known me entered into it, as if it
were the release of the dearest of their brothers. However,
the attempt was beset with difficulties, and time went with
terrible rapidity. I worked hard, writing late at night;
but my health improved, nevertheless, at a speed which I
found appalling. When I was let out into the yard for
the first time, I could only creep like a tortoise along the
footpath; now I felt strong enough to run. True, I continued to go at the same tortoise pace, lest my walks should
be stopped; but my natural vivacity might betray me at
any moment. And my comrades, in the mean time, had
to enlist more than a score of people in the affair, to find a
reliable horse and an experienced coachman, and to arrange
hundreds of unforeseen details which always spring up
around such conspiracies. The preparations took a month
or so, and any day I might be moved back to the house of
detention.

At last the day of the escape was settled. June 29, Old
Style, is the day of St. Peter and St. Paul. My friends,
throwing a touch of sentimentalism into their enterprise,
wanted to set me free on that day. They had let me

know that in reply to my signal "All right within" they would signal "All right outside" by sending up a red toy balloon. Then the carriage would come, and a song would be sung to let me know when the street was open.

I went out on the 29th, took off my hat, and waited for the balloon. But nothing of the kind was to be seen. Half an hour passed. I heard the rumble of a carriage in the street; I heard a man's voice singing a song unknown to me; but there was no balloon.

The hour was over, and with a broken heart I returned to my room. "Something must have gone wrong," I said to myself.

The impossible had happened that day. Hundreds of children's balloons are always on sale in St. Petersburg, near the Gostínoi Dvor. That morning there were none; not a single balloon was to be found. One was discovered at last, in the possession of a child, but it was old and would not fly. My friends rushed then to an optician's shop, bought an apparatus for making hydrogen, and filled the balloon with it; but it would not fly any better: the hydrogen had not been dried. Time pressed. Then a lady attached the balloon to her umbrella, and, holding the umbrella high over her head, walked up and down in the street along the high wall of our yard; but I saw nothing of it, — the wall being too high, and the lady too short.

As it turned out, nothing could have been better than that accident with the balloon. When the hour of my walk had passed, the carriage was driven along the streets which it was intended to follow after the escape; and there, in a narrow street, it was stopped by a dozen or more carts which were carrying wood to the hospital. The horses of the carts got into disorder, — some of them on the right side of the street, and some on the left, — and the carriage had to make its way at a slow pace amongst them; at a turning it was actually blocked. If I had been in it, we should have been caught.

Now a whole system of signals was established along the streets through which we should have to go after the escape, in order to give notice if the streets were not clear.   For a couple of miles from the hospital my comrades took the position of sentries.   One was to walk up and down with a handkerchief in his hand, which at the approach of the carts he was to put into his pocket; another was to sit on a stone and eat cherries, stopping when the carts came near; and so on.   All these signals, transmitted along the streets, were finally to reach the carriage.   My friends had also hired the gray bungalow that I had seen from the yard, and at an open window of that little house a violinist stood with his violin, ready to play when the signal "Street clear" reached him.

The attempt had been settled for the next day.   Further postponement would have been dangerous.   In fact, the carriage had been taken notice of by the hospital people, and something suspicious must have reached the ears of the authorities, as on the night before my escape I heard the patrol officer ask the sentry who stood opposite my window, "Where are your ball cartridges?"   The soldier began to take them in a clumsy way out of his cartridge pouch, spending a couple of minutes before he got them.   The patrol officer swore at him.   "Have you not been told to-night to keep four ball cartridges in the pocket of your coat?"   And he stood by the sentry till the latter put four cartridges into his pocket.   "Look sharp!" he said as he turned away.

The new arrangements concerning the signals had to be communicated to me at once; and at two on the next day a lady — a dear relative of mine — came to the prison, asking that a watch might be transmitted to me.   Everything had to go through the hands of the procureur; but as this was simply a watch, without a box, it was passed along. In it was a tiny cipher note which contained the whole plan. When I read it I was seized with terror, so daring was the feat. The lady, herself under pursuit by the police for political reasons, would have been arrested on the spot, if any one had chanced to open the lid of the watch. But I saw her calmly leave the prison and move slowly along the boulevard.

I came out at four, as usual, and gave my signal. I heard next the rumble of the carriage, and a few minutes later the tones of the violin in the gray house sounded through our yard. But I was then at the other end of the building. When I got back to the end of my path which was nearest the gate, — about a hundred paces from it, — the sentry was close upon my heels. "One turn more," I thought — but before I reached the farther end of the path the violin suddenly ceased playing.

More than a quarter of an hour passed, full of anxiety, before I understood the cause of the interruption. Then a dozen heavily loaded carts entered the gate and moved to the other end of the yard.

Immediately, the violinist — a good one, I must say — began a wildly exciting mazurka from Kontsky, as if to say, "Straight on now, — this is your time!" I moved slowly to the nearer end of the footpath, trembling at the thought that the mazurka might stop before I reached it.

When I was there I turned round. The sentry had stopped five or six paces behind me; he was looking the other way. "Now or never!" I remember that thought flashing through my head. I flung off my green flannel dressing-gown and began to run.

For many days in succession I had practiced how to get rid of that immeasurably long and cumbrous garment. It was so long that I carried the lower part on my left arm, as ladies carry the trains of their riding habits. Do what I might, it would not come off in one movement. I cut the seams under the armpits, but that did not help. Then

learn to throw it off in two movements: one
me end from my arm, the other dropping the gown
e floor. I practiced patiently in my room until I could
it as neatly as soldiers handle their rifles. "One, two,"
and it was on the ground.

I did not trust much to my vigor, and began to run
rather slowly, to economize my strength. But no sooner
had I taken a few steps than the peasants who were piling
the wood at the other end shouted, "He runs! Stop him!
Catch him!" and they hastened to intercept me at the
gate. Then I flew for my life. I thought of nothing but
running, — not even of the pit which the carts had dug
out at the gate. Run! run! full speed!

The sentry, I was told later by the friends who witnessed the scene from the gray house, ran after me, followed
by three soldiers who had been sitting on the doorsteps.
The sentry was so near to me that he felt sure of catching
me. Several times he flung his rifle forward, trying to give
me a blow in the back with the bayonet. One moment my
friends in the window thought he had me. He was so
convinced that he could stop me in this way that he did
not fire. But I kept my distance, and he had to give up
at the gate.

Safe out of the gate, I perceived, to my terror, that the
carriage was occupied by a civilian who wore a military cap.
He sat without turning his head to me. "Sold!" was my
first thought. The comrades had written in their last letter,
"Once in the street, don't give yourself up: there will be
friends to defend you in case of need," and I did not want
to jump into the carriage if it was occupied by an enemy.
However, as I got nearer to the carriage I noticed that the
man in it had sandy whiskers which seemed to be those of
a warm friend of mine. He did not belong to our circle,
but we were personal friends, and on more than one occasion
I had learned to know his admirable, daring courage, and

mune was voted, and the working population of Paris was in the streets to greet the returning Communards; it flocked by the thousand to cheer them at the meetings, and the socialist movement took a sudden expansion, carrying with it the radicals.

The time had not yet come for that revival, however, and one night in April, 1878, Costa and a French comrade were arrested. A police court condemned them to imprisonment for eighteen months as Internationalists. I escaped arrest only by mistake. The police wanted Levashóff, and went to arrest a Russian student whose name sounded very much like that. I had given my real name, and continued to stay at Paris under that name for another month. Then I was called to Switzerland.

wood, and which all of them had now deserted in their run
after me.   The turn was so sharp that the carriage was
nearly upset, when I flung myself inward, dragging toward
me my friend ; this sudden movement righted the carriage.

We trotted through the narrow lane and then turned to
the left.   Two gendarmes were standing there at the door
of a public house, and gave to the military cap of my companion the military salute.   "Hush! hush!" I said to
him, for he was still terribly excited.   "All goes well;
the gendarmes salute us!"   The coachman thereupon turned
his face toward me, and I recognized in him another friend,
who smiled with happiness.

Everywhere we saw friends, who winked to us or gave
us a Godspeed as we passed at the full trot of our beautiful horse.   Then we entered the large Nevsky Prospekt,
turned into a side street, and alighted at a door, sending
away the coachman.   I ran up a staircase, and at its top
fell into the arms of my sister-in-law, who had been waiting in painful anxiety.   She laughed and cried at the same
time, bidding me hurry to put on another dress and to crop
my conspicuous beard.   Ten minutes later my friend and I
left the house and took a cab.

In the meantime, the officer of the guard at the prison
and the hospital soldiers had rushed out into the street,
doubtful as to what measures they should take.   There was
not a cab for a mile round, every one having been hired by
my friends.   An old peasant woman from the crowd was
wiser than all the lot.   "Poor people," she said, as if talking to herself, "they are sure to come out on the Prospekt,
and there they will be caught if somebody runs along that
lane, which leads straight to the Prospekt."   She was quite
right, and the officer ran to the tramway car that stood close
by, and asked the men to let them have their horses to
send somebody on horseback to intercept us.   But the men
obstinately refused to give up their horses, and the officer
did not use force.

As to the violinist and the lady who had taken the gray house, they too rushed out and joined the crowd with the old woman, whom they heard giving advice, and when the crowd dispersed they went away also.

It was a fine afternoon. We drove to the islands where all the St. Petersburg aristocracy goes on bright spring days to see the sunset, and called on the way, in a remote street, at a barber's shop to shave off my beard, which operation changed me, of course, but not very much. We drove aimlessly up and down the islands, but, having been told not to reach our night quarters till late in the evening, did not know where to go. "What shall we do in the meantime?" I asked my friend. He also pondered over that question. "To Donon!" he suddenly called out to the cabman, naming one of the best St. Petersburg restaurants. "No one will ever think of looking for you at Donon," he calmly remarked. "They will hunt for you everywhere else, but not there; and we shall have a dinner, and a drink too, in honor of the success of your escape."

What could I reply to so reasonable a suggestion? So we went to Donon, passed the halls flooded with light and crowded with visitors at the dinner hour, and took a separate room, where we spent the evening till the time came when we were expected. The house where we had first alighted was searched less than two hours after we left, as were also the apartments of nearly all our friends. Nobody thought of making a search at Donon.

A couple of days later I was to take possession of an apartment which had been engaged for me, and which I could occupy under a false passport. But the lady who was to accompany me there in a carriage took the precaution of visiting the house first by herself. It was thickly surrounded by spies. So many of my friends had come to inquire whether I was safe there that the suspicions of the police had been aroused. Moreover, my portrait had been printed by the Third Section, and hundreds of copies had been distributed to policemen and watchmen. All the detectives who knew me by sight were looking for me in the streets; while those who did not were accompanied by soldiers and warders who had seen me during my imprisonment. The Tsar was furious that such an escape should have taken place in his capital in full daylight, and had given the order, " He *must* be found."

It was impossible to remain at St. Petersburg, and I concealed myself in country houses in its neighborhood. In company with half a dozen friends, I stayed at a village frequented at this time of the year by St. Petersburg people bent on picnicking. Then it was decided that I should go abroad. But from a foreign paper we had learned that all the frontier stations and railway termini in the Baltic provinces and Finland were closely watched by detectives who knew me by sight. So I determined to travel in a direction where I should be least expected. Armed with the passport of a friend, and accompanied by another friend, I crossed Finland, and went northward to a remote port on the Gulf of Bothnia, whence I crossed to Sweden.

After I had gone on board the steamer, and it was about to sail, the friend who was to accompany me to the frontier told me the St. Petersburg news, which he had promised our friends not to tell me before. My sister Hélène had been arrested, as well as the sister of my brother's wife, who had visited me in prison once a month after my brother and his wife went to Siberia.

My sister knew absolutely nothing of the preparations for my escape. Only after I had escaped a friend had hurried to her, to tell her the welcome news. She protested her ignorance in vain: she was taken from her children, and was kept imprisoned for a fortnight. As to the sister of my brother's wife, she had known vaguely that something was to be attempted, but she had had no part in the preparations. Common sense ought to have shown the authorities that a person who had officially visited me in prison would not be involved in such an affair. Nevertheless, she was kept in prison for over two months. Her husband, a well-known lawyer, vainly endeavored to obtain her release. "We are aware now," he was told by the gendarme officers, " that she has had nothing to do with the escape; but, you see, we reported to the Emperor, on the day we arrested her, that the person who had organized the escape was discovered and arrested. It will now take some time to prepare the Emperor to accept the idea that she is not the real culprit."

I crossed Sweden without stopping anywhere, and went to Christiania, where I waited a few days for a steamer to sail for Hull, gathering information in the meantime about the peasant party of the Norwegian Storthing. As I went to the steamer I asked myself with anxiety, "Under which flag does she sail, — Norwegian, German, English ? " Then I saw floating above the stern the union jack, — the flag under which so many refugees, Russian, Italian, French, Hungarian, and of all nations, have found an asylum. I greeted that flag from the depth of my heart.

PART SIXTH

WESTERN EUROPE

I

A STORM raged in the North Sea, as we approached the coasts of England. But I met the storm with delight. I enjoyed the struggle of our steamer against the furiously rolling waves, and sat for hours on the stem, the foam of the waves dashing into my face. After the two years that I had spent in a gloomy casemate, every fibre of my inner self seemed to be throbbing and eager to enjoy the full intensity of life.

My intention was not to stay abroad more than a few weeks or months: just enough time to allow the hue and cry caused by my escape to subside, and also to restore my health a little. I landed under the name of Levashóff, the name which I had used in leaving Russia; and avoiding London, where the spies of the Russian embassy would soon have been at my heels, I went first to Edinburgh.

It has so happened, however, that I have never returned to Russia. I was soon taken up by the wave of the anarchist movement, which was just then rising in Western Europe; and I felt that I should be more useful in helping that movement to find its proper expression than I could possibly be in Russia. In my mother country I was too well known to carry on an open propaganda, especially among the workers and the peasants; and later on, when the Russian movement became a conspiracy and an armed struggle against the representative of autocracy, all thought of a popular movement was necessarily abandoned; while my own inclinations drew me more and more intensely toward casting in my lot with the laboring and toiling masses. To bring to them such conceptions as would aid them to direct their efforts to the best advantage of all the workers; to deepen and to widen the ideals and principles which will underlie the coming social revolution; to develop these ideals and principles before the workers, not as an order coming from their leaders, but as a result of their own reason; and so to awaken their own initiative, now that they were called upon to appear in the historical arena as the builders of a new, equitable mode of organization of society, — this seemed to me as necessary for the development of mankind as anything I could accomplish in Russia at that time. Accordingly, I joined the few men who were working in that direction in Western Europe, relieving those of them who had been broken down by years of hard struggle.

When I landed at Hull and went to Edinburgh, I informed but a few friends in Russia and in the Jura Federation of my safe arrival in England. A socialist must always rely upon his own work for his living, and consequently, as soon as I was settled in the Scotch capital, in a small room in the suburbs, I tried to find some work.

Among the passengers on board our steamer there was a Norwegian professor, with whom I talked, trying to remember the little that I formerly had known of the Swedish language. He spoke German. "But as you speak some Norwegian," he said to me, "and are trying to learn it, let us both speak it."

"You mean Swedish?" I ventured to ask. "I speak Swedish, don't I?"

. "Well, I should say it is rather Norwegian; surely not Swedish," was his reply.

Thus happened to me what happened to one of Jules Verne's heroes, who had learned by mistake Portuguese instead of Spanish. At any rate, I talked a good deal with the professor, — let it be in Norwegian, — and he gave me a Christiania paper, which contained the reports of the Norwegian North Atlantic deep-sea expedition, just returned home.

As soon as I was at Edinburgh I wrote a note in English about these explorations, and sent it to "Nature," which my brother and I used regularly to read at St. Petersburg from its first appearance. The sub-editor acknowledged the note with thanks, remarking with an extreme leniency, which I have often met with since in England, that my English was "all right," and only required to be made "a little more idiomatic." I may say that I had learned English in Russia, and, with my brother, had translated Page's "Philosophy of Geology" and Herbert Spencer's "Principles of Biology." But I had learned it from books, and pronounced it very badly, so that I had the greatest difficulty in making myself understood by my Scotch landlady; her daughter and I used to write on scraps of paper what we had to say to each other; and as I had no idea of idiomatic English, I must have made the most amusing mistakes. I remember, at any rate, protesting once to her, in writing, that it was not a "cup of tea" that I expected at tea time, but many cups. I am afraid my landlady took me for a glutton, but I must say, by way of apology, that neither in the geological books I had read in English nor in Spencer's "Biology" was there any allusion to such an important matter as tea-drinking.

I got from Russia the Journal of the Russian Geographical Society, and soon began to supply the "Times" also with occasional paragraphs about Russian geographical explorations. Prjeválsky was at that time in Central Asia, and his progress was followed in England with interest.

However, the money I had brought with me was rapidly disappearing, and all my letters to Russia being intercepted, I could not succeed in making my address known to my relatives. So I moved in a few weeks to London, thinking I could find more regular work there. The old refugee, P. L. Lavróff, continued to edit at London his newspaper "Forward;" but as I hoped soon to return to Russia, and the editorial office of the Russian paper must have been closely watched by spies, I did not go there.

I went, very naturally, to the office of "Nature," where I was most cordially received by the sub-editor, Mr. J. Scott Keltie. The editor wanted to increase the column of Notes, and found that I wrote them exactly as they were required. A table was consequently assigned me in the office, and scientific reviews in all possible languages were piled upon it. "Come every Monday, Mr. Levashóff," I was told, "look over these reviews, and if there is any article that strikes you as worthy of notice, write a note, or mark the article; we will send it to a specialist." Mr. Keltie did not know, of course, that I used to rewrite each note three or four times before I dared to submit my English to him; but taking the scientific reviews home, I soon managed very nicely, with my "Nature" notes and my "Times" paragraphs, to get a living. I found that the weekly payment, on Thursday, of the paragraph contributors to the "Times" was an excellent institution. To be sure, there were weeks when there was no interesting news from Prjeválsky, and news from other parts of Russia was not found interesting; in such cases my fare was bread and tea only.

One day, however, Mr. Keltie took from the shelves several Russian books, asking me to review them for "Nature." I looked at the books, and, to my embarrassment, saw that they were my own works on the "Glacial Period" and the "Orography of Asia." My brother had not failed to send them to our favorite "Nature." I was in great perplexity, and, putting the books into my bag, took them home, to reflect upon the matter. "What shall I do with them?" I asked myself. "I cannot praise them, because they are mine; and I cannot be too sharp on the author, as I hold the views expressed in them." I decided to take them back next day, and explain to Mr. Keltie that, although I had introduced myself under the name of Levashóff, I was the author of these books, and could not review them.

Mr. Keltie knew from the papers about Kropótkin's escape, and was very much pleased to discover the refugee safe in England. As to my scruples, he remarked wisely that I need neither scold nor praise the author, but could simply tell the readers what the books were about. From that day a friendship, which still continues, grew up between us.

In November or December, 1876, seeing in the letter-box of P. L. Lavróff's paper an invitation for "K." to call at the editorial office to receive a letter from Russia, and thinking that the invitation was for me, I called at the office, and soon established friendship with the editor and the younger people who printed the paper.

When I called for the first time at the office — my beard shaved and my "top" hat on — and asked the lady who opened the door, in my very best English, "Is Mr. Lavróff in?" I imagined that no one would ever know who I was, as I had not mentioned my name. It appeared, however, that the lady, who did not know me at all, but well knew my brother while he stayed at Zürich, at once recognized me and ran upstairs to say who the visitor was. "I knew you immediately," she said afterwards, "by your eyes, which have much in common with those of your brother."

That time I did not stay long in England. I had been in lively correspondence with my friend James Guillaume, of the Jura Federation, and as soon as I found some permanent geographical work, which I could do in Switzerland as well as in London, I removed to Switzerland. The letters that I got at last from home told me that I might as well stay abroad, as there was nothing in particular to be done in Russia. A wave of enthusiasm was rolling over the country, at that time, in favor of the Slavonians who had revolted against the age-long Turkish oppression, and my best friends, Serghéi (Stepniák), Kelnitz, and several others, had gone to the Balkan peninsula to join the insurgents. " We read," my friends wrote, " the correspondence of the ' Daily News' about the horrors in Bulgaria; we weep at the reading, and go next to enlist either as volunteers in the Balkan insurgents' bands or as nurses."

I went to Switzerland, joined the Jura Federation of the International Workingmen's Association, and, following the advice of my Swiss friends, settled in La Chaux-de-Fonds.

II

THE Jura Federation has played an important part in the modern development of socialism.

It always happens that after a political party has set before itself a purpose, and has proclaimed that nothing short of the complete attainment of that aim will satisfy it, it divides into two factions. One of them remains what it was, while the other, although it professes not to have changed a word of its previous intentions, accepts some sort of compromise, and gradually, from compromise to compromise, is driven farther from its primitive programme, and becomes a party of modest makeshift reform.

Such a division had occurred within the International Workingmen's Association. Nothing less than an expropriation of the present owners of land and capital, and a transmission of all that is necessary for the production of wealth to the producers themselves, was the avowed aim of the association at the outset. The workers of all nations were called upon to form their own organizations for a direct struggle against capitalism; to work out the means of socializing the production of wealth and its consumption; and, when they should be ready to do so, to take possession of the necessaries for production, and to control production with no regard to the present political organization, which must undergo a complete reconstruction. The association had thus to be the means for preparing an immense revolution in men's minds, and later on in the very forms of life, — a revolution which would open to mankind a new era of progress based upon the solidarity of all. That was the ideal which aroused from their slumber millions of European workers, and attracted to the association its best intellectual forces.

However, two factions soon developed. When the war of 1870 had ended in a complete defeat of France, and the uprising of the Paris Commune had been crushed, and the Draconian laws which were passed against the association excluded the French workers from participation in it; and when, on the other hand, parliamentary rule had been introduced in "united Germany," — the goal of the radicals since 1848, — an effort was made by the Germans to modify the aims and the methods of the whole socialist movement. The "conquest of power *within the existing states*" became the watchword of that section, which took the name of "Social Democracy." The first electoral successes of this party at the elections to the German Reichstag aroused great hopes. The number of the social democratic deputies having grown from two to seven, and next to nine, it was confidently calculated by otherwise reasonable men that before the end of the century the social democrats would have a majority in the German parliament, and would then introduce the socialist "popular state" by means of suitable legislation. The socialist ideal of this party gradually lost the character of something that had to be worked out by the labor organizations themselves, and became state management of the industries, — in fact, state socialism; that is, state capitalism. To-day, in Switzerland, the efforts of the social democrats are directed in politics toward centralization as against federalism, and in the economic field to promoting the state management of railways and the state monopoly of banking and of the sale of spirits. The state management of the land and of the leading industries, and even of the consumption of riches, would be the next step in a more or less distant future.

Gradually, the life and activity of the German social democratic party was subordinated to electoral consider-

ations. Trade unions were treated with contempt and
strikes were met with disapproval, because both diverted
the attention of the workers from electoral struggles. Every
popular outbreak, every revolutionary agitation in any
country of Europe, was received in those years by the social
democratic leaders with even more animosity than by the
capitalist press.

In the Latin countries, however, this new departure
found but few adherents. The sections and federations of
the International remained true to the principles which had
prevailed at the foundation of the association. Federalist
by their history, hostile to the idea of a centralized state,
and possessed of revolutionary traditions, the Latin workers could not follow the evolution of the Germans.

The division between the two branches of the socialist
movement became apparent immediately after the Franco-
German war. The association, as I have already mentioned, had created a governing body in the shape of a
general council which resided at London ; and the leading
spirits of that council being two Germans, Engels and Marx,
the council became the stronghold of the new social democratic direction ; while the inspirers and intellectual leaders
of the Latin federations were Bakúnin and his friends.

The conflict between the Marxists and the Bakúnists was
not a personal affair. It was the necessary conflict between
the principles of federalism and those of centralization, the
free commune and the state's paternal rule, the free action
of the masses of the people and the betterment of existing
capitalist conditions through legislation, — a conflict between
the Latin spirit and the German *Geist*, which, after the
defeat of France on the battlefield, claimed supremacy in
science, politics, philosophy, and in socialism too, representing its own conception of socialism as " scientific," while all
other interpretations it described as " utopian."

At the Hague Congress of the International Association,

which was held in 1872, the London general council, by means of a fictitious majority, excluded Bakúnin, his friend Guillaume, and even the Jura Federation from the International. But as it was certain that most of what remained then of the International — that is, the Spanish, the Italian, and the Belgian federations — would side with the Jurassians, the congress tried to dissolve the association. A new general council, composed of a few social democrats, was nominated in New York, where there were no workmen's organizations belonging to the association to control it, and where it has never been heard of since. In the meantime, the Spanish, the Italian, the Belgian, and the Jura federations of the International continued to exist, and to meet as usual, for the next five or six years, in annual international congresses.

The Jura Federation, at the time when I came to Switzerland, was the centre and the leading voice of the International federations. Bakúnin had just died (July 1, 1876), but the federation retained the position it had taken under his impulse.

The conditions in France, Spain, and Italy were such that only the maintenance of the revolutionary spirit that had developed amongst the Internationalist workers previous to the Franco-German war prevented the governments from taking decisive steps toward crushing the whole labor movement, and inaugurating the reign of White Terror. It is well known that the reëstablishment of a Bourbon monarchy in France was very near becoming an accomplished fact. Marshal MacMahon was maintained as president of the republic only in order to prepare for a monarchist restoration; the very day of the solemn entry of Henry V. into Paris was settled, and even the harnesses of the horses, adorned with the pretender's crown and initials, were ready. And it is also known that it was only the fact that Gam-

betta and Clémenceau — the opportunist and the radical —
had covered wide portions of France with committees,
armed and ready to rise as soon as the *coup d'état* should
be made, which prevented the proposed restoration. But
the real strength of those committees was in the workers,
many of whom had formerly belonged to the International
and had retained the old spirit. Speaking from personal
knowledge, I may venture to say that the radical middle-
class leaders would have hesitated in case of emergency,
while the workers would have seized the first opportunity
for an uprising which, beginning with the defense of the
republic, might have gone farther on in the socialist direction.

The same was true in Spain. As soon as the clerical and
aristocratic surroundings of the king drove him to turn the
screws of reaction, the republicans menaced him with a
movement in which, they knew, the real fighting element
would be the workers. In Catalonia alone there were over
one hundred thousand men in strongly organized trade
unions, and more than eighty thousand Spaniards belonged
to the International, regularly holding congresses, and
punctually paying their contributions to the association with
a truly Spanish sense of duty. I can speak of these organizations from personal knowledge, gained on the spot, and I
know that they were ready to proclaim the United States
of Spain, abandon ruling the colonies, and in some of the
most advanced regions make serious attempts in the direction of collectivism. It was this permanent menace which
prevented the Spanish monarchy from suppressing all the
workers' and peasants' organizations, and from inaugurating
a frank clerical reaction.

Similar conditions prevailed also in Italy. The trade
unions in north Italy had not reached the strength they
have now; but parts of Italy were honeycombed with
International sections and republican groups. The monarchy

was kept under continual menace of being upset, should the middle-class republicans appeal to the revolutionary elements among the workers.

In short, looking back upon these years, from which we are separated now by a quarter of a century, I am firmly persuaded that if Europe did not pass through a period of stern reaction after 1871, this was mainly due to the spirit which was aroused in Western Europe before the Franco-German war, and has been maintained since by the anarchist Internationalists, the Blanquists, the Mazzinians, and the Spanish "cantonalist" republicans.

Of course, the Marxists, absorbed by their local electoral struggles, knew little of these conditions. Anxious not to draw the thunderbolts of Bismarck upon their heads, and fearing above all that a revolutionary spirit might make its appearance in Germany, and lead to repressions which they were not strong enough to face, they not only repudiated, for tactical purposes, all sympathy with the western revolutionists, but gradually became inspired with hatred toward the revolutionary spirit, and denounced it with virulence wheresoever it made its appearance, even when they saw its first signs in Russia.

No revolutionary papers could be printed in France at that time, under Marshal MacMahon. Even the singing of the "Marseillaise" was considered a crime; and I was once very much amazed at the terror which seized several of my co-passengers in a train when they heard a few recruits singing the revolutionary song (in May, 1878). "Is it permitted again to sing the 'Marseillaise'?" they asked one another with anxiety. The French press had consequently no socialist papers. The Spanish papers were very well edited, and some of the manifestoes of their congresses were admirable expositions of anarchist socialism; but who knows anything of Spanish ideas outside of Spain? As to the Italian papers they were all short-lived, appearing, disappearing, and reappearing elsewhere under different names; and admirable as some of them were, they did not spread beyond Italy.   Consequently, the Jura Federation, with its papers printed in French, became the centre for the maintenance and expression in the Latin countries of the spirit. which — I repeat it — saved Europe from a very dark period of reaction.   And it was also the ground upon which the theoretical conceptions of anarchism were worked out by Bakúnin and his followers in a language that was understood all over continental Europe.

III

Quite a number of remarkable men, of different nationalities, nearly all of whom had been personal friends of Bakúnin, belonged at that time to the Jura Federation. The editor of our chief paper, the Bulletin of the federation, was James Guillaume, a teacher by profession, who belonged to one of the aristocratic families of Neuchâtel. Small, thin, with the stiff appearance and resoluteness of Robespierre, and with a truly golden heart which opened only in the intimacy of friendship, he was a born leader by his phenomenal powers of work and his stern activity. For eight years he fought against all sorts of obstacles to maintain the paper in existence, taking the most active part in every detail of the federation, till he had to leave Switzerland, where he could find no work whatever, and settled in France, where his name will be quoted some day with the utmost respect in the history of education.

Adhémar Schwitzguébel, also a Swiss, was the type of the jovial, lively, clear-sighted French-speaking watchmakers of the Bernese Jura hills. A watch engraver by trade, he never attempted to abandon his position of manual worker, and, always merry and active, he supported his large family through the severest periods of slack trade and curtailed earnings. His gift of taking a difficult economic or political question, and, after much thought about it, considering it from the workingman's point of view, without divesting it of its deepest meaning, was wonderful. He was known far and wide in the " mountains," and with the workers of all countries he was a general favorite.

His direct counterpart was another Swiss, also a watch-

maker, Spichiger. He was a philosopher, slow in both
movement and thought, English in his physical aspect;
always trying to get at the full meaning of every fact, and
impressing all of us by the justness of the conclusions he
reached while he was pondering over all sorts of subjects
during his work of scooping out watch lids.

Round these three gathered a number of solid, stanch,
middle-aged or elderly workmen, passionate lovers of liberty,
happy to take part in such a promising movement, and a
hundred or so bright young men, also mostly watchmakers,
— all very independent and affectionate, very lively, and
ready to go to any length in self-sacrifice.

Several refugees of the Paris Commune had joined the
federation. Elisée Reclus, the great geographer, was of
their number, — a type of the true Puritan in his manner
of life, and of the French encyclopædist philosopher of
the last century in his mind; the man who inspires others,
but never has governed any one, and never will do so; the
anarchist whose anarchism is the epitome of his broad,
intimate knowledge of the forms of life of mankind under
all climates and in all stages of civilization; whose books
rank among the very best of the century; whose style, of
a striking beauty, moves the mind and the conscience; and
who, as he enters the office of an anarchist paper, says to
the editor, — maybe a boy in comparison to himself, —
"Tell me what I have to do," and will sit down, like a
newspaper subordinate, to fill up a gap of so many lines in
the current number of the paper. In the Paris Commune
he simply took a rifle and stood in the ranks; and if he
invites a contributor to work with him upon a volume of
his world-famed Geography, and the contributor timidly
asks, "What have I to do?" he replies: "Here are the
books, here is a table. Do as you like."

By his side was Lefrançais, an elderly man, formerly a
teacher, who had been thrice in his life an exile: after

June, 1848, after Napoleon's *coup d'état*, and after 1870. An ex-member of the Commune, and consequently one of those who were said to have left Paris carrying away millions in their pockets, he worked as a freight handler at the railway at Lausanne, and was nearly killed in that work, which required younger shoulders than his. His book on the Paris Commune is the one in which the real historical meaning of that movement was put in its proper light. " A communalist, not an anarchist, please," he would say. "I cannot work with such fools as you are; " and he worked with none but us, " because you fools," as he said, " are still the men whom I love best. With you one can work and remain one's self."

Another ex-member of the Paris Commune who was with us was Pindy, a carpenter from the north of France, an adopted child of Paris. He became widely known at Paris, during a strike supported by the International, for his vigor and bright intelligence, and was elected a member of the Commune, which nominated him commander of the Tuileries palace. When the Versailles troops entered Paris, shooting their prisoners by the hundred, three men, at least, were shot in different parts of the town, having been mistaken for Pindy. After the fight, however, he was concealed by a brave girl, a seamstress, who saved him by her calmness when the house was searched by the troops, and who afterward became his wife. Only twelve months later they succeeded in leaving Paris unnoticed, and came to Switzerland. Here Pindy learned assaying, at which he became skillful ; spending his days by the side of his red-hot stove, and at night devoting himself passionately to propaganda work, in which he admirably combined the passion of a revolutionist with the good sense and organizing powers characteristic of the Parisian worker.

Paul Brousse was then a young doctor, full of mental activity, uproarious, sharp, lively, ready to develop any idea

with a geometrical logic to its utmost consequences; powerful in his criticisms of the state and state organization;
finding enough time to edit two papers, in French and in
German, to write scores of voluminous letters, to be the
soul of a workmen's evening party; constantly active in
organizing men, with the subtle mind of a true "southerner."

Among the Italians who collaborated with us in Switzerland, two men whose names stood always associated, and
will be remembered in Italy by more than one generation,
two close personal friends of Bakúnin, were Cafiero and
Malatesta. Cafiero was an idealist of the highest and the
purest type, who gave his considerable fortune to the cause,
and who never after asked himself what he should live upon
in the future; a thinker plunged in philosophical speculation; a man who never would harm any one, and yet took
the rifle and marched in the mountains of Benevento, when
he and his friends thought that an uprising of a socialist
character might be attempted, were it only to show the
people that their uprisings ought to have a deeper meaning
than that of a mere revolt against tax collectors. Malatesta
was a student of medicine, who had left the medical profession and also his fortune for the sake of the revolution;
full of fire and intelligence, a pure idealist, who all his
life — and he is now approaching the age of fifty — has
never thought whether he would have a piece of bread for
his supper and a bed for the night. Without even so much
as a room that he could call his own, he would sell sherbet
in the streets of London to get his living, and in the evening
write brilliant articles for the Italian papers. Imprisoned
in France, released, expelled, re-condemned in Italy, confined in an island, escaped, and again in Italy in disguise;
always in the hottest of the struggle, whether it be in Italy
or elsewhere, — he has persevered in this life for thirty
years in succession. And when we meet him again, released from a prison or escaped from an island, we find him

just as we saw him last; always renewing the struggle, with the same love of men, the same absence of hatred toward his adversaries and jailers, the same hearty smile for a friend, the same caress for a child.

The Russians were few among us, most of them following the German social democrats. We had, however, Joukóvsky, a friend of Hérzen, who had left Russia in 1863, — a brilliant, elegant, highly intelligent nobleman, a favorite with the workers, — who better than any of the rest of us had what the French call *l'oreille du peuple* (the ear of the workers), because he knew how to fire them by showing them the great part they had to play in rebuilding society, to lift them by holding before them high historical views, to throw a flash of light on the most intricate economic problem, and to electrify them with his earnestness and sincerity. Sokolóff,- formerly an officer of the Russian general staff, an admirer of Paul Louis Courier for his boldness and of Proudhon for his philosophical ideas, who had made many a socialist in Russia by his review articles, was also with us temporarily.

I mention only those who became widely known as writers, or as delegates to congresses, or in some other way. And yet, I ask myself if I ought not rather to speak of those who never committed their names to print, but were as important in the life of the federation as any one of the writers; who fought in the ranks, and were always ready to join in any enterprise, never asking whether the work would be grand or small, distinguished or modest, — whether it would have great consequences, or simply result in infinite worry to themselves and their families.

I ought also to mention the Germans Werner and Rinke, the Spaniard Albarracin, and many others; but I am afraid that these faint sketches of mine may not convey to the reader the same feelings of respect and love with which every one of this little family inspired those who knew him or her personally.

IV

OF all the towns of Switzerland that I know, La Chaux-de-Fonds is perhaps the least attractive. It lies on a high plateau entirely devoid of any vegetation, open to bitterly cold winds in the winter, when the snow lies as deep as at Moscow, and melts and falls again as often as at St. Petersburg. But it was important to spread our ideas in that centre, and to give more life to the local propaganda. Pindy, Spichiger, Albarracin, the Blanquists Ferré and Jallot were there, and from time to time I could pay visits to Guillaume at Neuchâtel, and to Schwitzguébel in the valley of St. Imier.

A life full of work that I liked began now for me. We held many meetings, ourselves distributing our announcements in the cafés and the workshops. Once a week we held our section meetings, at which the most animated discussions took place, and we went also to preach anarchism at the gatherings convoked by the political parties. I traveled a good deal, visiting other sections and helping them.

During that winter we won the sympathy of many, but our regular work was very much hampered by a crisis in the watch trade. Half the workers were out of work or only partially employed, so that the municipality had to open dining-rooms to provide cheap meals at cost price. The co-operative workshop established by the anarchists at La Chaux-de-Fonds, in which the earnings were divided equally among all the members, had great difficulty in getting work, in spite of its high reputation, and Spichiger had to resort several times to wool-combing for an upholsterer, in order to get his living.

We all took part, that year, in a manifestation with the red flag at Bern. The wave of reaction spread to Switzerland, and the carrying of the workers' banner was prohibited by the Bern police, in defiance of the constitution. It was necessary, therefore, to show that at least here and there the workers would not have their rights trampled underfoot, and would offer resistance. We all went to Bern on the anniversary of the Paris Commune, to carry the red flag in the streets, notwithstanding the prohibition. Of course there was a collision with the police, in which two comrades received sword cuts and two police officers were rather seriously wounded. But the red flag was carried safe to the hall, where a most animated meeting was held. I hardly need say that the so-called leaders were in the ranks, and fought like all the rest. The trial involved nearly thirty Swiss citizens, all themselves demanding to be prosecuted, and those who had wounded the two police officers coming forward spontaneously to say that they had done it. A great deal of sympathy was won to the cause during the trial; it was understood that all liberties have to be defended jealously, in order not to be lost. The sentences were consequently very light, not exceeding three months' imprisonment.

However, the Bern government prohibited the carrying of the red flag anywhere in the canton; and the Jura Federation thereupon decided to carry it, in defiance of the prohibition, in St. Imier, where we held our congress that year. This time most of us were armed, and ready to defend our banner to the last extremity. A body of police had been placed in a square to stop our column; a detachment of the militia was kept in readiness in an adjoining field, under the pretext of target practice, — we distinctly heard their shots as we marched through the town. But when our column appeared in the square, and it was judged from its aspect that aggression would result in serious bloodshed, the mayor let us continue our march, undisturbed, to the hall where the meeting was to be held. None of us desired a fight; but the strain of that march, in fighting order, to the sound of a military band, was such that I do not know what feeling prevailed in most of us, during the first moments after we reached the hall, — relief at having been spared an undesired fight, or regret that the fight did not take place. Man is a very complex being.

Our main activity, however, was in working out the practical and theoretic aspects of anarchist socialism, and in this direction the federation has undoubtedly accomplished something that will last.

We saw that a new form of society is germinating in the civilized nations, and must take the place of the old one: a society of equals, who will not be compelled to sell their hands and brains to those who choose to employ them in a haphazard way, but who will be able to apply their knowledge and capacities to production, in an organism so constructed as to combine all the efforts for procuring the greatest sum possible of well-being for all, while full, free scope will be left for every individual initiative. This society will be composed of a multitude of associations, federated for all the purposes which require federation: trade federations for production of all sorts, — agricultural, industrial, intellectual, artistic; communes for consumption, making provision for dwellings, gas works, supplies of food, sanitary arrangements, etc.; federations of communes among themselves, and federations of communes with trade organizations; and finally, wider groups covering all the country, or several countries, composed of men who collaborate for the satisfaction of such economic, intellectual, artistic, and moral needs as are not limited to a given territory. All these will combine directly, by means of free agreements between them, just as the railway companies or the postal

departments of different countries coöperate now, without
having a central railway or postal government, — even
though the former are actuated by merely egotistic aims,
and the latter belong to different and often hostile states;
or as the meteorologists, the Alpine clubs, the lifeboat
stations in Great Britain, the cyclists, the teachers, and
so on, combine for all sorts of work in common, for intellectual pursuits, or simply for pleasure. There will be full
freedom for the development of new forms of production,
invention, and organization; individual initiative will be
encouraged, and the tendency toward uniformity and centralization will be discouraged. Moreover, this society will
not be crystallized into certain unchangeable forms, but will
continually modify its aspect, because it will be a living,
evolving organism; no need of government will be felt,
because free agreement and federation take its place in all
those functions which governments consider as theirs at the
present time, and because, the causes of conflict being reduced in number, those conflicts which may still arise can
be submitted to arbitration.

None of us minimized the importance and magnitude of
the change which we looked for. We understood that the
current opinions upon the necessity of private ownership in
land, factories, mines, dwelling-houses, and so on, as the
means of securing industrial progress, and of the wage-system as the means of compelling men to work, would not
soon give way to higher conceptions of socialized ownership
and production. We knew that a tedious propaganda and
a long succession of struggles, of individual and collective
revolts against the now prevailing forms of property-holding,
of individual self-sacrifice, of partial attempts at reconstruction and partial revolutions, would have to be lived through,
before the current ideas upon private ownership would be
modified. And we understood also that the prevalent
ideas concerning the necessity of authority — in which all

of us have been bred — would not and could not be abandoned by civilized mankind all at once. Long years of
propaganda and a long succession of partial acts of revolt
against authority, as well as a complete revision of the
teachings now derived from history, would be required before men would perceive that they had been mistaken in
attributing to their rulers and their laws what was derived
in reality from their own sociable feelings and habits. We
knew all that. But we also knew that in preaching reform
in both these directions, we should be working with the tide
of human progress.

When I made a closer acquaintance with the working
population and their sympathizers from the better educated
classes, I soon realized that they valued their personal
freedom even more than they valued their personal well-
being. Fifty years ago, the workers were ready to sell
their personal liberty to all sorts of rulers, and even to a
Cæsar, in exchange for a promise of material well-being ;
but now, this was no longer the case. I saw that the blind
faith in elected rulers, even if they were taken from amongst
the best leaders of the labor movement, was dying away
amongst the Latin workers. "We must know first what
we want, and then we can do it best ourselves," was an
idea which I found widely spread among them, — far more
widely than is generally believed. The sentence which
was put in the statutes of the International Association,
"The emancipation of the workers must be accomplished
by the workers themselves," had met with general sympathy,
and had taken root in minds. The sad experience of the
Paris Commune only confirmed it.

When the insurrection broke out, a considerable number
of men belonging to the middle classes themselves were prepared to make, or at least to accept, a new start in the social
direction. "When my brother and myself, coming from
our little room, went out into the streets," Elisée Reclus

said to me once, "we were asked on all sides by people belonging to the wealthier classes: 'Tell us what is to be done? We are ready to try a new start.' But *we* were not yet prepared to make the suggestions."

Never before had a government been as fairly representative of all the advanced parties as was the Council of the Commune, elected on the 25th of March, 1871. All shades of revolutionary opinion — Blanquists, Jacobinists, Internationalists — were represented in it in a true proportion. And yet, the workers themselves having no distinct ideas of social reform to impress upon their representatives, the Commune government did nothing in that direction. The very fact of having been isolated from the masses and shut up in the Hôtel de Ville paralyzed them. For the success of socialism, the ideas of no-government, of self-reliance, of free initiative of the individual, — of anarchism, in a word. — had thus to be preached side by side with those of socialized ownership and production.

We certainly foresaw that if full freedom were left to the individual for the expression of his ideas and for action, we should have to face a certain amount of extravagant exaggeration of our principles. I had seen it in the nihilist movement in Russia. But we trusted — and experience has proved that we were right — that social life itself, supported by a frank, open-minded criticism of opinions and actions, would be the most effective means for threshing out opinions and for divesting them of the unavoidable exaggerations. We acted, in fact, in accordance with the old saying that freedom remains still the wisest cure for freedom's temporary inconveniences. There is, in mankind, a nucleus of social habits — an inheritance from the past, not yet duly appreciated — which is *not* maintained by coercion and is superior to coercion. Upon it all the progress of mankind is based, and so long as mankind does not begin to deteriorate physically and mentally, it will not be destroyed by any amount of criticism or of occasional revolt against it. These were the opinions in which I grew confirmed more and more in proportion as my experience of men and things increased.

We understood at the same time that such a change cannot be produced by the conjectures of one man of genius, that it will not be one man's discovery, but that it must result from the constructive work of the masses, just as the forms of judicial procedure which were elaborated in the early mediæval period, the village community, the guild, the mediæval city, and the foundations of international law were worked out by the people.

Many of our predecessors had undertaken to picture ideal commonwealths, basing them sometimes upon the principle of authority, and, on some rare occasions, upon the principle of freedom. Robert Owen and Fourier had given the world their ideals of a free, organically developing society, in opposition to the pyramidal ideals which had been copied from the Roman Empire or from the Roman Church. Proudhon had continued their work, and Bakúnin, applying his wide and clear understanding of the philosophy of history to the criticism of present institutions, "built up while he was demolishing." But all that was preparatory work only.

The International Workingmen's Association inaugurated a new method of solving the problems of practical sociology by appealing to the workers themselves. The educated men who had joined the association undertook only to enlighten the workers as to what was going on in different countries of the world, to analyze the obtained results, and, later on, to aid them in formulating their conclusions. We did not pretend to evolve an ideal commonwealth out of our theoretical views as to what a society *ought to be*, but we invited the workers to investigate the causes of the present evils, and in their discussions and congresses to consider the practical aspects of a better social organization than the one we live in. A question raised at an international congress was recommended as a subject of study to all labor unions. In the course of the year it was discussed all over Europe, in the small meetings of the sections, with a full knowledge of the local needs of each trade and each locality; then the work of the sections was brought before the next congress of each federation, and finally it was submitted in a more elaborate form to the next international congress. The structure of the society which we longed for was thus worked out, in theory and practice, from beneath, and the Jura Federation took a large part in the elaboration of the anarchist ideal.

For myself, placed as I was in such favorable conditions, I gradually came to realize that anarchism represents more than a mere mode of action and a mere conception of a free society; that it is part of a philosophy, natural and social, which must be developed in a quite different way from the metaphysical or dialectic methods which have been employed in sciences dealing with man. I saw that it must be treated by the same methods as natural sciences; not, however, on the slippery ground of mere analogies such as Herbert Spencer accepts, but on the solid basis of induction applied to human institutions. And I did my best to accomplish what I could in that direction.

V

Two congresses were held in the autumn of 1877 in Belgium: one of the International Workingmen's Association at Verviers, and the other an international socialist congress at Ghent. The latter was especially important, as it was known that an attempt would be made by the German social democrats to bring all the labor movement of Europe under one organization, subject to a central committee, which would be the old general council of the International under a new name. It was therefore necessary to preserve the autonomy of the labor organizations in the Latin countries, and we did our best to be well represented at this congress. I went under the name of Levashóff; two Germans, the compositor Werner and the engineer Rinke, walked nearly all the distance from Basel to Belgium; and although we were only nine anarchists at Ghent, we succeeded in checking the centralization scheme.

Twenty-two years have passed since; a number of international socialist congresses have been held, and at every one of them the same struggle has been renewed, — the social democrats trying to enlist all the labor movement of Europe under their banner and to bring it under their control, and the anarchists opposing and preventing it. What an amount of wasted force, of bitter words exchanged and efforts divided, simply because those who have adopted the formula of "conquest of power within the existing states" do not understand that activity in this direction cannot embody all the socialist movement! From the outset socialism took three independent lines of development, which found their expression in Saint-Simon, Fourier, and

Robert Owen.   Saint-Simonism has developed into social democracy, and Fourierism into anarchism; while Owenism is developing, in England and America, into trade-unionism, coöperation, and the so-called municipal socialism, and remains hostile to social democratic state socialism, while it has many points of contact with anarchism.   But because of failure to recognize that the three move toward a common goal in three different ways, and that the two latter bring their own precious contribution to human progress, a quarter of a century has been given to endeavors to realize the unrealizable Utopia of a unique labor movement of the social democratic pattern.

The Ghent congress ended for me in an unexpected way. Three or four days after it had begun, the Belgian police learned who Levashóff was, and received the order to arrest me for a breach of police regulations which I had committed in giving at the hotel an assumed name.   My Belgian friends warned me.   They maintained that the clerical ministry which was in power was capable of giving me up to Russia, and insisted upon my leaving the congress at once.   They would not let me return to the hotel.   Guillaume barred the way, telling me that I should have to use force against him if I insisted upon returning thither.   I had to go with some Ghent comrades, and as soon as I joined them, muffled calls and whistling came from all corners of a dark square over which groups of workers were scattered.   It all looked very mysterious.   At last, after much whispering and subdued whistling, a group of comrades took me under escort to a social democrat worker, with whom I had to spend the night, and who received me, anarchist though I was, in the most touching way as a brother.   Next morning I left once more for England, on board a steamer, provoking a number of good-natured smiles from the British custom-house officers, who wanted me to show them my luggage, while I had nothing to show but a small hand-bag.

I did not stay long in London. In the admirable collections of the British Museum I studied the beginnings of the French Revolution, — how revolutions come to break out, — but I wanted more activity, and soon went to Paris. A revival of the labor movement was beginning there, after the rigid suppression of the Commune. With the Italian Costa and the few anarchist friends we had among the Paris workers, and with Jules Guesde and his colleagues, who were not strict social democrats at that time, we started the first socialist groups.

Our beginnings were ridiculously small. Half a dozen of us used to meet in cafés, and when we had an audience of a hundred persons at a meeting we felt happy. No one would have guessed then that two years later the movement would be in full swing. But France has its own ways of development. When a reaction has gained the upper hand, all visible traces of a movement disappear. Those who fight against the current are few. But in some mysterious way, by a sort of invisible infiltration of ideas, the reaction is undermined; a new current sets in, and then it appears, all of a sudden, that the idea which was thought to be dead was there alive, spreading and growing all the time; and as soon as public agitation becomes possible, thousands of adherents, whose existence nobody suspected, come to the front. "There are at Paris," old Blanqui used to say, "fifty thousand men who never come to a meeting or to a demonstration; but the moment they feel that the people can appear in the streets to manifest their opinion, they are there to storm the position." So it was then. There were not twenty of us to carry on the movement, not two hundred openly to support it. At the first commemoration of the Commune, in March, 1878, we surely were not two hundred. But two years later the amnesty for the Com-

roted, and the working population of Paris was
ts to greet the returning Communards; it flocked
usand to cheer them at the meetings, and the
vement took a sudden expansion, carrying with
als.

had not yet come for that revival, however, and
n April, 1878, Costa and a French comrade were
A police court condemned them to imprisonment
a months as Internationalists. I escaped arrest
stake. The police wanted Levashóff, and went
Russian student whose name sounded very much
I had given my real name, and continued to
is under that name for another month. Then
l to Switzerland.

VI

DURING this stay at Paris I made my first acquaintance with Turguéneff. He had expressed to our common friend P. L. Lavróff the desire to see me, and, as a true Russian, to celebrate my escape by a small friendly dinner. It was with a feeling almost of worship that I crossed the threshold of his room. If by his " Sportsman's Notebook " he rendered to Russia the immense service of throwing odium upon serfdom (I did not know at that time that he took a leading part in Hérzen's powerful " Bell "), he has rendered no less service through his later novels. He has shown what the Russian woman is, what treasuries of mind and heart she possesses, what she may be as an inspirer of men; and he has taught us how men who have a real claim to superiority look upon women, how they love. Upon me, and upon thousands of my contemporaries, this part of his teaching made an indelible impression, far more powerful than the best articles upon women's rights.

His appearance is well known. Tall, strongly built, the head covered with soft and thick gray hair, he was certainly beautiful; his eyes gleamed with intelligence, not devoid of a touch of humor, and his whole manner testified to that simplicity and absence of affectation which are characteristic of the best Russian writers. His fine head revealed a vast development of brain power, and when he died, and Paul Bert, with Paul Reclus (the surgeon), weighed his brain, it so much surpassed the heaviest brain then known, — that of Cuvier, — reaching something over two thousand grammes, that they would not trust to their scales, but got new ones, to repeat the weighing.

His talk was especially remarkable. He spoke, as he wrote, in images. When he wanted to develop an idea, he did not resort to arguments, although he was a master in philosophical discussions; he illustrated his idea by a scene presented in a form as beautiful as if it had been taken out of one of his novels.

"You must have had a great deal of experience in your life amongst Frenchmen, Germans, and other peoples," he said to me once. "Have you not remarked that there is a deep, unfathomable chasm between many of their conceptions and the views which we Russians hold on the same subjects, — that there are points upon which we can never agree?"

I replied that I had not noticed such points.

"Yes, there are some. Here is one of them. One night we were at the first representation of a new play. I was in a box with Flaubert, Daudet, Zola. [I am not quite sure whether he named both Daudet and Zola, but he certainly named one of the two.] All were men of advanced opinions. The subject of the play was this: A woman had separated from her husband. She had loved again, and now lived with another man. This man was represented in the play as an excellent person. For years they had been quite happy. Her two children — a girl and a boy — were babies at the time of the separation; now they had grown, and throughout all these years they had supposed the man to be their real father. The girl was about eighteen and the boy about seventeen. The man treated them quite as a father; they loved him, and he loved them. The scene represented the family meeting at breakfast. The girl comes in and approaches her supposed father, and he is going to kiss her, when the boy, who has learned in some way the true state of affairs, rushes forward and shouts, ' Don't dare!' (N'osez pas!)

"This exclamation brought down the house. There was

an outburst of frantic applause.   Flaubert and the others
joined in it.   I was disgusted.

" ' Why,' I said, ' this family was happy ; the man was
a better father to these children than their real father, . . .
their mother loved him and was happy with him. . . . This
mischievous, perverted boy ought simply to be whipped for
what he has said.' . . . It was of no use.   I discussed for
hours with them afterwards ; none of them could understand me ! "

I was, of course, fully in accordance with Turguéneff's
point of view.   I remarked, however, that his acquaintances were chiefly amongst the middle classes.   There, the
difference between nation and nation is immense indeed.
But my acquaintances were exclusively amongst the workers, and there is an immense resemblance between the
workers, and especially amongst the peasants, of all nations.

In so saying, I was quite wrong, however.   After I had
had the opportunity of making a closer acquaintance with
French workers, I often thought of the truth of Turguéneff's remark.   There is a real chasm indeed between
Russian conceptions of marriage relations and those which
prevail in France, amongst the workers as well as in the
middle classes ; and in many other things there is a similar
difference between the Russian point of view and that of
other nations.

It was said somewhere, after Turguéneff's death, that he
had intended to write a novel upon this subject.   If he had
begun it, the above-mentioned scene must be in his manuscript.   What a pity that he did not write it !   He, a
thorough " Occidental " in his ways of thinking, could have
said very deep things upon a subject which must have so
profoundly affected him personally throughout his life.

Of all novel-writers of our century, Turguéneff has certainly attained the greatest perfection as an artist, and his
prose sounds to the Russian ear like music, — music as deep

as that of Beethoven. His principal novels — the series of "Dmítri Rúdin," "A Nobleman's Retreat," "On the Eve," "Fathers and Sons," "Smoke," and "Virgin Soil" — represent the leading "history-making" types of the educated classes of Russia, which evolved in rapid succession after 1848; all sketched with a fullness of philosophical conception and humanitarian understanding and an artistic beauty which have no parallel in any other literature. Yet "Fathers and Sons" — a novel which he rightly considered his profoundest work — was received by the young people of Russia with a loud protest. Our youth declared that the nihilist Bazároff was by no means a true representation of his class; many described him even as a caricature of nihilism. This misunderstanding deeply affected Turguéneff, and, although a reconciliation between him and the young generation took place later on at St. Petersburg, after he had written "Virgin Soil," the wound inflicted upon him by these attacks was never healed.

He knew from Lavróff that I was an enthusiastic admirer of his writings; and one day, as we were returning in a carriage from a visit to Antokólsky's studio, he asked me what I thought of Bazároff. I frankly replied, "Bazároff is an admirable painting of the nihilist, but one feels that you did not love him as much as you did your other heroes."

"On the contrary, I loved him, intensely loved him," Turguéneff replied, with an unexpected vigor. "When we get home I will show you my diary, in which I have noted how I wept when I had ended the novel with Bazároff's death."

Turguéneff certainly loved the intellectual aspect of Bazároff. He so identified himself with the nihilist philosophy of his hero that he even kept a diary in his name, appreciating the current events from Bazároff's point of view. But I think that he admired him more than he

loved him. In a brilliant lecture on Hamlet and Don
Quixote, he divided the history makers of mankind into
two classes, represented by one or the other of these characters. "Analysis first of all, and then egotism, and therefore no faith, — an egotist cannot even believe in himself : "
so he characterized Hamlet. "Therefore he is a skeptic,
and never will achieve anything ; while Don Quixote, who
fights against windmills, and takes a barber's plate for the
magic helmet of Mambrino (who of us has never made the
same mistake ?), is a leader of the masses, because the masses
always follow those who, taking no heed of the sarcasms of
the majority, or even of persecutions, march straight forward, keeping their eyes fixed upon a goal which is seen,
perhaps, by no one but themselves. They search, they fall,
but they rise again, and find it, — and by right, too. Yet,
although Hamlet is a skeptic, and disbelieves in Good, he
does not disbelieve in Evil. He hates it ; Evil and Deceit
are his enemies ; and his skepticism is not indifferentism,
but only negation and doubt, which finally consume his
will."

These thoughts of Turguéneff give, I think, the true key
for understanding his relations to his heroes. He himself
and several of his best friends belonged more or less to the
Hamlets. He loved Hamlet, and admired Don Quixote.
So he admired also Bazároff. He represented his superiority admirably well, he understood the tragic character of
his isolated position, but he could not surround him with
that tender, poetical love which he bestowed as on a sick
friend, when his heroes approached the Hamlet type. It
would have been out of place.

"Did you know Mýshkin ? " he once asked me, in 1878.
At the trial of our circles Mýshkin revealed himself as the
most powerful personality. "I should like to know all
about him," he continued. "That *is* a man ; not the
slightest trace of Hamletism." And in so saying he was

obviously meditating on this new type in the Russian movement, which did not exist in the phase that Turguéneff
described in "Virgin Soil," but was to appear two years
later.

I saw him for the last time in the autumn of 1881. He
was very ill, and worried by the thought that it was his
duty to write to Alexander III., — who had just come to
the throne, and hesitated as to the policy he should follow,
— asking him to give Russia a constitution, and proving to
him by solid arguments the necessity of that step. With
evident grief he said to me: "I feel that I must do it, but
I feel that I shall not be able to do it." In fact, he was
already suffering awful pains occasioned by a cancer in the
spinal cord, and had the greatest difficulty even in sitting
up and talking for a few moments. He did not write then,
and a few weeks later it would have been useless. Alexander III. had announced in a manifesto his intention to
remain the absolute ruler of Russia.

VII

In the meantime affairs in Russia took quite a new turn.
The war which Russia began against Turkey in 1877 had
ended in general disappointment. There was in the country, before the war broke out, a great deal of enthusiasm
in favor of the Slavonians. Many believed, also, that a
war of liberation in the Balkans would result in a move in
the progressive direction in Russia itself. But the liberation of the Slavonian populations was only partly accomplished. The tremendous sacrifices which had been made
by the Russians were rendered ineffectual by the blunders
of the higher military authorities. Hundreds of thousands
of men had been slaughtered in battles which were only
half victories, and the concessions wrested from Turkey
were brought to naught at the Berlin congress. It was also
widely known that the embezzlement of state money went
on during this war on almost as large a scale as during the
Crimean war.

It was amidst the general dissatisfaction which prevailed
in Russia at the end of 1877 that one hundred and ninety-
three persons, arrested since 1873, in connection with our
agitation, were brought before a high court. The accused,
supported by a number of lawyers of talent, won at once
the sympathies of the great public. They produced a very
favorable impression upon St. Petersburg society ; and when
it became known that most of them had spent three or four
years in prison, waiting for this trial, and that no less than
twenty-one of them had either put an end to their lives by
suicide or become insane, the feeling grew still stronger in
their favor, even among the judges themselves. The court

pronounced very heavy sentences upon a few, and relatively
lenient ones upon the remainder, saying that the preliminary detention had lasted so long, and was so hard a
punishment in itself, that nothing could justly be added to
it. It was confidently expected that the Emperor would
still further mitigate the sentences. It happened, however,
to the astonishment of all, that he revised the sentences
only to increase them. Those whom the court had acquitted
were sent into exile in remote parts of Russia and Siberia,
and from five to twelve years of hard labor were inflicted
upon those whom the court had condemned to short terms
of imprisonment. This was the work of the chief of the
Third Section, General Mézentsoff.

At the same time, the chief of the St. Petersburg police,
General Trépoff, noticing, during a visit to the house of
detention, that one of the political prisoners, Bogolúboff,
did not take off his hat to greet the omnipotent satrap,
rushed upon him, gave him a blow, and, when the prisoner
resisted, ordered him to be flogged. The other prisoners,
learning the fact in their cells, loudly expressed their in-
dignation, and were in consequence fearfully beaten by the
warders and the police. The Russian political prisoners
bore without murmuring all hardships inflicted upon them
in Siberia or through hard labor, but they were firmly decided not to tolerate corporal punishment. A young girl,
Véra Zasúlich, who did not even personally know Bogolúboff, took a revolver, went to the chief of police, and shot
at him. Trépoff was only wounded. Alexander II. came
to look at the heroic girl, who must have impressed him
by her extremely sweet face and her modesty. Trépoff
had so many enemies at St. Petersburg that they managed
to bring the affair before a common-law jury, and Véra
Zasúlich declared in court that she had resorted to arms
only when all means for bringing the affair to public knowledge and obtaining some sort of redress had been ex-

hausted. Even the St. Petersburg correspondent of the London "Times" had been asked to mention the affair in his paper, but had not done so, perhaps thinking it improbable. Then, without telling any one her intentions, she went to shoot Trépoff. Now that the affair had become public, she was quite happy to know that he was but slightly wounded. The jury acquitted her unanimously; and when the police tried to rearrest her, as she was leaving the court house, the young men of St. Petersburg, who stood in crowds at the gates, saved her from their clutches. She went abroad, and soon was among us in Switzerland.

This affair produced quite a sensation throughout Europe. I was at Paris when the news of the acquittal came, and had to call that day on business at the offices of several newspapers. I found the editors fired with enthusiasm, and writing powerful articles to glorify the girl. Even the serious "Revue des Deux Mondes" wrote, in its review of the year, that the two persons who had most impressed public opinion in Europe during 1878 were Prince Gortcha-kóff at the Berlin congress and Véra Zasúlich. Their portraits were given side by side in several almanacs. Upon the workers in Europe the devotion of Véra Zasúlich produced a tremendous impression.

A few months after that, without any plot having been formed, four attempts were made against crowned heads in close succession. The worker Hoedel and Dr. Nobiling shot at the German Emperor; a few weeks later, a Spanish worker, Oliva Moncasi, followed with an attempt to shoot the King of Spain, and the cook Passanante rushed with his knife upon the King of Italy. The governments of Europe could not believe that such attempts upon the lives of three kings should have occurred without there being at the bottom some international conspiracy, and they jumped to the conclusion that the Jura Federation and the International Workingmen's Association were responsible.

More than twenty years have passed since then, and I
may say most positively that there was absolutely no ground
whatever for that supposition.   However, all the European
governments fell upon Switzerland, reproaching her with
harboring revolutionists, who organized such plots.   Paul
Brousse, the editor of our Jura newspaper, the "Avant-
Garde," was arrested and prosecuted.   The Swiss judges,
seeing there was not the slightest foundation for connecting Brousse or the Jura Federation with the recent attacks,
condemned Brousse to only a couple of months' imprisonment, for his articles ; but the paper was suppressed, and
all the printing-offices of Switzerland were asked by the
federal government not to publish this or any similar paper.
The Jura Federation thus remained without an organ.

Besides, the politicians of Switzerland, who looked with
an unfavorable eye on the anarchist agitation in their country, acted privately in such a way as to compel the leading
Swiss members of the Jura Federation either to retire from
public life or to starve.   Brousse was expelled from Switzerland.   James Guillaume, who for eight years had maintained against all obstacles the official organ of the federation,
and made his living chiefly by teaching, could obtain no
employment, and was compelled to leave Switzerland and
remove to France.   Adhémar Schwitzguébel found no work
in the watch trade, and, burdened as he was by a large
family, had to retire from the movement.   Spichiger was
in the same condition, and emigrated.   It thus happened
that I, a foreigner, had to undertake the editing of the
organ of the federation.   I hesitated, of course, but there
was nothing else to be done, and with two friends, Dumartheray and Herzig, I started a new fortnightly paper at
Geneva, in February, 1879, under the title of "Le Révolté."
I had to write most of it myself.   We had only twenty-
three francs (about four dollars) to start the paper, but we
all set to work to get subscriptions, and succeeded in issuing

our first number.   It was moderate in tone, but revolutionary in substance, and I did my best to write it in such a
style that complex historical and economical questions should
be comprehensible to every intelligent worker.   Six hundred was the utmost limit which the edition of our previous
papers had ever attained.   We printed two thousand copies
of " Le Révolté," and in a few days not one was left.   The
paper was a success, and still continues, at Paris, under the
name of " Temps Nouveaux."

Socialist papers have often a tendency to become mere
annals of complaints about existing conditions.   The oppression of the laborers in the mine, the factory, and the
field is related ; the misery and sufferings of the workers
during strikes are told in vivid pictures ; their helplessness
in the struggle against employers is insisted upon : and this
succession of hopeless efforts, related in the paper, exercises
a most depressing influence upon the reader.   To counter-
balance that effect, the editor has to rely chiefly upon burning words by means of which he tries to inspire his readers with energy and faith.   I thought, on the contrary,
that a revolutionary paper must be, above all, a record of
those symptoms which everywhere announce the coming of
a new era, the germination of new forms of social life, the
growing revolt against antiquated institutions.   These symptoms should be watched, brought together in their intimate
connection, and so grouped as to show to the hesitating
minds of the greater number the invisible and often unconscious support which advanced ideas find everywhere, when
a revival of thought takes place in society.   To make one
feel sympathy with the throbbing of the human heart all
over the world, with its revolt against age-long injustice,
with its attempts at working out new forms of life, — this
should be the chief duty of a revolutionary paper.   It is
hope, not despair, which makes successful revolutions.

Historians often tell us how this or that system of philosophy has accomplished a certain change in human thought, and subsequently in institutions. But this is not history. The greatest social philosophers have only caught the indications of coming changes, have understood their inner relations, and, aided by induction and intuition, have foretold what was to occur. It may also be easy to draw a plan of social organization, by starting from a few principles and developing them to their necessary consequences, like a geometrical conclusion from a few axioms; but this is not sociology. A correct social forecast cannot be made unless one keeps an eye on the thousands of signs of the new life, separating the occasional facts from those which are organically essential, and building the generalization upon that basis.

This was the method of thought with which I endeavored to familiarize my readers, using plain comprehensible words, so as to accustom the most modest of them to judge for himself whereunto society is moving, and himself to correct the thinker if the latter comes to wrong conclusions. As to the criticism of what exists, I went into it only to disentangle the roots of the evils, and to show that a deepseated and carefully-nurtured fetichism with regard to the antiquated survivals of past phases of human development, and a widespread cowardice of mind and will, are the main sources of all evils.

Dumartheray and Herzig gave me full support in that direction. Dumartheray was born in one of the poorest peasant families in Savoy. His schooling had not gone beyond the first rudiments of a primary school. Yet he was one of the most intelligent men I ever met. His appreciations of current events and men were so remarkable for their uncommon good sense that they were often prophetic. He was also one of the finest critics of the current socialist literature, and was never taken in by the mere display of fine words or would-be science. Herzig was a young clerk, born at Geneva; a man of suppressed emotions, shy, who would blush like a girl when he expressed an original thought, and who, after I was arrested, when he became responsible for the continuance of the journal, by sheer force of will learned to write very well. Boycotted by all Geneva employers, and fallen with his family into sheer misery, he nevertheless supported the paper till it became possible to transfer it to Paris.

To the judgment of these two friends I could trust implicitly. If Herzig frowned, muttering, " Yes — well — it may go," I knew that it would not do. And when Dumartherary, who always complained of the bad state of his spectacles when he had to read a not quite legibly written manuscript, and therefore generally read proofs only, interrupted his reading by exclaiming, " Non, ça ne va pas ! " I felt at once that it was not the proper thing, and tried to guess what thought or expression provoked his disapproval. I knew there was no use asking him, " Why will it not do ? " He would have answered : " Ah, that is not my affair; that 's yours. It won't do; that is all I can say." But I felt he was right, and I simply sat down to rewrite the passage, or, taking the composing-stick, set up in type a new passage instead.

I must own also that we had hard times with it. No sooner had we issued four or five numbers than the printer asked us to find another printing-office. For the workers and their publications the liberty of the press inscribed in the constitution has many limitations beside the paragraphs of the law. The printer had no objection to our paper : he liked it; but in Switzerland all printing-offices depend upon the government, which employs them more or less upon statistical reports and the like; and our printer was plainly told that if he continued to print the paper he need not expect to have any more orders from the Geneva government.   I made the tour of all the French-speaking part of Switzerland, and saw the heads of all the printing-offices, but everywhere, even from those who did not dislike the tendency of our paper, I received the same reply : " We could not live without work from the government, and we should have none if we undertook to print ' Le Révolté.' "

I returned to Geneva in very low spirits; but Dumartheray was only the more ardent and hopeful.   " It 's all very simple," he said.   " We buy our own printing-plant on a three months' credit, and in three months we shall have paid for it."   " But we have no money, only a few hundred francs," I objected.   " Money, nonsense !   We shall have it !   Let us only order the type at once and immediately issue our next number — and money will come ! " Once more his judgment was quite right.   When our next number came out from our own "Imprimerie Jurassienne," and we had told our difficulties and printed a couple of small pamphlets besides, — all of us helping in the printing, — the money came in ; mostly in coppers and small silver coins, but it came.   Over and over again in my life I have heard complaints among the advanced parties about the want of money ; but the longer I live, the more I am persuaded that our chief difficulty is not so much a lack of money as of *men* who will march firmly and steadily towards a given aim in the right direction, and inspire others. For twenty-one years our paper has now continued to live from hand to mouth, — appeals for funds appearing on the front page in almost every number ; but as long as there is a man who sticks to it and puts all his energy into it, as Herzig and Dumartheray did at Geneva, and as Grave has done for the last sixteen years at Paris, the money comes in, and a yearly debit of about eight hundred pounds is made up, — mainly out of the pennies and small silver coins of the workers, — to cover the yearly expenditure for printing the paper and the pamphlets.   For a paper, as for

everything else, men are of an infinitely greater value than
money.

We started our printing-office in a tiny room, and our
compositor was a man from Little Russia, who undertook
to put our paper in type for the very modest sum of sixty
francs a month. If he could only have his modest dinner
every day, and the possibility of going occasionally to the
opera, he cared for nothing more. " Going to the Turkish
bath, John ? " I asked him once as I met him at Geneva
in the street, with a brown-paper parcel under his arm.
" No, removing to a new lodging," he replied, in his usual
melodious voice, and with his customary smile.

Unfortunately, he knew no French. I used to write my
manuscript in the best of my handwriting, — often thinking with regret of the time I had wasted in the classes of
our good Ebert at school, — but John could read French
only indifferently well, and instead of " immédiatement "
he would read " immidiotermut " or " inmuidiatmunt," and
set up in type such wonderful words as these ; but as
he " kept the space," and the length of the line did not
have to be altered in making the corrections, there were
only four or five letters to be corrected in such uncouth
words as the above, and but one or two in each of the shorter
ones ; thus we managed pretty well. We were on the best
possible terms with him, and I soon learned a little type-
setting under his direction. The composition was always
finished in time to take the proofs to a Swiss comrade who
was the responsible editor, and to whom we submitted them
before going to press, and then one of us carted all the forms
to a printing-office. Our " Imprimerie Jurassienne " soon
became widely known for its publications, especially for its
pamphlets, which Dumartheray would never allow to be
sold at more than one penny. Quite a new style had to be
worked out for such pamphlets. I must say that I was
often wicked enough to envy those writers who could use

any number of pages for developing their ideas, and were
allowed to make the well-known excuse of Talleyrand : " I
have not had the time to be brief." When I had to con-
dense the results of several months' work — upon, let me
say, the origins of law — into a penny pamphlet, I had to
take the time to be brief. But we wrote for the workers,
and twenty centimes for a pamphlet is often too much for
the average worker. The result was that our penny and
half-penny pamphlets sold by the scores of thousands, and
were reproduced in many other countries in translations.
My leaders of that period were published later on, while I
was in prison, by Elisée Reclus, under the title of "The
Words of a Rebel," — *Paroles d'un Révolté*.

France was always the chief object of our aims ; but " Le
Révolté " was severely prohibited in France, and the smugglers had so many good things to import into France from
Switzerland that they did not care to meddle with our
paper. I went once with them, crossing in their company
the French frontier, and found that they were very brave
and reliable men, but I could not induce them to undertake
the smuggling of our paper. All we could do, therefore, was
to send it in sealed envelopes to about a hundred persons in
France. We charged nothing for postage, counting upon
voluntary contributions from our subscribers to cover our
extra expenses, — which they always did, — but we often
thought that the French police were missing a splendid
opportunity for ruining our paper by subscribing to a
hundred copies and sending no voluntary contributions.

For the first year we had to rely entirely upon ourselves ;
but gradually Elisée Reclus took a greater interest in the
work, and finally gave more life than ever to the paper
after my arrest. Reclus had invited me to aid him in the
preparation of the volume of his monumental Geography
which dealt with the Russian dominions in Asia. He had

learned Russian, but thought that, as I was well acquainted
with Siberia, I might be helpful; and as the health of my
wife was poor, and the doctor had ordered her to leave
Geneva with its cold winds at once, we removed early in
the spring of 1880 to Clarens, where Elisée Reclus lived
at that time. We settled above Clarens, in a small cottage
overlooking the blue waters of Lake Geneva, with the pure
snow of the Dent du Midi in the background. A streamlet
that thundered like a mighty torrent after rains, carrying
away immense rocks and digging for itself a new bed, ran
under our windows, and on the slope of the hill opposite
rose the old castle of Châtelard, of which the owners, up
to the revolution of the *burla papei* (the burners of the
papers) in 1799, levied upon the neighboring peasants servile taxes on the occasion of births, marriages, and deaths.
Here, aided by my wife, with whom I used to discuss every
event and every proposed paper, and who was a severe literary critic of my writings, I produced the best things that I
wrote for "Le Révolté," among them the address " To the
Young," which was spread in hundreds of thousands of copies in all languages. In fact, I worked out here the foundation of nearly all that I wrote later on. Contact with
educated men of similar ways of thinking is what we anarchist writers, scattered by proscription all over the world,
miss, perhaps, more than anything else. At Clarens I had
that contact with Elisée Reclus and Lefrançais, in addition
to permanent contact with the workers, which I continued
to maintain; and although I worked much for the Geography, I could produce even more than usual for the anarchist propaganda.

VIII

In Russia the struggle for freedom was taking on a
more and more acute character. Several political trials had
been brought before high courts, — the trial of "the hundred and ninety-three," of "the fifty," of "the Dolgúshin
circle," and so on, — and in all of them the same thing
was apparent. The youth had gone to the peasants and the
factory workers, preaching socialism to them; socialist pamphlets, printed abroad, had been distributed; appeals had
been made to revolt — in some vague, indeterminate way
— against the oppressive economical conditions. In short,
nothing was done that does not occur in socialist agitations
in every other country of the world. No traces of conspiracy against the Tsar, or even of preparations for revolutionary action, were found; in fact, there were none.
The great majority of our youth were at that time hostile
to such action. Nay, looking now over that movement of
the years 1870–78, I can say in full confidence that most of
them would have felt satisfied if they had been simply
allowed to live by the side of the peasants and the workers,
to teach them, to collaborate in any of the thousand capacities — private or as a part of the local self-government —
in which an educated and earnest man or woman can be
useful to the masses of the people. I knew the men, and
say so with full knowledge of them.

Yet the sentences were ferocious, — stupidly ferocious,
because the movement, which had grown out of the previous
state of Russia, was too deeply rooted to be crushed down
by mere brutality. Hard labor for six, ten, twelve years in
the mines, with subsequent exile to Siberia for life, was a

common sentence. There were such cases as that of a girl who got nine years' hard labor and life exile to Siberia, for giving one socialist pamphlet to a worker ; that was all her crime. Another girl of fourteen, Miss Gukóvskaya, was transported for life to a remote village of Siberia, for having tried, like Goethe's Klärchen, to excite an indifferent crowd to deliver Koválsky and his friends when they were going to be hanged, — an act the more natural in Russia, even from the authorities' standpoint, as there is no capital punishment in our country for common-law crimes, and the application of the death penalty to "politicals" was then a novelty, a return to almost forgotten traditions. Thrown into the wilderness, this young girl soon drowned herself in the Yeniséi. Even those who were acquitted by the courts were banished by the gendarmes to little hamlets in Siberia and Northeast Russia, where they had to starve on the government's monthly allowance, one dollar and fifty cents (three rubles). There are no industries in such hamlets, and the exiles were strictly prohibited from teaching.

As if to exasperate the youth still more, their condemned friends were not sent direct to Siberia. They were locked up, first, for a number of years, in central prisons, which made them envy the convict's life in Siberia. These prisons were awful indeed. In one of them — "a den of typhoid fever," as a priest of that particular jail said in a sermon — the mortality reached twenty per cent. in twelve months. In the central prisons, in the hard-labor prisons of Siberia, in the fortress, the prisoners had to resort to the strike of death, the famine strike, to protect themselves from the brutality of the warders, or to obtain conditions — some sort of work, or reading, in their cells — that would save them from being driven into insanity in a few months. The horror of such strikes, during which men and women refused to take any food for seven or eight days in succession, and then lay motionless, their minds wandering, seemed not to appeal to the gendarmes. At Khárkoff, the prostrated prisoners were tied up with ropes and fed by force, artificially.

Information of these horrors leaked out from the prisons, crossed the boundless distances of Siberia, and spread far and wide among the youth. There was a time when not a week passed without disclosing some new infamy of that sort, or even worse.

Sheer exasperation took hold of our young people. " In other countries," they began to say, " men have the courage to resist. An Englishman, a Frenchman, would not tolerate such outrages. How can we tolerate them ? Let us resist, arms in hands, the nocturnal raids of the gendarmes ; let them know, at least, that since arrest means a slow and infamous death at their hands, they will have to take us in a mortal struggle." At Odessa, Koválsky and his friends met with revolver shots the gendarmes who came one night to arrest them.

The reply of Alexander II. to this new move was the proclamation of a state of siege. Russia was divided into a number of districts, each of them under a governor-general, who received the order to hang offenders pitilessly. Koválsky and his friends — who, by the way, had killed no one by their shots — were executed. Hanging became the order of the day. Twenty-three persons perished in two years, including a boy of nineteen, who was caught posting a revolutionary proclamation at a railway station ; this act — I say it deliberately — was the only charge against him. He was a boy, but he died like a man.

Then the watchword of the revolutionists became " self-defense : " self-defense against the spies who introduced themselves into the circles under the mask of friendship, and denounced members right and left, simply because they would not be paid if they did not accuse large numbers of persons ; self-defense against those who ill-treated prisoners ;

self-defense against the omnipotent chiefs of the state police.

Three functionaries of mark and two or three small spies fell in that new phase of the struggle. General Mézentsoff, who had induced the Tsar to double the sentences after the trial of the hundred and ninety-three, was killed in broad daylight at St. Petersburg; a gendarme colonel, guilty of something worse than that, had the same fate at Kíeff; and the governor-general of Khárkoff — my cousin, Dmítri Kropótkin — was shot as he was returning home from a theatre. The central prison, in which the first famine strike and artificial feeding took place, was under his orders. In reality, he was not a bad man, — I know that his personal feelings were somewhat favorable to the political prisoners; but he was a weak man and a courtier, and he hesitated to interfere. One word from him would have stopped the illtreatment of the prisoners. Alexander II. liked him so much, and his position at the court was so strong, that his interference very probably would have been approved. "Thank you; you have acted according to my own wishes," the Tsar said to him, a couple of years before that date, when he came to St. Petersburg to report that he had taken a peaceful attitude in a riot of the poorer population of Khárkoff, and had treated the rioters very leniently. But this time he gave his approval to the jailers, and the young men of Khárkoff were so exasperated at the treatment of their friends that one of them shot him.

However, the personality of the Emperor was kept out of the struggle, and down to the year 1879 no attempt was made on his life. The person of the Liberator of the serfs was surrounded by an aureole which protected him infinitely better than the swarms of police officials. If Alexander II. had shown at this juncture the least desire to improve the state of affairs in Russia; if he had only called in one or two

of those men with whom he had collaborated during the reform period, and had ordered them to make an inquiry into
the conditions of the country, or merely of the peasantry;
if he had shown any intention of limiting the powers of
the secret police, his steps would have been hailed with
enthusiasm. A word would have made him "the Liberator" again, and once more the youth would have repeated
Hérzen's words: "Thou hast conquered, Galilean." But
just as during the Polish insurrection the despot awoke in
him, and, inspired by Katkóff, he resorted to hanging, so
now again, following the advice of his evil genius, Katkóff,
he found nothing to do but to nominate special military
governors — for hanging.

Then, and then only, a handful of revolutionists, — the
Executive Committee, — supported, I must say, by the
growing discontent in the educated classes, and even in
the Tsar's immediate surroundings, declared that war against
absolutism which, after several attempts, ended in 1881 in
the death of Alexander II.

Two men, I have said already, lived in Alexander II.,
and now the conflict between the two, which had grown
during all his life, assumed a really tragic aspect. When
he met Solovióff, who shot at him and missed the first shot,
he had the presence of mind to run to the nearest door, not
in a straight line, but in zigzags, while Solovióff continued
to fire; and he thus escaped with but a slight tearing of
his overcoat. On the day of his death, too, he gave a proof
of his undoubted courage. In the face of real danger he
was courageous; but he continually trembled before the
phantasms of his own imagination. Once he shot at an
aide-de-camp, when the latter had made an abrupt movement, and Alexander thought he was going to attempt his
life. Merely to save his life, he surrendered entirely all
his imperial powers into the hands of those who cared nothing for him, but only for their lucrative positions.

He undoubtedly retained an attachment to the mother of his children, even though he was then with the Princess Yurievski-Dolgorúki, whom he married immediately after the death of the Empress. "Don't speak to me of the Empress; it makes me suffer too much," he more than once said to Lóris Mélikoff. And yet he entirely abandoned the Empress Marie, who had stood faithfully by his side while he was the Liberator; he let her die in the palace in neglect. A well-known Russian doctor, now dead, told his friends that he, a stranger, felt shocked at the neglect with which the Empress was treated during her last illness, — deserted, of course, by the ladies of the court, having by her side but two ladies, deeply devoted to her, and receiving every day but a short official visit from her husband, who stayed in another palace in the meantime.

When the Executive Committee made the daring attempt to blow up the Winter Palace itself, Alexander II. took a step which had no precedent. He created a sort of dictatorship, vesting unlimited powers in Lóris Mélikoff. This general was an Armenian, to whom Alexander II. had once before given similar dictatorial powers, when the bubonic plague broke out on the Lower Vólga, and Germany threatened to mobilize her troops and put Russia under quarantine if the plague were not stopped. Now that Alexander II. saw that he could not have confidence in the vigilance of even the palace police, he gave dictatorial powers to Lóris Mélikoff, and as Mélikoff had the reputation of being a Liberal, this new move was interpreted as indicating that the convocation of a National Assembly would soon follow. As, however, no new attempts upon his life were made immediately after that explosion, the Tsar regained confidence, and a few months later, before Mélikoff had been allowed to do anything, he was dictator no longer, but simply minister of the interior. The sudden attacks of sadness of which I have already spoken, during which Alexander II.

reproached himself with the reactionary character that his reign had assumed, now took the shape of violent paroxysms of tears. He would sit weeping by the hour, bringing Mélikoff to despair. Then he would ask his minister, "When will your constitutional scheme be ready?" If, two days later, Mélikoff said that it was now ready, the Emperor seemed to have forgotten all about it. "Did I mention it?" he would ask. "What for? We had better leave it to my successor. That will be his gift to Russia."

When rumors of a new plot reached him, he was ready to undertake something; but when everything seemed to be quiet among the revolutionists, he turned his ear again to his reactionary advisers, and let things go. Every moment Mélikoff expected dismissal.

In February, 1881, Mélikoff reported that a new plot had been laid by the Executive Committee, but its plan could not be discovered by any amount of searching. Thereupon Alexander II. decided that a sort of deliberative assembly of delegates from the provinces should be called. Always under the idea that he would share the fate of Louis XVI., he described this gathering as an Assemblée des Notables, like the one convoked by Louis XVI. before the National Assembly in 1789. The scheme had to be laid before the council of state, but then again he hesitated. It was only on the morning of March 1 (13), 1881, after a final warning by Lóris Mélikoff, that he ordered it to be brought before the council on the following Thursday. This was on Sunday, and he was asked by Mélikoff not to go out to the parade that day, there being danger of an attempt on his life. Nevertheless, he went. He wanted to see the Grand Duchess Catherine (daughter of his aunt, Hélène Pávlovna, who had been one of the leaders of the emancipation party in 1861), and to carry her the welcome news, perhaps as an expiatory offering to the memory of the Empress Marie. He is said to have told her, "Je me suis décidé à convo-

quer une Assemblée des Notables." However, this belated
and half-hearted concession had not been announced, and
on his way back to the Winter Palace he was killed.

It is known how it happened. A bomb was thrown
under his iron-clad carriage, to stop it. Several Circassians
of the escort were wounded. Rysakóff, who flung the bomb,
was arrested on the spot. Then, although the coachman of
the Tsar earnestly advised him not to get out, saying that
he could drive him still in the slightly damaged carriage,
he insisted upon alighting. He felt that his military dignity required him to see the wounded Circassians, to con-
dole with them as he had done with the wounded during
the Turkish war, when a mad storming of Plevna, doomed
to end in a terrible disaster, was made on the day of his
fête. He approached Rysakóff and asked him something;
and as he passed close by another young man, Grinevétsky,
the latter threw a bomb between himself and Alexander II.,
so that both of them should be killed. They both lived
but a few hours.

There Alexander II. lay upon the snow, profusely bleeding, abandoned by every one of his followers! All had
disappeared. It was cadets, returning from the parade, who
lifted the suffering Tsar from the snow and put him in a
sledge, covering his shivering body with a cadet mantle and
his bare head with a cadet cap. And it was one of the terrorists, Emeliánoff, with a bomb wrapped in a paper under
his arm, who, at the risk of being arrested on the spot and
hanged, rushed with the cadets to the help of the wounded
man. Human nature is full of these contrasts.

Thus ended the tragedy of Alexander II.'s life. People
could not understand how it was possible that a Tsar who
had done so much for Russia should have met his death at
the hands of revolutionists. To me, who had the chance
of witnessing the first reactionary steps of Alexander II.
and his gradual deterioration, who had caught a glimpse of

his complex personality, — that of a born autocrat, whose violence was but partially mitigated by education, of a man possessed of military gallantry, but devoid of the courage of the statesman, of a man of strong passions and weak will, — it seemed that the tragedy developed with the unavoidable fatality of one of Shakespeare's dramas. Its last act was already written for me on the day when I heard him address us, the promoted officers, on June 13, 1862, immediately after he had ordered the first executions in Poland.

IX

A WILD panic seized the court circles at St. Petersburg. Alexander III., who, notwithstanding his colossal stature and force, was not a very courageous man, refused to move to the Winter Palace, and retired to the palace of his grandfather, Paul I., at Gatchina. I know that old building, planned as a Vauban fortress, surrounded by moats and protected by watchtowers, from the tops of which secret staircases lead to the Emperor's study. I have seen the trap-doors in the study, for suddenly throwing an enemy on the sharp rocks in the water underneath, and the secret staircase leading to underground prisons and to an underground passage which opens on a lake. All the palaces of Paul I. had been built on a similar plan. In the meantime, an underground gallery, supplied with automatic electric appliances to protect it from being undermined by the revolutionists, was dug round the Anichkoff palace, in which Alexander III. resided when he was heir apparent.

A secret league for the protection of the Tsar was started. Officers of all grades were induced by triple salaries to join it, and to undertake voluntary spying in all classes of society. Comical scenes followed, of course. Two officers, without knowing that they both belonged to the league, would entice each other into a disloyal conversation, during a railway journey, and then proceed to arrest each other, only to discover at the last moment that their pains had been labor lost. This league still exists in a more official shape, under the name of Okhrána (Protection), and from time to time frightens the present Tsar with all sorts of concocted "dangers," in order to maintain its existence.

A still more secret ... tion, the Holy League, was
formed at the same ... the leadership of the
brother of the ... purpose of opposing
the revoluti... of which was to
kill those ... d to have been
the lea... his number.
The ... ers of the
l... re were none
... such refugees ;
... hambre at the time
... nted by the league to

[card obscuring text reads:]
THE PAPER DOLL LOUNGE OR ANY OF ITS EMPLOYEES DO NOT ACCEPT
ANY RESPONSIBILITY FOR ITS MEMBERS AND/OR THEIR GUESTS THAT ARE IN
ROUTE FROM ABOVE NAMED CORPORATION TO USE AND LOUNGE. THIS MEMBERSHIP
ENTITLES EACH DUE'S PAID MEMBER TO USE AND ENJOY THE FACILITIES OF
THE CLUB AND ITS HOSPITALITY, NOT ABUSE THEM. THE CLUB MAINTAINS THE
RIGHT TO REFUSE SERVICE OR ADMISSION TO ANYONE THAT IS INTOXICATED
OR UNDESIRABLE. THE DISCRETION ID SOLELY UP TO MANAGEMENT OF THE
CLUB BY SIGNING THE DESIGNATED LINE AT THE BOTTOM OF
THIS CARD, THE APPLICANT AGREES TO ALL TERMS SET FORTH.
PERSONS USING FALSE ID WILL BE PROSECUTED
SIGNATURE

... gees abroad did not interfere
... ecutive Committee at St. Peters-
... irect conspiracies from Switzerland,
... s at St. Petersburg acted under a per-
m... death, would have been sheer nonsense;
and ... and I wrote several times, none of us would
have ac... the doubtful task of forming plans of action
without being on the spot. But of course it suited the
plans of the St. Petersburg police to maintain that they
were powerless to protect the Tsar because all plots were
devised abroad, and their spies — I know it well — amply
supplied them with the desired reports.

Skóbeleff, the hero of the Turkish war, was also asked
to join this league, but he blankly refused. It appears
from Lóris Mélikoff's posthumous papers, part of which
were published by a friend of his in London, that when
Alexander III. came to the throne, and hesitated to convoke the Assembly of Notables, Skóbeleff even made an
offer to Lóris Mélikoff and Count Ignátieff ("the lying
Pasha," as the Constantinople diplomatists used to nickname him), to arrest Alexander III., and compel him to
sign a constitutional manifesto ; whereupon Ignátieff is said

to have denounced the scheme to the Tsar, and thus to have obtained his nomination as prime minister, in which capacity he resorted, with the advice of M. Andrieux, the ex-prefect of police at Paris, to various stratagems in order to paralyze the revolutionists.

If the Russian Liberals had shown anything like a modest courage and some power of organized action, at that time, a National Assembly would have been convoked. From the same posthumous papers of Lóris Mélikoff it appears that Alexander III. was willing for a time to call one. He had made up his mind to do so, and had announced it to his brother. Old Wilhelm I. supported him in this intention. It was only when he saw that the Liberals undertook nothing, while the Katkóff party was busy in the opposite direction, — M. Andrieux advising him to crush the nihilists, and indicating how it ought to be done (his letter to this effect is in the pamphlet referred to), — that Alexander III. finally resolved to declare that he would continue to be absolute ruler of the empire.

I was expelled from Switzerland by order of the federal council a few months after the death of Alexander II. I did not take umbrage at this. Assailed by the monarchical powers on account of the asylum which Switzerland offered to refugees, and menaced by the Russian official press with a wholesale expulsion of all Swiss governesses and ladies' maids, who are numerous in Russia, the rulers of Switzerland, by banishing me, gave some sort of satisfaction to the Russian police. But I very much regret, for the sake of Switzerland itself, that that step was taken. It was a sanction given to the theory of "conspiracies concocted in Switzerland," and it was an acknowledgment of weakness, of which Italy and France took advantage at once. Two years later, when Jules Ferry proposed to Italy and Germany the partition of Switzerland, his argument must have been that the Swiss government itself had admitted that Switzerland was "a hotbed of international conspiracies." This first concession led to more arrogant demands, and has certainly placed Switzerland in a far less independent position than it might otherwise have occupied.

The decree of expulsion was delivered to me immediately after I had returned from London, where I was present at an anarchist congress in July, 1881. After that congress I had stayed for a few weeks in England, writing the first articles on Russian affairs from our standpoint for the "Newcastle Chronicle." The English press, at that time, was an echo of the opinions of Madame Novikóff, — that is, of Katkóff and the Russian state police, — and I was most happy when Mr. Joseph Cowen agreed to give me the hospitality of his paper in order to state our point of view.

I had just joined my wife in the high mountains where she was staying, near the abode of Elisée Reclus, when I was asked to leave Switzerland. We sent the little luggage we had to the next railway station and went on foot to Aigle, enjoying for the last time the sight of the mountains that we loved so much. We crossed the hills by taking short cuts over them, and laughed when we discovered that the short cuts led to long windings; and when we reached the bottom of the valley, we tramped along the dusty road. The comical incident which always comes in such cases was supplied by an English lady. A richly dressed dame, reclining by the side of a gentleman in a hired carriage, threw several tracts to the two poorly dressed tramps, as she passed them. I lifted the tracts from the dust. She was evidently one of those ladies who believe themselves to be Christians, and consider it their duty to distribute religious tracts among "dissolute foreigners." Thinking we were sure to overtake the lady at the railway station, I wrote on one of the pamphlets the well-known verse relative to the rich in the kingdom of God, and similarly appropriate quotations about the Pharisees being the worst enemies of Christianity. When we came to Aigle, the lady was taking refreshments in her carriage. She evidently preferred to continue the journey in this vehicle along the lovely valley, rather than to be shut up in a stuffy railway car. I returned her the pamphlets with politeness, saying that I had added to them something that she might find useful for her own instruction. The lady did not know whether to fly at me, or to accept the lesson with Christian patience. Her eyes expressed both impulses in rapid succession.

My wife was about to pass her examination for the degree of Bachelor of Science at the Geneva University, and we settled, therefore, in a tiny town of France, Thonon, situated on the Savoy coast of the Lake of Geneva, and stayed there a couple of months.

As to the death sentence of the Holy League, a warning reached me from one of the highest quarters of Russia. Even the name of the lady who was sent from St. Petersburg to Geneva to be the head centre of the conspiracy became known to me. So I simply communicated the fact and the names to the Geneva correspondent of the "Times," asking him to publish them if anything should happen, and I put a note to that effect in "Le Révolté." After that I did not trouble myself more about it. My wife did not take it so lightly, and the good peasant woman, Madame Sansaux, who gave us board and lodgings at Thonon, and who had learned of the plot in a different way (through her sister, who was a nurse in the family of a Russian agent), bestowed the most touching care upon me. Her cottage was out of town, and whenever I went to town at night — sometimes to meet my wife at the railway station — she always found a pretext to have me accompanied by her

husband with a lantern. "Wait only a moment, Monsieur
Kropótkin," she would say; "my husband is going that
way for purchases, and you know he always carries a lantern!" Or else she would send her brother to follow me
at a distance, without my noticing it.

X

In October or November, 1881, as soon as my wife had passed her examination, we removed from Thonon to London, where we stayed nearly twelve months. Few years separate us from that time, and yet I can say that the intellectual life of London and of all England was quite different then from what it became a little later. Every one knows that in the forties England stood almost at the head of the socialist movement in Europe; but during the years of reaction that followed, the great movement, which had deeply affected the working classes, and in which all that is now put forward as scientific or anarchist socialism had already been said, came to a standstill. It was forgotten, in England as well as on the Continent, and what the French writers describe as "the third awakening of the proletarians" had not yet begun in Britain. The labors of the agricultural commission of 1871, the propaganda amongst the agricultural laborers, and the previous efforts of the Christian socialists had certainly done something to prepare the way; but the outburst of socialist feeling in England which followed the publication of Henry George's "Progress and Poverty" had not yet taken place.

The year that I then passed in London was a year of real exile. For one who held advanced socialist opinions, there was no atmosphere to breathe in. There was no sign of that animated socialist movement which I found so largely developed on my return in 1886. Burns, Champion, Hardie, and the other labor leaders were not yet heard of; the Fabians did not exist; Morris had not declared himself a socialist; and the trade unions, limited in London to a few privileged trades only, were hostile to socialism. The only active and outspoken representatives of the socialist movement were Mr. and Mrs. Hyndman, with a very few workers grouped round them. They had held in the autumn of 1881 a small congress, and we used to say jokingly — but it was very nearly true — that Mrs. Hyndman had received all the congress in her house. Moreover, the more or less socialist radical movement which was certainly going on in the minds of men did not assert itself frankly and openly. That considerable number of educated men and women who appeared in public life four years later, and, without committing themselves to social-ism, took part in various movements connected with the well-being or the education of the masses, and who have now created in almost every city of England and Scotland a quite new atmosphere of reform and a new society of re-formers, had not then made themselves felt. They were there, of course; they thought and spoke; all the elements for a widespread movement were in existence; but, finding none of those centres of attraction which the socialist groups subsequently became, they were lost in the crowd; they did not know one another, or remained unconscious of their own selves.

Tchaykóvsky was then in London, and as in years past, we began a socialist propaganda amongst the workers. Aided by a few English workers whose acquaintance we had made at the congress of 1881, or whom the prosecu-tions against John Most had attracted to the socialists, we went to the radical clubs, speaking about Russian affairs, the movement of our youth toward the people, and socialism in general. We had ridiculously small audiences, seldom consisting of more than a dozen men. Occasionally some gray-bearded Chartist would rise from the audience and tell us that all we were saying had been said forty years before, and was greeted then with enthusiasm by crowds of workers, but that now all was dead, and there was no hope of reviving it.

Mr. Hyndman had just published his excellent exposition of Marxist socialism under the title of "England for All;" and I remember, one day in the summer of 1882, earnestly advising him to start a socialist paper. I told him what small means we had when we started "Le Révolté," and predicted a certain success if he would make the attempt. But so unpromising was its general outlook that even he thought the undertaking would be absolutely hopeless unless he had the means to defray all its expenses. Perhaps he was right; but when, less than three years later, he started "Justice," it found a hearty support among the workers, and early in 1886 there were three socialist papers, and the social democratic federation was an influential body.

In the summer of 1882 I spoke, in broken English, before the Durham miners at their annual gathering; I delivered lectures at Newcastle, Glasgow, and Edinburgh about the Russian movement, and was received with enthusiasm, a crowd of workers giving hearty cheers for the nihilists, after the meeting, in the street. But my wife and I felt so lonely in London, and our efforts to awaken a socialist movement in England seemed so hopeless, that in the autumn of 1882 we decided to remove again to France. We were sure that in France I should soon be arrested; but we often said to each other, "Better a French prison than this grave."

Those who are prone to speak of the slowness of evolution ought to study the development of socialism in England. Evolution *is* slow; but its rate is not uniform. It has its periods of slumber and its periods of sudden progress.

XI

We settled once more in Thonon, taking lodgings with our former hostess, Madame Sansaux. A brother of my wife, who was dying of consumption, and had come to Switzerland, joined us.

I never saw such numbers of Russian spies as during the two months that I remained at Thonon. To begin with, as soon as we had engaged lodgings, a suspicious character, who gave himself out for an Englishman, took the other part of the house. Flocks, literally flocks of Russian spies besieged the house, seeking admission under all possible pretexts, or simply tramping in pairs, trios, and quartettes in front of the house. I can imagine what wonderful reports they wrote. A spy must report. If he should merely say that he has stood for a week in the street without noticing anything mysterious, he would soon be put on the half-pay list or dismissed.

It was then the golden age of the Russian secret police. Ignátieff's policy had borne fruit. There were two or three bodies of police competing with one another, each having any amount of money at their disposal, and carrying on the boldest intrigues. Colonel Sudéikin, for instance, chief of one of the branches, — plotting with a certain Degáeff, who after all killed him, — denounced Ignátieff's agents to the revolutionists at Geneva, and offered to the terrorists in Russia all facilities for killing the minister of the interior, Count Tolstóy, and the Grand Duke Vladímir; adding that he himself would then be nominated minister of the interior, with dictatorial powers, and the Tsar would be entirely in his hands. This activity of the Russian police culminated, later on, in the kidnapping of the Prince of Battenberg from Bulgaria.

The French police, also, were on the alert. The question, "What is he doing at Thonon?" worried them. I continued to edit "Le Révolté," and wrote articles for the "Encyclopædia Britannica" and the "Newcastle Chronicle." But what reports could be made out of that? One day the local gendarme paid a visit to my landlady. He had heard from the street the rattling of some machine, and wished to report that I had in my house a secret printing-press. So he came in my absence and asked the lady to show him the press. She replied that there was none and suggested that perhaps the gendarme had overheard the noise of her sewing-machine. But he would not be convinced by so prosaic an explanation, and actually compelled the landlady to sew on her machine, while he listened inside the house and outside to make sure that the rattling he had heard was the same.

"What is he doing all day?" he asked the landlady.

"He writes."

"He cannot write all day long."

"He saws wood in the garden at midday, and he takes walks every afternoon between four and five." It was in November.

"Ah, that's it! When the dusk is coming on?" (A la tombée de la nuit?) And he wrote in his notebook, "Never goes out except at dusk."

I could not well explain at that time this special attention of the Russian spies; but it must have had some connection with the following. When Ignátieff was nominated prime minister, advised by the ex-prefect of Paris, Andrieux, he hit on a new plan. He sent a swarm of his agents into Switzerland, and one of them undertook the publication of a paper which slightly advocated the extension of provincial self-government in Russia, but whose chief purpose was to combat the revolutionists, and to rally to its standard those of the refugees who did not sympathize with terrorism. This was certainly a means of sowing division. Then, when nearly all the members of the Executive Committee had been arrested in Russia, and a couple of them had taken refuge at Paris, Ignátieff sent an agent to Paris to offer an armistice. He promised that there should be no further executions on account of the plots during the reign of Alexander II., even if those who had escaped arrest fell into the hands of the government; that Chernyshévsky should be released from Siberia; and that a commission should be nominated to review the cases of all those who had been exiled to Siberia without trial. On the other side, he asked the Executive Committee to promise to make no attempts against the Tsar's life until his coronation was over. Perhaps the reforms in favor of the peasants, which Alexander III. intended to make, were also mentioned. The agreement was made at Paris, and was kept on both sides. The terrorists suspended hostilities. Nobody was executed for complicity in the former conspiracies; those who were arrested later on under this indictment were immured in the Russian Bastille at Schlüsselburg, where nothing was heard of them for fifteen years, and where most of them still are. Chernyshévsky was brought back from Siberia, and ordered to stay at Astrakhan, where he was severed from all connection with the intellectual world of Russia, and soon died. A commission went through Siberia, releasing some of the exiles, and specifying terms of exile for the remainder. My brother Alexander received from it an additional five years.

While I was at London, in 1882, I was told one day that a man who pretended to be a *bona fide* agent of the Russian government, and could prove it, wanted to enter into negotiations with me. "Tell him that if he comes to my house I will throw him down the staircase," was my reply. Probably the result was that while Ignátieff considered the Tsar guaranteed from the attacks of the Executive Committee, he was afraid that the anarchists might make some attempt, and wanted to have me out of the way.

XII

THE anarchist movement had undergone a considerable development in France during the years 1881 and 1882. It was generally believed that the French mind was hostile to communism, and within the International Workingmen's Association "collectivism" was preached instead. It meant then the possession of the instruments of production in common, each separate group having to settle for itself whether the consumption of produce should be on individualistic or communistic lines. In reality, however, the French mind was hostile only to the monastic communism, to the *phalanstère* of the old schools. When the Jura Federation, at its congress of 1880, boldly declared itself anarchist-communist, — that is, in favor of free communism, — anarchism won wide sympathy in France. Our paper began to spread in that country, letters were exchanged in great numbers with French workers, and an anarchist movement of importance rapidly developed at Paris and in some of the provinces, especially in the Lyons region. When I crossed France in 1881, on my way from Thonon to London, I visited Lyons, St. Etienne, and Vienne, lecturing there, and I found in these cities a considerable number of workers ready to accept our ideas.

By the end of 1882 a terrible crisis prevailed in the Lyons region. The silk industry was paralyzed, and the misery among the weavers was so great that crowds of children stood every morning at the gates of the barracks, where the soldiers gave away what they could spare of their bread and soup. This was the beginning of the popularity of General Boulanger, who had permitted this distribution of food.   The miners of the region were also in a very precarious state.

I knew that there was a great deal of fermentation, but during the eleven months I had stayed at London I had lost close contact with the French movement.   A few weeks after I returned to Thonon I learned from the papers that the miners of Monceau-les-Mines, incensed at the vexations of the ultra-Catholic owners of the mines, had begun a sort of movement; they were holding secret meetings, talking of a general strike ; the stone crosses erected on all the roads round the mines were thrown down or blown up by dynamite cartridges, which are largely used by the miners in underground work, and often remain in their possession. The agitation at Lyons also took on a more violent character.   The anarchists, who were rather numerous in the city, allowed no meeting of the opportunist politicians to be held without obtaining a hearing for themselves, — storming the platform, as a last resource.   They brought forward resolutions to the effect that the mines and all necessaries for production, as well as the dwelling-houses, ought to be owned by the nation; and these resolutions were carried with enthusiasm, to the horror of the middle classes.

The feeling among the workers was growing every day against the opportunist town councilors and political leaders, as also against the press, which made light of a very acute crisis, while nothing was undertaken to relieve the widespread misery.   As is usual at such times, the fury of the poorer people turned especially against the places of amusement and debauch, which become only the more conspicuous in times of desolation and misery, as they impersonate for the worker the egotism and dissoluteness of the wealthier classes.   A place particularly hated by the workers was the underground café at the Théâtre Bellecour, which remained open all night, and where, in the small hours of the morning, one could see newspaper men and politicians feasting and drinking in company with gay women. Not a meeting was held but some menacing allusion was made to that café, and one night a dynamite cartridge was exploded in it by an unknown hand. A worker who was occasionally there, a socialist, jumped to blow out the lighted fuse of the cartridge, and was killed, while a few of the feasting politicians were slightly wounded. Next day a dynamite cartridge was exploded at the doors of a recruiting bureau, and it was said that the anarchists intended to blow up the huge statue of the Virgin which stands on one of the hills of Lyons. One must have lived at Lyons or in its neighborhood to realize the extent to which the population and the schools are still in the hands of the Catholic clergy, and to understand the hatred that the male portion of the population feel toward the clergy.

A panic now seized the wealthier classes of Lyons. Some sixty anarchists — all workers, and only one middle-class man, Emile Gautier, who was on a lecturing tour in the region — were arrested. The Lyons papers undertook at the same time to incite the government to arrest me, representing me as the leader of the agitation, who had come on purpose from England to direct the movement. Russian spies began to parade again in conspicuous numbers in our small town. Almost every day I received letters, evidently written by spies of the international police, mentioning some dynamite plot, or mysteriously announcing that consignments of dynamite had been shipped to me. I made quite a collection of these letters, writing on each of them "Police Internationale," and they were taken away by the French police when they made a search in my house. But they did not dare to produce these letters in court, nor did they ever restore them to me.

Not only was the house searched, but my wife, who was going to Geneva, was arrested at the station in Thonon, and searched. But of course absolutely nothing was found to compromise me or any one else.

Ten days passed, during which I was quite free to go away, if I wished to do so. I received several letters advising me to disappear, — one of them from an unknown Russian friend, perhaps a member of the diplomatic staff, who seemed to have known me, and wrote that I must leave at once, because otherwise I should be the first victim of the extradition treaty which was about to be concluded between France and Russia. I remained where I was; and when the "Times" inserted a telegram saying that I had disappeared from Thonon, I wrote a letter to the paper, giving my address. Since so many of my friends were arrested, I had no intention of leaving.

In the night of December 21 my brother-in-law died in my arms. We knew that his illness was incurable, but it is terrible to see a young life extinguished in your presence after a brave struggle against death. Both my wife and I were broken down. Three or four hours later, as the dull winter morning was dawning, gendarmes came to my house to arrest me. Seeing in what a state my wife was, I asked permission to remain with her till the burial was over, promising upon my word of honor to be at the prison door at a given hour; but it was refused, and the same night I was taken to Lyons. Elisée Reclus, notified by telegraph, came at once, bestowing on my wife all the gentleness of his golden heart; friends came from Geneva; and although the funeral was absolutely civil, which was a novelty in that little town, half of the population was at the burial, to show my wife that the hearts of the poorer classes and the simple Savoy peasants were with us, and not with their rulers. When my trial was going on, the peasants used to come from the mountain villages to town to get the papers, and to see how my affair stood before the court.

Another incident which profoundly touched me was the

arrival at Lyons of an English friend. He came on behalf
of a gentleman, well-known and esteemed in the English
political world, in whose family I had spent many happy
hours at London, in 1882. He was the bearer of a considerable sum of money for the purpose of obtaining my
release on bail, and he transmitted me at the same time the
message of my London friend that I need not care in the
least about the bail, but must leave France immediately.
In some mysterious way he had managed to see me freely,
— not in the double-grated iron cage in which I was allowed interviews with my wife, — and he was as much
affected by my refusal to accept the offer as I was by that
touching token of friendship on the part of one whom,
with his excellent wife, I had already learned to esteem so
highly.

The French government wanted to have one of those
great trials which produce an impression upon the population, but there was no possibility of prosecuting the arrested
anarchists for the explosions. It would have required
bringing us before a jury, which in all probability would
have acquitted us. Consequently, the government adopted
the Machiavellian course of prosecuting us for having
belonged to the International Workingmen's Association.
There is in France a law, passed immediately after the
fall of the Commune, under which men can be brought before a simple police court for having belonged to that association. The maximum penalty is five years' imprisonment;
and a police court is always sure to pronounce the sentences
which are wanted by the government.

The trial began at Lyons in the first days of January,
1883, and lasted about a fortnight. The accusation was
ridiculous, as every one knew that none of the Lyons workers had ever joined the International, and it entirely fell
through, as may be seen from the following episode. The
only witness for the prosecution was the chief of the secret

police at Lyons, an elderly man, who was treated at the court with the utmost respect. His report, I must say, was quite correct as concerns the facts. The anarchists, he said, had taken hold of the population; they had rendered opportunist meetings impossible, because they spoke at each meeting, preaching communism and anarchism, and carrying with them the audiences. Seeing that so far he had been fair in his testimony, I ventured to ask him a question: "Did you ever hear the International Workingmen's Association spoken of at Lyons?"

"Never," he replied sulkily.

"When I returned from the London congress of 1881, and did all I could to have the International reconstituted in France, did I succeed?"

"No. They did not find it revolutionary enough."

"Thank you," I said, and turning toward the procureur added, "There's all your prosecution overthrown by your own witness!"

Nevertheless, we were all condemned for having belonged to the International. Four of us got the maximum sentence, five years' imprisonment and four hundred dollars' fine; the remainder got from four years to one year. In fact, they never tried to prove anything concerning the International. It was quite forgotten. We were simply asked to speak about anarchism, and so we did. Not a word was said about the explosions; and when one or two of the Lyons comrades wanted to clear this point, they were bluntly told that they were not prosecuted for that, but for having belonged to the International, — to which I alone belonged.

There is always some comical incident in such trials, and this time it was supplied by a letter of mine. There was nothing upon which to base the accusation. Scores of searches had been made at the houses of French anarchists, but only two letters of mine had been found. The prosecution tried to make the best of them. One was written to a French worker when he was despondent. I spoke to him in my letter about the great times we were living in, the great changes coming, the birth and spreading of new ideas, and so on. The letter was not long, and little capital was made out of it by the procureur. As to the other letter, it was twelve pages long. I had written it to another French friend, a young shoemaker. He earned his living by making shoes in his own room. On his left side he used to have a small iron stove, upon which he himself cooked his daily meal, and upon his right a small stool upon which he wrote long letters to the comrades, without leaving his shoemaker's low bench. After he had made just as many pairs of shoes as were required to cover the expenses of his extremely modest living, and to send a few francs to his old mother in the country, he would spend long hours in writing letters in which he developed the theoretical principles of anarchism with admirable good sense and intelligence. He is now a writer well known in France and generally respected for the integrity of his character. Unfortunately, at that time he would cover eight or twelve pages of note paper without one single full stop, or even a comma. I once sat down and wrote a long letter in which I explained to him how our written thoughts subdivide into sentences, clauses, and phrases, each of which should end with its appropriate period, semicolon, or comma, and so on, — in short, gave him a little lesson in the elements of punctuation. I told him how much it would improve his writings if he adopted this simple plan.

This letter was read by the prosecutor before the court and elicited from him most pathetic comments. " You have heard, gentlemen, this letter " — he went on, addressing the Court. " You have listened to it. There is nothing particular in it at first sight. He gives a lesson in grammar to a worker. . . . But " — and here his voice vibrated with

accents of a deep emotion — "it was not in order to help
a poor worker in getting instruction which he, owing probably to laziness, failed to get at school. It was not to help
him to earn an honest living. No! gentlemen, it was written in order to inspire him with hatred for our grand and
beautiful institutions, in order only the better to infuse into
him the venom of anarchism, in order to make of him only
a more terrible enemy of society. Cursed be the day when
Kropótkin set his foot upon the soil of France!"

We could not help laughing like boys all the time he was
delivering that speech; the judges stared at him as if to tell
him that he was overdoing his rôle, but he seemed not to
notice anything, and, carried by his eloquence, went on
speaking with more and more theatrical gestures and intona-
tions. He really did his best to obtain his reward from the
Russian government.

Very soon after the condemnation the presiding magistrate was promoted to the magistracy of an assize court.
As to the procureur and another magistrate, — one would
hardly believe it, — the Russian government offered them
the Russian cross of Sainte-Anne, and they were allowed
by the republic to accept it! The famous Russian alliance
thus had its origin in the Lyons trial.

This trial — during which most brilliant anarchist
speeches, reported by all the papers, were made by such
first-rate speakers as the worker Bernard and Emile Gautier,
and during which all the accused took a very firm attitude,
preaching our doctrines for a fortnight — had a powerful
influence in clearing away false ideas about anarchism in
France, and surely contributed to some extent to the revival of socialism in other countries. As to the condemnation, it was so little justified by the proceedings that the
French press — with the exception of the papers devoted to
the government — openly blamed the magistrates. Even
the moderate "Journal des Economistes" found fault with

the verdict, which "nothing in the proceedings before the court could have made one foresee." The contest between the accusers and ourselves was won by us, in the public opinion. Immediately a proposition of amnesty was brought before the Chamber, and received about a hundred votes in support of it. It came up regularly every year, each time securing more and more voices, until we were released.

XIII

THE trial was over, but I remained for another couple of months in the Lyons prison. Most of my comrades had lodged an appeal against the decision of the police court, and we had to wait for its results. With four more comrades, I refused to take any part in that appeal to a higher court, and continued to work in my *pistole*. A great friend of mine — Martin, a clothier from Vienne — took another pistole by the side of the one which I occupied, and as we were already condemned, we were allowed to take our walks together; and when we had something to say to each other between the walks, we used to correspond by means of taps on the wall, just as in Russia.

During my sojourn at Lyons I began to realize the awfully demoralizing influence of the prisons upon the prisoners, which brought me later to condemn unconditionally the whole institution.

The Lyons prison is a "modern" structure, built in the shape of a star, on the cellular system. The spaces between the rays of the star are occupied by small asphalt paved yards, and, weather permitting, the inmates are taken to these yards to work outdoors. The chief occupation is the beating out of silk cocoons to obtain floss silk. Flocks of children are also taken at certain hours to these yards. Thin, enervated, underfed, — the shadows of children, — I often watched them from my window. Anæmia was plainly written on all the little faces and manifest in their thin, shivering bodies; and all day long — not only in the dormitories, but even in the yards, in the full light of the sun — they pursued their debilitating practices. What will become of them after they have passed through that schooling and come out with their health ruined, their wills annihilated, their energy reduced ? Anæmia, with its diminished energy, its unwillingness to work, its enfeebled will, weakened intellect, and perverted imagination, is responsible for crime to an infinitely greater extent than plethora, and it is precisely this enemy of the human race which is bred in prison. And then — the teachings which these children receive in their surroundings ! Mere isolation, even if it were rigorously carried out — and it cannot be — would be of little avail; the whole atmosphere of every prison is an atmosphere of glorification of that sort of gambling in " clever strokes " which constitutes the very essence of theft, swindling, and all sorts of similar anti-social deeds. Whole generations of future criminals are bred in these nurseries, which the state supports and which society tolerates, simply because it does not want to hear its own diseases spoken of and dissected. " Imprisoned in childhood, jail bird for life," is what I heard afterwards from all those who were interested in criminal matters. And when I saw these children, and realized what they have to expect in the future, I could not but continually ask myself : " Which of them is the worse criminal ? — this child or the judge who condemns every year hundreds of children to this fate ? " I gladly admit that the crime of the judge is unconscious. But are all the crimes for which people are sent to prison as conscious as they are supposed to be ?

There was another point which I vividly realized from the very first weeks of my imprisonment, but which in some inconceivable way has escaped the attention of both the judges and the writers on criminal law; namely, that imprisonment is in an immense number of cases a punishment which bears far more severely upon quite innocent people than upon the condemned prisoner himself.

Nearly every one of my comrades, who represented a fair

average of the working population, had either wife and children to support, or a sister or old mother who depended for her living upon his earnings. Now being left without support, all of these women did their best to get work, and some of them got it; but none of them succeeded in earning regularly even as much as thirty cents (1 fr. 50 c.) a day. Nine francs (less than two dollars) and often only a dollar and a half a week to support themselves and their children, — these were their earnings. And that meant, of course, underfeeding, privations of all sorts, and deterioration of health, weakened intellect, impaired energy and will power. I thus realized that what was going on in our law courts was in reality a condemnation of quite innocent people to all sorts of hardship; in most cases even worse than those to which the condemned man himself is subjected. The fiction is that the law punishes the man by inflicting upon him a variety of degrading physical and mental hardships. But man is so made that whatever hardships may be imposed upon him, he gradually grows accustomed to them. If he cannot modify them, he accepts them, and after a certain time he puts up with them, just as he puts up with a chronic disease, and grows insensible to them. But during his imprisonment what becomes of his wife and children, or of the other innocent people who depended upon his support? They are punished even more cruelly than he himself is. And, in our routine habits of thought, no one ever thinks of the immense injustice which is thus committed. I realized it only from actual experience.

In the middle of March, 1883, twenty-two of us, who had been condemned to more than one year of imprisonment, were removed in great secrecy to the central prison of Clairvaux. It was formerly an abbey of St. Bernard, of which the great Revolution had made a house for the poor.

Subsequently it became a house of detention and correction, which went among the prisoners and the officials themselves under the well-deserved nickname of "house of detention and corruption."

So long as we were kept at Lyons we were treated as the prisoners under preliminary arrest are treated in France; that is, we had our own clothes, we could get our own food from a restaurant, and one could hire for a few francs per month a larger cell, a pistole. I took advantage of this for working hard upon my articles for the "Encyclopædia Britannica" and the "Nineteenth Century." Now, the treatment we should have at Clairvaux was an open question. However, in France it is generally understood that, for political prisoners, the loss of liberty and the forced inactivity are in themselves so hard that there is no need to inflict additional hardships. Consequently, we were told that we should remain under the same régime that we had had at Lyons. We should have separate quarters, retain our own clothes, be free of compulsory work, and be allowed to smoke. "Those of you," the governor said, "who wish to earn something by manual work will be enabled to do so by sewing stays or engraving small things in mother of pearl. This work is poorly paid; but you could not be employed in the prison workshops for the fabrication of iron beds, picture frames, and so on, because that would require your lodging with the common-law prisoners." Like the other prisoners, we were allowed to buy from the prison canteen some additional food and a pint of claret every day, both being supplied at a very low price and of good quality.

The first impression which Clairvaux produced upon me was most favorable. We had been locked up and had been traveling all the day, from two or three o'clock in the morning, in those tiny cupboards into which the railway carriages used for the transportation of prisoners are usually divided. When we reached the central prison, we were

taken temporarily to the penal quarters, and were introduced into extremely clean cells. Hot food, plain but of
excellent quality, had been served to us notwithstanding
the late hour of the night, and we had been offered the
opportunity of having a half-pint each of the very good
vin du pays, which was sold at the prison canteen at the
extremely modest price of twenty-four centimes (less than
five cents) per quart. The governor and all the warders
were most polite to us.

Next day the governor of the prison took me to see the
rooms which he intended to give us, and when I remarked
that they were all right, only a little too small for such a
number, — we were twenty-two, — and that overcrowding
might result in illness, he gave us another set of rooms in
what had been in olden times the house of the superin-
tendent of the abbey, and was now the hospital. Our
windows looked down upon a little garden and off upon
beautiful views of the surrounding country. In another
room, on the same landing, old Blanqui had been kept the
last three or four years before his release. Before that he
was confined in one of the cells in the cellular house.

We obtained thus three spacious rooms, and a smaller
room was spared for Gautier and myself, so that we could
pursue our literary work. We probably owed this last
favor to the intervention of a considerable number of English men of science, who, as soon as I was condemned, had
signed a petition asking for my release. Many contributors
to the "Encyclopædia Britannica," Herbert Spencer, and
Swinburne were among the signers, while Victor Hugo had
added to his signature a few warm words. Altogether,
public opinion in France received our condemnation very
unfavorably ; and when my wife had mentioned at Paris
that I required books, the Academy of Sciences offered its
library, and Ernest Renan, in a charming letter, put his
private library at her service.

We had a small garden, where we could play ninepins or *jeu de boules,* and soon we managed to cultivate a narrow bed along the building's wall, in which, on a surface of some eighty square yards, we grew almost incredible quantities of lettuce and radishes, as well as some flowers. I need not say that at once we organized classes, and during the three years that we remained at Clairvaux I gave my comrades lessons in cosmography, geometry, or physics, also aiding them in the study of languages. Nearly every one learned at least one language, — English, German, Italian, or Spanish, — while a few learned two. We also managed to do some bookbinding, having learned how from one of those excellent Encyclopédie Roret booklets.

At the end of the first year, however, my health again gave way. Clairvaux is built on marshy ground, upon which malaria is endemic, and malaria, with scurvy, laid hold of me. Then my wife, who was studying at Paris, working in Würtz's laboratory and preparing to take an examination for the degree of Doctor of Science, abandoned everything, and came to the tiny hamlet of Clairvaux, which consists of less than a dozen houses grouped at the foot of an immense high wall which encircles the prison. Of course, her life in that hamlet, with the prison wall opposite, was anything but gay; yet she stayed there till I was released. During the first year she was allowed to see me only once in two months, and all interviews were held in the presence of a warder, who sat between us. But when she settled at Clairvaux, declaring her firm intention to remain there, she was soon permitted to see me every day, in one of the small houses within the prison walls where a post of warders was kept, and food was brought me from the inn where she stayed. Later, we were even allowed to take a walk in the governor's garden, closely watched all the time, and usually one of my comrades joined us in the walk.

I was quite astonished to discover that the central prison of Clairvaux had all the aspects of a small manufacturing town, surrounded by orchards and cornfields, all encircled by an outer wall. The fact is, that if in a French central prison the inmates are perhaps more dependent upon the fancies and caprices of the governor and the warders than they seem to be in English prisons, the treatment of the prisoners is far more humane than it is in the corresponding institutions on the other side of the Channel. The mediæval revengeful system which still prevails in English prisons has been given up long since in France. The imprisoned man is not compelled to sleep on planks, or to have a mattress on alternate days only; the day he comes to prison he gets a decent bed, and retains it. He is not compelled, either, to degrading work, such as to climb a wheel, or to pick oakum; he is employed, on the contrary, in useful work, and this is why the Clairvaux prison has the aspect of a manufacturing town, iron furniture, picture frames, looking-glasses, metric measures, velvet, linen, ladies' stays, small things in mother of pearl, wooden shoes, and so on, being made by the nearly sixteen hundred men who are kept there.

Moreover, if the punishment for insubordination is very cruel, there is, at least, none of the flogging which goes on still in English prisons. Such a punishment would be absolutely impossible in France. Altogether, the central prison at Clairvaux may be described as one of the best penal institutions in Europe. And, with all that, the results obtained at Clairvaux are as bad as in any of the prisons of the old type. "The watchword nowadays is that convicts are reformed in our prisons," one of the members of the prison administration once said to me. "This is all nonsense, and I shall never be induced to tell such a lie."

The pharmacy at Clairvaux was underneath the rooms

which we occupied, and we occasionally had some contact
with the prisoners who were employed in it. One of them
was a gray-haired man in his fifties, who ended his term
while we were there. It was touching to learn how he
parted with the prison. He knew that in a few months or
weeks he would be back, and begged the doctor to keep
the place at the pharmacy open for him. This was not his
first visit to Clairvaux, and he knew it would not be the
last. When he was set free he had not a soul in the world
to whom he might go to spend his old age. "Who will
care to employ me?" he said. "And what trade have I?
None! When I am out I must go to my old comrades;
they, at least, will surely receive me as an old friend."
Then would come a glass too much of drink in their company, excited talk about some capital fun, — some "new
stroke" to be made in the way of theft, — and, partly from
weakness of will, partly to oblige his only friends, he would
join in it, and would be locked up once more. So it had
been several times before in his life. Two months passed,
however, after his release, and he had not yet returned to
Clairvaux. Then the prisoners, and the warders too, began
to feel uneasy about him. "Has he had time to move to
another judicial district, that he is not yet back?" "One
can only hope that he has not been involved in some bad
affair," they would say, meaning something worse than
theft. "That would be a pity: he was such a nice, quiet
man." But it soon appeared that the first supposition was
the right one. Word came from another prison that the
old man was locked up there, and was now endeavoring to
be transferred to Clairvaux.

The old men were the most pitiful sight. Many of them
had begun their prison experience in childhood or early
youth; others at a riper age. But "once in prison, always in prison;" such is the saying derived from experience And now, having reached or passed beyond the age

of sixty, they knew that they must end their lives in prison. To quicken their departure from life the prison administration used to send them to the workshops where felt socks were made out of all sorts of woolen refuse. The dust in the workshop soon induced the consumption which finally released them. Then, four fellow prisoners would carry the old man to the common grave, the graveyard warder and his black dog being the only two beings to follow him; and while the prison priest marched in front of the procession, mechanically reciting his prayer and looking round at the chestnut or fir trees along the road, and the four comrades carrying the coffin were enjoying the momentary freedom from confinement, the black dog would be the only being affected by the solemnity of the ceremony.

When the reformed central prisons were introduced in France, it was believed that the principle of absolute silence could be maintained in them. But it is so contrary to human nature that its strict enforcement had to be abandoned.

To the outward observer the prison seems to be quite mute; but in reality life goes on in it as busily as in a small town. In suppressed voices, by means of whispers, hurriedly dropped words, and scraps of notes, all news of any interest spreads immediately throughout the prison. Nothing can happen either among the prisoners themselves, or in the "cour d'honneur," where the lodgings of the administration are situated, or in the village of Clairvaux, or in the wide world of Paris politics, that is not communicated at once throughout all the dormitories, workshops, and cells. Frenchmen are too communicative to admit of their underground telegraph ever being stopped. We had no intercourse with the common-law prisoners, and yet we knew all the news of the day. "John, the gardener, is back for two years." "Such an inspector's wife has had a fearful scrimmage with So and So's wife." "James, in the cells, has been caught transmitting a note of friendship to John of the framers' workshop." "That old beast So and So is no longer Minister of Justice; the ministry was upset;" and so on; and when the word goes that "Jack has got two five-penny packets of tobacco in exchange for two flannel jackets," it makes the tour of the prison very quickly. On one occasion a petty lawyer, detained in the prison, wished to transmit to me a note, in order to ask my wife, who was staying in the village, to see from time to time his wife, who was also there, — and quite a number of men took the liveliest interest in the transmission of that message, which had to pass through I don't know how many hands before it reached me. When there was something that might specially interest us in a paper, this paper, in some unaccountable way, would reach us, wrapped about a little stone and thrown over the high wall.

Confinement in a cell is no obstacle to communication. When we came to Clairvaux and were first lodged in the cellular quarter, it was bitterly cold in the cells; so cold, indeed, that I could hardly write, and when my wife, who was then at Paris, got my letter, she did not recognize my handwriting. The order came to heat the cells as much as possible; but do what they might, the cells remained as cold as ever. It appeared afterwards that all the hot air tubes were choked with scraps of paper, bits of notes, penknives, and all sorts of small things which several generations of prisoners had concealed in the pipes.

Martin, the same friend of mine whom I have already mentioned, obtained permission to serve part of his time in cellular confinement. He preferred isolation to life in a room with a dozen others, and so went to a cell. To his great astonishment he found that he was not at all alone. The walls and the keyholes spoke. In a short time all the inmates of the cells knew who he was, and he had

acquaintances all over the building.   Quite a life goes on,
as in a beehive, between the seemingly isolated cells; only
that life often takes such a character as to make it belong
entirely to the domain of psychopathy.   Kraft-Ebbing himself had no idea of the aspects it assumes with certain
prisoners in solitary confinement.

I will not repeat here what I have said in a book, "In
Russian and French Prisons," which I published in England in 1886, soon after my release from Clairvaux, upon
the moral influence of prisoners upon prisoners.   But there
is one thing which must be said.   The prison population
consists of heterogeneous elements; but, taking only those
who are usually described as "the criminals" proper, and
of whom we have heard so much lately from Lombroso and
his followers, what struck me most as regards them was
that the prisons, which are considered as preventive of anti-
social deeds, are exactly the institutions for breeding them.
Every one knows that absence of education, dislike of regular work, physical incapability of sustained effort, misdi-
rected love of adventure, gambling propensities, absence of
energy, an untrained will, and carelessness about the happiness of others are the causes which bring this class of
people before the courts.   Now I was deeply impressed
during my imprisonment by the fact that it is exactly these
defects of human nature — each one of them — which the
prison breeds in its inmates; and it is bound to breed them
because it is a prison, and will breed them so long as it
exists.   Incarceration in a prison of necessity entirely de-
stroys the energy of a man and annihilates his will.   In
prison life there is no room for exercising one's will; to
possess one's own will in prison means surely to get into
trouble.   The will of the prisoner *must* be killed, and it
is killed.   Still less room is there for exercising one's natural sympathies, everything being done to prevent free
contact with all those, outside and inside, with whom the

prisoner may have feelings of sympathy. Physically and mentally he is rendered less and less capable of sustained effort, and if he has had already a dislike for regular work, this dislike is only the more increased during his prison years. If, before he first came to the prison, he was easily wearied by monotonous work which he could not do properly, or had an antipathy to underpaid overwork, his dislike now becomes hatred. If he doubted about the social utility of current rules of morality, now after having cast a critical glance upon the official defenders of these rules, and learned his comrades' opinions of them, he openly throws these rules overboard. And if he has got into trouble in consequence of a morbid development of the passionate, sensual side of his nature, now, after having spent a number of years in prison, this morbid character is still more developed, in many cases to an appalling extent. In this last direction — the most dangerous of all — prison education is most effective.

In Siberia I had seen what sinks of filth and what hotbeds of physical and moral deterioration the dirty, overcrowded, " unreformed " Russian prisons were, and at the age of nineteen I imagined that if there were less overcrowding in the rooms and a certain classification of the prisoners, and if healthy occupations were provided for them, the institution might be substantially improved. Now I had to part with these illusions. I could convince myself that as regards their effects upon the prisoners and their results for society at large, the best " reformed " prisons — whether cellular or not — are as bad as, or even worse than the dirty prisons of old. They do not reform the prisoners. On the contrary, in the immense, overwhelming majority of cases they exercise upon them the most deteriorating effect. The thief, the swindler, the rough, who has spent some years in a prison, comes out of it more ready than ever to resume his former career; he is better prepared for it; he has learned to do it better; he is more embittered against society, and he finds a more solid justification for being in revolt against its laws and customs; necessarily, unavoidably, he is bound to sink deeper and deeper into the anti-social acts which first brought him before a law court. The offenses he will commit after his release will inevitably be graver than those which first got him into trouble; and he is doomed to finish his life in a prison or in a hard-labor colony. In the above-mentioned book I said that prisons are " universities of crime, maintained by the state." And now, thinking of it at fifteen years' distance, in the light of my subsequent experience, I can only confirm that statement of mine.

Personally, I have no reason whatever to complain of the years I spent in a French prison. For an active and independent man the restraint of liberty and activity is in itself so great a privation that all the remainder — all the petty miseries of prison life — are not worth speaking of. Of course, when we heard of the active political life which was going on in France, we resented very much our forced inactivity. The end of the first year, especially during a gloomy winter, is always hard for the prisoner. And when spring comes, one feels more strongly than ever the want of liberty. When I saw from our windows the meadows assuming their green garb, and the hills covered with a spring haze, or when I saw a train flying into a dale between the hills, I certainly felt a strong desire to follow it and to breathe the air of the woods, or to be carried along with the stream of human life in a busy town. But one who casts his lot with an advanced party must be prepared to spend a number of years in prison, and he need not grudge it. He feels that even during his imprisonment he remains not quite an inactive part of the movement which spreads and strengthens the ideas that are dear to him.

At Lyons, my comrades, my wife, and myself certainly

found the warders a very rough set of men. But after a couple of encounters all was set right. Moreover the prison administration knew that we had the Paris press with us, and they did not want to draw upon themselves the thunders of Rochefort or the cutting criticisms of Clémenceau. And at Clairvaux there was no need of such restraint. All the administration had been renewed a few months before we came thither. A prisoner had been killed by warders in his cell, and his corpse had been hanged to simulate suicide; but this time the affair leaked out through the doctor, the governor was dismissed, and altogether a better tone prevailed in the prison. I took away from Clairvaux the best recollection of its governor, and altogether, while I was there, I more than once thought that, after all, men are often better than the institutions they belong to. But, having no personal griefs, I can all the more freely and most unconditionally condemn the institution itself as a survival from the dark past, wrong in its principles, and a source of immeasurable evils to society.

One thing more I must mention, as it struck me perhaps even more forcibly than the demoralizing effects of prisons upon their inmates. What a nest of infection is every prison — and even every law court — for its neighborhood, for the people who live near it! Lombroso has made much of the "criminal type" which he believes he has discovered amongst the inmates of the prisons. If he had made the same efforts to observe the people who hang about the law courts, — detectives, spies, petty solicitors, informers, people preying upon the simpletons, and the like, — he would probably have concluded that his criminal type has a far greater geographical extension than the prison walls. I never saw such a collection of faces of the lowest human type as I saw around and within the Palais de Justice at Lyons, — certainly not within the prison walls of Clairvaux. Dickens and Cruikshank have immortalized a

few of these types ; but they represent quite a world which
revolves about the law courts and infuses its infection far
and wide around them.   And the same is true of each central prison, like Clairvaux.   It is an atmosphere of petty
thefts, petty swindlings, spying and corruption of all sorts,
which spreads like a blot of oil round the prison.

I saw all this ; and if before my condemnation I already
knew that society is wrong in its present system of punishments, after I left Clairvaux I knew that it is not only
wrong and unjust in this system, but that it is simply
foolish when, in its partly unconscious and partly willful
ignorance of realities, it maintains at its own expense these
universities of corruption, under the illusion that they are
necessary as a bridle to the criminal instincts of man.

XIV

EVERY revolutionist meets a number of spies and "*agents provocateurs*" in his way, and I have had my fair share of them. All governments spend considerable sums of money in maintaining this kind of reptile. However, they are mainly dangerous to young people only. One who has had some experience of life and men soon discovers that there is about these creatures something which puts him on his guard. They are recruited from the scum of society, amongst men of the lowest moral standard, and if one is watchful of the moral character of the men he meets with, he soon notices something in the manners of these "pillars of society" which shocks him, and then he asks himself the question: "What has brought this man to me? What in the world can he have in common with us?" In most cases this simple question is sufficient to put one on his guard.

When I first came to Geneva, the agent of the Russian government who had been commissioned to spy upon the refugees was well-known to all of us. He went under the title of Count; but as he had no footman and no carriage on which to emblazon his coronet and arms, he had had them embroidered on a sort of mantle which covered his tiny dog. We saw him occasionally in the cafés, without speaking to him; he was, in fact, an "innocent" who simply bought in the kiosques all the publications of the exiles, very probably adding to them such comments as he thought would please his chiefs.

Different men began to pour in, as Geneva began to fill up with refugees of the young generation; and yet, in one way or another, they also became known to us.

When a stranger appeared on our horizon, he was asked with the usual nihilist frankness about his past and his present prospects, and it soon appeared what sort of person he was. Frankness in mutual intercourse is alto gether the best way for bringing about proper relations be. tween men. In this case it was invaluable. Numbers of persons whom none of us had known or heard of in Russia — absolute strangers to the circles — came to Geneva, and many of them, a few days or even hours after their arrival, stood on the most friendly terms with the colony of refu- gees; but in some way or other the spies never succeeded in crossing the threshold of familiarity. A spy might name common acquaintances, he might give the best accounts, sometimes correct, of his past in Russia; he might possess in perfection the nihilist slang and manners, but he never could assimilate that sort of nihilist ethics which had grown up amongst the Russian youth; and this alone kept him at a distance from our colony. Spies can imitate anything else but ethics.

When I was working with Reclus, there was at Clarens one such individual, from whom we all kept aloof. We knew nothing bad about him, but we felt that he was not "ours," and as he tried only the more to penetrate into our society, we became suspicious of him. I never had said a word to him, and consequently he especially sought after me. Seeing that he could not approach me through the usual channels, he began to write me letters, giving me mysterious appointments for mysterious purposes in the woods and in similar places. For fun, I once accepted his invitation and went to the spot, with a good friend follow- ing me at a distance; but the man, who probably had a confederate, must have noticed that I was not alone, and did not appear. So I was spared the pleasure of ever say- ing to him a single word. Besides, I worked at that time so hard that every minute of my time was taken up either with the Geography or "Le Révolté," and I entered into no conspiracies. However, we learned later on that this man used to send to the Third Section detailed reports about the supposed conversations which he had had with me, my supposed confidences, and the terrible plots which I was manipulating at St. Petersburg against the Tsar's life! All that was taken for ready money at St. Petersburg, and in Italy, too. When Cafiero was arrested one day in Switzerland, he was shown formidable reports of Italian spies, who warned their government that Cafiero and I, loaded with bombs, were going to enter Italy. The fact was that I never was in Italy and never had had any intention of visiting the country.

In point of fact, however, the spies do not always make up reports out of whole cloth. They often tell things that are true, but all depends upon the way a story is told. We passed some most merry moments about a report which was addressed to the French government by a French spy who followed my wife and myself as we were traveling in 1881 from Paris to London. The spy, probably playing a double part, as is often done, had sold that report to Rochefort, who published it in his paper. Everything that the spy had stated was correct, — but the way he had told it!

He wrote, for instance : "I took the next compartment to the one that Kropótkin had taken with his wife." Quite true ; he was there. We noticed him, for he had managed at once to attract our attention by his sullen, unpleasant face. "They spoke Russian all the time, in order not to be understood by the passengers." Very true again; we spoke Russian, as we always do. "When they came to Calais, they both took a bouillon." Most correct again : we took a bouillon. But here the mysterious part of the journey begins. "After that, they both suddenly disappeared, and I looked for them in vain, on the platform and elsewhere; and when they reappeared, he was in disguise, and was followed by a Russian priest, who never left him after that until they arrived in London, where I lost sight of the priest." All that was true again. My wife had a tooth slightly aching, and I asked the permission of the keeper of the restaurant to go to his private room, where my wife could ease her tooth. So we had "disappeared" indeed; and as we had to cross the Channel, I put my soft felt hat into my pocket and put on a fur cap; I was "in disguise." As to the mysterious priest, he was also there. He was not a Russian, but that is irrelevant: he wore at any rate the dress of the Greek priests. I saw him standing at the counter and asking something which no one understood. "Agua, agua," he repeated, in a woeful tone. "Give the gentleman a glass of water," I said to the waiter. Whereupon the priest, struck by my wonderful linguistic capacities, began to thank me for my intervention with a truly Eastern effusion. My wife took pity on him and spoke to him in different languages, but he understood none of them. It appeared at last that he knew a few words in one of the South Slavonian languages, and we could make out: "I am a Greek; Turkish embassy, London." We told him, mostly by signs, that we, too, were going to London, and that he might travel with us.

The most amusing part of the story was that I really found for him the address of the Turkish embassy even before we had reached Charing Cross. The train stopped at some station on the way, and two elegant ladies entered our already full third-class compartment. Both had newspapers in their hands. One was English, and the other — a handsome woman, who spoke good French — pretended to be English. After exchanging a few words, the latter asked me à brûle pourpoint: "What do you think of Count Ignátieff?" and immediately after that: "Are you soon going to kill the new Tsar?" I was clear as to her profession from these two questions, but thinking of my priest, I said to her: " Do you happen to know the address of the Turkish embassy ? "   " Street so and so, number so and so," she replied without hesitation, like a schoolgirl in a class.   " You could, I suppose, also give the address of the Russian embassy ? " I asked her, and the address having been given with the same readiness, I communicated both to the priest.   When we reached Charing Cross, the lady was so obsequiously anxious to attend to my luggage, and even to carry a heavy package herself with her glóved hands, that I finally told her, much to her surprise: "Enough of this : ladies don't carry gentlemen's luggage. Go away ! "

But to return to my trustworthy French spy. "He alighted at Charing Cross," he wrote in his report, "but for more than half an hour after the arrival of the train he did not leave the station, until he had ascertained that every one else had left it. I kept aloof in the meantime, concealing myself behind a pillar. Having ascertained that all passengers had left the platform, they both suddenly jumped into a cab. I followed them nevertheless, and overheard the address which the cabman gave at the gate to the policeman, — 12, Street So and So, — and ran after the cab. There were no cabs in the neighborhood; so I ran up to Trafalgar Square, where I got one.   I then drove after him, and he alighted at the above address."

Every fact of it is true again, — the address and everything; but how mysterious it all reads. I had warned a Russian friend of my arrival, but there was a dense fog that morning, and he overslept. We waited for him half an hour, and then, leaving our luggage in the cloak-room, drove to his house.

"There they sat till two o'clock with drawn curtains, and then only a tall man came out of the house, and returned one hour later with their baggage." Even the remark about the curtains was correct; we had to light the gas on account of the fog, and drew down the curtains to get rid of the ugly sight of a small Islington street wrapped in a dense fog.

When I was working with Elisée Reclus at Clarens, I used to go every fortnight to Geneva to see to the bringing out of "Le Révolté." One day when I reached our print-ing-office, I was told that a Russian gentleman wanted to see me. He had already seen my friends, and had told them that he came to induce me to start a paper, like "Le Révolté," in Russian. He offered for that purpose all the money that might be required. I went to meet him in a café, where he gave me a German name, — Tohnlehm, let us say, — and told me that he was a native of the Baltic provinces. He boasted of possessing a large fortune in cer-tain estates and manufactures, and he was extremely angry against the Russian government for their Russianizing schemes. On the whole he produced a somewhat indeter-minate impression, so that my friends insisted upon my accepting his offer; but I did not much like the man from first sight.

From the café he took me to his rooms in a hotel, and there he began to show less reserve, and to appear more like himself and still more unpleasant. "Don't doubt my for-tune," he said to me, "I have also a capital invention. There's a lot of money in it. I shall patent it, and get a considerable sum of money for it, — all for the cause of the revolution in Russia." And he showed me, to my astonish-ment, a miserable candlestick, the originality of which was that it was awfully ugly and had three bits of wire to put the candle in. The poorest housewife would not have cared for such a candlestick, and even if it could have been patented, no manufacturer would have paid the patentee more than ten dollars. "A rich man placing his hopes on such a candlestick! This man," I thought to myself, "can never have seen better ones," and my opinion about him was made up. He was no rich man at all, and the money he offered was not his own. So I bluntly told him, " Very well, if you are so anxious to have a Russian revolutionary paper, and hold the flattering opinion about myself that you have expressed, you will have to deposit your money in my name at a bank, and at my entire disposal. But I warn you that you will have absolutely nothing to do with the paper." " Of course, of course," he said, " but just see to it, and sometimes advise you, and aid you in smuggling it into Russia." " No, nothing of the sort ! You need not see me at all." My friends thought that I was too hard upon the man, but some time after that a letter was received from St. Petersburg warning us that we would receive the visit of a spy of the Third Section, Tohnlehm by name. The candlestick had thus rendered us a good service.

Whether by candlesticks or something else, these people almost always betray themselves in one way or another. When we were at London in 1881, we received on a foggy morning a visit from two Russians. I knew one of them by name; the other, a young man whom he recommended as his friend, was a stranger. The latter had volunteered to accompany his friend on a few days' visit to London. As he was introduced by a friend, I had no suspicions whatever about him; but I was very busy that day and asked another friend, who lived near by, to find them a room and take them about to see London. My wife had not yet seen England, either, and she went with them. In the afternoon she returned, saying to me : " Do you know, I dislike that man very much. Beware of him." " But why ? What's the matter ?" I asked. " Nothing, absolutely nothing, but he is surely not 'ours.' By the way he treated the waiter in a café, and the way he handles money, I saw at once he is not ' ours,' and if he is not, why should

he come to us ? " She was so certain of the justice of her
suspicions that while she performed her duties of hospitality, she nevertheless managed never to leave that young
man alone in my study even for one minute. We had a
chat, and the visitor began to exhibit himself more and
more under such a low moral aspect that even his friend
blushed for him, and when I asked more details about him,
the explanations they both gave were still less satisfactory.
We were both on our guard. In short, they left London
in a couple of days, and a fortnight later I got a letter
from my Russian friend, full of excuses for having introduced the young man, who, they had found out at Paris,
was a spy in the service of the Russian embassy. I looked
then into a list of Russian secret service agents in France
and Switzerland, which we refugees had received lately
from the Executive Committee, — they had their men
everywhere at St. Petersburg, — and I found the name of
that young man on the list, with one letter only altered
in it.

To start a paper, subsidized by the police, with a police
agent at its head, is an old plan, and the prefect of the
Paris police, Andrieux, resorted to it in 1881. I was staying with Elisée Reclus in the mountains, when we received
a letter from a Frenchman, or rather a Belgian, who announced to us that he was going to start an anarchist paper
at Paris, and asked our collaboration. The letter, full of
flatteries, produced upon us an unfavorable impression, and
Reclus had, moreover, some vague recollection of having
heard the name of the writer in some unfavorable connection. We decided to refuse collaboration, and I wrote to a
Paris friend that we must first of all ascertain whence
the money came with which the paper was going to be
started. It might come from the Orleanists, — an old trick
of the family, — and we must know its origin. My Paris

friend, with a workman's straightforwardness, read that letter at a meeting at which the would-be editor of the paper was present. He simulated offense, and I had to answer several letters on this subject; but I stuck to my words: "If the man is in earnest, he must show us the origin of the money."

And so he did at last. Pressed by questions, he said that the money came from his aunt, a rich lady of antiquated opinions, who yielded, however, to his fancy of having a paper, and had parted with the money. The lady was not in France; she was staying at London. We insisted nevertheless upon having her name and address, and our friend Malatesta volunteered to see her. He went with an Italian friend who was connected with the second-hand trade in furniture. They found the lady occupying a small flat, and while Malatesta spoke to her and was more and more convinced that she was simply playing the aunt's part in the comedy, the furniture friend, looking round at the chairs and tables, discovered that all of them had been taken the day before — probably hired — from a second-hand furniture dealer, his neighbor. The labels of the dealer were still fastened to the chairs and the tables. This did not prove much, but naturally reinforced our suspicions. I absolutely refused to have anything to do with the paper.

The paper was of an unheard-of violence; burning, assassination, dynamite bombs, — there was nothing but that in it. I met the man, the editor of the paper, when I went to the London congress, and the moment I saw his sullen face and heard a bit of his talk and caught a glimpse of the sort of women with whom he always went about, my opinions concerning him were settled. At the congress, during which he introduced all sorts of terrible resolutions, all present kept aloof from him; and when he insisted upon having the addresses of all anarchists throughout the world, the refusal was made in anything but a flattering manner.

To make a long story short, he was unmasked a couple of months later, and the paper was stopped forever on the very next day. Then, a couple of years after that, the prefect of police, Andrieux, published his Memoirs, and in this book he told all about the paper which he had started, and the explosions which his agents had organized at Paris, by putting sardine-boxes filled with something under the statue of Thiers.

One can imagine the quantities of money all these things cost the French and other nations.

I might write several chapters on this subject, but I will mention only one more story, of two adventurers at Clairvaux.

My wife stayed in the only inn of the little village which has grown up under the shadow of the prison wall. One day the landlady entered her room with a message from two gentlemen, who came to the hotel and wanted to see my wife. The landlady interceded with all her eloquence in their favor. "Oh, I know the world," she said, "and I assure you, madame, that they are the most correct gentlemen. Nothing could be more *comme-il-faut*. One of them gave the name of a German officer. He is surely a baron, or a 'milord,' and the other is his interpreter. They know you perfectly well. The baron is going now to Africa, perhaps never to return, and he wants to see you before he leaves."

My wife looked at the visiting card, which bore "A Madame la *Principesse* Kropotkine. Quand à voir?" and needed no more commentaries about the comme-il-faut of the two gentlemen. As to the contents of the message, they were even worse than the address. Against all rules of grammar and common sense the "baron" wrote about a mysterious communication which he had to make. She refused point blank to receive the writer and his interpreter.

Thereupon the baron wrote to my wife letter upon letter, which she returned without opening them. All the village soon became divided into two parties, — one siding with the baron and led by the landlady, the other against him and headed, as a matter of fact, by the landlady's husband. Quite a romance was circulated. The baron had known my wife before her marriage. He had danced with her many times at the Russian embassy in Vienna. He was still in love with her, but she, the cruel one, refused even to allow him a glimpse of her before he went upon his perilous expedition.

Then came the mysterious story of a boy, whom we were said to conceal. "Where is their boy?" the baron wanted to know. "They have a son, six years old by this time, — where is he?" "She never would part with a boy if she had one," the one party said. "Yes, they have one, but they conceal him," the other party maintained.

For us two this contest contained a very interesting revelation. It proved to us that my letters were not only read by the prison authorities, but that their contents were made known to the Russian embassy as well. When I was at Lyons, and my wife had gone to see Elisée Reclus in Switzerland, she wrote to me once that "our boy" was getting on very well; his health was excellent, and they all spent a very nice evening at the anniversary of his fifth birthday. I knew that she meant "Le Révolté," which we often used to name in conversations "our *gamin*," — our naughty boy. But now that these gentlemen were inquiring about "our gamin," and even designated so correctly his age, it was evident that the letter had passed through other hands than those of the governor. It was well to know this.

Nothing escapes the attention of village-folk in the country, and the baron soon awakened suspicions. He wrote a new letter to my wife, even more wordy than the former

ones. Now he asked her pardon for having tried to introduce himself as an acquaintance. He owned that she did
not know him; but nevertheless he was a well-wisher. He
had a most important communication to make to her. My
life was in danger, and he wanted to warn her. The
baron and his secretary took an outing in the fields to read
this letter together and to consult about its tenor, — the
forest-guard following them at a distance; but they quarreled about it, and the letter was torn to pieces and thrown
on the ground. The forester waited till they were out of
sight, gathered the pieces, connected them, and read the
letter. In an hour's time the village knew that the baron
had never really been acquainted with my wife; the romance which was so sentimentally repeated by the baron's
party crumbled to pieces.

"Ah, then they are not what they pretended to be,"
the *brigadier de gendarmerie* concluded in his turn; "then
they must be German spies;" and he arrested them.

It must be said in his behalf that a German spy had
really been at Clairvaux shortly before. In time of war
the vast buildings of the prison might serve as depots for
provisions or barracks for the army, and the German general staff was surely interested to know the inner capacity
of the prison buildings. Accordingly a jovial traveling
photographer came to our village, made friends with every
one by photographing all of them for nothing, and was admitted to photograph not only the inside of the prison
yards, but also the dormitories. Having done this, he traveled to some other town on the eastern frontier, and was
there arrested by the French authorities, as a man found
in possession of compromising military documents. The
brigadier, fresh from the impression of that visit, jumped
to the conclusion that the baron and his secretary were also
German spies, and took them in custody to the little town
of Bar-sur-Aube. There they were released next morning,

the local paper stating that they were not German spies, but "persons commissioned by another more friendly power."

Now public opinion turned entirely against the baron and his secretary, who had to live through more adventures. After their release they entered a small village café, and there ventilated their griefs in German in a friendly conversation over a bottle of wine. "You were stupid, you were a coward," the self-styled interpreter said to the self-styled baron. "If *I* had been in your place, I would have shot that examining magistrate with this revolver. Let him only repeat that with *me*, — he will have these bullets in his head!" And so on.

A commercial traveler who sat quietly in a corner of the room rushed at once to the brigadier to report the conversation which he had overheard. The brigadier made an official report immediately, and again arrested the secretary, — a pharmacist from Strasburg. He was taken before a police court at the same town of Bar-sur-Aube, and got a full month's imprisonment "for menaces uttered against a magistrate in a public place." After that the baron had more adventures, and the village did not resume its usual quietness till after the departure of the two strangers.

I have here related only a very few of the spy stories that I might tell. But when one thinks of the thousands of villains going about the world in the pay of all governments, — and very often well paid for their villainies, — of the traps they lay for all sorts of artless people, of the vast sums of money thrown away in the maintenance of that army, which is recruited in the lowest strata of society and from the population of the prisons, of the corruption of all sorts which they pour into society at large, nay, even into families, one cannot but be appalled at the immensity of the evil which is thus done.

XV

DEMANDS for our release were continually raised, both
in the press and in the Chamber of Deputies, — the more
so as about the same time that we were condemned Louise
Michel was condemned, too, for robbery! Louise Michel —
who always gives literally her last shawl or cloak to the
woman who is in need of it, and who never could be compelled, during her imprisonment, to have better food than
her fellow prisoners, because she always gave them what
was sent to her — was condemned, together with another
comrade, Pouget, to nine years' imprisonment for highway
robbery! That sounded too bad even for the middle-class
opportunists. She marched one day at the head of a procession of the unemployed, and, entering a baker's shop,
took a few loaves from it and distributed them to the
hungry column: this was her robbery. The release of the
anarchists thus became a war-cry against the government,
and in the autumn of 1885 all my comrades save three were
set at liberty by a decree of President Grévy. Then the
outcry in behalf of Louise Michel and myself became still
louder. However, Alexander III. objected to it; and one
day the prime minister, M. Freycinet, answering an inter-
pellation in the Chamber, said that "diplomatic difficulties
stood in the way of Kropótkin's release." Strange words in
the mouth of the prime minister of an independent country;
but still stranger words have been heard since in connection
with that ill-omened alliance of France with imperial Russia.

In the middle of January, 1886, both Louise Michel and
Pouget, as well as the four of us who were still at Clairvaux, were set free.

My release meant also the release of my wife from her voluntary imprisonment in the little village at the prison gates, which began to tell upon her health, and we went to Paris to stay there for a few weeks with our friend, Elie Reclus, — a writer of great power in anthropology, who is often mistaken outside France for his younger brother, the geographer, Elisée. A close friendship has united the two brothers from early youth. When the time came for them to enter a university, they went together from a small country place in the valley of the Gironde to Strasburg, making the journey on foot, — accompanied, like true wandering students, by their dog; and when they stayed at some village, it was the dog which got the bowl of soup, while the two brothers' supper very often consisted only of bread with a few apples. From Strasburg the younger brother went to Berlin, whither he was attracted by the lectures of the great Ritter. Later on, in the forties, they were both at Paris. Elie Reclus became a convinced Fourierist, and both saw in the republic of 1848 the coming of a new era of social evolution. Consequently, after Napoleon III.'s *coup d'état*, they both had to leave France, and emigrated to England. When the amnesty was voted, and they returned to Paris, Elie edited there a Fourierist coöperative paper, which circulated widely among the workers. It is not generally known, but may be interesting to note, that Napoleon III., who played the part of a Cæsar, — interested, as behooves a Cæsar, in the conditions of the working classes, — used to send one of his aides-de-camp to the printing-office of the paper, each time it was printed, to take to the Tuileries the first sheet issued from the press. He was, later on, even ready to patronize the International Working-men's Association, on the condition that it should put in one of its reports a few words of confidence in the great socialist plans of the Cæsar; and he ordered its prosecution when the Internationalists refused point blank to do any thing of the sort.

When the Commune was proclaimed, both brothers heartily joined it, and Elie accepted the post of keeper of the National Library and the Louvre Museum under Vaillant. It was, to a great extent, to his foresight and to his hard work that we owe the preservation of the invaluable treasures of human knowledge and art accumulated in these two institutions, during the bombardment of Paris by the armies of Thiers and the subsequent conflagration. A passionate lover of Greek art, and profoundly acquainted with it, he had had all the most precious statues and vases of the Louvre packed and placed in the vaults, while the greatest precautions were taken to store in a safe place the most precious books of the National Library, and to protect the building from the conflagration which raged round it. His wife, a courageous woman, a worthy companion of the philosopher, followed in the streets by her two little boys, organized in the meantime in her own quarter of the town a system of feeding the people, who had been reduced to sheer destitution during the second siege. In the last few weeks of its existence the Commune finally realized that a supply of food for the people, who were deprived of the means of earning it for themselves, ought to have been the Commune's first care, and volunteers organized the relief. It was by mere accident that Elie Reclus, who had kept to his post till the last moment, escaped being shot by the Versailles troops; and a sentence of deportation having been pronounced upon him, — for having dared to accept so necessary a service under the Commune, — he went with his family into exile. Now, on his return to Paris, he had resumed the work of his life, ethnology. What this work is may be judged from a few, a very few chapters of it, published in book form under the titles of "Primitive Folk" and "The Australians," as well as from the history of the origin of religions, which forms the substance of his lectures at the Ecole des Hautes Etudes, at Brussels, — a foundation of his brother. In the whole range of ethnological literature there are not many works imbued to the same extent with a thorough and sympathetic understanding of the true nature of primitive man. As to his history of religions (part of which was published in the review "Société Nouvelle," and which is now being continued in its successor, "Humanité Nouvelle"), it is, I venture to say, the best work on the subject that has yet appeared; undoubtedly superior to Herbert Spencer's attempt in the same direction, because Herbert Spencer, with all his immense intellect, does not possess that understanding of the artless and simple nature of the primitive man which Elie Reclus possesses to a rare perfection, and to which he has added an extremely wide knowledge of a rather neglected branch of folk-psychology, — the evolution and transformation of beliefs. It is needless to speak of Elie Reclus' infinite good nature and modesty, or of his superior intelligence and vast knowledge of all subjects relating to humanity; it is all comprehended in his style, which is his and no one else's. With his modesty, his calm manner, and his deep philosophical insight, he is the type of the Greek philosopher of antiquity. In a society less fond of patented tuition and of piecemeal instruction, and more appreciative of the development of wide humanitarian conceptions, he would be surrounded by flocks of pupils, like one of his Greek prototypes.

A very animated socialist and anarchist movement was going on at Paris while we stayed there. Louise Michel lectured every night, and aroused the enthusiasm of her audiences, whether they consisted of workingmen or were made up of middle-class people. Her already great popularity became still greater, and spread even amongst the university students, who might hate advanced ideas, but worshiped in her the ideal woman. While I was at Paris a riot, caused by some one speaking disrespectfully of Louise

Michel in the presence of students, took place in a café. The young men took up her defense and made a great uproar, smashing all the tables and glasses in the café. I also lectured once, on anarchism, before an audience of several thousand people, and left Paris immediately after that lecture, before the government could obey the injunctions of the reactionary and pro-Russian press, which insisted upon my being expelled from France.

From Paris we went to London, where I found once more my two old friends, Stepniák and Tchaykóvsky. Life in London was no more the dull, vegetating existence that it had been for me four years before. We settled in a small cottage at Harrow. We cared little about the furniture of the cottage, a good part of which I made myself with the aid of Tchaykóvsky, — he had been in the United States and had learned some carpentering, — but we rejoiced immensely at having a small plot of heavy Middlesex clay in our garden. My wife and I went with much enthusiasm into gardening, the admirable results of which I had before realized after having made acquaintance with the writings of Toubeau, and some Paris market-gardeners, and after our own experiment in the prison garden at Clairvaux. As for my wife, who had typhoid fever soon after we settled at Harrow, the work in the garden during the period of convalescence was more completely restorative than a stay at the very best sanatorium would have been.

Near the end of the summer a heavy blow fell upon me. I learned that my brother Alexander was no longer living.

During the years that I had been abroad before my imprisonment in France we had never corresponded with each other. In the eyes of the Russian government, to love a brother who is persecuted for his political opinions is itself a sin. To maintain relations with him after he has become a refugee is a crime. A subject of the Tsar must hate all

the rebels against the supreme ruler's authority, — and
Alexander was in the clutches of the Russian police.   I
persistently refused, therefore, to write to him or to any
other of my relatives.   After the Tsar had written on the
petition of our sister Hélène, "Let him remain there,"
there was no hope of a speedy release for my brother.   Two
years after that a committee was nominated to settle terms
for those who had been exiled to Siberia without judgment,
for an undetermined time, and my brother got five years.
That made seven, with the two which he had already been
kept there.   Then a new committee was nominated under
Lóris Mélikoff, and added another five years.   My brother
was thus to be liberated in October, 1886.   That made
twelve years of exile, first in a tiny town of East Siberia,
and afterwards at Tomsk, — that is, in the lowlands of
West Siberia, where he had not even the dry and healthy
climate of the high prairies further east.

When I was imprisoned at Clairvaux he wrote to me,
and we exchanged a few letters.   He wrote that though
our letters would be read by the Russian police in Siberia,
and by the French prison authorities in France, we might
as well write to each other even under this double supervision.   He spoke of his family life, of his three children,
whom he described interestingly, and of his work.   He
earnestly advised me to keep a watchful eye upon the development of science in Italy, where excellent and original
researches are conducted, but remain unknown in the scientific world until they have been exploited in Germany; and
he gave me his opinions about the probable progress of political life in Russia.   He did not believe in the possibility
with us, in a near future, of constitutional rule on the pattern of the West European parliaments; but he looked forward — and found it quite sufficient for the moment — to
the convocation of a sort of deliberative National Assembly
(*Zémskiy Sobór* or *Etats Généraux*).   It would not make

laws, but would only work out the schemes of laws, to which the imperial power and the Council of State would give definitive form and final sanction.

Above all he wrote to me about his scientific work. He had always had a decided leaning towards astronomy, and when we were at St. Petersburg he had published in Russian an excellent summary of all our knowledge of the shooting stars. With his fine critical mind he soon saw the strong or the weak points of different hypotheses; and without sufficient knowledge of mathematics, but endowed with a powerful imagination, he succeeded in grasping the results of the most intricate mathematical researches. Living with his imagination amongst the moving celestial bodies, he realized their complex movements often better than some mathematicians, — especially the pure algebraists, — who are apt to lose sight of the realities of the physical world and see nothing but their own formulæ. Our St. Petersburg astronomers spoke to me with great appreciation of that work of my brother's. Now, he undertook to study the structure of the universe; to analyze the data and the hypotheses about the worlds of suns, star-clusters, and nebulæ in the infinite space, and to work out the problems of their grouping, their life, and the laws of their evolution and decay. The Púlkova astronomer, Gyldén, spoke highly of this new work of Alexander's, and introduced him by correspondence to Mr. Holden in the United States, from whom, while at Washington lately, I had the pleasure of hearing an appreciative estimate of the value of these researches. Science is greatly in need, from time to time, of such scientific speculations of a higher standard, made by a scrupulously laborious, critical, and, at the same time, imaginative mind.

But in a small town of Siberia, far away from all the libraries, unable to follow the progress of science, he had only succeeded in embodying in his work the researches which had been made up to the date of his exile. Some capital work had been done since. He knew it, but how could he get access to the necessary books, so long as he remained in Siberia ? The approach of the time of his liberation did not inspire him with hope either. He knew that he would not be allowed to stay in any of the university towns of Russia, or of Western Europe, but that his exile to Siberia would be followed by a second exile, perhaps even worse than the first, to some hamlet of Eastern Russia.

"A despair like Faust's takes hold of me at times," he wrote to me. When the time of his liberation was at hand, he sent his wife and children to Russia, taking advantage of one of the last steamers before the close of navigation, and, on a gloomy night, this despair put an end to his life.

A dark cloud hung upon our cottage for many months, — until a flash of light pierced it, when, the next spring, a tiny being, a girl who bears my brother's name, came into the world, and with her helpless cry set new strings vibrating in my heart.

XVI

In 1886 the socialist movement in England was in full
swing. Large bodies of workers had openly joined it in all
the principal towns, as well as a number of middle-class
people, chiefly young, who helped it in different ways. An
acute industrial crisis prevailed that year in most trades, and
every morning, and often all the day long, I heard groups
of workers going about in the streets singing "We've got
no work to do," or some hymn, and begging for bread.
People flocked at night into Trafalgar Square, to sleep there
in the open air, in the wind and the rain, between two
newspapers; and one day in February a crowd, after having listened to the speeches of Burns, Hyndman, and
Champion, rushed into Piccadilly and broke a few windows
in the great shops. Far more important, however, than
this outbreak of discontent was the spirit which prevailed
amongst the poorer portion of the working population in
the outskirts of London. It was such that if the leaders
of the movement, who were prosecuted for the riots, had
received severe sentences, a spirit of hatred and revenge,
hitherto unknown in the recent history of the labor movement in England, but the symptoms of which were very well
marked in 1886, would have been developed, and would
have impressed its stamp upon the subsequent movement
for a long time to come. However, the middle classes
seemed to have realized the danger. Considerable sums
of money were immediately subscribed in the West End
for the relief of misery in the East End, — certainly quite
inadequate to relieve a widely spread destitution, but sufficient to show, at least, good intentions. As to the

sentences which were passed upon the prosecuted leaders, they were limited to two or three months' imprisonment.

The amount of interest in socialism and all sorts of schemes of reform and reconstruction of society was very great among all classes of people. Beginning with the autumn and throughout all the winter I was asked to lecture all over the country, partly on prisons but mainly on anarchist socialism, and I visited in this way nearly every large town of England and Scotland. As a rule I accepted the first invitation I received for entertainment on the night of the lecture, and consequently it happened that I stayed one night in a rich man's mansion, and the next in the narrow quarters of a working family. Every night I saw considerable numbers of people of all classes; and whether it was in the worker's small parlor, or in the reception-room of the wealthy, the most animated discussions went on about socialism and anarchism till a late hour, — with hope in the workman's house, with apprehension in the mansion, but everywhere with the same earnestness.

In the mansion the main questions asked were, " What do the socialists want ? What do they intend to do ? " and next, " What are the concessions which it is absolutely necessary to make at some given moment in order to avoid serious conflicts ? " In our conversations I seldom heard the justice of the socialist contention simply denied, or described as sheer nonsense. But I found a firm conviction that a revolution was impossible in England; that the claims of the mass of the workers had not yet reached the precision nor the extent of the claims of the socialists, and that the workers would be satisfied with much less; so that secondary concessions, amounting to a prospect of a slight increase of well-being or of leisure, would be accepted by the working classes of England as a pledge, in the meantime, of still more in the future. " We are a left-centre country; we live by compromise," I was once told by an

aged member of Parliament who had had a wide experience
of the life of his mother country.

In workmen's dwellings, too, I noticed a difference in
the questions which were addressed to me in England from
those which I was asked on the Continent. General principles, of which the partial applications will be determined
by the principles themselves, deeply interest the Latin workers. If this or that municipal council votes funds in support of a strike, or provides for the feeding of the children at
the schools, no importance is attached to such steps. They
are taken as a matter of fact. " Of course a hungry child
cannot learn," a French worker says, " it must be fed."
" Of course the employer was wrong in forcing the workers
to strike." That is all that is said, and no praise is
given to such minor concessions by the present individual-
ist society to communist principles. The thought of the
worker goes beyond the period of such concessions, and he
asks whether it is the commune or the unions of workers,
or the state which ought to undertake the organization of
production ; whether free agreement alone will be sufficient
to maintain society in working order, and what could
be the moral restraint if society parted with its present
repressive agencies ; whether an elected democratic government would be capable of accomplishing serious changes
in the socialist direction, and whether accomplished facts
ought not to precede legislation ; and so on. In England, it
was upon a series of palliative concessions, gradually growing in importance, that the chief weight was laid. But on
the other hand the impossibility of state administration of industries seemed to have been settled long before in the workers' minds, while what chiefly interested most of them was
matters of constructive realization, as well as how to attain
the conditions which would make such a realization possible.
" Well, Kropótkin, suppose that to-morrow we were to take

possession of the docks of our town. What's your idea about how to manage them?" would be asked, for instance, as soon as we had sat down in a workingman's parlor. Or, "We don't like the idea of state management of railways, and the present management by private companies is organized robbery. But suppose the workers own all the railways. How could the working of them be organized?" The lack of general ideas was thus supplemented by a desire of going deeper into the details of the realities.

Another feature of the movement in England was the considerable number of middle-class people who gave it their support in different ways, — some of them frankly joining it, while others helped it from the outside. In France and in Switzerland the two parties — the workers and the middle classes — stood arrayed against each other, sharply separated from each other. So it was, at least, in the years 1876–85. When I was in Switzerland I could say that during my three or four years' stay in the country I was acquainted with none but workers. I hardly knew more than a couple of middle-class men. In England this would have been impossible. We found quite a number of middle-class men and women who did not hesitate to appear openly, both in London and in the provinces, as helpers in organizing socialist meetings, or in going about during a strike with boxes to collect coppers in the parks. Besides, we saw a movement similar to what we had had in Russia in the early seventies, when our youth rushed "to the people," though by no means so intense, so full of self-sacrifice, and so utterly devoid of the idea of "charity." Here also, in England, a considerable number of people went in all sorts of capacities to live near the workers, in the slums, in people's palaces, in Toynbee Hall, and the like. It must be said that there was a great deal of enthusiasm at that time. Many probably thought that a social revolution had already commenced.   As always happens, however, with such enthusiasts, when they saw that in England, as everywhere, there was a long, tedious, preparatory uphill work to be done, very many of them retired from active work, and now stand outside of it as mere sympathetic onlookers.

XVII

I took a lively part in this movement, and with a few English comrades I started, in addition to the three socialist papers already in existence, an anarchist-communist monthly, "Freedom," which continues to live up to the present hour. At the same time I resumed my work on anarchism where I had had to interrupt it at the time of my arrest. The critical part of it was published by Elisée Reclus, during my Clairvaux imprisonment, under the title, "Paroles d'un Révolté." Now I began to work out the constructive part of an anarchist-communist society, — so far as it could be forecast, — in a series of articles published at Paris in "La Révolte." "Our boy," prosecuted for anti-militarist propaganda, had been compelled to change its title-page, and now appeared under a feminine name. Later on these articles were published in a more elaborate form in a book, "La Conquête du Pain."

These researches caused me to study more thoroughly certain points in the economic life of the civilized nations of to-day. Most socialists had hitherto said that in our present civilized societies we actually produce much more than is necessary for guaranteeing full well-being to all; that it was only the distribution which was defective; and, if a social revolution took place, all that was required would be for every one to return to his factory or workshop, — society taking possession for itself of the "surplus value," or benefits, which now went to the capitalist. I thought, on the contrary, that under the present conditions of private ownership production itself had taken a wrong turn, and was entirely inadequate even as regards the very necessaries of life. None of these necessaries are produced in greater quantities than would be required to secure well-being for all; and the over-production, so often spoken of, means nothing but that the masses are too poor to buy even what is now considered as necessary for a decent existence. But in all civilized countries the production, both agricultural and industrial, ought to and easily might be immensely increased, so as to secure a reign of plenty for all. This brought me to consider the possibilities of modern agriculture, as well as those of an education which would give to every one the possibility of carrying on at the same time both enjoyable manual work and brain work. I developed these ideas in a series of articles in the "Nineteenth Century," which are now published as a book under the title of "Fields, Factories, and Workshops."

Another great question also engrossed my attention. It is known to what conclusions Darwin's formula, the "struggle for existence," had been developed by his followers generally, even the most intelligent of them, such as Huxley. There is no infamy in civilized society, or in the relations of the whites towards the so-called lower races, or of the strong towards the weak, which would not have found its excuse in this formula.

Even during my stay at Clairvaux I saw the necessity of completely revising the formula itself and its applications to human affairs. The attempts which had been made by a few socialists in this direction did not satisfy me, but I found in a lecture by a Russian zoölogist, Professor Kessler, a true expression of the law of struggle for life. "Mutual aid," he said in that lecture, "is as much a law of nature as mutual struggle; but for the *progressive* evolution of the species the former is far more important than the latter." These few words — confirmed unfortunately by only a couple of illustrations (to which Syévertsoff, the zoölogist of whom I have spoken in an earlier chapter, added one or

two more) — contained for me the key of the whole problem. When Huxley published in 1888 his atrocious article,
"The Struggle for Existence; a Program," I decided to put
in a readable form my objections to his way of understanding the struggle for life, among animals as well as among
men, the materials for which I had been accumulating
for two years. I spoke of it to my friends. However,
I found that the interpretation of " struggle for life " in
the sense of a war-cry of " Woe to the Weak," raised to
the height of a commandment of nature revealed by science,
was so deeply rooted in this country that it had become
almost a matter of religion. Two persons only supported
me in my revolt against this misinterpretation of the facts
of nature. The editor of the " Nineteenth Century," Mr.
James Knowles, with his admirable perspicacity, at once
seized the gist of the matter, and with a truly youthful
energy encouraged me to take it in hand. The other sup-
porter was the regretted H. W. Bates, whom Darwin, in his
" Autobiography," described as one of the most intelligent
men he ever met. He was secretary of the Geographical
Society, and I knew him ; so I spoke to him of my intention. He was delighted with it. " Yes, most assuredly
write it," he said. " That is true Darwinism. It is a
shame to think of what they have made of Darwin's ideas.
Write it, and when you have published it, I will write
you a letter of commendation which you may publish." I
could not have had better encouragement, and I began the
work, which was published in the " Nineteenth Century "
under the titles of " Mutual Aid among Animals," " Among
Savages," " Among Barbarians," " In the Mediæval City,"
and " Amongst Ourselves." Unfortunately I neglected to
submit to Bates the first two articles of this series, dealing
with animals, which were published during his lifetime ; I
hoped to be soon ready with the second part of the work,
" Mutual Aid among Men ; " but it took me several years

to complete it, and in the meantime Bates passed from among us.

The researches which I had to make during these studies, in order to acquaint myself with the institutions of the barbarian period and with those of the mediæval free cities, led me to another important research : the part played in history by the state during its latest manifestation in Europe, in the last three centuries. And on the other hand, the study of the mutual support institutions at different stages of civilization led me to examine the evolutionist bases of the senses of justice and morality in man.

Within the last ten years the growth of socialism in England has taken on a new aspect. Those who judge only by the numbers of socialist and anarchist meetings held in the country, and the audiences attracted by these meetings, are prone to conclude that socialist propaganda is now on the decline. And those who judge the progress of it by the numbers of votes that are given to those who claim to represent socialism in Parliament jump to the conclusion that there is now hardly any socialist work going on in England. But the depth and the penetration of the socialist ideas can nowhere be judged by the numbers of votes given in favor of those who bring more or less socialism into their electoral programmes. Especially is this the case in England. The fact is, that of the three systems of socialism which were formulated by Fourier, Saint-Simon, and Robert Owen, it is the last-named which prevails in England and Scotland. Consequently it is not so much by the number of meetings or of socialist votes that the intensity of the movement must be judged, but by the infiltration of the socialist point of view into the trade-unionist, the co-operative, and the so-called municipal socialist movements, as well as the general infiltration of socialist ideas all over the country. Under this aspect, the extent to which the socialist views have penetrated is immense in comparison with what it was in 1886; and I do not hesitate to say that it is simply colossal in comparison with what it was in the years 1876–82.   And I may also add that the persevering endeavors of the small anarchist groups have contributed, to an extent which makes us feel that we have not wasted our time, to spread the ideas of no-government, of the rights of the individual, of local action and free agreement, as against those of state supremacy, centralization, and discipline, which were dominant twenty years ago.

All Europe is now going through a very bad phase of the development of the military spirit.   This was an unavoidable consequence of the victory obtained by the German military empire, with its universal military service system, over France in 1871, and it was already then foreseen, and foretold by many, in an especially impressive form by Bakúnin.   But the counter-current already begins to make itself felt in modern life.

Communist ideas, divested of their monastic form, have penetrated in Europe and America to an immense extent during the twenty-seven years in which I have taken an active part in the socialist movement and could observe their growth.   When I think of the vague, confused, timid ideas which were expressed by the workers at the first congresses of the International Workingmen's Association, or which were current at Paris during the Commune insurrection, even among the most thoughtful of the leaders, and compare them with those which have been arrived at to-day by a vast number of workers, I must say that they seem to me to belong to two entirely different worlds.

There is no period in history — with the exception, perhaps, of the period of the insurrections in the twelfth and thirteenth centuries, which led to the birth of the mediæval Communes — during which a similarly deep change has taken place in the current conceptions of society.   And

now, in my fifty-seventh year, I am even more deeply convinced than I was twenty-five years ago that a chance combination of accidental circumstances may bring about in
Europe a revolution as wide-spread as that of 1848, and
far more important ; not in the sense of mere fighting between different parties, but in the sense of a profound and
rapid social reconstruction ; and I am convinced that whatever character such a movement may take in different countries, there will be displayed everywhere a far deeper com-
prehension of the required changes than has ever been
displayed within the last six centuries; while the resistance
which the movement will meet in the privileged classes
will hardly have the character of obtuse obstinacy which
made the revolutions of times past so violent.

To obtain this great result is well worth the efforts which
so many thousands of men and women of all nations and all
classes have made within the last thirty years.

NOTES TO THE TEXT
BY NICOLAS WALTER

The numbers at the head of these notes refer to pages of the text. Dates of events in Russia are given in the Old Style (Julian Calendar) which was used there until 1918. During the nineteenth century this was twelve days behind the New Style (Gregorian Calendar) which was already in use in the West; to calculate a date in New Style, add twelve days to that given. Names of Russian people and publications are given in a modern transliteration of the original Russian. This is not always the same as the transliteration in the text; for instance, "Ekaterína Nicoláevna Kropótkin" will appear here as Yekaterina Nikolayevna Kropotkina. The sources for the notes have not been given for reasons of space; they are mainly the standard reference works of the relevant countries, supplemented by standard biographies and histories. A particularly useful book is the most recent Russian edition of Kropotkin's memoirs: P. A. Kropotkin, *Zapiski revolyutsionera* (Moscow, 1966), with introduction, commentary and annotated index by Valentina Aleksandrovna Tvardovskaya. Other informative books are as follows—for the life and work of Kropotkin: George Woodcock and Ivan Avakumović, *The Anarchist Prince* (London, 1950); for the anarchist background: George Woodcock, *Anarchism* (Cleveland, 1962); for the Russian background: Franco Venturi, *Il populismo russo* (Milan, 1952), translated as *Roots of Revolution* (London, 1960); for the French background: Jean Maitron, *Le mouvement anarchiste en France* (Paris, 1951); for the English background: E. P. Thompson, *William Morris: Romantic to Revolutionary* (London, 1955). I am grateful to the staff of the British Museum Reading Room, London, and of the Library of the School of Slavonic and East European Studies, University of London, where most of the information was obtained, and also to Paul Avrich, Marianne Enckell, Ivor Guest, John Hewetson, R. W. Thomson, Ruth Walter and Colin Ward for help with various points.

1. The Zamoskvorechie (Trans-Moskva district) is in central Moscow, south of the Moskva river. The "Old Faith" (*Staraya vera*) was the traditional Russian religion, many of whose followers left the Orthodox Church when it was reformed in the seventeenth century; they were called "Old Believers" (*Starovery*) or "Nonconformists" (*Raskolniki*), and split into many sects. The Kremlin (*Kreml*), the citadel of Moscow, is now the seat of the government of the Soviet Union; the "immense space in front of it" is the Red Square. Tverskaya and Kuznetski Most (Smiths' Bridge) are fashionable streets in central Moscow. Plyushchikha and Dorogomilovka are suburbs of Moscow.

2. The Staraya Konyushennaya, between the Arbat and the Prechistenka (now Kropotkinskaya Ulitsa—Kropotkin Street), is in the west of central Moscow. Pyotr (Peter) I built St. Petersburg on the river Neva and moved the capital there from Moscow in 1712. He frequently promoted *raznochintsy* ("men of various ranks") instead of relying on the old aristocracy.

5. Pyotr Alekseyevich Kropotkin (pronounced *Krahpáwtkeen*) was born on November 27 (December 9, New Style), 1842, at 26 Shtatny Pereulok (now Kropotkinski Pereulok).

6. Yekaterina Nikolayevna Kropotkina, the author's mother, was born in 1810 and died in 1846. Aleksandr Alekseyevich Kropotkin ("Sasha") was born in 1840.

7. Nikolai Alekseyevich Kropotkin was born in 1834, and Yelena Alekseyevna Kropotkina in 1836.

8. Ryurik was a Scandinavian adventurer who traditionally founded the Russian monarchy in the ninth century. Smolensk was ruled by Grand Princes of Kiev, descended from Ryurik, until the

mid-eleventh century, and then by independent Princes, also descended from Ryurik, until it was conquered by Lithuania in the early fifteenth century. Rostislav Mstislavich was Prince of Smolensk and then Grand Prince of Kiev in the mid-twelfth century; he was a grandson of Vladimir Monomakh, Grand Prince of Kiev in the early twelfth century. According to the parchment, the Kropotkin family was descended from Dmitri Vasilievich Kropotki, a grandson of Svyatoslav Ivanovich, the penultimate Prince of Smolensk in the late fourteenth century—according to another account, from Dmitri Vasilievich Smolenski and his wife Kropotka, a granddaughter of Svyatoslav Ivanovich (*kropotki* and *kropotka* are masculine and feminine forms of a word meaning "painstaking").

9. Kropotkin's paternal grandparents were Pyotr Nikolayevich Kropotkin and Praskovia Alekseyevna Gagarina (1770–1850). The Gagarins were another family of princes descended from Ryurik. Ivan Alekseyevich Gagarin (1771–1832) behaved even more scandalously than Kropotkin remembered: he lived with Yekaterina Semyonovna Semyonova (1786–1849) for fifteen years before marrying her in 1828.

10. Mikhail Pavlovich (1798–1848) was a younger brother of Nikolai I. Russia invaded the Balkans in May, 1828, under the command of Ivan Ivanovich Dibich (1785–1831); the Turks were forced to accept the Treaty of Adrianople in September, 1829.

11. The Polish rising against Russia began in November, 1830, and was crushed by the Russian army between February and October, 1831. Ivan Fyodorovich Paskevich (1782–1856) was commander-in-chief of the First Russian Army and viceroy of Poland from 1831 to 1856. Kropotkin's grandfather, Nikolai Semyonovich Sulima (1777–1840), was wounded in the head at Austerlitz in 1804, not during Napoleon's invasion of Russia in 1812; he was Governor-General first of East Siberia (1833–1834) and then of West Siberia (1834–1836), not the other way round. The Ukrainian Cossacks rose against Polish rule in 1648 under the leadership of Bogdan Khmelnitski (1595–1657), who transferred allegiance from the King of Poland to the Emperor of Russia. Ivan Mikhailovich Sulima, a "hetman" (= colonel) of the Zaporozhe Cossacks of the Dnieper River, was captured by the Poles and executed in Warsaw in 1635.

14. Vasili Ivanovich Timofeyev (1770–1850) was Commander of the Sixth Army Corps from 1842 to 1848. Aleksei Kropotkin married Yelizaveta Markovna Karandino in 1848.

15. Mikhail Nikolayevich Zagoskin (1789–1852) was a well-known Russian playwright and novelist.

17. The Yekaterinski Institut was a leading girls' school in Moscow.

20. Fanny Elssler (1810–1884), the Austrian dancer, performed in Moscow at the end of her career, in 1850 and 1851. *La Gitana* was first performed in St. Petersburg in 1839, the main role of Lauretta being created by Elssler's rival, Maria Taglioni (1804–1884); another version of the same ballet, *La Gypsi*, was first performed in Paris at the same time, the main role of Sarah being created by Fanny Elssler herself. But she performed neither ballet in Moscow.

22. Mikhail Semyonovich Shchepkin (1788–1863), Prov Mikhailovich Sadovski (1818–1872) and Sergei Vasilievich Shumski (1821–1878) were three leading actors at the Moscow Maly theater. *Revizor* (The Inspector-General), the best-known play by Nikolai Vasilievich Gogol (1809–1852), was first performed in 1836.

23. Vladimir Ivanovich Nazimov (1802–1874) was governor-general of Vilna from 1855 to 1863.

24. "My uncle, Prince Gagárin" was Aleksandr Ivanovich Gagarin (1801–1857), a military administrator.

25. The heir to the throne was Aleksandr, who later ruled as Aleksandr II. His wife was Marie (1824–1880), daughter of Ludwig II of Hesse; they were married in 1841, and she was known in Russia as Mariya Aleksandrovna. The child she was carrying cannot have been her third, Aleksandr (who later ruled as Aleksandr III), for he was born in 1845, or her fourth, Vladimir, who was born in 1847, or her sixth, Mariya, who was born in 1853; but her fifth, Aleksei, was born in January, 1850, so the ball may have been earlier than Kropotkin remembered—and the royal family did go to Moscow for a ball celebrating the completion of the Great Kremlin Palace in spring, 1849.

26. The Corps of Pages (*Pazheski Korpus*) was an elite cadet school in St. Petersburg which was formed in 1759 and re-formed in 1802. The Izmailovsk Regiment was formed in 1730 and re-formed in 1801.

31. "General D——" = Durnovo, brother of a prominent administrator.

33. Ivan Sergeyevich Gagarin (1814–1882) left Russia in 1843 and became a Jesuit scholar in France. "Mirski" = Dmitri Sergeyevich Drutskoi.

43. Kropotkin's impression of Napoleon's retreat from Moscow is confused. In October, 1812, the French route was barred by the Russian army; at the battle of Vinkovo near Tarutino, on October 18, the Russians worsted the French in a skirmish, and at the battle of Maloyaroslavets, on October 24, the Russians decisively defeated the French; the two battles together forced Napoleon to abandon the southern route and retreat to Smolensk. Louis-Nicolas Davout

(1770–1823) was commander of the French First Corps. Mikhail Illarionovich Kutuzov (1745–1813) was commander-in-chief of the Russian army.

45. Polina Alekseyevna Kropotkina was born in 1850 and died in 1924.

46. The French campaign in Spain lasted from 1808 to 1814. Yakov Nikolayevich Repninski (1740–1790) served in the army from 1756; his daughter Yelena married N. S. Sulima.

47. *L'Illustration* was a weekly paper published in Paris from 1843 to 1944. The Orleanists were liberal monarchists who supported the heirs of Louis-Philippe of Orléans, king of France from 1830 to 1848.

48. Kropotkin attended the Pervaya Gimnaziya, a leading boys' school in Moscow, from 1853 to 1857.

57. *Mumu* was published in 1852. Dmitri Vasilievich Grigorovich (1822–1899) was a novelist who pioneered the genre of stories about the life of serfs in *Derevnya* (The Village) and *Anton Goremyka,* which were published in 1846 and 1847.

62. "T——" = Ivan Sidorovich Tolmachov.

63. Nikolai Kropotkin became an alcoholic, was sent to a monastery, escaped in 1862, and disappeared.

67. *Gore ot uma* (Misfortune from Intelligence, or Wit Works Woe), the masterpiece of Aleksandr Sergeyevich Griboyedov (1795–1829), was completed in 1824 but could not be performed because of its satire on Moscow society; it circulated in manuscript, but no authentic version survived. Aleksei Konstantinovich Tolstoi (1817–1875) was a writer who was a personal friend of Aleksandr II but was still censored. Countess Yelizaveta Vasilievna Salias de Turnemir (1815–1892) wrote popular novels under the name "Eugénie Tour." Gogol died in February, 1852, not in 1851. Turgenev's article on Gogol's death was written for the *Peterburgskiye Vedomosti* (St. Petersburg Gazette) but rejected by the censor, so he sent it to the *Moskovskiye Vedomosti* (Moscow Gazette); it was published on March 13, 1852, and Turgenev was arrested on April 16 and exiled for two years. Pushkin's *Yevgeni Onegin* was published in 1833.

68. Kropotkin's novel was called *Istoriya grivennika* (The Story of a Ten-Kopeck Piece). His daily paper was called *Dnevnye Vedomosti* (Daily Gazette); a 32mo volume would be about 4½ × 3 inches in size.

69. Kropotkin's monthly paper was called *Vremennik* (Chronicle); it was produced from 1855 to 1857.

72. Pavel Petrovich fon Vinkler was inspector at the Corps of

Pages from 1856 to 1865. Vladislav Konstantinovich Chigarev taught arithmetic at the Corps of Pages from 1855 to 1865.

73. Aleksandr Nikolayevich Ostrovski (1823–1886) was a well-known dramatist in the mid-nineteenth century. Vladimir Petrovich Zheltukhin (1798–1878) was director of the Corps of Pages from 1854 to 1861. Karl Karlovich Zhirardot was company commander at the Corps of Pages from 1831 to 1840 and from 1843 to 1859.

75. Fyodor (Theodore) M. Tolstoi's novel, *Bolezni voli*, was published in 1866.

77. The "page de chambre with carroty hair" was Vasilchikov.

78. "Selanoff" = Sevastianov.

80. Nikolai Ulianovich Zenkevich was doctor at the Corps of Pages from 1857 to 1885.

84. Sukhonin taught algebra at the Corps of Pages from 1847 to 1864. Nikolai Aleksandrovich was born in September, 1843, and died in April, 1865. Vladimir Ignatievich Klassovski (1815–1877), a well-known Russian and classical scholar, taught Russian at the Corps of Pages from 1851 to 1867. Karl Andreyevich Beker taught German at the Corps of Pages from 1856 to 1862. Kamchatka is a remote and barren peninsula in the far east of Russia.

86. Kropotkin's quotation from Goethe's *Faust* is from the English translation by the American writer Bayard Taylor (1825–1878), published in 1870–1871. Turgenev's novel *Faust* was published in 1856.

87. "Dauroff" = Donaurov. "Von Kleinau" = Klyuki-fon-Klyugenau.

88. The first volume of Humboldt's masterpiece, *Kosmos*, was published in 1845.

89. "Ebert" = Ivan Stanislavovich Obert, who taught writing at the Corps of Pages from 1856 to 1861.

90. Feliks Feliksovich Gants taught drawing at the Corps of Pages from 1854 to 1866.

92. "Nesadoff" = Nesterov.

94. The letters between the Kropotkin brothers were not in fact seized by the police, but were preserved by friends and relatives, and published in 1932.

95. *Otsy i deti* (Fathers and Sons [Children]) was published in 1862.

96. The quotation from Goethe is again from *Faust*. Servetus—

Miguel Servet (1511–1553)—was a Spanish scientist whose religious views were condemned by both Catholics and Protestants; he was arrested by the Inquisition and burnt by Calvin. Jules Michelet (1798–1874), the French historian, did not write a book on him, though he did describe his life in the twelfth volume of his *Histoire de France*, which was published in 1858—Kropotkin may have meant his book on Luther, *Mémoires de Luther*, which was published in 1835. The Confession of Augsburg is the Lutheran creed.

97. Yelena Kropotkina married Nikolai Pavlovich Kravchenko.

98. Karl Frantsevich Rulie (1814–1858), the Russian zoologist, was a professor at Moscow university from 1842, and edited *Vestnik Yestestvennykh Nauk* (Natural Science Herald) from 1854. August Weismann (1834–1914) was a German biologist; Herbert Spencer (1820–1903) was an English scientist and sociologist; their controversy concerned the mechanism of evolution—Weismann held that acquired characteristics could not be inherited, Spencer held that they could. Francis Galton (1822–1911), the English scientist (and a cousin of Darwin), also opposed the theory of the inheritance of acquired characteristics, and founded the science of eugenics. The Neo-Lamarckians were the later followers of Jean-Baptiste Lamarck (1744–1829), the French naturalist who anticipated the theory of evolution, and held that it occurred through the inheritance of characteristics acquired in response to the environment. *Économie politique* by Jean-Baptiste Say (1767–1832), the French economist, was published in 1803.

102. Ivan Sergeyevich Aksakov (1823–1886) published *Issledovaniye o torgovle na ukrainskikh yarmarkakh* (An Investigation of Trade in Ukrainian Fairs) in 1858.

106. The man who ran the carriages between Kaluga and Moscow was called Kozyol (which means "buck [billygoat]" in Russian).

108. "Captain B——" = Fyodor Kondratievich fon Brevern, who was company commander at the Corps of Pages from 1859 to 1865.

109. The wife of Nikolai I was Frederika, daughter of Friedrich Wilhelm III of Prussia; she was born in 1798, married Nikolai in 1817, was known in Russia as Aleksandra Fyodorovna, and died in October, 1860.

110. Konstantin Nikolayevich (1827–1892) was a younger brother of Aleksandr II; his eldest son, Nikolai Konstantinovich, was born in 1850.

112. Friedrich III (1831–1888) was king of Prussia and emperor of Germany for a few months before his death.

114. Nikolai Ivanovich Cherukhin taught physics at the Corps of Pages from 1854 to 1861. The physics textbook was by Emili Khristianovich Lents (1804–1865), a well-known physicist.

115. Vasili Fomich Petrushevski (1829–1891) taught chemistry at the Corps of Pages from 1857 to 1875. Kropotkin compressed into three years the work of many more: William Grove (1811–1896), the English physicist, established the theory of mutual convertibility of forces in 1846; Rudolph Julius Clausius (1822–1888), the German physicist, introduced the idea of entropy into thermodynamics and formulated the second law in 1850; James Joule (1818–1889), the English physicist, determined the mechanical equivalent of heat in 1849; Marc Séguin (1786–1875), the French engineer, pioneered the technology of steam locomotion in the 1820's and 1830's; Hermann Helmholtz (1821–1894), the German physiologist and physicist, laid the foundations of scientific acoustics in 1862; John Tyndall (1820–1893), the Irish physicist, was well known for his popular lectures on science from the 1850's to the 1870's; Charles Gerhardt (1816–1856), the French chemist, developed a unitary system which combined the substitution and radicle theories in the early 1850's; Amedeo Avogadro (1776–1856), the Italian chemist, formulated the law that equal volumes of gases at equal temperatures under equal pressures contain the same number of molecules; Dmitri Ivanovich Mendeleyev (1834–1907), the Russian chemist, Lothar Meyer (1830–1895), the German chemist, and John Newlands (1838–1898), the English chemist, formulated the periodic law of physical elements; Karl Vogt (1817–1895), the Swiss naturalist, and Jacob Moleschott (1822–1893), the Dutch-Italian scientist, were both strong supporters of evolution; Claude Bernard (1813–1878), the French physiologist, pioneered the study of experimental medicine. Julius Adolph Stöckhardt (1809–1886), the German chemist, published the first edition of *Die Schule der Chemie* in 1846; many editions followed. "Zasetsky" = Zamytski; Dmitri Petrovich Zamytski (c. 1780–1879) was an admiral who lived in retirement from 1859.

117. Ivan Petrovich Shulgin (1795–1869) taught history at the Corps of Pages from 1831 to 1863.

119. Angiolina Bosio (1824–1859), the Italian singer, died in St. Petersburg.

126. Nikolai Platonovich Ogaryov (1813–1877) was a writer who was closely associated with Herzen. Konstantin Dmitrievich Kavelin (1818–1885) was a liberal philosopher and historian. Dostoyevski was a moderate socialist in his youth. Kropotkin's cousin Varvara Dmitrievna Drutskaya, the daughter of Dmitri Sergeyevich Drutskoi

and Yelena Petrovna Drutskaya, fell in love with Ivan Ivanovich Musin-Pushkin.

127. *Polyarnaya Zvezda* (The Pole Star), which was named after a Decembrist paper of the 1820's, was a mainly literary paper which actually began publication in August, 1855. Herzen's paper *Kolokol* (The Bell), which was more political, cheaper and more widely circulated than *Polyarnaya Zvezda*, began publication in July, 1857. Kropotkin's paper, which was called *Otgoloski iz Korpusa* (Echoes from the Corps), was actually produced in 1858.

129. Yelena Pavlovna (1806–1873) was the wife of the grand-duke Mikhail Pavlovich. Aleksandr II did not quote Herzen's words in March, 1856; it was Herzen who quoted Aleksandr's words in August, 1857, at the beginning of his article "The Russian Revolution" in the second issue of *Kolokol*.

130. Aleksandr's Rescript to Nazimov was issued on November 20, 1857. Herzen's article "In Three Years," which opened with the last words of the Roman Emperor Julian the Apostate—"Thou hast conquered, O Galilean"—was published in *Kolokol* in February, 1858. Peasant insurrections actually increased after 1857.

131. Nikolai Chernyshevski was born in 1828 and became a socialist in 1848; in 1854 he became the leading contributor to *Sovremennik* (The Contemporary), and by 1862 he was involved in the revolutionary movement. Ivan Dmitrievich Belyayev (1810–1873), the Russian historian, was professor at Moscow University from 1852.

132. Nikolai Alekseyevich Milyutin (1818–1872) was joint minister of internal affairs, with responsibility for the organization of the emancipation of the serfs, from 1859; he was dismissed in March, 1861. Dmitri Alekseyevich Milyutin (1816–1912) was minister of war from 1861 to 1881. Pyotr Aleksandrovich Valuyev (1814–1890) was minister of internal affairs from 1861 to 1876. "Princess X." = Aleksandra Sergeyevna Dolgorukaya, the mistress of Aleksandr around 1860 (she should not be confused with her distant relative, Yekaterina Mikhailovna Dolgorukaya, who became Aleksandr's mistress in 1866); she married Pyotr Pavlovich Albedinski (1826–1883), a military administrator.

134. Filaret, whose real name was Vasili Mikhailovich Drozdov (1782–1867), was Metropolitan (archbishop) of Moscow from 1826.

135. Mikhail Nikolayevich Muraviov (1796–1866) was put in charge of the suppression of the Polish rising of 1863, as governor-general of Lithuania, and was nicknamed *Veshatel* (the Hangman) because of his methods. Herzen's article, "Mater Dolorosa"—ending

with the words: "Only forty days! Why did not *this man* die on the day when the emancipation manifesto was proclaimed to the Russian people?"—appeared in *Kolokol* not after the Polish rising of 1863 but in May, 1861, after Russian soldiers had savagely crushed a demonstration in Warsaw on February 15. Peasant uprisings actually increased in 1861.

145. Fyodor Fedorovich Trepov (1803–1889) was chief of the St. Petersburg police from 1868 to 1878. The Third Section (*Tretie Otdeleniye*) was the Russian political police organization from 1826 to 1880.

146. The governor-general of East Siberia from 1847 to 1861 was Nikolai Nikolayevich Muraviov (1809–1881). Pyotr Andreyevich Shuvalov (1827–1889) was chief of the St. Petersburg police from 1857 to 1866, and of the national police from 1866 to 1873. Nikolai Pavlovich Ignatiev (1832–1908) was first a diplomat, and then held many political offices from 1861 to 1882.

149. Nikolai Nikolayevich (1831–1891) and Mikhail Nikolayevich (1832–1909) were younger brothers of Aleksandr II who were both soldiers and administrators. Aleksandr Vladimirovich Adlerberg (1819–1888) succeeded his father as minister of the imperial household and estates from 1872 to 1881.

150. The student disorders of 1861 began at St. Petersburg in the autumn term; the students held the first political demonstration in the city since the Decembrists on September 23, and the university was closed the next day; similar demonstrations followed in Moscow and Kazan during October, 1861.

151. Cassius Marcellus Clay (1810–1903), the abolitionist politician, was American minister in Russia from 1861 to 1862 and from 1863 to 1869; he arrived in St. Petersburg in June, 1861, and was received by the Tsar in July. Konstantin Dmitrievich Ushinski (1824–1870) was a well-known Russian educationist in the mid-nineteenth century.

152. Pavel (Paul) I lived at Gatchina Palace from 1784, and was killed there by his own courtiers in 1801.

153. Aleksandr married Princess Dagmar of Denmark (1847–1928) in 1866; in 1864 she had been engaged to his elder brother Nikolai, who died in 1865; in Russia she was known as Mariya Fyodorovna.

155. The Amur region was ceded to Russia by the Treaty of Aigun in 1858. Humboldt explored Siberia in 1829, and wrote *Fragments de géologie et de climatologie asiatiques* (1831) and *Asie centrale* (1843). Karl Ritter (1779–1859), the German geographer, wrote about Asia in the second edition of *Erdkunde* (Geography), which was

published in 19 volumes from 1822 to 1859. The Cossacks of the Amur were formed in 1858, and the Mounted Cossacks of the Amur in 1860.

156. Sergei Petrovich Ozerov (1809–1884) was director of the Corps of Pages from 1861 to 1865. The assistant to Mikhail Nikolayevich was Nikita Vasilievich Korsakov (1821–1890).

159. Ivan Vasilievich Annenkov (1813–1887) was chief of the St. Petersburg police from 1862 to 1867. Pavel Vasilievich Annenkov (1812–1887) was a liberal critic. Lyudvig Lyudvigovich Gosse was adjutant at the Corps of Pages from 1854 to 1870.

160. Aleksandr Arkadievich Suvorov (1804–1882) was governor-general of St. Petersburg from 1861 to 1866.

162. Mikhail Nikiforovich Katkov (1818–1883), who belonged to the liberal circle at Moscow University in the 1830's, was a leading reactionary intellectual from the 1850's to the 1870's; he was editor of *Moskovskiye Vedomosti* (Moscow Gazette). He did not in fact fight a duel with Bakunin; when they quarreled in 1840, Bakunin refused to fight.

163. The "secret revolutionary government" in the Polish rising of 1863 was the Rzad Narodowy (Popular Administration), which made contact with Herzen, Ogaryov and Bakunin in London. Aleksandr Nikolayevich Liders (1790–1874), the Russian soldier, was viceroy of Poland from 1861 to 1862 and was shot at on June 27, 1862. Konstantin Nikolayevich was viceroy of Poland from 1862 to 1863. Aleksander Wielopolski (1803–1877), the Polish politician, was head of the civil administration in Poland from 1862 to 1863. The main revolutionary proclamation issued in May, 1862, was called *Molodaya Rossiya* (Young Russia) and was written in prison by the socialist P. G. Zaichnevski (1842–1896), who began revolutionary activity in 1859 and spent most of the rest of his life in prison and exile.

164. Semyon Romanovich Zhdanov (1803–1865) became a member of the Senate in 1864; he was a member of the commission which investigated political disturbances in Kazan in 1863, and died on his way back to St. Petersburg from carrying out a similar investigation in Siberia in 1864.

165. *Sovremennik* and several other radical papers were suppressed in June, 1862.

167. Kropotkin left St. Petersburg in June, 1862.

168. Kropotkin's diary for the period he spent in Siberia (1862–1867) survived and was published in 1923.

169. Muraviov's second cousin Bakunin was exiled to Siberia

in 1857 and escaped in July, 1861. Kropotkin arrived in Irkutsk in September, 1862. Mikháil Semyonovich Korsakov (1826–1871) was governor-general of East Siberia from 1861 to 1870. Boleslav-Viktor Kazimirovich Kukel, a Lithuanian, was acting governor of Transbaikalia from 1862 to 1863.

170. Kropotkin arrived in Chita in October, 1862. K. N. Pedashenko was commander of the Transbaikalian Cossacks. The "well-meaning civil service officials" were Adolf Leopoldovich Shanyavski (1837–1905) and Nikolai Mikhailovich Yadrintsev (1842–1894).

171. The "district chief" was Markovich; Kropotkin carried out the investigation in November, 1862.

172. Mikhail Illarionovich Mikhailov (1826–1865) was a poet and journalist who was close to Chernyshevski; in 1861 he helped to write the manifesto *K molodomu pokoleniyu* (To the Younger Generation), for which he was arrested and sent to Siberia at the end of the year; he died not "a few months later" but after more than three years. Kropotkin went to Kadaya near Nerchinsk to warn him in November, 1862, and he introduced Kropotkin to anarchist ideas by recommending Proudhon's *Système des contradictions économiques*.

174. I. S. Aksakov published the periodical *Den* (The Day) from 1861 to 1865; the article on Poland appeared in November, 1861.

177. Nikolai Milyutin was secretary of state in Poland from 1863 to 1864. Vladimir Aleksandrovich Cherkasski (1824–1878), a Russian politician also involved in administering the emancipation of the serfs, was in charge of internal affairs in Poland from 1864 to 1866.

181. The new governor-general of Transbaikalia was Yevgeni Mikhailovich Zhukovski (1814–1883). George Kennan visited Siberia from 1885 to 1886 and published his findings in *Siberia and the Exile System* (New York, 1891).

184. Kropotkin traveled on the Amur from June to September, 1863.

186. Innokenti, whose real name was Ivan Yevseyevich Popov-Veniaminov (1791–1879), was bishop of Kamchatka from 1840 to 1867.

187. "Marovsky" = Anton Ivanovich Malinovski.

196. The high functionary who spoke French was Vladimir Petrovich Butkov (1814–1881), head of the Siberian Committee of the Council of Ministers. Vyacheslav Grigorievich Shvarts (1838–1869) was a Russian artist whose painting *Ioann Grozny u tela ubitogo im syna* (Ivan the Terrible by the Body of His Murdered Son) was done

in cartoon in 1861 and in oils in 1864; Ivan IV murdered his son
Ivan in 1580. Chernyshevski was arrested in July, 1862, imprisoned
until 1864, and exiled to Siberia until 1883; he died in 1889.

197. Ignatiev was head of the Asian department at the Ministry of
Foreign Affairs from 1860 to 1864.

198. Kropotkin returned to Irkutsk in February, 1864.

199. Kropotkin traveled across Manchuria from April to June,
1864.

200. K'an-Hsi (1654–1722), who ruled as the second Manchu
emperor of China from 1662, made use of Jesuit missionaries as
advisers, scholars and explorers; the Flemish Jesuit, Ferdinand
Verbiest (1623–1688), accompanied him on a journey into Manchuria
in 1683.

208. Kropotkin traveled down the Amur in the summer and
up the Sungari in the autumn of 1864. The Russian consul from Urga
was Shishmarev.

209. Mikhail Grigorievich Chernyayev (1828–1898) was the
commander of a Cossack brigade; the doctor was Konradi, and the
astronomer was Fyodor Usoltsev.

212. The reports of the Manchurian expeditions were published
in the *Zapiski* (Memoirs) of the Siberian Section of the Imperial
Russian Geographical Society in 1865.

214. Kropotkin's report of his expedition in the Western Sayans
was published in the *Zapiski* of the Siberian Section of the Imperial
Russian Geographical Society in 1867. The map was shown to
Kropotkin by the explorer M. V. Rukhlov.

215. Alfred Russel Wallace (1823–1913), the English naturalist
who developed the theory of evolution at the same time as Darwin,
explored South America from 1848 to 1852 and was much impressed
by the primitive people he met there. Ivan Semyonovich Polyakov
(1847–1887), the Russian zoologist and anthropologist, made several
expeditions between 1866 and 1880, and wrote a great many articles;
Kropotkin met him again in Switzerland in 1878; he was later the
curator of the Zoological Museum of the Russian Academy of Sciences.
The topographer was P. N. Moshinski. Kropotkin received the gold
medal of the Imperial Russian Geographical Society for the Vitim-
Olyokma expedition, and the mountain range he crossed was named
Khrebet Kropotkina (Kropotkin's Range).

217. Raphael Pumpelly (1837–1923), the American geologist,
surveyed Japan and China from 1861 to 1865, and visited Irkutsk
on his way home. Adolph Bastian (1826–1905), the German pioneer

of ethnography, traveled in the Far East from 1861 to 1866, and visited Irkutsk in 1865.

218. "Potaloff" = Porokhov. Kropotkin's five anonymous reports of the courts-martial were published in the *Birzhevye Vedomosti* (Exchange Gazette) in December, 1866.

223. Aleksandr Kropotkin had married Vera Sevastianovna Chaikovskaya, daughter of Sevastian Chaikovski, a Polish revolutionary.

224. When Kropotkin left the army he was officially transferred to the civil service; in January, 1868, he was given the rank of Titular Councilor in the Ministry of Internal Affairs, and was attached to the statistical committee under Pyotr Petrovich Semyonov (1827–1914), a leading geographer.

225. "L. Schwartz" = Julius Schwartz (1822–1894), the German astronomer, who explored Siberia from 1855 to 1858.

227. Kropotkin's revision of the orography of Asia was published in the *Zapiski* of the Imperial Russian Geographical Society in 1875. August Petermann (1822–1878) was a German cartographer who spent much of his life in Britain. His map of Asia was for the sixth edition of *Stielers Handatlas*, which was published in 1871–1875.

228. Nikolai Alekseyevich Severtsov (1827–1885), the Russian zoologist, made many expeditions in Central Asia from 1857, and actually published several important articles and books from 1867. Nikolai Nikolayevich Miklukha-Maklai (1846–1888), the Russian explorer, studied in Germany, where he was a pupil of Ernst Heinrich Haeckel (1834–1919), the German biologist, and went on expeditions in several places from 1866; he traveled to the Red Sea in 1869, and to New Guinea in the ship *Vityaz* (Champion) in 1870, and lived in Australia for most of the time from 1878 to 1886; he actually wrote many important articles.

230. Aleksei Pavlovich Fedchenko (1844–1873) and Olga Aleksandrovna Fedchenko (1845–1921), the Russian naturalists, made expeditions all over the world from 1868; *Puteshestviye v Turkestan A. P. Fedchenko* (A. P. Fedchenko's Travels in Turkestan) was published between 1872 and 1877; their son, Boris Alekseyevich Fedchenko (1872–1947), was a botanist who made expeditions from 1908 to 1917 and was a professor at Leningrad from 1918 to 1931. Nikolai Mikhailovich Przhevalski (Przewalski) (1839–1888) made five expeditions in Central Asia between 1867 and 1888.

231. Mikhail Vasilievich Pevtsov (1843–1902), Vsevolod Ivanovich Roborovski (1856–1910) and Pyotr Kuzmich Kozlov (1863–1935) were colleagues of Przhevalski who made many expeditions

in Central Asia. Mikhail Konstantinovich Sidorov (1823–1887) wrote about Arctic navigation in the 1870's.

232. Willem Barentz (1550–1597), the Dutch explorer, attempted to discover the Northeast Passage round Russia three times in the 1590's and died in the attempt. Nils Adolf Nordenskjöld (1832–1901), the Swedish geologist, was the first to navigate the Northeast Passage in the 1870's. Robert Edwin Peary (1856–1920), the American explorer, traveled to North Greenland in the 1890's. Fridtjof Nansen (1861–1930), the Norwegian explorer, traveled in the Arctic in the *Fram* from 1893 to 1895. (The final success came when Peary reached the North Pole in 1909.) Kropotkin's report advocating a Russian Arctic expedition was published by the Imperial Russian Geographical Society in 1871.

233. Nikolai Gustavovich Shilling (1828–1911) and Fyodor Petrovich Litke (1797–1882) were Russian geographers and explorers.

234. Elling Carlsen (1819–1900) and Edvard Johannesen (1844–1901) were Norwegian explorers. Julius von Payer (1842–1915) and Karl Weyprecht (1838–1881), the Austrian and German explorers, discovered Franz-Josef Land in 1874. (Severnaya Zemlya, northwest of Novaya Zemlya, was discovered in 1913.) Grigori Petrovich Gelmersen (1803–1885), the Russian geologist, made many expeditions and was director of the St. Petersburg Mining Institute from 1865 to 1872. Fyodor Bogdanovich Schmidt (1832–1908), the Russian geologist, explored Siberia between 1859 and 1862.

236. The outgoing secretary of the Imperial Russian Geographical Society was Fyodor Romanovich Osten-Saken, an administrator and explorer.

242. Apollon Nikolayevich Maikov (1821–1897) was a minor romantic poet. The "high dignitary" in the Ministry of Foreign Affairs was Osten-Saken.

243. Émile-Félix Fleury (1815–1884) was a close associate of Louis Napoléon (whose *coup d'état* was on December 2, 1851, not 1852); he became aide-de-camp to the Emperor in 1856, and was French ambassador in Russia from 1863 to 1870; Compiègne was the favorite residence of Napoleon III.

244. Shuvalov was Russian ambassador in Britain from 1874 to 1879. Aleksandr Lvovich Potapov (1818–1886) was chief of police from 1874 to 1876.

245. Potapov's friend was Tokarev, governor of Minsk, and his main ally in the Ministry of Internal Affairs was Loshkarev.

246. The navy was "in the pockets" of Andrei Aleksandrovich Popov (1821–1898), a prominent official in charge of shipbuilding

during the 1870's, who made a fortune by bribery and peculation. The grand duke who arranged orgies was Vladimir Aleksandrovich (1847–1909), a son of Aleksandr II and a military administrator. The grand duke who became psychopathic was Sergei Aleksandrovich (1857–1905), another son of Aleksandr II; he was later governor-general of Moscow and was assassinated by a revolutionary.

247. The grand duke who stole his mother's diamonds was Nikolai Konstantinovich, son of Konstantin Nikolayevich and Aleksandra Iosifovna (1830–1912), who was born in 1850.

249. Pyotr Lavrovich Lavrov (1823–1900) was a Russian political writer who was exiled in 1866 and escaped abroad in 1870; he was influential among Russian refugees and in Russia itself as a moderate socialist. Dmitri Ivanovich Pisarev (1840–1868) was a leading writer in *Sovremennik*; he was influential as an extreme nihilist (in the original sense), was arrested in 1862, and was imprisoned until his death. Velikorus (the Great Russian) was a group of intellectuals who produced a paper with that name in 1861; it is still not known who they were. The first Zemlya i Volya (Land and Liberty) was a populist group formed in 1861; its members were soon arrested, but for a few months it united the various revolutionary tendencies, and the name was revived by a much larger organization in the 1870's.

251. "Madame Kohanovsky" = Nadezhda Dmitrievna Khvosh-chinskaya (1825–1889), a well-known writer who used the pseudonym V. Krestovski. Vsevolod Vladimirovich Krestovski (1840–1895) was a well-known writer in the mid-nineteenth century.

252. The "vulgar theatre" was the Berg. *La Belle Hélène* was performed at the Aleksandrinski theatre, with Vera Alekseyevna Lyadova (1839–1870) in the title role. Dmitri Vladimirovich Kara-kozov (1840–1866) began revolutionary activity in 1861; he became a member of Ishutin's organization, and made an individual attempt to assassinate Aleksandr II on April 4, 1866; he was hanged on October 3.

253. Nikolai Andreyevich Ishutin (1840–1879) began revolutionary activity in 1863 and formed his Organizatsiya (Organization) in 1865; its members were arrested after Karakozov, and Ishutin was condemned to death but reprieved; he went mad and died in prison. The quotation is from Heine.

256. "Adrian Saburov" = Aleksei Dmitrievich Oboleshev (1854–1881), alias Saburov, a member of Zemlya i Volya (Land and Liberty), who took part in Kropotkin's escape from prison and in the assassination of Mezentsov. He was arrested in 1879, and died in the Peter-Paul Fortress.

259. Ventseslav Leopoldovich Gruber (1814–1890), the Russian anatomist, was professor at the St. Petersburg Medical Academy from 1858.

260. Sofia Vasilievna Kovalevskaya (1850–1891) was professor of mathematics at Stockholm University from 1884. Karl Weierstrass (1815–1897) was professor of mathematics at Berlin University from 1864.

261. Russia invaded the Balkans in April, 1877; the Turks were forced to accept the Treaty of San Stefano in March, 1878. The "greater 'criminal'" of the two nurses was Sofia Nikolayevna Lavrova (1841–1916), sister of Aleksandr's wife Vera, who had been adopted by N. N. Muraviov; she was involved in the revolutionary movement, imprisoned and exiled, and later lived in France.

263. Nadezhda Vasilievna Stasova (1822–1895) was an active feminist leader. Nikolai Aleksandrovich Korf (1834–1883) was a well-known educationist.

265. Aleksei Kropotkin died on September 7, 1871, and was buried in the church of Ioann Predtecha (John the Precursor).

266. "General N——" = Pyotr Pavlovich Durnovo, an administrator who was for a time governor of Moscow. His daughter, Yelizaveta Petrovna Durnovo (1854–1910) was an active revolutionary from the 1870's to 1907, when she emigrated to France, where she committed suicide. Natalia Aleksandrovna Armfeldt (1850–1887) began revolutionary activity in the early 1870's, was arrested and released in 1874, was arrested again in 1879, imprisoned until 1884, and then sent to Siberia, where she died; Kennan met her at Kara in November, 1885.

268. Kropotkin left Russia in February, 1872.

270. Charles Fourier (1772–1837) was a French utopian socialist with libertarian tendencies; Henri de Saint-Simon (1760–1825) was a French utopian socialist with authoritarian tendencies; Robert Owen (1771–1858) was the main founder of the trade-union and cooperative movement in Britain. Pierre Dupont (1821–1870) was a French revolutionary singer. Young Italy, Young Germany, Young Hungary, etc., were the titles of progressive nationalist movements.

274. Ferdinand Lassalle (1825–1864), the main founder of the German socialist movement, formed the Allgemeiner Deutscher Arbeiterverein (General German Workers Union) in 1863; the Marxist Sozialdemokratische Arbeiterpartei (Social-Democratic Workers Party) was formed in 1869, and they merged in 1875. Kropotkin's sister-in-law at Zurich was Sofia Lavrova.

276. Nikolai Isaakovich Utin (1845–1883) began revolutionary activity in the early 1860's, fled from Russia in 1863, and joined the revolutionary refugees in Switzerland. "Madame Olga" = Olga S. Levashova, ˉa Russian revolutionary who also settled in Switzerland and patronized revolutionary activity there. They became associated in 1868, and with her money and his ability they became the leading Russian Marxists in Switzerland, but in 1872 they abandoned revolutionary activity and became reformist socialists. In 1877 Utin recanted and was pardoned by the Russian government, and in 1880 he returned to Russia and became an army contractor.

278. *The Career of a Nihilist* was a novel by Stepniak written in English and published in London in 1889 (Kropotkin edited a Russian translation published in Geneva in 1898). The meeting at which Kropotkin realized he must join the revolutionary movement was held in memory of the Paris Commune on its first anniversary, March 18, 1872.

279. "Monsieur A." = Amberny. The *Journal de Genève* was (and still is) a leading Geneva newspaper. The Geneva builders' strike of 1869 was encouraged by the local section of the First International, under the leadership of Bakunin. The new strike was threatened in March, 1872.

280. Nikolai Ivanovich Zhukovski (1842–1895) began revolutionary activity in the early 1860's, fled from Russia in 1863, and settled in Switzerland; there he was closely associated with Bakunin, and played a leading part in the Swiss anarchist movement for many years.

281. The Fédération Jurassienne was formed in 1871 by Bakunin-ists driven out of the Fédération Romande by the Marxists in 1870.

282. James Guillaume (1844–1916) was a teacher at Le Locle, where he formed a branch of the First International in 1866, until he was dismissed for his political activity in 1869, and became a printer; he was one of the leading anti-Marxists in the International, and was expelled with Bakunin in 1872. For ten years he produced anarchist papers—*Le Progrès* (Progress) from 1868 to 1870, *Solidarité* (Solidarity) from 1870 to 1871, and the *Bulletin* of the Jura Federation from 1872 to 1878. Then he gave up political activity and went to France, where he became a well-known educationist, and took French nationality in 1889. He returned to political activity at the time of the syndicalist movement in the 1890's; he and Kropotkin resumed contact in 1902; during the last ten years of his life he produced a long history of the First International and edited the works of Bakunin; he supported the First World War. He did not translate

for a living in 1872, and when he did so, in 1875, he was paid 60 francs for 32 pages; the local paper was *Lectures Populaires*, which began publication in April, 1872.

283. The "French communard" was André Bastélica (1845–1884), a Corsican printer who was the leading Bakuninist in Marseille in the late 1860's and took part in the Lyon Commune of 1870 and the Paris Commune of 1871. Benoît Malon (1841–1893) was a journalist who became the leading anarchist in the Paris section of the First International during the 1860's; he lived in Switzerland from 1871 to 1880, and wrote a book on the Paris Commune, *La troisième défaite du prolétariat français*, which was published in 1871; when he returned to France he became a reformist socialist. Eugène Varlin (1839–1871), who was one of the earliest anarchists in the First International during the 1860's, led the rising which began the Paris Commune, was arrested and shot. Jean-Louis Pindy (1840–1917), who was a Blanquist in the First International, settled in Switzerland in 1872; he helped to produce *L'Avant-Garde* (The Vanguard) from 1877 to 1878, and was later active in the free-thought movement.

284. Charles Delécluze (1809–1871) was a journalist who took part in the risings of 1830 and 1848 as well as that of 1871; he was the last military commander of the Paris Commune, and died on the barricades.

285. Raoul Rigault (1846–1871), the youngest leader of the Paris Commune, was in charge of the hostages as Procurator General and Chief of Police, but he was killed in the May street-fighting before their execution began. Gaston Gallifet (1830–1909), who commanded a brigade of the army which suppressed the Paris Commune under the orders of the government at Versailles, behaved particularly cruelly. *Le livre rouge de la justice rurale*, a documentary account of the suppression of the Commune, was prepared by Jules Guesde and published in 1871. The *Standard* (now the *Evening Standard*), the *Daily Telegraph*, and the *Times* were already leading daily newspapers in London; *Le Figaro* was even then the leading conservative daily newspaper in Paris.

286. Adhémar Schwitzguébel (1844–1895) joined the First International in 1866 and became a Bakuninist; he was a leading member of the Jura Federation with strong syndicalist tendencies; Guillaume published a collection of his writings, *Quelques écrits*, in 1908.

288. Bakunin lived at Locarno from October, 1870, to September, 1872; Guillaume's paper at Le Locle was *Le Progrès*; they met in 1869. Giuseppe Fanelli (1827–1877), an Italian parliamentary deputy who had taken part in the Risorgimento, became a Bakuninist

in 1866, and traveled to Spain, where he founded the anarchist movement in 1868.

295. Kropotkin returned to Russia in May, 1872; in the same month he resigned from the Ministry of Internal Affairs, and was given the honorary rank of Collegiate Assessor.

301. Chernyshevski's novel *Chto delat?* (What Is To Be Done?), which was written in prison, was published in 1863. *V narod!* (To the People!) was the key phrase of an influential article by Herzen in *Kolokol* in November, 1861.

303. "Kelnitz" = Dmitri Aleksandrovich Klements (1848–1914), who began revolutionary activity in the 1860's, lived abroad from 1875 to 1878, was arrested in 1879, and was sent to Siberia in 1881; he made several expeditions in Central Asia and became a prominent ethnologist.

304. The Chaikovski Circle (*Kruzhok Chaikovtsev*) was one of the most important groups in the Russian populist movement. Nikolai Vasilievich Chaikovski (1850–1926) was active from 1869, and led the group from 1871 until he left Russia in 1874; he lived in the United States and then in England, where he was active for a time in the anarchist movement. He returned to Russia in 1907 and became a prominent Social Revolutionary leader; after the 1917 Revolution he was for a time the head of an anti-Bolshevik government at Archangel; he left Russia in 1918 and settled in the United States. Sergei Gennadievich Nechayev (1847–1882) began revolutionary activity in 1869, and during that year he left Russia, visited Bakunin in Switzerland, returned to Russia, formed a secret group in Moscow, murdered one of its members (Ivan Ivanovich Ivanov), and escaped to Switzerland; he was extradited to Russia in 1872 and imprisoned in 1873. He continued revolutionary activity in the Peter-Paul Fortress, but died there after ten years' solitary confinement.

305. The best known of Lassalle's many works was the *Arbeiterprogramm* (Workers' Program) of 1862. Vasili Vasilievich Bervi (1829–1918) was a civil servant who was dismissed for protesting against government policy in 1861, then detained and exiled in many parts of Russia until 1870; he used his experience in his first book, *Polozheniye rabochego klassa v Rossii* (The Situation of the Working Class in Russia), which was published under the pseudonym N. Flerovski in 1869; he was arrested in 1873 and exiled until he escaped to England in 1893.

310. The officer who had been interested in the Zemstvos was Leonid Emmanuilovich Shishko (1852–1910); he was arrested in 1874 and imprisoned and exiled until he escaped to England in 1890.

313. John Wyclif (c. 1330–1384), the English religious reformer, did not preach to the people, though his followers, the Lollards, did. The "peasant dissenters in South Russia" were the Shtundists, a baptist sect in the Ukraine.

315. The Executive Committee (*Ispolnitelny Komitet*) was the central organ of Narodnaya Volya (the People's Will, or the People's Liberty) from 1879; it eventually carried out the assassination of the Tsar.

317. Kropotkin included an account of his expedition in Finland in his major investigation of the ice age, which was published in the *Zapiski* of the Imperial Russian Geographical Society in 1876. Sofia Lvovna Perovskaya (1853–1881) began revolutionary activity in 1872, was arrested in 1874, was released and exiled in 1878, and became a leader of Narodnaya Volya in 1879; she led the assassination of Aleksandr II in 1881 and was hanged. Her father was Lyov Nikolayevich Perovski (1816–1890), vice-governor of St. Petersburg from 1861 to 1865 and governor from 1865 to 1866 (he was dismissed after Karakozov's attempt to assassinate Aleksandr II); her mother was Varvara Stepanovna Veselovskaya.

318. The Kornilov sisters—Vera (1848–1875), Lyubov (1852–1892) and Aleksandra (1853–1930)—were daughters of Ivan Kornilov, grandson of the founder of the Kornilov porcelain business in 1791.

319. Mikhail Vasilievich Kupriyanov (1854–1878) was arrested in 1874 and died in prison. "Varvara B." = Varvara Nikolayevna Batyushkova (1852–1894), who was arrested in 1875 and imprisoned and exiled. Sergei Mikhailovich Kravchinski (1851–1895) began revolutionary activity in 1872, left Russia in 1873, joined the Slav rising against the Turks in the Balkans in 1875 and an anarchist rising in Italy in 1877, returned to Russia and became a leader of the second Zemlya i Volya (Land and Liberty), assassinated Mezentsov, left Russia again in 1878, and settled in England, where he was active as a propagandist for the Russian revolutionary movement.

320. Henry Morton Stanley (1841–1909), the Anglo-American explorer, published *How I Found Livingstone* in 1872.

322. Dmitri Mikhailovich Rogachov (1851–1884) was very active in the movement to the people in St. Petersburg and on the Volga and Don; he was arrested in 1876 and sent to prison, where he died.

323. Porfiri Ivanovich Voinaralski (1844–1898) began revolutionary activity in 1861 and was arrested several times; he was arrested in 1874, imprisoned until 1883, and exiled until 1897.

324. Kravchinski's pamphlets were *Slovo na veliki pyatok* (The

Lay of the Great Five-Kopeck Piece) in the style of Félicité de Lamennais (1782–1854), the French Christian socialist writer; and *Skazka o Mudritse Naumovne* (The Tale of Mudritsa Naumovna), a fairy-tale exposition of Marxist socialism. Kropotkin also wrote two pamphlets for the Chaikovski Circle—*Skazka o chetyryokh bratiakh* (The Tale of Four Brothers) and *Yemelian Ivanovich Pugachov* (a history of the Pugachov rising), both printed in Switzerland in 1873 —in collaboration with Lyov Aleksandrovich Tikhomirov (1852–1923), a member of the Chaikovski Circle who was later a leading member of Zemlya i Volya and Narodnaya Volya, but became a reactionary in 1888.

325. Anatoli Ivanovich Serdyukov was frequently arrested, and committed suicide in prison in 1878. Henry Thomas Buckle (1821–1862) was an English social historian with liberal rationalist views. John Stuart Mill (1806–1873) was a British utilitarian philosopher who became a moderate socialist. John William Draper (1811–1882) was an American scientist who became a rationalist historian of ideas. Friedrich Spielhagen (1829–1911) was a German novelist with strong social interests. Kropotkin's lectures to the St. Petersburg workers were about the First International and the Paris Commune.

326. The other two members in contact with the workers were Sergei Silych Sinegub (1851–1907) and Nikolai Apollonovich Charushin (1851–1937), who both spent much time in prison and exile.

327. Émile Erckmann (1822–1899) and Alexandre Chatrian (1826–1890) were French historical novelists who wrote together under the name Erckmann-Chatrian; their *L'histoire d'un paysan* (The Story of a Peasant), a popular account of the French Revolution, was published in four volumes from 1868 to 1870; the Russian adaptation, which was written by Klements, was called *Istoriya odnogo frantsuzskogo krestianina* (The Story of a French Peasant) and was printed in Switzerland in 1873.

330. The settlement raided in November, 1873, was in the Narva district of St. Petersburg, and was connected with the Tortoni factory.

331. The settlement raided in January, 1874, was in the Vyborg district of St. Petersburg, and was connected with the Nikolski factory. Aleksandr Vasilievich Nizovkin (1854–1879) was arrested in 1874 and betrayed his friends; in 1878 he was sentenced to imprisonment but released.

333. Kropotkin's speech to the Imperial Russian Geographical Society was given on March 21, and was reported in its *Zapiski* on August 15, 1874. Nikolai Pavlovich Barbot-de-Marni (1829–

1877) was professor of geology at the St. Petersburg Mining Institute from 1863.

334. Kropotkin was arrested on March 25, 1874.

336. The "Secret Department" was the Preobrazhenski Prikaz (the Preobrazhenski Department), which was established in the 1690's; it was followed by the Preobrazhenskaya Kantselyariya (the Preobrazhenski Chancery) in the early eighteenth century, and then by the Tainaya Kantselyariya (the Secret Chancery) under the empresses Yelizaveta and Yekaterina later in the eighteenth century. Burkhardt Christoph Münnich (1683–1767), known in Russia as Khristofor Antonovich Minikh, was a German adventurer in the Russian service who was briefly prime minister during the reign of Anna Leopoldovna (1718–1745), from 1740 to 1741, but was imprisoned from 1741 to 1762; the specialist in terror was actually his rival, Ernst Johann Biron (1690–1772), another German adventurer who was Lord Chamberlain during the reign of Anna Ivanovna (1693–1740), from 1730 until he was supplanted by Minikh in 1740.

337. The procurator (public prosecutor) was Maslovski.

343. Aleksei Petrovich (1690–1718) was murdered by or at the orders of his father. Tarakanova, a pretender to the Russian throne who claimed to be a daughter of the empress Yelizaveta (1741–1762), died soon after her arrest in 1775. Yekaterina (Catherine) II deposed her husband, Pyotr III, in 1762 and had him murdered. Taras Shevchenko (1814–1861), the greatest Ukrainian poet, was arrested for anti-Russian activity in 1847 and imprisoned and exiled until 1857. Dostoyevski was arrested for being a member of the moderate socialist Petrashevski Circle in 1849 and imprisoned until 1853.

344. Bakunin was arrested in Dresden in 1849 and imprisoned in Germany from 1849 to 1850 and in Austria from 1850 to 1851 (being chained to the wall at Olmütz for two months), before being returned to Russia and imprisoned from 1851 to 1857; he did not in fact manage to maintain his vigor, and wrote a detailed confession to Nikolai I in 1851.

346. The governor of the Peter-Paul Fortress was Bogorodski.

347. George Lewes (1817–1878) was an English writer who lived with the novelist George Eliot as her husband; his *Physiology of Common Life* was published in 1859. Eugène Sue (1804–1857), the French novelist, published *Les mystères du peuple* (Mysteries of the People) between 1849 and 1856. Aleksandr Kropotkin went to Switzerland in 1872 and returned to Russia in 1874; the brothers met in

September. Aleksandr's child who died of cholera was called Pyotr, and the one who died of tuberculosis was called Aleksandr.

348. John Bright (1811–1889) was a Radical leader in Parliament from 1843 to 1887. Louis Blanc (1811–1882) and Alexandre-Auguste Ledru-Rollin (1807–1874) were moderate socialists who were members of the provisional government after the 1848 Revolution; the Paris workers rose against it in June, 1848, and were savagely suppressed. Lavrov lived in Zurich from 1872 to 1874.

351. Kropotkin's first volume on the ice age was published in the *Zapiski* of the Imperial Russian Geographical Society in 1876.

353. The son of the governor was Nikolai Nikolayevich Bogorodski (1853–1920), who began revolutionary activity in 1874 and was later the Narodnaya Volya contact in the Peter-Paul Fortress; he was arrested in 1881 and sent to Siberia, where he settled.

354. Kropotkin met Yelena and Aleksandr on December 21, his name day.

355. Aleksandr Kropotkin was arrested in December, 1874 (he had been arrested for a brief period in 1858 for possessing a copy of Emerson's *Self-Reliance*). Lavrov published *Vperyod!* (Forward!) in London from 1874 to 1876.

357. Aleksandr Kropotkin lived in Siberia from 1875 to 1886; George Kennan met him in Tomsk in August, 1885.

359. The woman prisoner was Platonova. The peasant was Govorukha.

361. The Marquis of Posa is a character in Schiller's play *Don Carlos* (1787). The Decembrist whom Kropotkin knew in Siberia was Dmitri Irinarkhovich Zavalishin (1804–1892), who was exiled to Siberia in 1826; Kropotkin met him in Chita in October, 1862, and was impressed by his opposition to the Russian authorities there.

365. The doctor who transferred Kropotkin to the Nikolayevski Military Hospital was Ivan Mikhailovich Sechenov (1829–1905).

369. The lady with the balloon was M. P. Leshern-fon-Gertsfeld.

370. The man who ate cherries was Aron Isaakovich Zundelevich (1854–1923), later a leading member of Zemlya i Volya and Narodnaya Volya, who was arrested in 1879 and imprisoned and exiled until 1905. The gray bungalow was hired by M. P. Leshern-fon-Gertsfeld and Eduard Eduardovich Veimar.

371. Apollinari Kontski (1825–1879) was a Polish violinist and composer.

372. The man in the carriage was Orest Eduardovich Veimar

(1845–1885), brother of Eduard, a doctor who had treated the Empress Mariya Aleksandrovna; he was arrested in 1878 and sent to Siberia, where he died.

373. The horse, which was called Varvara, was used for other escapes. The man who diverted the soldier was Yuri Nikolayevich Bogdanovich (1850–1888), who was later a leading member of Narodnaya Volya, was involved in the assassination of Aleksandr II, was arrested in 1882, and died in prison.

374. The coachman was Mark Andreyevich Natanson (1850–1919), who in 1869 had formed a student group which later grew into the Chaikovski Circle, and was arrested in 1871 and exiled; he was a leading member of Zemlya i Volya, and was again arrested in 1877 and exiled; in 1890 he formed a populist party and was yet again arrested in 1894 and exiled; he left Russia in 1904 and became active in the Social-Revolutionary Party; in 1918 he became a leading Left Social-Revolutionary.

376. The friend who accompanied Kropotkin to the Russian frontier was Aleksandr Konstantinovich Levashov (1851–1902), a member of the Chaikovski Circle, with whose passport and under whose name Kropotkin traveled for four years.

377. Sofia Lavrova was actually released after less than a month.

378. Kropotkin arrived in England in August, 1876; he did not return to Russia until 1917.

380. Paganel, the geographer in Jules Verne's *Les enfants du Capitaine Grant* (1867–1868), learns Portuguese by mistake instead of Spanish. *Nature* is a scientific weekly paper published in London; Kropotkin's first note about the Norwegian North Atlantic expedition was published on July 13, 1876. In the late 1860's the Kropotkin brothers had translated *The Philosophy of Geology* (1863) by David Page (1814–1879), the British geologist, and *Principles of Biology* (1864–1867) by Herbert Spencer.

381. John Scott Keltie (1840–1927), the British geographer, was sub-editor of *Nature* from 1873, and was later librarian, assistant secretary and secretary of the Royal Geographical Society, and editor of its *Geographical Journal*.

382. Kropotkin's review of his own book on the ice age was published in *Nature* on June 28, 1877; no review of his book on Asian orography was published.

383. The Slavs rose against Turkish rule in the Balkans in 1875; Stepniak, Klements and many others went there that summer; the *Daily News* was an English liberal newspaper. Kropotkin went to Switzerland in January, 1877.

387. The Hague Congress of the International was held in September, 1872. The anti-authoritarian International held congresses at St. Imier in 1872, at Geneva in 1873, at Brussels in 1874, at Berne in 1876, and at Verviers in 1877. Bakunin died in Berne at the age of sixty-two. Edmé MacMahon (1808–1893) was a French soldier who commanded the army which crushed the Paris Commune in 1871 and was president of France from 1873 to 1879; he attempted to bring about the restoration of the monarchy in 1873. Henri de Bourbon, Comte de Chambord (1820–1883), was the pretender to the French throne from 1836, under the name Henri V; the main reason for the failure of the restoration was that he quarreled with MacMahon.

388. Léon Gambetta (1838–1882) was a republican politician from the 1860's, who led the patriotic reaction to the defeat by Prussia in 1870 and the republican resistance to the monarchists during the 1870's; he was prime minister from 1881 to 1882. Georges Clemenceau (1841–1929) was a radical politician from the 1860's, who led the radical resistance to the monarchists during the 1870's; he was prime minister twice after 1906. The Spanish monarchy was restored after a short republican regime in 1874.

389. Louis-Auguste Blanqui (1805–1881) was the main revolutionary socialist leader in France from the 1830's to the 1870's. The Cantonalists were republicans who rose against the Spanish government in 1873 in favor of an extreme federalist system. Bismarck began a twelve-year campaign against the socialists in 1878.

391. The *Bulletin de la Fédération Jurassienne* was published from 1872 to 1878.

392. Auguste Spichiger (1842–1919) was active in the labor movement during the 1870's, and helped to produce *L'Avant-Garde* from 1877 to 1878. Élisée Reclus (1830–1905), the French geographer, was also an active anarchist who lived in exile in Britain, America, Switzerland and Belgium for much of his life; he published the *Nouvelle géographie universelle* in Paris in twenty volumes from 1876 to 1894. Gustave Lefrançais (1826–1901) was a teacher who became the first chairman of the Paris Commune and was later responsible for finance; he wrote a book on the Commune, *Étude sur le mouvement communaliste à Paris en 1871*, which was published in 1872; he returned to France in 1881 and became a reformist socialist.

393. Paul Brousse (1844–1912) began political activity as a radical in 1869 and became an anarchist in 1872; he had to leave France because of his support for the Commune, and lived in Spain in 1873 and in Switzerland from 1873 to 1879; he led the Berne section of the Jura Federation, and edited the *Arbeiterzeitung* (Workers' Gazette) from 1876 to 1877 and *L'Avant-Garde* from 1877

to 1878; he was imprisoned for a month for leading a demonstration at Berne in 1877 and for two months for editing *L'Avant-Garde* in 1879, and then expelled from Switzerland.

394. Carlo Cafiero (1846–1892) was a Marxist in the International who became an anarchist in 1871 and was active in Switzerland and Italy until he became a social democrat in 1882; in 1883 he went mad, and he died in a lunatic asylum. Errico Malatesta (1853–1932) joined the International in 1871 and immediately became an anarchist; he was active not only in Switzerland and Italy but in many other places in Europe, North Africa, and North and South America; in 1919 he returned to Italy permanently; he was the main figure in the Italian anarchist movement for half a century. Malatesta and Cafiero led an abortive rising in the province of Benevento, near Naples, in April, 1877.

395. Nikolai Vasilievich Sokolov (1832–1889) left the Russian army in 1863 and became a radical journalist, writing in *Russkoye Slovo* (the Russian Word); he was arrested and exiled in 1867, escaped from Russia in 1872, and settled in Switzerland in 1873. Paul-Louis Courier (1772–1825) was a French scholar and pamphleteer who opposed the royalist reaction after the restoration of the monarchy in 1815, and was murdered. Severino Albarracín was a Spanish schoolteacher who led the first general strike in Spain, at Alcoy in 1873, and fled to Switzerland; he returned to Spain in 1877. Otto Rinke (b. 1853) and Emil Werner (b. 1846) were leaders of the German Swiss anarchist movement who helped to produce the *Arbeiterzeitung* from 1876 to 1877; they were later active in Britain and the United States.

396. Hippolyte Ferré (d. 1913)—brother of Charles-Théophile Ferré (1845–1871), a leading member of the Paris Commune, who was shot—and P. Jeallot were French Blanquists who lived in Switzerland during the 1870's.

397. The demonstration with a red flag at Berne was on March 18, 1877 (the sixth anniversary of the Paris Commune). The Annual Congress of the Jura Federation was held from August 4 to 6. The demonstration with a red flag at St. Imier was on August 5; this was the nearest Kropotkin ever came to fighting in his life.

404. The Congress of the International was held at Verviers from September 6 to 8. The Socialist World Congress was held at Ghent from September 9 to 15.

405. Kropotkin left Ghent for Antwerp on September 11 and sailed for England.

406. Kropotkin's study of the history of the French Revolution

led to several articles and finally a book, *The Great French Revolution* (1909). Andrea Costa (1851–1910) was an Italian republican who joined the International in 1871 and became a Bakuninist; he was very active in Italy and Switzerland during the 1870's, and took refuge in France in 1877; he was imprisoned in 1878 and expelled from France in 1879, by which time he had abandoned anarchism; he became a leading reformist socialist in Italy. Jules Guesde, whose real name was Jules-Mathieu Basile (1845–1922), was a French radical journalist who became a Bakuninist in the early 1870's, and then the leading French Marxist in the late 1870's.

407. Costa and Pédoussaut were arrested on March 22, 1878, and were sent to prison for two years and thirteen months, respectively. From Switzerland Kropotkin went straight to Spain, where he stayed from May to August.

408. Turgenev lived in or near Paris from 1871 until his death in 1883. He published the stories of *Zapiski okhotnika* (Sportsman's Notes) from 1847 to 1851. Paul Bert (1833–1886) was a French physiologist and republican politician; Paul Reclus (1847–1914), nephew of Élisée Reclus, was a French surgeon. Georges Cuvier (1769–1832) was a French anatomist.

409. Flaubert, Daudet and Zola were all close friends of Turgenev in Paris. The play was *Madame Caverlet* by Émile Augier (1820–1889), which was performed at the Vaudeville theatre in February, 1876.

411. *Nov* (Virgin Soil) was published in 1877. Mark Matveyevich Antokolski (1842–1902) was a Russian sculptor who spent much of his life abroad; he made a sculpture of Turgenev in Paris in 1880.

412. Turgenev's lecture on Hamlet and Don Quixote was published in *Sovremennik* in January, 1860. Ippolit Nikitich Myshkin (1848–1885) began revolutionary activity in 1873, tried to organize the escape of Chernyshevski in 1875, but was arrested; he made a remarkable speech at the Trial of 193 and was sentenced to ten years' imprisonment; he escaped but was recaptured, and was eventually executed for insulting the governor of Shlisselburg prison near St. Petersburg.

413. Aleksandr III issued the manifesto proclaiming his intention of maintaining the autocracy on April 29, 1881.

415. At the Trial of 193, five people were sentenced to prison for ten years, ten for nine years, and three for five years; forty were exiled; most were freed. Nikolai Vladimirovich Mezentsov (1827–1878) was chief of the police and head of the Third Section from 1876. Bogolyubov, whose real name was Aleksei Stepanovich Yemelianov (1852–1885), was arrested for his part in the workers' demonstration

at the Kazan Cathedral Square in St. Petersburg on December 6, 1876, and sentenced to fifteen years' imprisonment; he was flogged in prison in St. Petersburg in July, 1877, and went mad. Vera Ivanovna Zasulich (1849–1919) began revolutionary activity in the 1860's, was arrested in 1869, imprisoned until 1871, and exiled until 1873; she shot Trepov on January 24, 1878, and was acquitted on April 1, 1878; she later became a leading Russian Marxist.

416. The *Revue des Deux Mondes* was published in Paris from 1829 to 1940. Aleksandr Mikhailovich Gorchakov (1798–1883) was the Russian minister of foreign affairs from 1856 to 1882, and led the Russian delegation at the Congress of Berlin. Emil Hoedel, a socialist tinsmith, tried to shoot Wilhelm I in Berlin on May 11, 1878; he was hanged. Karl Nobiling (1840–1878), a republican scholar, shot at Wilhelm I in Berlin on June 2, 1878; he died from his own wounds. Juan Oliva Moncasi, a socialist cooper, shot at Alfonso XII in Madrid on October 25, 1878; he was garrotted. Giovanni Passanante, a republican cook, tried to stab Umberto I in Naples on November 17, 1878; he was sentenced to death but reprieved.

417. *L'Avant-Garde* (The Vanguard) was published at La Chaux-de-Fonds from June, 1877, to December, 1878. Brousse was tried in April, 1879, sent to prison, and expelled from Switzerland in June; he went to Belgium and then England, and returned to France in 1880, when he began activity as a leading reformist socialist. *Le Révolté* (The Rebel) began publication at Geneva on February 22, 1879; it moved to Paris in April, 1885, and the name was changed to *La Révolte* (Rebellion) in September, 1887; it ceased publication in March, 1894, but was revived in May, 1895, as *Les Temps Nouveaux* (New Times), and continued publication until August, 1914. François Dumartheray (1842–1931) and Georges Herzig (1856–1923) attended the London Congress in 1881 and were later involved in the Swiss anarchist paper *Le Réveil* (The Alarm); Kropotkin met them again when he visited Switzerland in 1909.

421. The Imprimerie Jurassienne (Jura Press) started in May, 1879. Jean Grave (1854–1939) became an anarchist in the 1870's; in 1883 he took over *Le Révolté*, and he edited it and its successors up to 1914; he also wrote several books; he was imprisoned from 1894 to 1895; he supported the First World War in 1914.

423. *Paroles d'un Révolté* (Words of a Rebel) was published in Paris in 1885. Volume 6 of the *Nouvelle géographie universelle— L'Asie russe*—was published in 1881.

424. Kropotkin married Sofia Grigorievna Ananieva-Rabinovich (1856–1938) on October 8, 1878; she came from a bourgeois Jewish family in Kiev, grew up in Tomsk, became a revolutionary agitator

in 1873. She had gone to Switzerland to recover her health. Chillon Castle was captured by the citizens of Vevey and Montreux in 1798 during the revolutionary upheaval following the French invasion. The Bourla Papey was a rising of peasants round Lake Geneva in 1802; dissatisfied with the survival of feudal dues after 1798, they seized and burnt the archives recording them (the dues were legally abolished in 1804). *Aux jeunes gens* (To the Young) was published in *Le Révolté* in 1880 and as a pamphlet in 1881; the first English translation appeared in 1885 (it has been the most frequently translated and widely circulated of all anarchist writings).

425. The Trial of Fifty was held in Moscow in March, 1877; the leading figures were Pyotr Alekseyevich Alekseyev (1849–1891) and Sofia Illarionovna Bardina (1853–1883). The Trial of 193 was held in St. Petersburg from October, 1877, to January, 1878; the leading figure was Ippolit Nikitich Myshkin. Most of the accused in these two trials had been members of the Chaikovski Circle. The Trial of the Dolgushin Circle was held in Moscow in July, 1874; Aleksandr Vasilievich Dolgushin (1848–1885) began revolutionary activity in 1866, formed a group in St. Petersburg in 1872, moved to Moscow in 1873, was arrested and died in prison.

426. Viktoriya Leontievna Gukovskaya (1864–1881) was a leader of a violent demonstration against Kovalski's trial in Odessa on July 24, 1878; Clärchen is a character in Goethe's play *Egmont* (1788).

427. The members of the Dolgushin Circle held in Kharkov prison were treated so badly that they went on hunger strike; Dolgushin wrote a pamphlet about the conditions, *Zazhivo pogrebyonnye* (Buried Alive), which was smuggled out of the prison and published in 1878. Ivan Martynovich Kovalski (1850–1878) began revolutionary activity and formed a group in Odessa in 1876; when they were raided by police on January 30, 1878, they defended themselves; Kovalski was hanged on August 2, 1878. A state of emergency was proclaimed in the metropolitan areas of European Russia on April 5, 1879. The boy who posted a revolutionary proclamation was Iosif Isaakovich Rozovski, a Kiev student, who was arrested in December, 1879, and hanged in March, 1880.

428. Mezentsov was stabbed by Stepniak in St. Petersburg on August 4, 1878, in revenge for Kovalski; Baron Geiking was stabbed by Grigori Anfimovich Popko in Kiev on May 25, 1878; Dmitri Kropotkin was shot by Grigori Goldenberg in Kharkov on February 9, 1879.

429. Aleksandr II was formally sentenced to death by the Executive Committee of Narodnaya Volya on August 26, 1879. Aleksandr

Konstantinovich Soloviov (1846–1879) began revolutionary activity in the late 1870's, and attempted to shoot Aleksandr II on April 2, 1879; he was hanged on May 28.

430. Yekaterina Mikhailovna Dolgorukaya (1847–1922) became the ward of Aleksandr II after the death of her father in 1860; she became his mistress in 1866. Mariya Aleksandrovna died in May, 1880, and in July Aleksandr married Yekaterina and made her Princess Yurievskaya. The "well-known Russian doctor" was Orest Veimar, who helped Kropotkin to escape from prison. Mikhail Tarielovich Loris-Melikov (1825–1888) was made governor-general of Kharkov in January, 1879, head of the Supreme Administrative Commission in February, 1880, and minister of the interior in August, 1880. Part of the Winter Palace was blown up on February 5, 1880, by Stepan Nikolayevich Khalturin (1857–1882), who began revolutionary activity in 1875, joined Narodnaya Volya in 1879, and got a job in the palace as a workman; the Tsar was not harmed, and Khalturin was not caught.

431. Yekaterina Mikhailovna (1827–1894) was the daughter of Mikhail Pavlovich and Yelena Pavlovna.

432. Nikolai Ivanovich Rysakov (1861–1881) was a worker who joined Narodnaya Volya in 1880; he was the only person arrested at the time of the assassination, and betrayed all his friends, but he was still hanged. Plevna, in northern Bulgaria, was attacked by the Russians during the Turkish war of 1877–1878, and fell after a five months' siege in December, 1877. Ignati Yoakhimovich Grinevitski (1856–1881) was a Polish student (the Polish form of his name was Ignacy Hryniewiecki) who joined Narodnaya Volya in 1879. Ivan Pantaleimovich Yemilianov (1861–1916) was a student who joined Narodnaya Volya in 1880; he was arrested later in 1881 and imprisoned until 1905.

434. Sébastien le Prestre de Vauban (1633–1717) was a French military engineer who specialized in fortification. The Okhrana, or Okhrannoye Otdeleniye (Protective Section) was the main political police organization from 1881 to 1917.

435. Vladimir Aleksandrovich was now military governor of St. Petersburg. Mikhail Dmitrievich Skobelev (1843–1882) was a Russian soldier who distinguished himself not only in the Turkish war of 1877–1878, but also in conquering much of Central Asia.

436. Loris-Melikov resigned in May, 1881, and left Russia. Ignatiev was minister of internal affairs from May, 1881, to May, 1882. Louis Andrieux (1840–1931) was a French lawyer and journalist who

was chief of the Paris police from 1879 to 1881. The pamphlet containing information about Loris-Melikov, *Konstitutsiya Grafa Loris-Melikova* (The Constitution of Count Loris-Melikov), was published in London in 1893. Jules Ferry (1832–1893) was prime minister of France for the second time from 1883 to 1885; he was an enthusiastic imperialist.

437. The International Revolutionary Socialist Congress (which was dominated by anarchists) was held in London from July 14 to July 20, 1881. Joseph Cowen (1831–1900) was a radical journalist and politician who supported European revolutionary movements and was a Liberal member of parliament from 1873 to 1885; he acquired the *Newcastle Chronicle* in 1859 and controlled it until his death; Kropotkin's articles were published anonymously in August and September, 1881. Olga Alekseyevna Novikova (1840–1914) was a Russian reactionary journalist who lived in England during the 1870's and 1880's. The Swiss Federal Council ordered Kropotkin's expulsion on August 23, and he left the country on August 30, 1881.

438. Kropotkin was warned about the death sentence of the Holy League by Lavrov, who got the message indirectly from Loris-Melikov. A report about the plans of the Holy League was published in *Le Révolté* on October 1, 1881. The Russian agent was Arkadi Pavlovich Malshinski (1841–1899), a reactionary journalist.

440. Kropotkin left Thonon in October and arrived in London in November, 1881. Henry George (1839–1897), the American founder of the single-tax movement, was an influential writer and speaker on both sides of the Atlantic; his *Progress and Poverty*, which was published in the United States in 1879, appeared in England in 1881, and in the same year he began his first tour of Britain. John Burns (1858–1943) was a British labor leader who was a militant socialist from 1884 to 1889, a Liberal member of parliament from 1892 to 1918, and a member of the Liberal cabinet from 1905 to 1914; he was one of the main figures in the great dock strike of 1889, and wrote a pamphlet about it with Kropotkin. Henry Hyde Champion (d. 1928) was an army officer who resigned because of Britain's imperialist policies and became an active socialist, in the Democratic Federation and Social Democratic Federation, in the Fabian Society, and in the Scottish Labour Party; he emigrated to Australia in 1892. James Keir Hardie (1856–1915) was the leader of the parliamentary labor movement from his first election as a member of parliament until his death, and the main figure in the Independent Labour Party. The Fabian Society was a group of moderate socialist intellectuals, formed in 1884. William Morris (1834–1896), the English writer and artist, became a socialist in 1883, was active in the Democratic

Federation and the Social Democratic Federation, and in the Fabian Society, and was the main figure in the Socialist League from 1885 to 1890; he was one of the greatest of all English socialist writers.

441. Henry Mayers Hyndman (1842–1921) was the leading British Marxist up to the First World War; in 1880 he read *Das Kapital* and met Karl Marx; in 1881 he formed the Democratic Federation, which became the Social Democratic Federation in 1884 and the British Socialist Party in 1911. Hyndman was its leader until 1916, when he was driven out for supporting the First World War; he formed the National Socialist Party, which became the Social Democratic Federation in 1919 and survived until the Second World War. The inaugural conference of the Democratic Federation was held in June, 1881. Johann Most (1846–1906) was a German socialist who was elected to the Reichstag in 1874 and fled from persecution to England in 1878; he became an anarchist, and in January, 1879, he began publication of *Die Freiheit* (Freedom), the first anarchist paper in Britain; he was arrested in March, 1881, for an article welcoming the assassination of Aleksandr II, and was sentenced to sixteen months' hard labor. In 1882 he was expelled from England and settled in the United States, where he resumed publication of *Die Freiheit* and became the leader of the extreme anarchists.

442. *England for All*, which drew heavily on Marx, was published in 1881. *Justice* began publication in January, 1884, and remained Hyndman's mouthpiece until his death; at first it was financed not only by him but also by William Morris and by Edward Carpenter (1844–1929), another middle-class socialist. In 1886 there were in fact more than three socialist papers; the most important, apart from *Justice*, were *The Christian Socialist*, *The Commonweal*, *Our Corner*, *The Practical Socialist* and *Today*.

443. Kropotkin returned to Thonon in October, 1882. The golden age of the Russian secret police was during the period that Ignatiev was minister of the interior. Dmitri Andreyevich Tolstoi (1823–1889) was minister of education from 1866 to 1880 and minister of internal affairs from 1882. G. P. Sudeikin, head of the Okhrana, was murdered in 1883 by Sergei Petrovich Degayev (1854–1908), a leading member of Narodnaya Volya after 1881 who betrayed all his friends to the police; he left Russia and settled in the United States.

444. Alexander of Battenberg (1857–1893), son of Alexander of Hesse and Julia, Princess of Battenberg, and nephew of empress Mariya Aleksandrovna, was made prince of Bulgaria in 1879 through the influence of Aleksandr II; but he quarreled with Aleksandr III after 1881, and in 1886 he was kidnapped and handed over to

the Russian authorities; he abdicated and joined the Austrian army.
Kropotkin contributed to the ninth, tenth and eleventh editions of the
Encyclopaedia Britannica, which were published in Britain between
1875 and 1911. The Russian constitutionalist paper in Switzerland
was *Volnoye Slovo* (The Free Word), which Malshinski produced from
1881 to 1883.

445. The two members of the Executive Committee in Paris were
Tikhomirov and Mariya Nikolayevna Oshanina (1853–1898). Oshanina
began revolutionary activity in the early 1870's, was a leading member
of Zemlya i Volya and Narodnaya Volya, and left Russia in 1882.
Ignatiev's agent was Niko Yakovlevich Nikoladze (1843–1928), a
Georgian journalist; the agreement was made at the end of 1882,
and Aleksandr III was crowned in May, 1883. The prisoners in the
Shlisselburg prison were freed by the 1905 Revolution; Chernyshevski was released from exile in July, 1883.

447. Georges Boulanger (1837–1891), the French soldier, helped
to suppress the Paris Commune in 1871, became minister of war in
1886, and almost attempted a *coup d'état* in 1889, but lost his nerve
and fled to Belgium, where he shot himself.

448. The events at Montceau-les-Mines in 1882 provided material
for Zola's novel *Germinal* (1885); the attacks on the crosses began
in August, and several miners were tried and imprisoned at the end
of the year.

449. The explosions in Lyon occurred on October 22 and 23,
1882; fifty-one anarchists were arrested from October to December
(fourteen escaped arrest). Émile Gautier (1853–1937) was a leading
anarchist in Paris, but he also carried out propaganda in southern
France; he was sentenced to five years' imprisonment at the Lyon
trial, but he abandoned anarchism in prison, was released in 1885,
and became a radical journalist under the name "Raoul de Lucet."
Kropotkin's house was searched on December 15, 1882.

450. The *Times* published a report that Kropotkin had left
Thonon on November 22, and his correction on November 28, 1882.
Ananiev died on December 19, and Kropotkin was arrested on the
afternoon of December 20.

451. The English "gentleman" was Joseph Cowen. The Lyon
trial was held from January 8 to 18, 1883.

453. The "young shoemaker" was Jean Grave.

454. Joseph Bernard was the leading anarchist in Lyon at the
beginning of the 1880's; he made a considerable impression at the
trial, and was sentenced to five years' imprisonment; he abandoned
anarchism in prison, was released in 1885, and became a parliamentary socialist. The *Journal des Économistes* was a liberal periodical
in Paris.

456. Pierre Martin (1856–1916), nicknamed *le Bossu* ("the Hunch-back"), was active at Vienne before the Lyon trial, when he was sentenced to four years' imprisonment; he was the main figure in a May Day riot at Vienne in 1890, and was sentenced to five years' imprisonment; in the early years of the twentieth century he was one of the leading contributors to the French anarchist paper *Le Libertaire* (The Libertarian).

459. *The Nineteenth Century* was a monthly paper published in London from 1877, and Kropotkin was a frequent contributor; he wrote seven articles for it while he was in prison in France, mostly about the Russian prison system.

460. Blanqui, who spent almost half his life in prison, was at Clairvaux during his last term from 1872 to 1879. The petition for Kropotkin's release was presented in March, 1883; Herbert Spencer did not in fact sign it; Algernon Charles Swinburne (1837–1909), the English poet, had strong republican and atheist beliefs; other signatories included Joseph Cowen, William Morris and A. R. Wallace; Victor Hugo (1802–1885), the French writer, added the following message to the petition: "I am interested in all petitions for amnesty. This one affects me deeply, and I support it."

461. The *Encyclopédie Roret* series of practical handbooks was begun by Nicolas-Edmé Roret (1797–1860), the French publisher, in 1825; the booklet on bookbinding—*Reliure*, by Louis-Sébastien Le Normand—was published in 1827. Charles Adolphe Würtz (1817–1884) was professor of organic chemistry at the Sorbonne from 1875.

466. Richard von Krafft-Ebing (1840–1902), the German psychologist, specialized in the psychopathology of crime and sex. *In Russian and French Prisons*, which was based partly on articles published in *The Nineteenth Century* from 1883 to 1886, was published in London in 1887. Cesare Lombroso (1835–1909), the Italian criminologist, suggested—especially in *L'uomo delinquente* (1876)—that criminals belonged to a specific physical and psychological type.

469. Henri Rochefort (1831–1913) published *L'Intransigeant* from 1881, and Clemenceau published *La Justice* from 1880—both extreme republican papers. George Cruikshank (1792–1878) illustrated several of Dickens's novels, especially *Oliver Twist* (1837).

473. Reports of the French system of spying on Russian revolutionary exiles were published in *L'Intransigeant* from June 26 to July 1, 1882; the story of Hermanovich, the spy who followed Kropotkin from Paris to London in November, 1881, was published on July 1.

475. In 1881 Kropotkin stayed in Islington with Lyov Nikolayevich Gartman (1850–1913), a member of Narodnaya Volya who left

Russia in 1879 but was arrested in Paris in 1880; he was released after a public campaign against his extradition to Russia, and he settled in England.

476. "Tohnlehm" = Kaldenbach.

478. Andrieux subsidized a weekly anarchist paper called *La Révolution Sociale* (Social Revolution) from September, 1880, to September, 1881; the editor was a Belgian agent-provocateur called Égide Spilleux, who used the pseudonym Serreaux.

480. *Souvenirs d'un Préfet de Police* (Memories of a Chief of Police) was published in 1885; Andrieux claimed that by encouraging the harmless attack on the statue of Thiers in June, 1881, he diverted the Paris anarchists from a dangerous attack on the Palais Bourbon.

484. Louise Michel (1830–1905) was a French schoolteacher who took an active part in the Paris Commune and was transported to New Caledonia (in the South Pacific) from 1871 to 1879. Émile Pouget (1860–1931) was a French journalist who became a militant trade unionist in 1879. They both attended the London Congress in 1881, and they both took a leading part in an unemployed demonstration in Paris on March 9, 1883, for which he got eight and she got six years' imprisonment; they were amnestied in 1886. She got another four months' imprisonment for an inflammatory speech in June, 1886. In 1888 she was shot by a madman in Le Havre, but recovered and not only refused to take proceedings against him but campaigned for his release. She was arrested for taking part in a May Day riot at Vienne in 1890, but was released; she lived in England from 1890 to 1895. Pouget edited a series of anarchist papers from 1889 to 1900, living in England from 1894 to 1895 to avoid arrest. He took a leading part in the French syndicalist movement, being for a time joint secretary of the Confédération Générale du Travail and editor of its paper. Jules Grévy (1807–1891) was president of France from 1879 until his death. Charles de Freycinet (1828–1923) was prime minister for the third time from January to December, 1886; he worked for the alliance with Russia which was concluded in the 1890's. The remaining anarchists in prison were pardoned on January 14, 1886, to mark Grévy's re-election; Kropotkin was released on January 15.

485. Élie Reclus (1827–1904) was a French anthropologist who, though not as committed an anarchist as his brother Élisée, was an important libertarian writer. Their walk, which was from Strasbourg to the Gironde and not the other way round, took place when they had completed their education, in 1851. Élie Reclus produced *L'Association* and *Coopération* from 1864 to 1868.

486. Édouard Vaillant (1840–1915), the French socialist, was

a leading member of the First International and of the Paris Commune, in which he was responsible for education; he lived in England from 1871 to 1880, then returned to France and became a leading parliamentary socialist. Adolphe Thiers (1797–1877), the French liberal politician, was head of the government in 1871 and crushed the Paris Commune; he was then president of France until 1873. *Les primitifs* was published in 1885, *Le primitif d'Australie* in 1894, and *La formation des religions* also in 1894; the École des Hautes Études was a free university formed by Élisée Reclus in 1893, when he was deprived of his professorship at Brussels University; Élie Reclus was professor of comparative mythology there.

487. *La Société Nouvelle* (New Society) was published in Brussels from 1885 to 1897, and *L'Humanité Nouvelle* (New Humanity) in Paris from 1897 to 1903. Reclus's book *Les croyances populaires* (Popular Beliefs) was published in 1908.

488. Kropotkin's lecture, *L'anarchisme dans l'évolution socialiste* (Anarchism in Socialist Evolution), was given on February 28, 1886; it was published in *Le Révolté* in 1886 and as a pamphlet in 1887; the first English translation appeared in 1886. Kropotkin arrived in London early in March, 1886, and after staying with Stepniak for a month lived at 17 Roxborough Road, Harrow, until 1892. Albert Toubeau was a French writer on agriculture and economics.

490. Pulkovo, near St. Petersburg, was (and still is) the site of the main observatory in Russia; Johan Gylden (1841–1896), the Swedish astronomer, worked there from 1863 to 1871. Edward Singleton Holden (1846–1914) was a well-known American astronomer in the late nineteenth century.

491. Aleksandr Kropotkin shot himself on July 25, 1886. Aleksandra Petrovna Kropotkina was born on April 15, 1887, and died in New York on July 4, 1966.

492. The unemployed riot in London was on February 8, 1886; Burns, Hyndman and Champion were the main leaders of the Social Democratic Federation.

494. The "aged member of Parliament" was Joseph Cowen, who was fifty-five years old in 1886.

495. Toynbee Hall, which was opened in 1884, was then, as it is now, a social settlement house in the East End of London.

497. *Freedom* began publication in October, 1886; today it is still the main anarchist paper in Britain. In addition to the many socialist papers in existence in 1886, there was also an anarchist paper, *The Anarchist*, which Kropotkin was involved with during the spring

of 1886. *Paroles d'un révolté* (Words of a Rebel) was published in Paris in 1885; it has not yet been translated into English. *La conquête du pain* (The Conquest of Bread) was published in Paris in 1892; an English translation appeared in London in 1906.

498. *Fields, Factories and Workshops* was published in London in 1899. Thomas Henry Huxley (1825–1895), the English biologist, was a well-known popularizer of the theory of evolution. Karel Fedorovich Kessler (1815–1881), the Russian zoologist, gave his lecture on "Mutual aid as a law of nature and the chief factor of evolution" in St. Petersburg on January 8, 1880; it was published in the *Trudy* (Transactions) of the St. Petersburg Naturalist Society in 1880.

499. Huxley's article was published in *The Nineteenth Century* in February, 1888. James Knowles (1831–1908), the English architect and writer, founded *The Nineteenth Century* in 1877 and edited it and its successor *The Nineteenth Century and After* until his death. Henry Walter Bates (1825–1892), the English naturalist, explored South America during the 1840's and 1850's, and was assistant secretary of the Royal Geographical Society from 1864 until his death.

500. *Mutual Aid*, which was based on articles published in *The Nineteenth Century* from 1890 to 1896, was published in London in 1902. *L'état: son rôle historique* (The State: Its Historic Role) was written as a lecture to be given in Paris on March 7, 1896, but the French authorities refused to let Kropotkin enter the country; it was published in *Les Temps Nouveaux* in 1896–1897, and as a pamphlet in 1897; the first English translation appeared in 1898, and the most recent in 1969. Kropotkin's early articles on ethics were published in *The Nineteenth Century and After* in 1904–1905; he resumed work on the subject in 1919, and the first part of his unfinished book on ethics was published in Moscow in 1922; an English translation appeared in New York in 1924.

INDEX

INDEX

ADLERBERG, Count, 149.

Agents, government. *See* Spies.

Agriculture, in Finland and other parts of Russia, 237–239.

Aigle, Switzerland, 437, 438.

Aigún, Manchuria, 206.

Aksákoff, Iván, 131, 174.

Albarracin, a member of the Jura Federation, 395, 396.

Alexander II., at the funeral of the Dowager-Empress, 111, 120; attends the manœuvres of the military schools, 121–123; takes the first steps towards the abolition of serfdom, 129, 130; hesitates to proclaim freedom, 130–132; issues manifesto of emancipation, 132–134; meets with popular approval, 134, 135; his court life, 141–144; his relations with a certain princess, 144, 145; closely watched by the police, 145, 146; his moods, 146; an incident at a parade of the garrison, 146, 147; his character, 148–151; his policy becoming reactionary, 148–151; 152; surrenders to the reactionaries, 163, 164; his address to the newly promoted officers, 165, 166; his talk with Kropótkin before the latter's departure for Siberia, 166, 167; his betrayal of the reform movement, 183; retains Dmítri Milútin as minister of war, 242; a tool of Shuváloff and Trépoff, 242, 243; as a bear hunter, 243, 244; his courage, cowardice, brutality, and cruelty, 244; official corruption under, 245, 246; restriction of education under, 247, 248; shot at by Kara-kózoff, 253, 254; 260, 261, 310; protected by the very men whom he afterwards exiled, 315, 316; 344, 349; refuses to liberate Alexander Kropótkin, 357; 376, 377; increases the sentences of socialists, 415; adopts severe measures against the revolutionary move-

ment, 427–429; his relations with Dmítri Kropótkin, 428; his courage and cowardice again, 429; his relations with Princess Yu-rievski-Dolgorúki and the Empress, 430; alarmed by an attempt to blow up the Winter Palace he creates a sort of dictatorship, which he soon abolishes, 430; wavers between constitutionalism and absolutism, 431; decides to convoke a deliberative assembly, 431; his assassination, 431, 432; the tragedy of his life, 432, 433.

Alexander III., a true descendant of Paul I., 152, 153; his lack of education, 152, 153; his haughtiness and impetuosity, 153; 246, 413; fears assassination on his accession, 434; organizations for the protection of, 434, 435; at first willing to convoke a National Assembly, he finally resolves to remain absolute ruler, 436; an arrangement to protect him until after his coronation, 445, 446; objects to Kropótkin's release from Clairvaux, 484.

Amúr, the river, 184–186; barge navigation on, 186–189, 191–193; scenery on, 189; a post boat journey on, 189, 190; floods and high seas in the rainy season, 190, 191; a typhoon on, 191; a perilous journey on, 192, 193; a steamer on, 193, 194; 206, 208.

Amúr region, the, annexation to Russia, 184; settlement of, 184–186. *See* Manchuria, Siberia, Transbaikália.

Anarchism, the first spark of, 282; the aim of the Jura Federation, 287; gaining headway in Western Europe, 378; its presence saves Europe from a period of reaction, 387–390; the red flag, 397, 398; the ideal society under, 398, 399; a long struggle necessary to bring about the change, 399, 400; asso-

A CATALOG OF SELECTED

DOVER BOOKS

IN ALL FIELDS OF INTEREST

A CATALOG OF SELECTED DOVER
BOOKS IN ALL FIELDS OF INTEREST

100 BEST-LOVED POEMS, Edited by Philip Smith. "The Passionate Shepherd to His Love," "Shall I compare thee to a summer's day?" "Death, be not proud," "The Raven," "The Road Not Taken," plus works by Blake, Wordsworth, Byron, Shelley, Keats,m anyot hers. 96pp. 5³⁄₁₆ x 8¼.   0-486-28553-7

100 SMALL HOUSES OF THE THIRTIES, Brown-Blodgett Company. Exterior photographs and floor plans for 100 charming structures. Illustrations of models accompanied by descriptions of interiors, color schemes, closet space, and other amenities.2 00illu strations. 112pp. 8⅜ x 11.   0-486-44131-8

1000 TURN-OF-THE-CENTURY HOUSES: With Illustrations and Floor Plans, Herbert C. Chivers. Reproduced from a rare edition, this showcase of homes ranges from cottages and bungalows to sprawling mansions. Each house is meticulously illustrated and accompanied by complete floor plans. 256pp. 9⅜ x 12¼.
     0-486-45596-3

101 GREAT AMERICAN POEMS, Edited by The American Poetry & Literacy Project. Rich treasury of verse from the 19th and 20th centuries includes works by Edgar Allan Poe, Robert Frost, Walt Whitman, Langston Hughes, Emily Dickinson, T. S. Eliot, other notables. 96pp. 5³⁄₁₆ x 8¼.   0-486-40158-8

101 GREAT SAMURAI PRINTS, Utagawa Kuniyoshi. Kuniyoshi was a master of the warrior woodblock print — and these 18th-century illustrations represent the pinnacle of his craft. Full-color portraits of renowned Japanese samurais pulse with movement, passion, and remarkably fine detail. 112pp. 8⅜ x 11.   0-486-46523-3

ABC OF BALLET, Janet Grosser. Clearly worded, abundantly illustrated little guide defines basic ballet-related terms: arabesque, battement, pas de chat, relevé, sissonne, many others. Pronunciation guide included. Excellent primer. 48pp. 4³⁄₁₆ x 5¾.
     0-486-40871-X

ACCESSORIES OF DRESS: An Illustrated Encyclopedia, Katherine Lester and Bess Viola Oerke. Illustrations of hats, veils, wigs, cravats, shawls, shoes, gloves, and other accessories enhance an engaging commentary that reveals the humor and charm of the many-sided story of accessorized apparel. 644 figures and 59 plates. 608pp. 6 ⅛ x 9¼.
     0-486-43378-1

ADVENTURES OF HUCKLEBERRY FINN, Mark Twain. Join Huck and Jim as their boyhood adventures along the Mississippi River lead them into a world of excitement, danger, and self-discovery. Humorous narrative, lyrical descriptions of the Mississippi valley, and memorable characters. 224pp. 5³⁄₁₆ x 8¼.   0-486-28061-6

ALICE STARMORE'S BOOK OF FAIR ISLE KNITTING, Alice Starmore. A noted designer from the region of Scotland's Fair Isle explores the history and techniques of this distinctive, stranded-color knitting style and provides copious illustrated instructions for 14 original knitwear designs. 208pp. 8⅜ x 10⅞.   0-486-47218-3

Browse over 9,000 books at www.doverpublications.com

ALICE'S ADVENTURES IN WONDERLAND, Lewis Carroll. Beloved classic about a little girl lost in a topsy-turvy land and her encounters with the White Rabbit, March Hare, Mad Hatter, Cheshire Cat, and other delightfully improbable characters. 42 illustrations by Sir John Tenniel. 96pp. 5³⁄₁₆ x 8¼.   0-486-27543-4

AMERICA'S LIGHTHOUSES: An Illustrated History, Francis Ross Holland. Profusely illustrated fact-filled survey of American lighthouses since 1716. Over 200 stations — East, Gulf, and West coasts, Great Lakes, Hawaii, Alaska, Puerto Rico, the Virgin Islands, and the Mississippi and St. Lawrence Rivers. 240pp. 8 x 10¾.
    0-486-25576-X

AN ENCYCLOPEDIA OF THE VIOLIN, Alberto Bachmann. Translated by Frederick H. Martens. Introduction by Eugene Ysaye. First published in 1925, this renowned reference remains unsurpassed as a source of essential information, from construction and evolution to repertoire and technique. Includes a glossary and 73 illustrations. 496pp. 6⅛ x 9¼.   0-486-46618-3

ANIMALS: 1,419 Copyright-Free Illustrations of Mammals, Birds, Fish, Insects, etc., Selected by Jim Harter. Selected for its visual impact and ease of use, this outstanding collection of wood engravings presents over 1,000 species of animals in extremely lifelike poses. Includes mammals, birds, reptiles, amphibians, fish, insects, and otherin vertebrates. 284pp. 9x 1 2.   0-486-23766-4

THE ANNALS, Tacitus. Translated by Alfred John Church and William Jackson Brodribb. This vital chronicle of Imperial Rome, written by the era's great historian, spans A.D. 14-68 and paints incisive psychological portraits of major figures, from Tiberiust oNero. 416pp. 5³⁄₁₆ x 8¼.   0-486-45236-0

ANTIGONE, Sophocles. Filled with passionate speeches and sensitive probing of moral and philosophical issues, this powerful and often-performed Greek drama reveals the grim fate that befalls the children of Oedipus. Footnotes. 64pp. 5³⁄₁₆ x 8 ¼.   0-486-27804-2

ART DECO DECORATIVE PATTERNS IN FULL COLOR, Christian Stoll. Reprinted from a rare 1910 portfolio, 160 sensuous and exotic images depict a breathtaking array of florals, geometrics, and abstracts — all elegant in their stark simplicity. 64pp. 8⅜ x 11.   0-486-44862-2

THE ARTHUR RACKHAM TREASURY: 86 Full-Color Illustrations, Arthur Rackham. Selected and Edited by Jeff A. Menges. A stunning treasury of 86 full-page plates span the famed English artist's career, from *Rip Van Winkle* (1905) to masterworks such as *Undine, A Midsummer Night's Dream,* and *Wind in the Willows* (1939). 96pp. 8⅜ x 11.
    0-486-44685-9

THE AUTHENTIC GILBERT & SULLIVAN SONGBOOK, W. S. Gilbert and A. S. Sullivan. The most comprehensive collection available, this songbook includes selections from every one of Gilbert and Sullivan's light operas. Ninety-two numbers are presented uncut and unedited, and in their original keys. 410pp. 9 x 12.
    0-486-23482-7

THE AWAKENING, Kate Chopin. First published in 1899, this controversial novel of a New Orleans wife's search for love outside a stifling marriage shocked readers. Today, it remains a first-rate narrative with superb characterization. New introductoryNot e. 128pp. 5³⁄₁₆ x 8¼.   0-486-27786-0

BASIC DRAWING, Louis Priscilla. Beginning with perspective, this commonsense manual progresses to the figure in movement, light and shade, anatomy, drapery, composition, trees and landscape, and outdoor sketching. Black-and-white illustrationst hroughout. 128pp. 8⅜ x 11.   0-486-45815-6

THE BATTLES THAT CHANGED HISTORY, Fletcher Pratt. Historian profiles 16 crucial conflicts, ancient to modern, that changed the course of Western civilization. Gripping accounts of battles led by Alexander the Great, Joan of Arc, Ulysses S. Grant, other commanders. 27 maps. 352pp. 5⅜ x 8½. 0-486-41129-X

BEETHOVEN'S LETTERS, Ludwig van Beethoven. Edited by Dr. A. C. Kalischer. Features 457 letters to fellow musicians, friends, greats, patrons, and literary men. Reveals musical thoughts, quirks of personality, insights, and daily events. Includes 15p lates. 410pp. 5⅜ x 8½. 0-486-22769-3

BERNICE BOBS HER HAIR AND OTHER STORIES, F. Scott Fitzgerald. This brilliant anthology includes 6 of Fitzgerald's most popular stories: "The Diamond as Big as the Ritz," the title tale, "The Offshore Pirate," "The Ice Palace," "The Jelly Bean," and"M ayD ay." 176pp. 5⅜ x 8½. 0-486-47049-0

BESLER'S BOOK OF FLOWERS AND PLANTS: 73 Full-Color Plates from Hortus Eystettensis, 1613, Basilius Besler. Here is a selection of magnificent plates from the *Hortus Eystettensis,* which vividly illustrated and identified the plants, flowers, and trees that thrived in the legendary German garden at Eichstätt. 80pp. 8⅜x 1 1. 0-486-46005-3

THE BOOK OF KELLS, Edited by Blanche Cirker. Painstakingly reproduced from a rare facsimile edition, this volume contains full-page decorations, portraits, illustrations, plus a sampling of textual leaves with exquisite calligraphy and ornamentation. 32 full-color illustrations. 32pp. 9⅜ x 12¼. 0-486-24345-1

THE BOOK OF THE CROSSBOW: With an Additional Section on Catapults and Other Siege Engines, Ralph Payne-Gallwey. Fascinating study traces history and use of crossbow as military and sporting weapon, from Middle Ages to modern times. Also covers related weapons: balistas, catapults, Turkish bows, more. Over 240 illustrations. 400pp. 7¼ x 10⅛. 0-486-28720-3

THE BUNGALOW BOOK: Floor Plans and Photos of 112 Houses, 1910, Henry L. Wilson. Here are 112 of the most popular and economic blueprints of the early 20th century — plus an illustration or photograph of each completed house. A wonderful time capsule that still offers a wealth of valuable insights. 160pp. 8⅜ x 11. 0-486-45104-6

THE CALL OF THE WILD, Jack London. A classic novel of adventure, drawn from London's own experiences as a Klondike adventurer, relating the story of a heroic dog caught in the brutal life of the Alaska Gold Rush. Note. 64pp. 5³⁄₁₆ x 8¼. 0-486-26472-6

CANDIDE, Voltaire. Edited by Francois-Marie Arouet. One of the world's great satires since its first publication in 1759. Witty, caustic skewering of romance, science, philosophy, religion, government — nearly all human ideals and institutions. 112pp. 5³⁄₁₆ x 8¼. 0-486-26689-3

CELEBRATED IN THEIR TIME: Photographic Portraits from the George Grantham Bain Collection, Edited by Amy Pastan. With an Introduction by Michael Carlebach. Remarkable portrait gallery features 112 rare images of Albert Einstein, Charlie Chaplin, the Wright Brothers, Henry Ford, and other luminaries from the worlds of politics, art, entertainment, and industry. 128pp. 8⅜ x 11. 0-486-46754-6

CHARIOTS FOR APOLLO: The NASA History of Manned Lunar Spacecraft to 1969, Courtney G. Brooks, James M. Grimwood, and Loyd S. Swenson, Jr. This illustrated history by a trio of experts is the definitive reference on the Apollo spacecraft and lunar modules. It traces the vehicles' design, development, and operation in space. More than 100 photographs and illustrations. 576pp. 6¾ x 9¼. 0-486-46756-2

A CHRISTMAS CAROL, Charles Dickens. This engrossing tale relates Ebenezer Scrooge's ghostly journeys through Christmases past, present, and future and his ultimate transformation from a harsh and grasping old miser to a charitable and compassionateh umanbein g. 80pp. 5³⁄₁₆ x 8¼. 0-486-26865-9

COMMON SENSE, Thomas Paine. First published in January of 1776, this highly influential landmark document clearly and persuasively argued for American separation from Great Britain and paved the way for the Declaration of Independence. 64pp. 5³⁄₁₆ x 8¼. 0-486-29602-4

THE COMPLETE SHORT STORIES OF OSCAR WILDE, Oscar Wilde. Complete texts of "The Happy Prince and Other Tales," "A House of Pomegranates," "Lord Arthur Savile's Crime and Other Stories," "Poems in Prose," and "The Portrait of Mr.W .H ." 208pp. 5³⁄₁₆ x 8¼. 0-486-45216-6

COMPLETE SONNETS, William Shakespeare. Over 150 exquisite poems deal with love, friendship, the tyranny of time, beauty's evanescence, death, and other themes in language of remarkable power, precision, and beauty. Glossary of archaic terms. 80pp. 5³⁄₁₆ x 8¼. 0-486-26686-9

THE COUNT OF MONTE CRISTO: Abridged Edition, Alexandre Dumas. Falsely accused of treason, Edmond Dantès is imprisoned in the bleak Chateau d'If. After a hair-raising escape, he launches an elaborate plot to extract a bitter revenge against those who betrayed him. 448pp. 5³⁄₁₆ x 8¼. 0-486-45643-9

CRAFTSMAN BUNGALOWS: Designs from the Pacific Northwest, Yoho & Merritt. This reprint of a rare catalog, showcasing the charming simplicity and cozy style of Craftsman bungalows, is filled with photos of completed homes, plus floor plans and estimated costs. An indispensable resource for architects, historians, and illustrators. 112pp. 10x 7 . 0-486-46875-5

CRAFTSMAN BUNGALOWS: 59 Homes from "The Craftsman," Edited by Gustav Stickley. Best and most attractive designs from Arts and Crafts Movement publication — 1903–1916 — includes sketches, photographs of homes, floor plans, descriptivet ext. 128pp. 8¼ x 11. 0-486-25829-7

CRIME AND PUNISHMENT, Fyodor Dostoyevsky. Translated by Constance Garnett. Supreme masterpiece tells the story of Raskolnikov, a student tormented by his own thoughts after he murders an old woman. Overwhelmed by guilt and terror, he confesses and goes to prison. 480pp. 5³⁄₁₆ x 8¼. 0-486-41587-2

THE DECLARATION OF INDEPENDENCE AND OTHER GREAT DOCUMENTS OF AMERICAN HISTORY: 1775-1865, Edited by John Grafton. Thirteen compelling and influential documents: Henry's "Give Me Liberty or Give Me Death," Declaration of Independence, The Constitution, Washington's First Inaugural Address, The Monroe Doctrine, The Emancipation Proclamation, Gettysburg Address,m ore. 64pp. 5³⁄₁₆ x 8¼. 0-486-41124-9

THE DESERT AND THE SOWN: Travels in Palestine and Syria, Gertrude Bell. "The female Lawrence of Arabia," Gertrude Bell wrote captivating, perceptive accounts of her travels in the Middle East. This intriguing narrative, accompanied by 160 photos, traces her 1905 sojourn in Lebanon, Syria, and Palestine. 368pp. 5⅜ x 8½. 0-486-46876-3

A DOLL'S HOUSE, Henrik Ibsen. Ibsen's best-known play displays his genius for realistic prose drama. An expression of women's rights, the play climaxes when the central character, Nora, rejects a smothering marriage and life in "a doll's house." 80pp. 5³⁄₁₆ x 8¼. 0-486-27062-9

Browse over 9,000 books at www.doverpublications.com

DOOMED SHIPS: Great Ocean Liner Disasters, William H. Miller, Jr. Nearly 200 photographs, many from private collections, highlight tales of some of the vessels whose pleasure cruises ended in catastrophe: the *Morro Castle, Normandie, Andrea Doria, Europa,*an dm anyot hers. 128pp. 8⅞ x 11¾.   0-486-45366-9

THE DORÉ BIBLE ILLUSTRATIONS, Gustave Doré. Detailed plates from the Bible: the Creation scenes, Adam and Eve, horrifying visions of the Flood, the battle sequences with their monumental crowds, depictions of the life of Jesus, 241 plates inall. 241pp. 9x 1 2.   0-486-23004-X

DRAWING DRAPERY FROM HEAD TO TOE, Cliff Young. Expert guidance on how to draw shirts, pants, skirts, gloves, hats, and coats on the human figure, including folds in relation to the body, pull and crush, action folds, creases, more. Over 200 drawings. 48pp. 8¼ x 11.   0-486-45591-2

DUBLINERS, James Joyce. A fine and accessible introduction to the work of one of the 20th century's most influential writers, this collection features 15 tales, including a masterpiece of the short-story genre, "The Dead." 160pp. 5³⁄₁₆ x 8¼.

0-486-26870-5

EASY-TO-MAKE POP-UPS, Joan Irvine. Illustrated by Barbara Reid. Dozens of wonderful ideas for three-dimensional paper fun — from holiday greeting cards with moving parts to a pop-up menagerie. Easy-to-follow, illustrated instructions for more than 30 projects. 299 black-and-white illustrations. 96pp. 8⅜ x 11.

0-486-44622-0

EASY-TO-MAKE STORYBOOK DOLLS: A "Novel" Approach to Cloth Dollmaking, Sherralyn St. Clair. Favorite fictional characters come alive in this unique beginner's dollmaking guide. Includes patterns for Pollyanna, Dorothy from *The Wonderful Wizard of Oz,* Mary of *The Secret Garden,* plus easy-to-follow instructions, 263 black-and-white illustrations, and an 8-page color insert. 112pp. 8¼ x 11.   0-486-47360-0

EINSTEIN'S ESSAYS IN SCIENCE, Albert Einstein. Speeches and essays in accessible, everyday language profile influential physicists such as Niels Bohr and Isaac Newton. They also explore areas of physics to which the author made major contributions. 128pp. 5x 8 .   0-486-47011-3

EL DORADO: Further Adventures of the Scarlet Pimpernel, Baroness Orczy. A popular sequel to *The Scarlet Pimpernel,* this suspenseful story recounts the Pimpernel's attempts to rescue the Dauphin from imprisonment during the French Revolution. An irresistible blend of intrigue, period detail, and vibrant characterizations. 352pp. 5³⁄₁₆ x 8¼.   0-486-44026-5

ELEGANT SMALL HOMES OF THE TWENTIES: 99 Designs from a Competition, Chicago Tribune. Nearly 100 designs for five- and six-room houses feature New England and Southern colonials, Normandy cottages, stately Italianate dwellings, and other fascinating snapshots of American domestic architecture of the 1920s. 112pp. 9x 1 2.   0-486-46910-7

THE ELEMENTS OF STYLE: The Original Edition, William Strunk, Jr. This is the book that generations of writers have relied upon for timeless advice on grammar, diction, syntax, and other essentials. In concise terms, it identifies the principal requirements of proper style and common errors. 64pp. 5⅜ x 8¼.   0-486-44798-7

THE ELUSIVE PIMPERNEL, Baroness Orczy. Robespierre's revolutionaries find their wicked schemes thwarted by the heroic Pimpernel — Sir Percival Blakeney. In this thrilling sequel, Chauvelin devises a plot to eliminate the Pimpernel and his wife. 272pp. 5³⁄₁₆ x 8¼.   0-486-45464-9

AN ENCYCLOPEDIA OF BATTLES: Accounts of Over 1,560 Battles from 1479 B.C. to the Present, David Eggenberger. Essential details of every major battle in recorded history from the first battle of Megiddo in 1479 B.C. to Grenada in 1984. List of battle maps. 99 illustrations. 544pp. 6½ x 9¼. 0-486-24913-1

ENCYCLOPEDIA OF EMBROIDERY STITCHES, INCLUDING CREWEL, Marion Nichols. Precise explanations and instructions, clearly illustrated, on how to work chain, back, cross, knotted, woven stitches, and many more — 178 in all, including Cable Outline, Whipped Satin, and Eyelet Buttonhole. Over 1400 illustrations. 219pp. 8⅜ x 11¼. 0-486-22929-7

ENTER JEEVES: 15 Early Stories, P. G. Wodehouse. Splendid collection contains first 8 stories featuring Bertie Wooster, the deliciously dim aristocrat and Jeeves, his brainy, imperturbable manservant. Also, the complete Reggie Pepper (Bertie's prototype)s eries. 288pp. 5⅜ x 8½. 0-486-29717-9

ERIC SLOANE'S AMERICA: Paintings in Oil, Michael Wigley. With a Foreword by Mimi Sloane. Eric Sloane's evocative oils of America's landscape and material culture shimmer with immense historical and nostalgic appeal. This original hardcover collection gathers nearly a hundred of his finest paintings, with subjects ranging from New England to the American Southwest. 128pp. 10⅝ x 9. 0-486-46525-X

ETHAN FROME, Edith Wharton. Classic story of wasted lives, set against a bleak New England background. Superbly delineated characters in a hauntingly grim tale of thwarted love. Considered by many to be Wharton's masterpiece. 96pp. 5³⁄₁₆ x 8 ¼. 0-486-26690-7

THE EVERLASTING MAN, G. K. Chesterton. Chesterton's view of Christianity — as a blend of philosophy and mythology, satisfying intellect and spirit — applies to his brilliant book, which appeals to readers' heads as well as their hearts. 288pp. 5⅜ x 8½. 0-486-46036-3

THE FIELD AND FOREST HANDY BOOK, Daniel Beard. Written by a co-founder of the Boy Scouts, this appealing guide offers illustrated instructions for building kites, birdhouses, boats, igloos, and other fun projects, plus numerous helpful tips forc ampers. 448pp. 5³⁄₁₆ x 8¼. 0-486-46191-2

FINDING YOUR WAY WITHOUT MAP OR COMPASS, Harold Gatty. Useful, instructive manual shows would-be explorers, hikers, bikers, scouts, sailors, and survivalists how to find their way outdoors by observing animals, weather patterns, shifting sands, and other elements of nature. 288pp. 5⅜ x 8½. 0-486-40613-X

FIRST FRENCH READER: A Beginner's Dual-Language Book, Edited and Translated by Stanley Appelbaum. This anthology introduces 50 legendary writers — Voltaire, Balzac, Baudelaire, Proust, more — through passages from *The Red and the Black, Les Misérables, Madame Bovary,* and other classics. Original French text plus English translation on facing pages. 240pp. 5⅜ x 8½. 0-486-46178-5

FIRST GERMAN READER: A Beginner's Dual-Language Book, Edited by Harry Steinhauer. Specially chosen for their power to evoke German life and culture, these short, simple readings include poems, stories, essays, and anecdotes by Goethe, Hesse, Heine, Schiller, and others. 224pp. 5⅜ x 8½. 0-486-46179-3

FIRST SPANISH READER: A Beginner's Dual-Language Book, Angel Flores. Delightful stories, other material based on works of Don Juan Manuel, Luis Taboada, Ricardo Palma, other noted writers. Complete faithful English translations on facingp ages.Ex ercises. 176pp. 5⅜ x 8½. 0-486-25810-6

FIVE ACRES AND INDEPENDENCE, Maurice G. Kains. Great back-to-the-land classic explains basics of self-sufficient farming. The one book to get. 95 illustrations. 397pp. 5⅜ x 8½. 0-486-20974-1

FLAGG'S SMALL HOUSES: Their Economic Design and Construction, 1922, Ernest Flagg. Although most famous for his skyscrapers, Flagg was also a proponent of the well-designed single-family dwelling. His classic treatise features innovations that save space, materials, and cost. 526 illustrations. 160pp. 9⅜ x 12¼. 0-486-45197-6

FLATLAND: A Romance of Many Dimensions, Edwin A. Abbott. Classic of science (and mathematical) fiction — charmingly illustrated by the author — describes the adventures of A. Square, a resident of Flatland, in Spaceland (three dimensions), Lineland (one dimension), and Pointland (no dimensions). 96pp. 5$\frac{3}{16}$ x 8¼. 0-486-27263-X

FRANKENSTEIN, Mary Shelley. The story of Victor Frankenstein's monstrous creation and the havoc it caused has enthralled generations of readers and inspired countless writers of horror and suspense. With the author's own 1831 introduction. 176pp. 5$\frac{3}{16}$ x 8¼. 0-486-28211-2

THE GARGOYLE BOOK: 572 Examples from Gothic Architecture, Lester Burbank Bridaham. Dispelling the conventional wisdom that French Gothic architectural flourishes were born of despair or gloom, Bridaham reveals the whimsical nature of these creations and the ingenious artisans who made them. 572 illustrations. 224pp. 8⅜ x 11. 0-486-44754-5

THE GIFT OF THE MAGI AND OTHER SHORT STORIES, O. Henry. Sixteen captivating stories by one of America's most popular storytellers. Included are such classics as "The Gift of the Magi," "The Last Leaf," and "The Ransom of Red Chief." Publisher'sN ote. 96pp. 5$\frac{3}{16}$ x 8¼. 0-486-27061-0

THE GOETHE TREASURY: Selected Prose and Poetry, Johann Wolfgang von Goethe. Edited, Selected, and with an Introduction by Thomas Mann. In addition to his lyric poetry, Goethe wrote travel sketches, autobiographical studies, essays, letters, and proverbs in rhyme and prose. This collection presents outstanding examples from each genre. 368pp. 5⅜ x 8½. 0-486-44780-4

GREAT EXPECTATIONS, Charles Dickens. Orphaned Pip is apprenticed to the dirty work of the forge but dreams of becoming a gentleman — and one day finds himself in possession of "great expectations." Dickens' finest novel. 400pp. 5$\frac{3}{16}$ x 8¼. 0-486-41586-4

GREAT WRITERS ON THE ART OF FICTION: From Mark Twain to Joyce Carol Oates, Edited by James Daley. An indispensable source of advice and inspiration, this anthology features essays by Henry James, Kate Chopin, Willa Cather, Sinclair Lewis, Jack London, Raymond Chandler, Raymond Carver, Eudora Welty, and Kurt Vonnegut,Jr. 192pp. 5⅜ x 8½. 0-486-45128-3

HAMLET, William Shakespeare. The quintessential Shakespearean tragedy, whose highly charged confrontations and anguished soliloquies probe depths of human feeling rarely sounded in any art. Reprinted from an authoritative British edition complete with illuminating footnotes. 128pp. 5$\frac{3}{16}$ x 8¼. 0-486-27278-8

THE HAUNTED HOUSE, Charles Dickens. A Yuletide gathering in an eerie country retreat provides the backdrop for Dickens and his friends — including Elizabeth Gaskell and Wilkie Collins — who take turns spinning supernatural yarns. 144pp. 5⅜ x 8½. 0-486-46309-5

HEART OF DARKNESS, Joseph Conrad. Dark allegory of a journey up the Congo River and the narrator's encounter with the mysterious Mr. Kurtz. Masterly blend of adventure, character study, psychological penetration. For many, Conrad's finest, mosten igmatics tory. 80pp. 5³⁄₁₆ x 8¼.　　　　　0-486-26464-5

HENSON AT THE NORTH POLE, Matthew A. Henson. This thrilling memoir by the heroic African-American who was Peary's companion through two decades of Arctic exploration recounts a tale of danger, courage, and determination. "Fascinating and exciting." — *Commonweal.* 128pp. 5⅜ x 8½.　　　　　0-486-45472-X

HISTORIC COSTUMES AND HOW TO MAKE THEM, Mary Fernald and E. Shenton. Practical, informative guidebook shows how to create everything from short tunics worn by Saxon men in the fifth century to a lady's bustle dress of the late 1800s. 81 illustrations. 176pp. 5⅜ x 8½.　　　　　0-486-44906-8

THE HOUND OF THE BASKERVILLES, Arthur Conan Doyle. A deadly curse in the form of a legendary ferocious beast continues to claim its victims from the Baskerville family until Holmes and Watson intervene. Often called the best detective story ever written. 128pp. 5³⁄₁₆ x 8¼.　　　　　0-486-28214-7

THE HOUSE BEHIND THE CEDARS, Charles W. Chesnutt. Originally published in 1900, this groundbreaking novel by a distinguished African-American author recounts the drama of a brother and sister who "pass for white" during the dangerous days of Reconstruction. 208pp. 5⅜ x 8½.　　　　　0-486-46144-0

THE HUMAN FIGURE IN MOTION, Eadweard Muybridge. The 4,789 photographs in this definitive selection show the human figure — models almost all undraped — engaged in over 160 different types of action: running, climbing stairs, etc. 390pp. 7⅞ x 10⅝.　　　　　0-486-20204-6

THE IMPORTANCE OF BEING EARNEST, Oscar Wilde. Wilde's witty and buoyant comedy of manners, filled with some of literature's most famous epigrams, reprinted from an authoritative British edition. Considered Wilde's most perfect work. 64pp. 5³⁄₁₆ x 8¼.　　　　　0-486-26478-5

THE INFERNO, Dante Alighieri. Translated and with notes by Henry Wadsworth Longfellow. The first stop on Dante's famous journey from Hell to Purgatory to Paradise, this 14th-century allegorical poem blends vivid and shocking imagery with graceful lyricism. Translated by the beloved 19th-century poet, Henry Wadsworth Longfellow. 256pp. 5³⁄₁₆ x 8¼.　　　　　0-486-44288-8

JANE EYRE, Charlotte Brontë. Written in 1847, *Jane Eyre* tells the tale of an orphan girl's progress from the custody of cruel relatives to an oppressive boarding school and its culmination in a troubled career as a governess. 448pp. 5³⁄₁₆ x 8¼.

0-486-42449-9

JAPANESE WOODBLOCK FLOWER PRINTS, Tanigami Kônan. Extraordinary collection of Japanese woodblock prints by a well-known artist features 120 plates in brilliant color. Realistic images from a rare edition include daffodils, tulips, and other familiar and unusual flowers. 128pp. 11 x 8¼.　　　　　0-486-46442-3

JEWELRY MAKING AND DESIGN, Augustus F. Rose and Antonio Cirino. Professional secrets of jewelry making are revealed in a thorough, practical guide. Over2 00illu strations. 306pp. 5⅜ x 8½.　　　　　0-486-21750-7

JULIUS CAESAR, William Shakespeare. Great tragedy based on Plutarch's account of the lives of Brutus, Julius Caesar and Mark Antony. Evil plotting, ringing oratory, high tragedy with Shakespeare's incomparable insight, dramatic power. Explanatory footnotes. 96pp. 5³⁄₁₆ x 8¼.　　　　　0-486-26876-4

Browse over 9,000 books at www.doverpublications.com

THE JUNGLE, Upton Sinclair. 1906 bestseller shockingly reveals intolerable labor practices and working conditions in the Chicago stockyards as it tells the grim story of a Slavic family that emigrates to America full of optimism but soon faces despair. 320pp. 5³⁄₁₆ x 8¼. 0-486-41923-1

THE KINGDOM OF GOD IS WITHIN YOU, Leo Tolstoy. The soul-searching book that inspired Gandhi to embrace the concept of passive resistance, Tolstoy's 1894 polemic clearly outlines a radical, well-reasoned revision of traditional Christian thinking. 352pp. 5³⁄₁₆ x 8¼. 0-486-45138-0

THE LADY OR THE TIGER?: and Other Logic Puzzles, Raymond M. Smullyan. Created by a renowned puzzle master, these whimsically themed challenges involve paradoxes about probability, time, and change; metapuzzles; and self-referentiality. Nineteen chapters advance in difficulty from relatively simple to highly complex. 1982ed ition. 240pp. 5⅜ x 8½. 0-486-47027-X

LEAVES OF GRASS: The Original 1855 Edition, Walt Whitman. Whitman's immortal collection includes some of the greatest poems of modern times, including his masterpiece, "Song of Myself." Shattering standard conventions, it stands as an unabashed celebration of body and nature. 128pp. 5³⁄₁₆ x 8¼. 0-486-45676-5

LES MISÉRABLES, Victor Hugo. Translated by Charles E. Wilbour. Abridged by James K. Robinson. A convict's heroic struggle for justice and redemption plays out against a fiery backdrop of the Napoleonic wars. This edition features the excellent original translation and a sensitive abridgment. 304pp. 6⅛ x 9¼.

0-486-45789-3

LILITH: A Romance, George MacDonald. In this novel by the father of fantasy literature, a man travels through time to meet Adam and Eve and to explore humanity's fall from grace and ultimate redemption. 240pp. 5⅜ x 8½.

0-486-46818-6

THE LOST LANGUAGE OF SYMBOLISM, Harold Bayley. This remarkable book reveals the hidden meaning behind familiar images and words, from the origins of Santa Claus to the fleur-de-lys, drawing from mythology, folklore, religious texts, and fairy tales. 1,418 illustrations. 784pp. 5⅜ x 8½. 0-486-44787-1

MACBETH, William Shakespeare. A Scottish nobleman murders the king in order to succeed to the throne. Tortured by his conscience and fearful of discovery, he becomes tangled in a web of treachery and deceit that ultimately spells his doom. 96pp. 5³⁄₁₆ x 8¼. 0-486-27802-6

MAKING AUTHENTIC CRAFTSMAN FURNITURE: Instructions and Plans for 62 Projects, Gustav Stickley. Make authentic reproductions of handsome, functional, durable furniture: tables, chairs, wall cabinets, desks, a hall tree, and more. Construction plans with drawings, schematics, dimensions, and lumber specs reprinted from 1900s *The Craftsman*m agazine. 128pp. 8⅛ x 11. 0-486-25000-8

MATHEMATICS FOR THE NONMATHEMATICIAN, Morris Kline. Erudite and entertaining overview follows development of mathematics from ancient Greeks to present. Topics include logic and mathematics, the fundamental concept, differential calculus, probability theory, much more. Exercises and problems. 641pp. 5⅜ x 8½. 0-486-24823-2

MEMOIRS OF AN ARABIAN PRINCESS FROM ZANZIBAR, Emily Ruete. This 19th-century autobiography offers a rare inside look at the society surrounding a sultan's palace. A real-life princess in exile recalls her vanished world of harems, slave trading, and court intrigues. 288pp. 5⅜ x 8½. 0-486-47121-7

THE METAMORPHOSIS AND OTHER STORIES, Franz Kafka. Excellent new English translations of title story (considered by many critics Kafka's most perfect work), plus "The Judgment," "In the Penal Colony," "A Country Doctor," and "A Report to an Academy." Note. 96pp. 5³⁄₁₆ x 8¼. 0-486-29030-1

MICROSCOPIC ART FORMS FROM THE PLANT WORLD, R. Anheisser. From undulating curves to complex geometrics, a world of fascinating images abound in this classic, illustrated survey of microscopic plants. Features 400 detailed illustrations of nature's minute but magnificent handiwork. The accompanying CD-ROM includes all of the images in the book. 128pp. 9 x 9. 0-486-46013-4

A MIDSUMMER NIGHT'S DREAM, William Shakespeare. Among the most popular of Shakespeare's comedies, this enchanting play humorously celebrates the vagaries of love as it focuses upon the intertwined romances of several pairs of lovers. Explanatory footnotes. 80pp. 5³⁄₁₆ x 8¼. 0-486-27067-X

THE MONEY CHANGERS, Upton Sinclair. Originally published in 1908, this cautionary novel from the author of *The Jungle* explores corruption within the American system as a group of power brokers joins forces for personal gain, triggering a crash on Wall Street. 192pp. 5⅜ x 8½. 0-486-46917-4

THE MOST POPULAR HOMES OF THE TWENTIES, William A. Radford. With a New Introduction by Daniel D. Reiff. Based on a rare 1925 catalog, this architectural showcase features floor plans, construction details, and photos of 26 homes, plus articles on entrances, porches, garages, and more. 250 illustrations, 21 color plates. 176pp. 8⅜ x 11. 0-486-47028-8

MY 66 YEARS IN THE BIG LEAGUES, Connie Mack. With a New Introduction by Rich Westcott. A Founding Father of modern baseball, Mack holds the record for most wins — and losses — by a major league manager. Enhanced by 70 photographs, his warmhearted autobiography is populated by many legends of the game. 288pp. 5⅜ x 8½. 0-486-47184-5

NARRATIVE OF THE LIFE OF FREDERICK DOUGLASS, Frederick Douglass. Douglass's graphic depictions of slavery, harrowing escape to freedom, and life as a newspaper editor, eloquent orator, and impassioned abolitionist. 96pp. 5³⁄₁₆ x 8¼. 0-486-28499-9

THE NIGHTLESS CITY: Geisha and Courtesan Life in Old Tokyo, J. E. de Becker. This unsurpassed study from 100 years ago ventured into Tokyo's red-light district to survey geisha and courtesan life and offer meticulous descriptions of training, dress, social hierarchy, and erotic practices. 49 black-and-white illustrations; 2 maps. 496pp. 5⅜ x 8½. 0-486-45563-7

THE ODYSSEY, Homer. Excellent prose translation of ancient epic recounts adventures of the homeward-bound Odysseus. Fantastic cast of gods, giants, cannibals, sirens, other supernatural creatures — true classic of Western literature. 256pp. 5³⁄₁₆ x 8¼. 0-486-40654-7

OEDIPUS REX, Sophocles. Landmark of Western drama concerns the catastrophe that ensues when King Oedipus discovers he has inadvertently killed his father and married his mother. Masterly construction, dramatic irony. Explanatory footnotes. 64pp. 5³⁄₁₆ x 8¼. 0-486-26877-2

ONCE UPON A TIME: The Way America Was, Eric Sloane. Nostalgic text and drawings brim with gentle philosophies and descriptions of how we used to live — self-sufficiently — on the land, in homes, and among the things built by hand. 44 line illustrations. 64pp. 8⅜ x 11. 0-486-44411-2